MUSIC OF EXILE

MUSIC OF EXILE

THE UNTOLD STORY OF THE COMPOSERS WHO FLED HITLER

MICHAEL HAAS

YALE UNIVERSITY PRESS
NEW HAVEN AND LONDON

For information about this and other Yale University Press publications, please contact:
U.S. Office: sales.press@yale.edu   yalebooks.com
Europe Office: sales@yaleup.co.uk   yalebooks.co.uk

Set in Adobe Caslon Pro by IDSUK (DataConnection) Ltd
Printed in Great Britain by TJ Books Limited, Padstow, Cornwall

Library of Congress Control Number: 2023938935

ISBN 978-0-300-26650-4

A catalogue record for this book is available from the British Library.

10 9 8 7 6 5 4 3 2 1

This book is dedicated to the founding team of the Exilarte Center at Vienna's University of Music and Performing Arts and to my colleagues Professor Gerold Gruber, Dr Ulrike Anton, Katharina Reischl, Nobuko Nakamura, Lucia Lajčáková and Ulrike Sych, the President of the University who was able to make it happen. I also include Geraldine Auerbach, former Director and founder of London University's Jewish Music Institute, to whom I owe an enormous debt of gratitude.

CONTENTS

ILLUSTRATIONS

FOREWORD

Trautwein hatte geglaubt, das Exil zu kennen. Das war ein Irrtum. [. . .] Er begriff, daß er bisher immer nur Einzelheiten gesehen hatte, ein Nacheinander, ein Nebeneinander. Jetzt sah er in einem die Größe und Erbärmlichkeit des Exils, seine Weite und Enge. Keine Schilderung, keine Erfahrung, kein Erlebnis vermochte diese Ganzheit des Exils, seine innere Wahrheit, zu offenbaren; nur die Kunst.

Trautwein believed he knew all about exile. That was a mistake. [. . .] He now realised that he only saw singular details of successive and parallel events. He now saw in its entirety the enormity and wretchedness of exile, with all of its vastness and constraints. No narrative, experience or expertise could reveal the totality, or inner truth of exile. Only art could do that.

Lion Feuchtwanger's novel *Exil*, 1940[1]

In my previous book, *Forbidden Music: The Jewish Composers Banned by the Nazis*, published by Yale University Press in 2013, I largely dealt with musical developments in Germany and Austria where Jewish composers were not only participants but catalysts. The Epilogue of *Forbidden Music* was a plea for a place where the musical legacies of those forced into exile could be recovered, restored and essentially returned to the audiences from whom they had been taken. So it was that with the founding of the Exilarte Research Center and Archive at Vienna's University of Music and Performing Arts (the former Academy founded by Antonio Salieri in 1817), we were able to create such a repository for the musical estates of exiled musicians, singers, performers, people who worked in the music business and, above all, composers. With each arrival, a new story of exile emerged, often stories that were overlooked, or simply never considered by previous scholars. As so many of the major émigré musical estates have already landed in established archives, we took the decision to take any musical estate regardless of genre and the profile of the individual. We have been fortunate in still attracting many important names that one would have assumed had already been housed by national libraries, or at the very least by important university collections: Hans Gál, Wilhelm Grosz, Walter Susskind, Georg Tintner and even items from Erich Korngold's estate. All are copiously represented by recordings either as composers or conductors. Yet it was the estates of individuals with less prominent profiles who often revealed the true costs of loss and exile. Just as it was only those with luck, connections and, most often, relatives and funds abroad, who could escape Hitler, it was also largely only a lucky few who managed to make successful careers in their new homelands. We think we know their stories because we are grateful for the contributions they made to the countries and communities that took them in. What has often been casually passed over is an examination of the nature of the changes that were necessary in order to survive professionally. Much of this story is the story of music post-war, and as a result may come across as something of a follow-up to *Forbidden Music*.

Exile is a familiar concept that most often applies to writers and artists. It has more recently become associated with composers and musicians as well. In German, the expression *Exilmusik* is used to cover all music and musicians persecuted and censored by the Nazis. It is strictly speaking inaccurate since composers were also banned who were never in exile, such as Franz Schreker or even Felix Mendelssohn; nor could it be applied to composers or musicians murdered in Nazi death camps, since they too were not exiled, but deported and interned. Exile is a term that allows a wide-ranging genre to be classified without resorting to the Nazi word 'entartet', usually translated as 'degenerate', but more accurately meaning 'deformed'. Paradoxically, the term 'entartet' was conceived by the Zionist doctor and philosopher Max Nordau in 1892 in his publication *Entartung*. What the Nazis banned and persecuted goes beyond strict classification because it covered everything from popular music, cabaret and operetta to applied music, the avant-garde, concert works and opera. By evading Nazi terminology and resorting to the euphemistic notion of 'exile music', they placed the real music of exile into a perpetual no man's land. It was classified as music written by exiles, but rarely examined as 'exile music'.

When music and exile are considered, it is usually the nineteenth century that comes to mind. One need only think of Chopin or Wagner as examples. Their sense of identity was tied to a specific concept of national self-determination. The idea of returning home through music is not new. In the nineteenth century, however, the idea of 'home' was most often replaced by 'homeland'. This difference becomes apparent with every performance of a Chopin polonaise or mazurka. It is music that expresses defiance rather than loss. Yet the nineteenth-century desire for national self-determination, defined by homogeneous communities collected into nation states, was different from the experiences of composers and musicians forced to flee Nazi Europe. The subversive nationalists of the nineteenth century, living abroad and pitching themselves against supranational foreign rulers, were not comparable with musicians and composers in the mid-twentieth century, oppressed because of what victims saw as religious persecution, and what oppressors saw as 'racial cleansing'.

A political refugee has a sense of identity and homeland that is different from the Jewish composer or musician who is told they are no longer part, and indeed, have never been part of the national narrative. To object to such mendacity and insist on defiantly refusing to leave one's homeland would prove tantamount to suicide. It is here that we see an important difference: the political exile leaves for reasons of conscience; the persecuted Jew flees the genocide of 'ethnic cleansing'. The hurt and indignation of being told one does not, and can never, belong to the communities in which one has lived for generations, is often translated into an even stronger sense of entitlement. Anger and a coming to terms with injustice were frequently expressed in works consigned to desk drawers in distant countries. This is music that springs from a deep need to demonstrate birthright, along with the necessity to accommodate new and complex situations and the bewilderment of learning strange new languages. This is not just music written by exiles, this is indeed the music of exile.

It was on a visit in San Diego, California, to see the Viennese-born composer Robert Fürstenthal[2] that I first stumbled on a hitherto unresolved discrepancy between music written by successful composers in former homelands and the aesthetic and stylistic changes required in countries where they found refuge. Fürstenthal was not a composer prior to his arrival in the United States in 1939, but a casual comment he made regarding his need to maintain a cultural identity, threatened by displacement, was revealing. He first came to my notice while I was working as music curator at Vienna's Jewish Museum, when I received copies of manuscripts sent by the Hugo Wolf Society. Its representative told me about an American composer, formerly from Vienna, who so admired Hugo Wolf that his compositions, including string quartets, chamber works and Lieder, could be seen as something of an extension of Wolf's own music. I assumed this would have been a composer born around 1870, or perhaps 1880, and was not prepared when it turned out to be Robert Fürstenthal, an accounts auditor living in San Diego and born in Vienna in 1920. Several years later, having left the Museum and co-founded the Exilarte Center with the professor of theory Gerold Gruber, I had an opportunity to meet Robert Fürstenthal and his Viennese wife in San Diego. It was there that he said something that unexpectedly clarified my perspective and perhaps explains the provenance of this book. When asked why he had over the previous decades continued to compose in the manner of Hugo Wolf, Gustav Mahler, Richard Strauss and Joseph Marx, he answered, 'Wenn ich komponiere, bin ich wieder in Wien' – 'When I compose, I'm back in Vienna.' This concept of 'return' while composing in new homelands was the spark that over time began to offer explanations for a number of questions and paradoxes encountered while going over the works of other, more established composers.

Fürstenthal was too young to have lived in the Vienna of Mahler and Wolf. But this was the Vienna to which he returned when he composed. To quote Orson Welles, 'The true Vienna lover lives on borrowed memories. With a bittersweet pang of nostalgia, he remembers things he never knew. The Vienna that is, is as nice a town as there is. But the Vienna that never was is the grandest city ever.'[3] Alternatively, as the philosopher Ernst Bloch put it, 'Homeland is a place where nobody has been, but is present in every memory of childhood.'[4]

This book looks at the attempts to explore the more intimate conflicts arising from the loss of homeland and identity, and the need to return and often to heal, as expressed in music. It would of course be a task of many volumes to cover every composer or musician who fled Hitler and the Nazis. The selection of composers to profile and the contexts in which they lived and worked is perhaps arbitrary and subjective, but behind every one of these figures – some well-known and established, others totally forgotten – stand many others. The selection made for this book should be seen as representative rather than comprehensive. It is not my intention to profile every significant composer forced into exile, but to describe the varied experiences of exile that can then be applied to different individuals. For that reason, this is not meant to be read as a lexicon of composers, but a selection of lives and experiences of exile, from which others may be extrapolated. By describing different aspects and experiences of exile, we often encounter the same composer in different chapters. If each composer was to be treated individually, then this work would have indeed become closer to a lexicon than an examination of different aspects of music exile.

In my forty-odd years as a recording producer, it was my good fortune to meet, work and come to know a number of musical survivors. If I do not reference every analysis made by countless academic colleagues, it is because I am presenting my own conclusions, drawn from my own experiences. I was lucky that my professional life would dovetail with working with this generation of exceptional musicians, performers and composers. As Music Curator at Vienna's Jewish Museum and then as co-founder of the Exilarte Center at Vienna's University of Music and Performing Arts (the former Music Academy where so many of the subjects discussed in this book studied or taught), I met their families and heard their stories. Interviews undertaken by many composers and musicians with German and Austrian broadcasters would inevitably offer a more candid appraisal of their individual experiences of loss. Interviews conducted for media or oral history projects in new homelands were more inclined to emphasise the gratitude that composers and musicians felt at being given a second chance, even if it meant losing what they had already accomplished. It is with these interviews to hand that I have been able to compile and organise the various complex categories and experiences that are presented in this book.

My thanks go to my colleagues mentioned in the dedication along with the many individuals who have followed, along with young students who have proven that the restitution of these legacies is relevant. Tanya Tintner has been a close friend and challenging editor. She has lived through many of the issues described and her input always went beyond correcting spelling and punctuation. But other friends who read the manuscript searching for typos and inconsistencies also need mentioning, such as Evelyn Chan and my neighbour, the now retired Professor Christopher Taylor. I'm also enormously grateful to Yale University Press's team of Julian Loose and Frazer Martin, along with their invaluable, one-to-one editor, Richard Mason. Above all, however, my thanks go to the families who held on to the musical estates of their forebears kept in basements, in lofts and under beds until they believed they had found an archive and research centre that could understand and honour the legacies of parents and grandparents who had worked, performed and composed in lost homelands.

All translations are by myself unless otherwise stated.

Michael Haas
May 2023

Introduction

Scholars who specialise in music during the Hitler years frequently reach for the term 'inner emigration'. It was a formulation conceived by the writer Frank Thiess[1] in August 1945 in response to Thomas Mann, who had spent the years of the Nazi dictatorship in Switzerland and the United States. Thiess, though not sympathetic to the Nazis, had nonetheless chosen to remain in Germany. Its relevance to musicians usually refers to composers who either withheld their works from performance in Nazi-occupied Europe, such as Karl Amadeus Hartmann, or who, like Walter Braunfels, lived in secluded isolation. There were composers such as Max Butting, Felix Petyrek or Eduard Erdmann who were not in sympathy with Hitler, but found they needed to join the NSDAP[2] if they wished to continue a career as performer or teacher. Their works were, if not directly banned, often tacitly removed from performance schedules. The concept of 'Cultural Bolshevism' hovered over works composed by those who were former members of the left-wing November Group. Joining the NSDAP, even if seen as an expedient means of continuing a professional existence, would cost them dearly after the war. In the shadow of genocide, any concessions to the Nazis, even those made by people with few or no options to emigrate, were seen as damaging and viewed as being, at the very least, a form of complicity. Over time, more sympathy has emerged for these composers as it has been recognised that not everyone could leave, even if they wanted to. Also, such dilemmas need to be seen in light of the fact that refugee quotas in many countries were already filled with Jews. Musicians who hated the Hitler regime but were otherwise not politically exposed would have taken places needed by Jewish musicians who would have been murdered had they remained in countries controlled by the Nazis.

Thus, the logical inverse of 'inner emigration' becomes 'immigration' or flight to another country. It refers largely to composers and musicians who would have been most exposed had they remained. 'Inner emigration' for them would have meant waiting for deportation to a certain death. These were usually Jewish musicians, or musicians deemed Jewish by Nazi race laws, or composers who had written works that were publicly discredited by the new regime, such as Ernst Krenek or Paul Hindemith. Both Jewish and politically exposed composers would experience persecution and the full brunt of expulsion. What Jewish musicians experienced, however, was very different: a loss of identity. The Nazis had quite deliberately removed two layers of identity: the one that allowed Jews to be culturally German, and the one that allowed anyone to be nationally Austrian, following Austria's annexation by Nazi Germany in March 1938. For many musicians, being an Austrian Jew, therefore, was to lose all sense of who you were. Countries offering refuge had been too quick in shrugging off the loss of Austria's sovereignty, and considered all refugees from Austria as Germans, for which there were set quotas. The Nazis, on the other hand, had removed German citizenship from all Jews. Those expelled for political reasons, or those who left because they could not live under the Nazi regime, would never be compelled to deny their sense of national or cultural identity. For that reason, this book takes as its premise the idea that 'inner return' is the more accurate inverse of 'inner emigration'. It is the restoration of identity, and sense of belonging, that was officially removed by a criminal regime. It is the 'restitution' of self. If what Hitler decreed was accepted internationally and Austrians were classified as Germans, but Jews were not allowed to be Germans, then it should come as no surprise that resistance and a need to return was most often expressed in works confined to the desk drawer.

Although refuge was also found in the Far East and South America, most countries offering a safe haven for escaping musicians were English-speaking, and given the vast colonial heritage of Great Britain, most of these English-speaking countries were 'New World' and strange to Central Europeans. If they spoke a second language, it was most likely French rather than English. New World countries came with different cultural priorities and traditions demanding considerable accommodation. Performances of new music from Germany conducted by Otto Klemperer would have been met with bemused, polite interest by audiences in Los Angeles rather than the enthusiastic admiration, or pink-faced indignation, of audiences in Berlin. At some point, attempts to ignite the same reactions and discourses in new homelands would come across as patronising. Americans, Canadians, Australians and New Zealanders had very different ideas regarding new music and, while welcoming the wisdom, skills and depth of knowledge offered by refugees, chose their own direction of cultural travel, often rejecting their underpinning Old World values. Musical developments in Europe may have illustrated moves from tonality to atonality, from consonance to dissonance, from the subjective to the objective; but to many pre-war New World audiences they came across as abrupt ruptures.

Over the last decades, a number of British and American books have been published about the positive contributions made to the cultural lives of countries that offered refuge to the artists, writers, composers and performers exiled by Hitler's 'Third Reich'.[3] These studies have generally been triumphalist in perspective, underlining the gains made by countries that took in Hitler's unwanted Jews and dissidents. Few have stopped to examine the losses that individual composers and performers experienced. The overall theme of these books was that Hitler's refugees came to new pastures and were hugely successful to the benefit of themselves as well as to their new homelands. These examinations did not ignore stylistic or aesthetic changes that took place, but too infrequently questioned what these changes might have cost the individual. Nor did these examinations tend to take much account of an inner urge to return to symphonic, sonata and quartet composition from composers who, prior to immigration, had assumed these forms to be superseded. Comments about changes of style and aesthetics were put down to the needs of communicating with new publics in new countries, but few, unless writing about Arnold Schoenberg, asked what these changes cost musicians artistically and whether these changes were organic, or made out of existential necessity.[4] If Schoenberg was presented more objectively, it was because of his undisputed importance in moving music away from the diatonic, a crucial development in twentieth-century music that would germinate much of the post-war avant-garde.

Missing answers to previously unasked questions start to become more pressing. For example, if Erich Wolfgang Korngold was such a successful film music composer, why did he leave Hollywood as soon as the war was over? Why is this period in his life so briefly covered in the memoirs of his wife Luzi Korngold, and why are his film scores, for which he is justifiably famous, so casually dismissed in family correspondence? He and other refugees made indisputable contributions to a fledgling industry, empowering it with their music at least as much if not more than even the most glamorous movie star. As John Mauceri argues in his book *The War on Music*, they represented an organic transition from one century to the next.[5] Yet to Korngold, Ernst Toch, Erich Zeisl and others, what started out as an exciting experiment with a new medium became a means of survival and a limitation of possibilities of artistic development. The inability to move into other genres during the war was unquestionably seen by Korngold and his family as a rupture.

4

Britain is deservedly proud of having taken in a number of musical refugees including the composers Hans Gál and Egon Wellesz, both highly successful opera composers before 1938. Their contributions to post-war British scholarship can hardly be contested. Much of Britain's early music research may be traced back to Wellesz while Gál is remembered today as a co-founder of the Edinburgh Festival and guiding spirit at Edinburgh University's music department. Other than an opera by Wellesz, written as a submission for a competition held by the Arts Council of England, neither composer would write another opera. Nor would they ever hear another note of any of their operas that had previously enjoyed regular performances in German and Austrian houses. Their lives had been saved, but their legacies lost. Much of the music composed in new homelands, often in the privacy of their studios, may be seen as attempts to find connections between past and current situations. Perhaps Hans Gál's arid *24 Preludes and Fugues*, composed for himself in the 1980s and 1990s, can be taken as an example.

Another example might be Karol Rathaus, a composer whose success in Berlin during the interwar years can hardly be overestimated. As nearly 1,000 letters held in the archive of Universal Edition attest, he was one of Germany's headline composers.[6] His operas and ballets were performed at Berlin's State Opera; his orchestral works were performed by the Berlin Philharmonic and conducted by Wilhelm Furtwängler. Rathaus's collaboration with Alfred Döblin briefly threatened the hegemony of Brecht and Weill; Rathaus was the first classical composer to write a film score. He remained successful as a composer of film music in Paris and London after fleeing Berlin in 1933. He even composed a ballet, which was performed at the Royal Opera House, Covent Garden.[7] When war threatened Europe, he managed to save himself and his family, taking a low-paid job in a recently founded college on New York's Long Island. From the moment his worldly possessions, still in London, were destroyed by a German V2 rocket in 1940, he devoted himself to teaching and building up the music department of Queens College in New York. Rathaus never spoke of his past to any of his students and he avoided contact with former colleagues and friends who were successfully conducting concert and opera performances in nearby Manhattan.

Yet all of these composers continued to write music. Sometimes it was didactic material for local educational authorities, at other times it was an attempt to present themselves in a more exposed context to local audiences; but very often it was simply for themselves and their desk drawer, or even more occasionally, for places of worship.

Since establishing the Exilarte Center, we have looked for lost musical estates beyond the obvious countries of exile. It has taken us to the Far East, the South Pacific, Central and South America. Of course, we have also taken in a number of 'orphaned' estates from North America and Great Britain. If the estates were of composers, it has been surprising to see how many wrote music for themselves, friends and family, without any intention of having it published. Other works that these composers did intend for wider dissemination were often stylistically distinct from what they had composed before, though there was little accompanying information as to why or how these changes had been made. Only a hint in a letter might offer an explanation. The reasons for such changes can only be surmised. As we so often heard from their surviving children and grandchildren, these composers were grateful for simply having been able to survive.

Yet many composers felt that Hitler had successfully smothered their European creativity. Moreover, it wasn't only composers and musicians who were lucky enough to flee from the Nazis, it was also their audiences with whom they were engaged in a creative dialogue. The public reception of new works was just as important in music's European development as the creativity of individual composers. With both public and composers severely constrained, exiled creativity was forced to turn to new audiences. Dialogues with new

1. Richard Strauss rehearsing the Vienna Symphony Orchestra on 22 January 1929. Subsequent research carried out by Mark Latimer identified members of the orchestra who were murdered or forced into exile. He also identified Nazi facilitators and party members.[8]

audiences were difficult to establish. Kurt Weill's successes on Broadway must stand as a singular exception, but do we know that he fully understood his creative conversation with New York's public, and was he in full command of his dialogue with them? Or was he writing works in the blind hope they would be understood and appreciated? His early death at the age of fifty precluded any certain answers to such questions. In any case, Lys Symonette, a singer close to Kurt Weill and Lotte Lenya, told the author that it was 'the pain of losing Germany and the German language that killed him'.[9] A weak heart and smoking would not have helped Weill's chances, but we cannot know the degree and nature of the stress that ultimately took his life. There is no 'like-with-like' comparison available, as he was the only refugee from Nazi Europe who arrived in America and went on to make a success on Broadway. Can we assume he did not give a second thought to the composers who had been equally successful in Germany before Hitler, who then found themselves struggling in American exile? Composers such as Paul Benatzky, Friedrich Hollaender, Emmerich Kálmán, Paul Abraham and Jaromír Weinberger represented different genres of Central European light musical theatre. They nevertheless enjoyed enormous success in Europe prior to emigration, and unlike Weill, did not manage to replicate their successes and continue their artistic development in America. Weill must have felt like a lottery winner surrounded by needy relatives.

Considering the output of composers prior to and post-immigration into America, one can detect many consistent patterns despite enormous stylistic differences. One of these patterns is the need to reconnect to a place or a fundamental identity that is put in question by transplantation. Sometimes it can be detected in a certain choice of poetry for song settings, or a return to quintessentially European forms. The return to classical ideas has already been mentioned, but also the works written as exercises in 'Aufarbeiten' – a German word that means 'coming to terms', though the German expression is active rather than passive. A more complete translation of 'Aufarbeiten' would be 'working one's way through to reality'. Other composers felt bludgeoned into accepting racial and religious identities they had previously discarded, for example embracing their long-forgotten Jewish faith or bypassing confessional identities, embracing Zionism. Returning to a Jewish identity, either confessional or political, was also an act of personal restitution.

Music that was banned, forgotten, suppressed and then deemed inappropriate for a post-Hitler Europe in need of re-education is too stylistically varied in too many genres to be classified in one category. The closest one can come to an umbrella term is the Nazi word 'entartet', which is the worst possible solution to a complex question of semantics. But so too is the classification 'exile music' or *Exilmusik*. It is too vague and refers to the situation of individual composers rather than the music they produced. The music of exile was the means by which composers could return to a sense of inner stability. Exile for composers thrown out of Hitler's Europe meant something broader than physical expulsion and was a loss of more than place: it was a state of physical and mental transplantation. For many composers, it could only be allayed through composing works that suggested return and offered a sense of inner restitution. This was more than just music written by composers forced by Hitler to live in faraway exotic places. It makes its own statement. It is music that could never have been written by a composer of the same generation and hailing from the same homeland, but not forced into exile. Nor is it music that a composer could have written who was native-born in those countries that became new homelands for refugees. The music of exile was a unique synthesis written by a composer in a place to which they did not fully belong. As such, it came across as too foreign for local audiences while remaining alien to audiences in former homelands. It is music that, with its unique synthesis emerging from displacement, deserves its own chapter within the broader story of twentieth-century music.

1

The *'Hanswurst'* of Havoc

Damals . . . lachten wir über diesen Hitler. Ein Verrückter, sagten wir, ein' Hanswurst, ein Idiot; von der Sorte haben wir viele. Produkte des Krieges. Gesundbeter und stigmatisierte Jungfrauen und Propheten, Putschisten und Mörder und wer weiß, was sonst noch alles. Aber ihre Zeit ist vorbei. Nach und nach werden sie ja wohl zu sich kommen und den Mund halten.

Back then . . . we laughed at this Hitler character. He was a nut, we told ourselves, a provincial and an idiot – the likes of many others knocking about at the time. He's a product of the War: Messianic healers, virgins with the stigmata and prophets, revolutionaries, murderers and who knows what else. But their time has come and gone. Slowly they'll start to sober up and shut up.

Memoirs of the writer and journalist Vicki Baum[1]

Two quite incompatible strands existed in Nazi cultural ideology. One strand designated any modernist development that nationalist arbiters found offensive under the vague classification of 'Cultural Bolshevism'. The other strand of works deemed 'undesirable' was the result of something referred to as 'race', a wildly misunderstood concept that was applied as freely to nationalities as it was to non-European physiognomy and skin colour. Nazi cultural arbiters conjoined these two disparate concepts by surmising that only representatives of a foreign race could be capable of producing or influencing works of 'Cultural Bolshevism'.

Included in these pseudo-scientific concepts were romanticised ideals of the German people as Europe's dominant 'race'. This view had evolved during a time when Germany was not a unified nation state but a network of German-speaking, self-governing units, some of which were too small to qualify as anything more than a personal 'estate' (Liechtenstein), whereas others were large and powerful kingdoms. The only idea that could unite this diverse group, each speaking their variant dialect, was the German of Luther's Bible, along with medieval or Norse mythology. The mid-nineteenth century was an age that produced the poems of *Des Knaben Wunderhorn* and thousand-page novels about knights and castles by authors such as Adalbert Stifter. It was an age that craved national self-determination. The French had shown what advantages were to be found in the cohesion of the nation state. As a result, there was not a linguistic community in Europe that did not strive to achieve the same status of nation-state sovereignty.

The default setting of Europe was rule by foreign emperors, whether it was the nominal head of the German Confederation, until 1866 the Austrian Emperor, who also held large tracts of Central Europe, Italy and the Adriatic – or the French. The rulers of Europe came from a limited number of aristocratic families evenly divided between Catholics and Protestants. Protestants ruled in Great Britain, much of Germany, Holland and Scandinavia, and Catholics ruled the rest of Europe, including much of southern Germany and Austria. It was incomprehensible to most Europeans that a continent of nation states based on communities who spoke the same language and practised the same religion was possible. At the same time, such a Europe that used these markers for self-determination could not avoid the pseudo-science emerging around Darwinism, eugenics and the concept that certain communities in Europe had developed in particular ways because of some mysterious physical component. One saw it in cattle, why shouldn't it apply to people as well? Racism had risen its very ugly head and would continue to reverberate throughout the following century. It was one of the driving philosophies behind German aggression in the First World War, and with Europe's new settlement of nation states, tidily organised into self-contained republics, it would become an even more deadly component of political philosophy leading into the Second World War. The homogenised nation state had no use for the Emperor as a unifying element in a network of disparate peoples. Language and religion were all that were necessary. Such limiting criteria inevitably led to debates as to who could belong and who should be excluded. Early twentieth-century racism was the malevolent shadow of new nationhood. Jews, Roma and Sinti all found themselves vulnerable to exclusion, as were any number of individuals deemed incompatible with the racial ideal.

Liberal constitutions in both Germany and Austria-Hungary towards the final quarter of the nineteenth century had granted all citizens, including Jews, full emancipation with the freedom to live and work without hindrance. Individual rights had to be fought through courts and parliaments, such as the right for Jews to marry non-Jews or the right to attend or teach in universities or join the military or civil service. By the start of the twentieth century, legal equality had been achieved, but social prejudice continued. For some antisemites, Jews were antagonistic to Christianity and had been murderers of Christ. Unless they converted, they were condemned by God. To others, Jews were representative of an outside interest, another nation and therefore another 'race'. They could convert all they wanted. It would never result in the Jew becoming a fellow citizen. As Richard Wagner wrote, 'The Jew could no more become a German than an African could become a white European.'[2]

This concept of 'foreign' would be extrapolated into making Jews responsible for every modernist development in the twentieth century, all of which were deemed as 'non-German'. Perhaps this was the greatest and most damaging of all racist lies. Far from being behind movements that wished to tip over the apple carts of convention, Jews were assimilating and had subsumed conventions so thoroughly that they initially showed a reluctance to deviate from them. The most popular genres exploded with Jewish creativity, a thorn in the flesh of the antisemite. If Jews were behind the most popular songs, the most popular operettas, that could only have a negative influence on the purity of the German non-Jew. This disregarded the fact that large communities of Jews had lived in what would become Germany before the arrival of Teutonic tribes and had intermarried with locals for millennia. The Russian Empress Catherine the Great may have confined Jews in her realm to the strip of the Empire called the Pale of Settlement, but it did not make them any less a European people. They were simply a non-Christian European people, something that disturbed Catholic, Orthodox and Protestant clergy and the uneducated masses even more. Nevertheless, the Eastern European, as opposed to the German, Jew was usually seen as a shtetl Jew, or a Jew from the ghetto, and no matter how educated and assimilated, the traces of accent and the sound of their spoken language continued to betray them, even if they were tall, blonde and blue-eyed.

This short excursion into German antisemitism is intended to demonstrate the synthesis of nationalism, racism and *avant le mot*, denunciations of 'cultural appropriation'. The Jew was, according to the nationalist antisemite (of which Richard Wagner was something of a prototype), as incapable of composing a symphony or a sonata as today's claims that whites are incapable of writing from the viewpoint of someone who is black, or a man is of writing from the viewpoint of a woman. No matter how worthy, good and admirable such a work might come across, it could only be viewed as imitation and artificial. The closeness of 'art' to 'artificial' in English is even closer in German, with the concepts being 'Kunst' and 'künstlich'.[3] All art is by its nature artifice, even the *Gesamtkunst* works of Wagner.[4] But racism, the draw of science, the traditions of religion all conspired against anyone Jewish. If they were successful in business, medicine and law, professions in which Jews were particularly prominent, this was seen as an insidious rather than a benevolent development emerging from the Liberal constitutions of the late nineteenth century.

Antisemitism in the early years of the twentieth century, camouflaged as nationalists protecting 'native' German culture, had become ingrained in the public discourse, with even Jewish writers and critics disparaging Jewish composers.[5] When dissonance was left unresolved in music, it must have been the fault of a Jewish composer, since no 'German' (i.e. non-Jewish) composer would dream of such a thing ... *pace* Bach, Beethoven, Brahms and of course Richard Strauss. The same view was held in questions of departures from tonality, or the transition from artistic subjectivity to objectivity. All of these departures and deviations were 'non-German', and it was easy for German antisemites to make German Jews into scapegoats.[6] The German Jew could never win, could never fit in, and could never be allowed to participate or contribute to the narrative of German culture. Those who did, such as Heinrich Heine or Felix Mendelssohn, were simply denounced as frauds and their admirers were told they had been taken for fools, incapable of seeing the deceit.

But Jews were crucial to German culture and tacitly accepted by even the likes of Richard Wagner, whose final opera *Parsifal* was given over to the Jewish conductor Hermann Levi. Heine's poems had been set by every important composer in the nineteenth century and even Wagner's *Flying Dutchman* can cite Heine as its original source. No amount of antisemitism could remove the appeal of Offenbach's operettas, Meyerbeer's operas, or the overwhelming popularity of Mendelssohn. *Nathan the Wise* may not have been written by a Jew, but Gotthold Ephraim Lessing's play demonstrated Jewish entitlement. Because of intermarriage and assimilation, some of the greatest writers of the German language would later be wilfully suppressed, and their books burned. No matter how great their poetry, how compelling their plays or popular their novels, they simply could not represent German culture for the reason that they were Jews.

It should come as no surprise that Jewish writers, composers and artists did not see things in the same way. Twentieth-century Austrian Jewish composers as different as Hans Gál, Erich Zeisl and Arnold Schoenberg saw themselves as products and arbiters of a musical culture that was innately German. In 1919 the half-Jewish composer Franz Schreker was officially anointed the only conceivable successor to Richard Wagner, by the half-Jewish journalist Paul Bekker writing in the influential *Frankfurter Zeitung*. It was a red rag to antisemites who believed, justifiably or not, that Richard Strauss or Hans Pfitzner were the more deserving candidates. Neither Bekker nor Schreker were practising Jews, yet both believed themselves to be profoundly involved in the narrative of German music in the twentieth century.

The overwhelming emphasis on Jewish Austrian composers is no coincidence. Vienna was a magnet for musical genius in the nineteenth century and a producer of musical genius in the twentieth. The sheer number of prominent composers in the twentieth century with Jewish parents and grandparents (the criterion for exclusion by Nazi cultural arbiters) from Austria is overwhelming: Gustav Mahler, Arnold Schoenberg, Alexander Zemlinsky, Franz Schreker, Erich Korngold, Egon Wellesz, Hans Gál, Hanns Eisler, Ernst Toch are just the names of the so-called 'serious music' composers. When it comes to composers of operettas, film music and popular music, Austrians continue to outweigh in prominence their German neighbours. Of course, there were many important composers banned from Germany due to their Jewish parentage, such as Kurt Weill and Walter Braunfels, but Austria had another issue. It had never been part of Bismarck's project because most Austrians were not Germanic. Post-1918, this was no longer the case. Austria's claim to German cultural identity was profound. For most German-speaking Austrians, the creation of a separate German-speaking Austria after 1918 was nonsense. In their view, it should have been folded into the German nation state, as Bismarck would have done forty-five years earlier had Habsburg Austria been less Slavic. As if to prove the point, nearly all the composers mentioned above either moved to Germany or their careers and their successes were based in Germany.

The double loss of identity, however, with Austria's annexation (*Anschluss*) by Nazi Germany in March 1938 was profound. With Austria's dissolution as a separate country, all Austrians became German nationals, except Jews, who were not allowed the 'privilege' of German citizenship. These various losses were hugely felt and often reflected in music written in exile.

Jewish composers in the rest of Europe were altogether less fortunate. Few survived. Germans knew what was happening to Jewish fellow citizens after 1933, and when Austria fell in March 1938 there was just enough time for those with resources to leave. The rest of Europe was less fortunate. Czechoslovakia fell to the Nazis in March 1939 and war broke out in September. Nearly an entire generation of Czech composers was murdered. The rest of Europe suffered similar losses, though cultural excavations are still taking place in France, Poland, Hungary, Romania, Greece and the Netherlands. The inability to escape left a vast vacuum in European musical creativity. It distorted what we believe we know. We consider today's capitals of what we think of as 'modern music' as being Berlin, Vienna or Paris, but we cannot know what might have come out of Prague, Warsaw, Amsterdam and Budapest. All had separate, independent musical biotopes. Some were influenced by Berlin, Vienna or Paris, but many developed in parallel, producing distinctive musical idioms.

Their music of exile is difficult to classify for the simple reason that so few lived to experience exile. The closest we can come to examining the music by non-German and Austrian composers that grew out of exile is the Czech composer Hans Winterberg, discussed later in this book. As with Winterberg, the music of exile was also largely the music of post-war Europe.

An Overview of the Obvious Options

If Anglo-American historians have been triumphalist in writing about the gains made by those nations that took in Hitler's refugees, they have been slow to draw conclusions as to why this was the case. The obvious fact remains that only those with international connections, funds or incredibly good luck managed to escape Hitler's murderous regime. To observe the influx of refugees arriving in England, one might have assumed that all Jews were doctors, lawyers, scientists, industrialists, academics or classical musicians. The reality, however, was that only these sectors had the wherewithal and resources to escape. Jews, like any other community, had as many tinkers and tailors as it had lawyers and doctors. The tinkers and tailors had no access to a workable exit strategy, no relatives living abroad, no funds held in foreign bank accounts, no connections through business contacts. They rarely spoke another language. If the cream of the European haute bourgeoisie were taken in as refugees, it should come as no surprise that, offered the opportunity, their contributions would turn out to be considerable.

It was no different for musicians. Classical musicians were often international whereas popular musicians were more local. *Schlager* – hit songs – weren't performed in English, as is so often the case today, but in native languages addressing local features, often written in local dialects. The songs may have sounded jazzy and pseudo-American, but the topics being sung about were totally provincial. The composer Walter Arlen wrote a piano fantasy on just such a hit song called *Wenn die letzte Blaue geht* (*When the Last Blue Goes*). Even for a German-speaking audience, its reference could be unclear, as the 'last blue' referred to the blue light on the back of the last tram at night in Vienna. If you missed the 'last blue tram', you had to wait until four o'clock the next morning or walk home. In Arlen's fantasy, simply called *Die letzte Blaue*, he incorporated identifiable musical motifs that referred to Vienna, using quotes from *Die Fledermaus* and bits of the *Blue Danube Waltz* in order to provide commentary on a lost locality. Though the music of the original *Schlager* was composed by Willy Engel-Berger, who continued to work throughout the Nazi years as a film composer, the author of the text, Artur Rebner, only managed to escape to France, where he was interned before immigrating to Mexico. Arlen's piano fantasy in some ways stands as a memorial to the countless Jewish composers and librettists who composed such numbers by the dozen. Many were murdered in camps, or only managed to escape to some of the few countries still willing to take refugees, such as Mexico, India, various Latin American countries, the Far East and China. The works of these composers and poets would have been rarely, if ever, heard or performed outside the individual towns or cities in which they were composed. What was true of Vienna was equally true of Munich, Cologne, Hamburg, Berlin, or anywhere that had a strong local culture that could be referenced in song. There was little infrastructure available for selling popular songs as sheet music or 78 rpm discs outside of specific geographical markets. As a result, *Schlager* composers and lyricists had few, if any, international contacts they could call upon.

Of course, there were also the hit songs from the movies that spread across the German-speaking world. Until the Nazis came to power, the film industry in Berlin had been private, allowing some Jewish input to continue. The most successful composers of film chansons and cabaret did have the international contacts to be able to escape. Werner Richard Heymann and Friedrich Hollaender managed to make it to Hollywood via Paris. But even enormous popularity could not always guarantee special treatment or an easy exit. The Austrian cabaret composer Hermann Leopoldi was arrested and sent to Dachau after attempting to enter Czechoslovakia. Colleagues such as Fritz Grünbaum, Fritz Löhner-Beda and Paul

Morgen were murdered. Family members who had successfully managed to immigrate to America were able to bribe officials so that Leopoldi could follow. His colleague Karl Farkas also initially made it to Paris, where he was interned before arriving in America where, lacking an affidavit, he narrowly avoided being sent back to Europe. These, however, were the best-known composers, performers and entertainers working in German-language popular music and cabaret. For every one of these better-known names, dozens of lesser, younger names perished, unable to negotiate the complex machinations of finding a safe haven, lacking international contacts, or simply too poor, too old, too monoglot or too frightened to flee.

The composer Berthold Goldschmidt was a member of the music staff of Berlin's Charlottenburg Opera in 1935. He told the story of being summoned before a Nazi official. In the course of the interview, the conversation switched to classical music. The Nazi official confided to Goldschmidt that his daughter was studying piano, at which point they started discussing which works she might be learning. Suddenly, the official leaned over the desk and hissed *sotto voce* that Goldschmidt needed to get out of the country as quickly as possible. During these first years of the Hitler dictatorship, it was not clear how things would develop for Germany's Jews, so the warning coming early from an official sufficed for Goldschmidt to prepare his departure for England, where former Charlottenburg colleagues were already developing Glyndebourne Opera in Sussex.

Considered closely, this account underscores the unspoken solidarity of what in German is referred to as the *Bildungsbürgertum*, a word that describes the bourgeois citizen who invests in self-cultivation. It's a demographic that could be understood as the educated middle class. The same Nazi official would probably have had less tolerance for the likes of Artur Rebner, or Engel-Berger had he actually been Jewish. In addition, Goldschmidt was in a position of being able to contact colleagues in England who were already engaged within a well-connected network to help facilitate his departure from Germany. Walter Arlen, the composer of *Die letzte Blaue*, came from the Dichter family who not only owned a large department store in Vienna but were related to the wealthy American Pritzker family, who provided affidavits and funds. The more one deals with the music of exile, the more one confronts the fact that much of the music was not just a 'return' to a country, a homeland, a language, but also to a particular way of life, a loss of privilege and position within an educated and cultivated society. Even composers with communist sympathies such as Hanns Eisler or Paul Dessau came from Germany's *Bildungsbürgertum*, with its inbuilt network of international connections.

Escaping Hitler's Germany is largely seen today as escaping unavoidable and fully visible annihilation. Yet genocide was a policy only consciously adopted at the so-called Wannsee Conference in January 1942. The activities of SS Einsatzgruppen in Eastern Europe were kept under wraps. The marginalisation of Germany's Jews had been deliberate, venal and often brutal, but at no point was there an impression that they would be the victims of mass murder and wiped out of European history and culture. For that reason, there remained kernels of hope that the situation would eventually return to normal despite a process of marginalisation that made it more and more imperative for Jews to leave. This was initially the intention of the Nazis, but without funds, family or help abroad, leaving Germany meant losing everything except for the minimum one was allowed to take.

Jews who were on the public payroll lost their jobs with the so-called *Wiederherstellung des Berufsbeamtentums* (Law for the Restoration of the Professional Civil Service), passed on 7 April 1933, a week after the official boycott of Jewish businesses and professional services and two weeks before Jewish children were banned from state education. The Restoration of the Professional Civil Service meant that Jews teaching or performing, or working in any capacity in publicly funded institutions, were dismissed. This law gave notice to a sector that was by definition part of the *Bildungsbürgertum* – the educated middle class, as entry to public positions was largely limited to the qualified or professional. Tradespeople and employees in the private sector would not have been affected. As classical musicians were publicly employed, they were effectively given advance notice of how things might develop. Composers writing popular hit songs for Berlin's film industry, or writing and performing cabaret or performing as part of an independent ensemble, would have carried on as normal. They would have noticed discrimination when venues operating with public money cancelled performances. However, the threat of not earning a livelihood had not yet happened to those Jewish musicians, performers and composers working in the private sector.

There were of course situations in which even the best connected found it difficult to emigrate, just as there were many musicians without contacts who still managed to escape Germany. Erich Zeisl was only thirty-three when Hitler's troops marched into Vienna in March 1938. Due to Germany's embargo of any work by a Jewish composer in the previous five years, Zeisl's international career was reduced to occasional performances in Czechoslovakia or Switzerland. He was little known outside of Austria, despite his growing reputation as a local composer of considerable promise. Zeisl and his wife nevertheless managed to flee to Paris, an option that was still reasonably viable following Austria's annexation. They searched through American telephone books on the look-out for people with the same surname, which produced moments of hope that quickly evaporated until one of the American 'Zeisls' provided their much-needed affidavit. Despite having important contacts in Paris among refugees who were already leaving for safer countries, the Zeisls only managed to escape by actively creating their own 'good luck'.

The opposite was true of Franz Schreker, a composer and teacher so embedded in the Austro-German music establishment that it remains baffling today why he never managed to find the support necessary to emigrate. He had very different issues to deal with. His

2. The Zeisl family at home in Vienna, 10 November 1938, the day after *Kristallnacht* and their last day in Austria. From left to right: Ilona Jellinek, Gertrud Zeisl (née Jellinek), family friend Hilde Hirschenhauser and Erich Zeisl.

wife was not Jewish, and as Schreker himself was only half-Jewish their children were therefore only quarter-Jewish, meaning nobody in the Schreker household, other than Schreker himself, considered themselves in immediate danger. After losing his position at Berlin's Prussian Academy of Arts, Schreker was faced with the difficult task of convincing his family of the gravity of the situation. His wife was disinclined to leave Berlin and was in any case deeply involved in an affair with another woman. The stress of Schreker's professional situation, perhaps the vulnerability of his marriage and other factors, resulted in a stroke that left him paralysed before his death in 1934.

Such blindness to how things could develop was shared by many, and often by people who should have been more sensitive. When Schreker appealed for help from Joseph Marx, one of Vienna's most noted composition teachers and head of the Academy, in the hope of returning to his former teaching position in Vienna, Marx replied in a letter that Jews were themselves to blame for their present predicament.[7] Marx had a number of Jewish pupils, including Erich Zeisl, so his lack of sympathy for a former colleague and friend is chilling in light of the events to come.

In July 1938 the Americans convened a conference in Évian in France in order to come to some sort of agreement as to how to accommodate internationally the impending wave of refugees fleeing Germany and former Austria, following the Nazi annexation in March of that year. Refugees were mostly Jewish, or those deemed Jewish by Nazi race laws, and the conference ended as a propaganda coup for the Nazis, who proudly reported that nobody in the world was prepared to take Germany's Jews, thereby suggesting international acquiescence in their policy of Jewish expatriation and expropriation. Emboldened by seeming international indifference, they unleashed their grotesque pogrom in November 1938 known as *Kristallnacht*, the so-called 'Night of Broken Glass', in a brutal attempt to intimidate Jewish stragglers into emigrating.

Mexico was one of the few countries that did not recognise the legality of Germany's annexation of Austria. As a result, Mexico continued to view Austrian citizenship as valid and its diplomatic offices in Vienna began offering large numbers of visas to Austrians, and especially Jews, who were otherwise without international connections or funds. Other countries simply followed Berlin's lead and closed their embassies in Vienna, as it was no longer a capital city. Officially, Mexico was prepared only to take political refugees, but as many of these were Jewish, or at least 'non-Aryan', the categories often overlapped. Mexico's bold stand in 1938 is today remembered with the name 'Mexico Square' in Vienna's predominantly Jewish Second District.

The situation in Austria was precarious as the Roman Catholic clerical dictatorship of Engelbert Dollfuß, followed by Kurt Schuschnigg, persecuted Social Democrats, Communists and members of the outlawed German Nazi Party, sending all of them to Austria's recently established Mauthausen concentration camp. As many German Austrians still resented the fact that the treaties following the First World War had not allowed Austria to become part of Germany, sympathy for the *Anschluss* was widespread. Suppression of pan-German aspirations by the Dollfuß/Schuschnigg regime only resulted in the removal of any potential opposition to Hitler coming from the political left. The recognition of various international diplomats in Mexico, China and Japan is all the more remarkable given the generally wide support for the Nazi annexation.

It seems paradoxical that the official Nazi policy prior to the Wannsee Conference was to make Germany so impossible for Jews that they would be compelled to leave, and then placing so many obstacles in their way that many of the best-made emigration plans were thwarted. Leaving Germany, especially following the annexation of Austria, became a bureaucratic, Kafkaesque nightmare of smoke and mirrors: documents requiring counter-documents that required previous documents only being obtained by presentation of the documents yet to be acquired. This sent frustrated Jews into endless circles, even those who had come to terms with leaving all of their worldly goods behind and handing over their bank accounts to local officials. It was not just a question of having international contacts or access to funds in foreign bank accounts; it was also a question of perseverance and patience, of having to smile while being insulted and abused. Most Jews in Vienna were not wealthy. Of the nearly 200,000 Jews living in Austria, only 48,000 were wealthy enough to pay their synagogue membership fees.[8]

The options of where to go were becoming increasingly limited. With Austria's annexation, followed by the so-called Nazi Protectorate of Bohemia and Moravia just months before the outbreak of war, quotas were already filling up. America was hardly taking any more German émigrés and while Canada had agreed to take refugees, it specifically excluded Jews. Ultimately, Canada and Australia would end up taking Jewish refugees who were deported from Great Britain as enemy aliens.

From 1933 onwards, neighbouring states took in the largest number of refugees: France, Belgium and the Netherlands each took in 30,000; America took in over 100,000, while Israel came in with the next largest number of 55,000, followed by Argentina with 45,000. South Africa took in 26,000, while 20,000 made it to Shanghai. Australia and Brazil took in approximately 8,000 refugees each, with Bolivia taking in the next largest number of 7,000. All of these numbers are admittedly conservative estimates offered by Amsterdam's Anne Frank House.[9]

From Switzerland to France, Spain, Portugal, the Netherlands, Scandinavia

Escape to Switzerland, France, Spain or Portugal was always a temporary solution. These countries saw themselves primarily as transit stations, offering those with funds and potential connections just enough time to organise onward travel plans. With the declaration of war, Germans and Austrians were interned in camps as 'enemy aliens', while Switzerland requested that Germany begin identifying Jews with a 'J' on passports and other travel documents. We know from Korngold family correspondence how difficult it was to remain in Switzerland. The musicologist Alfred Einstein also decided that the only reasonable escape route was to leave Switzerland, travel to Italy, and pay a local fisherman to take him and his family to France. The wait for American visas in Switzerland was particularly long, while the country maintained strict rules forbidding refugees from taking employment. The Hungarian conductor Georg Solti mentioned endless evenings of bridge with the composer Vladimir Vogel. From

Solti's conversation, it was clear that he had no idea that Vogel was a composer, and presumably Vogel only knew Solti as an out-of-work pianist and répétiteur.[10] Fame and reputation were of little importance. The movie star and heart-throb tenor Joseph Schmidt, famous through his nine films and recordings, one of which was *Ein Lied geht um die Welt*, known in English as *A Song Goes Round the World*, one of the most popular songs of the age, was interned in Switzerland. He died of heart failure in 1942 aged thirty-eight after a short release had allowed him to recover from a throat infection.

Portugal was operating as something of a free port, with people arriving from all corners of Europe, often via North Africa, from where they could travel by ship to the United States and Latin America. The Portuguese consul in Bordeaux, Aristides de Sousa Mendes, disobeyed the instructions from Portugal's dictator António de Oliveira Salazar, and issued some 30,000 transit visas and passports. Ultimately, nearly 100,000 Jews immigrated via Lisbon on the passenger liners *Mouzinho*, *Nyassa*, *Serpa Pinto* or *Nea Hellas* to Brazil, Argentina, Cuba or North America. Alma Mahler and her third husband, the writer Franz Werfel, along with the cabaret composer and performer Karl Farkas, were led on foot across the Pyrenees by special guides facilitated by Eleanor Roosevelt. Other notables who escaped via Portugal included Otto von Habsburg, who travelled under the name of Otto Bar. A small émigré cabaret called *Bompernasse* – a pun on Paris's *Montparnasse* with *Bom* the Portuguese word for 'good' and *parnasse* punning with the Portuguese for 'legs', *pernas* – was opened near Lisbon's train station, where charity performances were mounted by Farkas and others. All of this was possible because of Salazar's decision to remain neutral and profit from both warring factions. Few musicians, however, chose to remain in Portugal, despite its representing for many some sort of paradise. Salazar's rule was called 'a dictatorship in slippers'.[11] Escape to Portugal offered the context for the film *Casablanca*, where desperate refugees awaited visas and passage to North and South America.

France, however, was not yet a 'transit country' and it took in many fleeing Jewish refugees. In fact, just under half of the 330,000 Jews in France were refugees from Germany, Austria and Czechoslovakia. Antisemitism had died down after the exoneration of Alfred Dreyfus in 1906, but flared up again in the 1930s. Nevertheless, until its fall to the Germans in 1940, Paris offered a safe haven where many thought they could settle permanently, establish careers and pick up where they had left off in their homelands. Sadly, this was not to be; restrictions made it difficult to impossible to employ refugees. Accounts of Jewish refugee life in France are offered by the writers Soma Morgenstern, in his memoirs, and Lion Feuchtwanger, in his novel *Paris Gazette*.[12]

Yet refugee life in Paris provided an interesting dynamic to fleeing Jews. It offered a Zionist identity exclusive of confessional dogmas – in other words, being a Jew transcended religious adherence and was understood as a cultural, indeed, a *national* identity. There is a lack of clarity as to the extent that such Zionism was actively looking for a homeland. In the case of Arnold Schoenberg's Zionism in Paris, it amounted to establishing a dynamic political movement that would ultimately lead to a nation state for Jews. Many Jews arriving in Paris were confronted with their Jewish identity for the first time. Schoenberg had converted to Protestantism in 1898. He returned to Judaism in 1933, while nevertheless being aware of his Jewish heritage in 1914 when he wrote the libretto to his unfinished oratorio *Die Jakobsleiter* (*Jacob's Ladder*). In the mid-1920s he wrote his play *Der biblische Weg* (*The Biblical Way*), generally accepted as a template of his unfinished opera *Moses und Aron*. In a letter from Hôtel Régina with a presumed date of May 1933, he wrote to Ernst Toch:

Dear Dr Toch,
The mistake always made by the Jews was relying on the help of others and taking comfort in the belief that their charitable acts,

like all undertakings, actually served towards an end [handwritten in the margin: *Like Zionism*].

We could say that this has been the state of play for the last 150 years (though perhaps Russian and Polish Jews would disagree!). Today, however, such sleepy confidence would only lead to the end of Jews both collectively and individually.

For that reason, I wish to create a movement in which Jews return to being a nation, living in their own country and united as a state. We must resort to all the well-known means that history has given us without consideration of any conventional beliefs that Jews and non-Jews hold regarding the question of what it is to be Jewish. With consideration against the self-imposed Jewish sense of purpose as God's chosen people – a people whose sole purpose is to maintain this concept – this idea of an unimaginable God. One needs a man for this, prepared to run against brick walls and [someone who] is equally prepared to run around everyone who [thinks the solution is] simply to sit down and talk, discuss, and debate in parliaments [and pay lip-service] to support: to put it bluntly, [the people who only] want to dampen everything down. I've decided, in lieu of anyone better, for the time being to make a start. One thing is for sure, I'm known for running against brick walls and it's quite visibly not done me any harm.

One can follow me until someone better shows up. In any case, I don't want to halt what I feel I must carry out. Please let me know how you feel.

Warm wishes,

Your,

Arnold Schönberg

[handwritten] *And another thing. It would be pointless to take up other opportunities such as conspiring against Germany. We should do only what's useful to us – not undertake actions against others. Everything for the Jews.*[13]

Toch's thoughts on Judaism were less strident, and more considered. Only later in American exile did he express them in a variety of lectures, papers and essays with titles such as 'The Teutons are Blond', 'Nazism as a Political Power' and 'The Attitude of Jews'. His sojourn in Paris was brief and but a stepping stone before he left for the United States.

The father of Schoenberg's future daughter-in-law, the composer Erich Zeisl,[14] had a different experience altogether. Although nearly thirty years younger than Schoenberg, he too was a child of Vienna's Second District, Leopoldstadt, called colloquially the 'Matzos Island' as it was located on an artificial island between the Danube to the north and a long crescent-shaped canal that fed into the centre of the city. It was where poorer working-class Jews tended to live. Despite being raised in a traditionally observant family, Zeisl saw himself as a child of enlightened German culture. Like many Austrian Jews of his generation, he was a proud 'German-Austrian'. The First Republic of Austria, despite its changed status from the core of a vast Central European empire to a small Alpine republic, rightly viewed itself and its capital Vienna as one of the centres of German letters and music. For Vienna's Jews to be excluded from this legacy by the likes of Adolf Hitler and the thugs who made up his government was not just an insult but an injury that wounded them deeply. Hitler's demented adoration of Wagner did not qualify him to be the arbiter of who was and who was not entitled to a German cultural inheritance. But Jewish exclusion had already begun under the dictatorships of Engelbert Dollfuß and Kurt Schuschnigg, who viewed Austrian exceptionalism as paramount, locating it in its Catholicism and transnational aristocracy. Their imposition of a Roman Catholic clerical dictatorship paradoxically led many Austrian Jews to identify themselves even more resolutely with German culture, dismissing Austrian citizenship as little more than a bureaucratic necessity.

If such anger and frustration would turn Schoenberg into a militant, the reaction of Zeisl was different but equally important.

Perhaps in light of the pseudo-biological arguments being bandied about (and not just by Nazis) that Jews were not a European people but exotic and oriental, incompatible with the biological make-up of the 'German race', Zeisl decided that if he was a Jew, he needed to compose like a Jew. What that meant was as unclear to him as it was to others. He had no desire to evoke the shtetl or even the synagogue, but this left a massive hole in the concept of what sort of music a Jew might compose.

Clarity was gained following the death of the Austrian writer and journalist Joseph Roth. He had been living in Paris for a number of years and witnessed the exodus of Jews from Germany. In his slim volume *Juden auf Wanderschaft* (*Jews on a Journey*), he wrote colourfully about the German Jews' having forgotten what being Jewish meant. He described their bewilderment and confusion upon arriving in Paris after banishment from what they had assumed to be their German homeland. It was an observation that clearly resonated with Zeisl.

Another work by Roth was a novel called *Hiob* (*Job*), a contemporary account of the biblical story of Job. The novel was criticised at the time as sentimental, offering a cringe-inducing recollection of the shtetl, which German and Austrian Jews believed to be a long-superseded irrelevance. The preceding generations of many German Jews had no experience of Eastern European shtetls or ghettos, having lived in Jewish communities that had existed in Germany since Roman times. With the arrival of the Nazi Party in power, the story of Job took on enormous significance. After Roth's death from alcohol abuse at the age of forty-four in Paris, the Viennese journalist Hans Kafka adapted the novel into a play and commissioned Zeisl to write the accompanying music.[15]

The inclination of Austrian Jews since the so-called 'December Constitution' of 1867 was to assimilate.[16] The Zionist movement was founded with the view that assimilation was incapable of making a difference. Proof was provided in enlightened France by the Dreyfus Affair in 1894. Debates were held as to whether assimilation within the diaspora was preferable to a Jewish nation as a means of dealing with European antisemitism. Zeisl was definitely an assimilationist until his arrival in Paris and his encounter with Roth's *Job*.

Initially, in correspondence with his friend the novelist Hilde Spiel, Zeisl wrote that Paris offered everything anyone could hope for, as if arriving in Cockaigne.[17] Such a view was deceptive and without the help and friendship of Darius Milhaud, the Zeisls would have found themselves on the same bureaucratic carousel as countless other refugees, racing from one official bureau to the next in order to find a place to live and a chance to work.

Many members of Max Reinhardt's ensemble had gathered in Paris and would take part in Hans Kafka's adaptation of Roth's novel, including Josef Meinrad, Hugo Haas (the brother of the composer Pavel Haas) and Leon Askin. In Roth's adaptation of the biblical *Job*, Mendel Singer is a teacher of the Torah in an Eastern European shtetl. The family is poor but devout. Together with his wife Deborah, they have two sons and a daughter. A third son, Menuchim, is born who appears to be epileptic, brain-damaged and in need of constant care. Mendel's faith in God keeps him from doing what is necessary and possible for his family's welfare – especially that of his severely handicapped son. His daughter becomes the plaything of a nearby Russian garrison and his two other sons are called into the army. One bribes his way out while the other remains. The son who escapes military service travels to America and much later pays for his family to follow. Mendel and Deborah decide to leave Menuchim in the care of neighbours, but their arrival in America is anything but successful. One son dies fighting for the Americans during the First World War, the other is listed as missing in action, and their daughter has a mental breakdown. Mendel desperately misses his old life and, above all, the son he abandoned. He ceases to believe in a merciful God and no longer dresses as or maintains the daily devotionals of a religious Jew. Ultimately, when all appears irredeemably lost, he returns to his former faith with the unexpected arrival of his much-loved but abandoned son Menuchim, healed and now a world-famous musician. Menuchim rescues his father from further misery and hardship.

The play was a success and ran in the Théâtre Pigalle. Harry Kahn wrote in the German-language *Pariser Tageszeitung* on 5 June 1938:

> Joseph Roth's novel *Job* is more than a historical retrospective and preview: it is a review of the beginning and end of all times, a metaphysical review, the mythological concentration into a single destiny of the fate of an entire people kat'exochin [Ancient Greek κατ' ἐξοχήν: 'par excellence'], the fate of humanity on this Earth.[18]

The music for *Job* represented a turning point in Zeisl's compositional direction. Until then, his output had largely been art song, built on templates already established by Schubert. The last German text he set, 'Komm, süßer Tod' ('Come, Sweet Death'), is the same text as set by Bach from Schemelli's *Musical Song Book* of 1736, and was composed shortly before leaving Austria. It can be thought of as Zeisl's final defiant affirmation of his entitlement to German identity.

The music of *Job* represented a major stylistic change, perhaps best represented in the number 'Menuchim's Song', with its predominant augmented second interval in both melody and accompaniment, its unstructured, improvisational, occasionally recitative character. Zeisl moves his musical language eastwards, though in later compositions the inflection is more subtle and attempts to evoke a Jewish sound world without resorting to either the ethnic modes of klezmer or the synagogue.

The exiled musician was clearly such a characteristic feature of Paris that Lion Feuchtwanger incorporated it in his novel *Paris Gazette* in the figure of Sepp Trautwein. Zeisl was active in a wide circle of émigrés, soon to be refugees. He was joined by Marcel Rubin, Ernst Toch, Arnold Schoenberg and Paul Stefan along with Alma Mahler-Werfel. An important figure in Zeisl's development was Hans Kafka, with whom he would work on turning *Job* into a full-length opera during his remaining years, leaving the work incomplete upon his death in 1957. The story of a son rescuing the father perhaps resonated with Zeisl. He was unable to rescue his own father, who died in a Nazi camp. It nevertheless became the vehicle of Jewish musical identity. It was undoubtedly a difficult transition to make from assimilation, and Zeisl never went so far as to become a musical Zionist. Zeisl's musical identity would continue to be characterised by modal harmonies and melodies, but often these were so subtly placed as to be undetected by the passive listener. It was more like a personal reminder to himself and to those who knew where to look and how to listen.

The Netherlands was another obvious destination for refugees immediately following Hitler's seizure of power. Like France, it was not a transit country and was welcoming to refugees. The composer Wilhelm Rettich, who arrived in 1933, felt so comfortable in the Netherlands that he took the decision to remain.[19] Only when in hiding during the Nazi occupation did he begin to acknowledge his Jewish identity, composing in a cupboard his piano concerto, *Variations on a Hebrew Theme*, and his *Sinfonia Giudaica*. Rettich was lucky; his mother and other members of the family were denounced, deported and murdered.

Similarly, James Simon (1880–1944) felt no need to leave the Netherlands and refused several offers to immigrate, even an offer to bring him to America. He too began to incorporate Eastern references in his otherwise late-Romantic musical language. These are heard in his 'Lament for Cello and Piano', based on a Yemenite melody. Simon is one of the composers forgotten when mentioning the notorious transport from Theresienstadt to Auschwitz on 12 October 1944. He was murdered, along with Viktor Ullmann, Pavel Haas and Hans Krása.

Hans Lachman (originally Heinz Lachmann: 1906–90) fled Berlin for Amsterdam in 1933 where he became an important composer of film and light music. After surviving the war in hiding in the Dutch town of Limburg, he too began to reassess his Jewish identity, composing a cantata called *Stammen van Israël* (*Tribes of Israel*), accompanying singers of Yiddish songs, and later arranging Jewish songs, incorporating elements into his own music.

Hans Krieg (1899–1961), already a self-acknowledged composer of Jewish music, a scholar and collector of Jewish music, also found life in the Netherlands safe and the public welcoming after leaving Berlin in 1933. Incredibly, he survived Westerbork, Bergen-Belsen and Theresienstadt, and after the war felt happy returning to live in the Netherlands, much like Wilhelm Rettich.

Yet, for many, escape to the Netherlands would prove to be a deadly mirage. Even the most welcoming people could not stop the antisemitic purges. Other refugees, such as Paul Hermann (1902–44), along with James Simon, would not survive. Even the man who was responsible for the Jewish Cultural League, Kurt Singer, would be arrested and deported from the Netherlands.[20] In the case of Paul Hermann, a Hungarian hidden by Dutch friends in Vichy France, he was arrested in Toulouse and deported to Drancy, before being sent to Auschwitz on 15 May 1944.

Scandinavia seemed a possible, albeit temporary, option. All of the countries were exposed and vulnerable. Sweden was neutral but harboured sympathisers for the Nazis in its governmental ranks and, as in Switzerland, was forced into the day-to-day existence of 'Realpolitik'. The Austrian Jewish composer Hans Holewa (1905–91) felt these restrictions throughout the war, though afterwards he remained in Sweden and became a major figure in post-war musical life and a representative of Vienna's Second School in a country that was otherwise unreceptive to new musical developments. Denmark, Finland and Norway were equally vulnerable. Either they were physically vulnerable, because of their geographical proximity to Germany, or politically vulnerable as in the case of Norway whose prime minister, Vidkun Quisling, was executed in 1945 for collaboration.

This left Iceland, which became the last possible port of call for the Austrian composer Victor Urbancic (1903–58). He wasn't Jewish himself, though his wife, the actress Melitta Grünbaum, was. He refused to divorce her despite political pressure to do so. As with Holewa, who remained in Sweden after the war, Urbancic also chose to remain in Iceland and would go on to be a major influence on musical life in Reykjavik and the rest of the country until his death in 1958. The musicians who managed to escape to Sweden were more often than not the 'jobbing' musicians, orchestral players or members of groups and ensembles. They were constantly aware of their exposure. It was a vulnerability expressed by Bertolt Brecht in some of his Steffin Poems later set by Hanns Eisler, such as *An den kleinen Radioapparat* (*To the Little Transistor Radio*).

To Great Britain, Canada and Australia

Great Britain, on the other hand, was not a country so receptive to immigration and after 1938 demanded visas for entry. It took the advice of leading members of the Jewish community not to emphasise the fact that most of the refugees arriving were Jewish. Antisemitism was alive in Great Britain as well, and there was a genuine concern that advertising the fact that Britain was perhaps taking in some of Germany's Jews would cause enormous problems for the local Jewish community. Even Kindertransport children were not usually designated as being Jewish, leading many to be taken in by families who, with the best intentions, proceeded to bring the children up as Christians.

The consequences of this decision for musicians were not positive. Because refugees were presented as Germans, followed by the declaration of war on Germany in 1939, British music teachers and orchestral players were conscripted, leaving their positions open, potentially to be taken by recently arrived refugees. The Incorporated Society of Musicians (ISM) lobbied the government to restrict employment possibilities for refugees. Correspondence in *The Times* offered a lively debate on the subject. It was clear that musicians arriving from Germany and Austria were better trained than locals. In addition, they came equipped with huge technical advantages and a wider grasp of music historiography and aesthetics. British musicians, many of whom were already unemployed following the advent of sound cinema, could not compete and had to endure the spectacle of highly trained Central Europeans taking up temporary positions while British musicians were conscripted.

Unlike France, there does not seem to have been a huge revival of Jewish identity in Britain. If anything, pressure to assimilate into a local way of life was even greater. Names like Rosenkrantz, or Rosengarten, were shortened to 'Rose'; other names were completely anglicised as soon as feasible. It was ironic in retrospect that the German conductor Hans Bernstein should choose to change his name to Harold Byrns, convinced that someone named 'Bernstein' could not make a career in Great Britain or America as a conductor.

The Soviets financed various refugee centres for Germans and, surprisingly, for Austrians; surprising because Austria did not officially exist and its annexation by Nazi Germany in 1938 was accepted as a natural evolution that would have happened anyway and probably should have been permitted in November 1918. It was not until the Moscow Conference of 1943 that Austria was officially declared the first of Hitler's illegally occupied states. Regardless of how popular the annexation may have been among the Austrian population, it was ultimately deemed illegal, making Austria the official 'first victim' of Nazi aggression, a status it exploited shamelessly after the war. In any case, refugee venues opened and financed by the Soviets offered language courses, newspapers, concerts, lectures and a cultural life not otherwise available to immigrants. In accordance with the Soviet policy of 'socialism in one country', these centres were kept non-political, and until the Hitler–Stalin Pact they were allowed to become centres for anti-Nazi activities. Mostly, the centres were used to facilitate contacts abroad so that refugees could continue their journeys to the United States or South America, or wherever a guarantor might be found.

Refugees, if not free to be engaged by British orchestras or institutions, were still free to run their own venues and recitals – much to the irritation of the ISM, which had to stand by and watch as English audiences joined queues to hear German and Austrian musicians perform. The composer Georg Knepler and Webern pupil and pianist Peter Stadlen mentioned in two separate interviews that Franz Osborn and Berthold Goldschmidt's performances of Hans Gál's reductions of Mahler symphonies on two pianos planted the seed of Mahler in Great Britain, with the country becoming a Mahlerian stronghold post-war.[21]

With the outbreak of war, many Jewish musicians found themselves trapped in Britain, with any plans to leave now thwarted. In 1940 they were nearly all interned and those too young or unwilling to fight were often deported to Australia or Canada. There were particular horrors experienced by refugees on transport ships that were either torpedoed or, like the *Dunera*, turned into floating concentration camps. The *Dunera* arrived in Sydney Harbour with its passengers having been so badly treated that the harbour master had the entire crew arrested. It didn't stop the Australians taking the refugees to a camp in southern New South Wales, where the lack of shade, the ferocious heat and meagre food and water rations left internees with no idea how or if they would survive.[22]

If Canada took in Jewish refugees, it was only against the will of its government. It expressed a willingness to take in refugees following the outbreak of war, but under no circumstances should these be Jewish. In fact, Great Britain would send several ships of internees to Canada, most of whom would have been Jewish. Canada notoriously joined Cuba and the United States in not allowing the *St Louis* to dock, forcing the return of its refugees to Europe. The *Arandora Star*, one of several ships transporting 'enemy aliens', was torpedoed en

3. Refugees from Germany and Austria arriving for deportation to British internment camps as 'enemy aliens', May 1940.

route to Canada. Survivors were later put on board the *Dunera* to Australia.

The composer Hans Gál's memoirs of his own period in a British internment camp do not totally support the propaganda pitch that these were not so much internment camps as holiday camps with faculties springing up to teach music, painting, architecture, physics, philosophy and almost every other academic discipline. Members of the Amadeus Quartet did come together in one of the Isle of Man camps, and the names of those who agreed to teach, or at least supervise activities, is impressive. The extent to which such 'faculties' and activities were permitted depended on individual camp directors. Some encouraged these activities, but as Gál relates, most did not. The composer Egon Wellesz's Oxford diary remains empty from his first day of internment until a later entry reading only 'Schöne Müllerin – Nervenzusammenbruch' ('Schöne Müllerin – nervous breakdown').

The pianist and organiser of London's lunchtime concerts at the emptied National Gallery (its works of art brought to safety outside of the city), Myra Hess, showed no hesitation in engaging refugee musicians, almost openly daring the ISM to object. As she was herself Jewish, she was better informed regarding the persecution of arriving refugees than most. She, along with Ralph Vaughan Williams, would play crucial roles later in freeing musicians such as Egon Wellesz from internment camps.

In Britain, Jewish refugees were confronted with a need to become as British as possible. An interesting synthesis of such an aesthetic transformation can be heard in the works of the young German composer Franz Reizenstein, formerly a pupil of Paul Hindemith and in England a pupil of Vaughan Williams. German New Objectivity is reimagined via modal impressionism. Berthold Goldschmidt also adjusted his musical language, moving it closer to Benjamin Britten and Michael Tippett and away from his Berlin roots. It was a futile and short-lived experiment that ultimately silenced him for a quarter of a century. If in Germany he was told that, as a Jew, he was only 'imitating' German music, in Great Britain he was made to understand that as a German he was only 'imitating' English music.

A competition for a new opera in English was held by the Arts Council of England after the war and refugee composers enthusiastically competed, winning the top two spots: Karl Rankl with his *Deirdre of the Sorrows* and Berthold Goldschmidt with *Beatrice Cenci*. Egon Wellesz also submitted an opera based on William Congreve's play *Incognita*, though it was excluded in one of the opening rounds. Rankl and Goldschmidt had moved quite far from their native roots. Rankl's First Symphony, composed in 1938, would be well received in Liverpool in 1953, which, given the antagonism shown to other refugee composers, was something of a surprise. Kurt Weill's operetta *A Kingdom for a Cow* and Ernst Toch's Piano Concerto, premiered in one of the Promenade concerts and conducted by Sir Henry Wood, were met with critical opprobrium – indeed, attacks on the music and the composers were in some cases mere dog-whistles for antisemites. Both composers subsequently left for the greener pastures of the United States.

Even if refugee musicians were forbidden from taking the positions left vacant in orchestras and conservatories, film studios continued to hire them, with Ernst Toch, Karol Rathaus, Mischa Spoliansky, Hanns Eisler and Allan Gray (originally Józef Żmigrod) out of the ISM's firing range. As already stated, concerts for and by refugees became increasingly popular with the general population. Even nightclubs and cabarets were opened exclusively for refugees from Austria, Germany and Czechoslovakia. The ballet dancer Anita Bild (1915–2012), born Anita Lelewer, was the daughter of one of Austria's most prominent high court judges. Fortunately for her, he was a fairly capable amateur pianist as well, and could fill in the harmonies of the cabaret songs she composed and performed in the Austrian cabaret nightclub *Das Laternderl* (*The Little Streetlight*).

When Europe Was Too Close

The ultimate intention of nearly all refugees was to arrive in the United States. With its quotas continuously tightened, this became less of an option as the Nazi advancement across Europe continued. Thousands of Austrians managed to flee to Latin America thanks to the efforts of Gilberto Bosques at the Mexican Embassy in Vienna. Similarly, Chiune Sugihara issued thousands of transit visas for Japan to Jews in Lithuania. Some musicians such as Thomas Mann's brother-in-law Klaus Pringsheim (1882–1972) and Manfred Gurlitt (1890–1972), who were already in Japan, remained in the country, making significant contributions to Japanese musical life.

Others, such as Philip Herschkowitz to whom we return later, fled east to the Soviet Union. Herschkowitz, a pupil of Alban Berg and Anton Webern, would go on to teach an entire generation of post-Soviet composers, including Alfred Schnittke, Edison Denisov, Sofia Gubaidulina and Elena Firsova, among many others. He was luckier than most; though never granted an official post in any of Moscow's music institutions, he taught privately and survived Stalin's purges.

Thousands of German Communists who did not give a second thought about fleeing to the USSR would be less fortunate. Even the Czech composer Erwin Schulhoff had taken Soviet citizenship, resulting in internment as an 'enemy alien' following the Nazi absorption of Bohemia and Moravia. He died in Wülzburg internment camp before he could emigrate. In addition to Herschkowitz, Kurt Sanderling and Mieczysław Weinberg also managed to escape Stalin's purges, mostly thanks to the intervention of Dmitri Shostakovich.

We will return to a number of these individuals later on, but in conclusion, it is enormously difficult to evaluate the options available to Jewish musicians following the appointment of Hitler as chancellor in January 1933 and his subsequent consolidation of power. There were potentially more possibilities available to political refugees who were not Jewish. Openings for immigration would have been very different in 1933 and 1938. By 1938, it was clear that the United States was probably not a realistic choice unless one was exceptionally well connected or, like the Zeisls, very lucky. Austrians who made it to America had generally arrived before the annexation of Austria and fall of Czechoslovakia. From 1933 until 1938, France, the Netherlands and even Great Britain seemed reasonable immigration destinations. A large war was not on the immediate horizon, only a determination to remove Jews and those deemed politically undesirable from Germany.

An example of the thinking of the time can be gleaned from the British Home Office, ranking refugees according to various categories following the fall of Czechoslovakia, which Britain had largely facilitated through Neville Chamberlain's signing of the Munich Agreement with Hitler in September 1938. The refugees with the highest priority were those politically opposed to Hitler's annexation of the Sudetenland following the Munich Agreement; next came Austrian political refugees who had fled to Czechoslovakia after the Nazi annexation of Austria in March 1938. From a post-Holocaust perspective, placing Jews in the lowest category as 'economic migrants', since most had lost employment due to Nazi purges, seems callous, stupid and short-sighted. Largely incomprehensible to us today was the profound degree of antisemitism in all countries.[23]

Yet the issues were different for different people. In some ways, Jews were more fortunate than refugees who were not Jewish but classed as such by Nazi race laws: children of so-called 'mixed race' marriages, for example, if the Jewish parent was a father rather than the mother, or people who had converted or whose parents or grandparents had converted but had married other converted Jews. Jewish refugee charities were simply not in a position to help people who were deemed Jewish by Nazi race laws, but not Jewish according to religious laws. Other charities had to act, most notably those run by Quakers. Following the results of the Évian Conference in July 1938, Hitler's propaganda machine argued that the Germans were simply doing what every nation state would do if given the political opportunity: ridding itself of its Jews. Only a few wise prophets such as Joseph Roth in his novel from 1923, *The Spider's Web*, could see where such purges would ultimately, and inevitably, end.

2

Exile in Germany
Of Jewish Destiny, the Composer Richard Fuchs and the Jewish Kulturbund

Ich hatte einst ein schönes Vaterland
Der Eichenbaum wuchs dort so hoch,
Die Veilchen nickten sanft
Es war ein Traum, es war ein Traum

I once had a beautiful Fatherland
The oak there grew so tall,
The violets swayed gently
It was a dream, it was a dream

'In der Fremde' by Heinrich Heine, as set by
Richard Fuchs in 1937

Much has been written about the Jewish Cultural League in recent years, though the material available in English tends to focus on the Berlin Chapter of the league. This is understandable as it was the league closest to the Nazi overlords on whose existence it depended.[1]

The story of the Jewish Cultural League, or the *Kulturbund* as it was known, represents one of the most grotesque exercises in Nazi cynicism and their means of dealing with the perceived paradoxes of

Jews and German culture. An early example of such Nazi cynicism was their insistence on changing its original name *Kulturbund deutscher Juden* ('Cultural League for German Jews') to *Kulturbund der Juden in Deutschland* ('Cultural League for Jews in Germany'). For the Nazis, it was impossible to be a German Jew. One could at best be a Jew in Germany. The mendacity that lay behind this Nazi project for the Jews is understood when viewed today through the lens of the Holocaust. It can be more clearly seen as an attempt to ghettoise Jewish cultural activities as the first step towards genocide. Yet, at the time, the Kulturbund was the only possible means of employment for Jewish performers, administrators or technicians, along with a ready audience that, despite progressive marginalisation, was unwilling or unable to emigrate. At the same time, it absolved the Nazi regime from having to pay unemployment benefits to thousands of people they themselves had rendered unemployable.

Thus, the history of the Kulturbund confronts us with a number of ethical dilemmas. Jews active in the performing arts, regardless of whether onstage or behind it, were the earliest victims of Hitler's initial purges. In retrospect, musicians, actors and various backstage facilitators were offered a certain advantage, though most could not believe such official policies of Jewish exclusion were tenable in the long term and decided to wait things out. A policy of removing Jews from Germany's cultural life would not alter the situation of the 24,000 unemployed musicians along with thousands more who barely earned enough to live on. The enactment of the so-called 'Law for the Restoration of the Professional Civil Service' (known in German as the *Berufsbeamtengesetz*) in early April 1933 led to the instant dismissal of Jewish musicians, writers, composers and actors who were on the public payroll. With nearly all theatres, orchestras and opera houses publicly supported, this amounted to an instantaneous decimation of staffing within institutional operations. It also left vast holes in performance schedules and gaps within orchestras. It led to fear and confusion. People with names that could be construed as

'Jewish-sounding' took out advertisements in newspapers, offering to prove their 'Aryan birth lineage'. On the other hand, there were thousands more who were unaware they were Jewish and therefore vulnerable to the new laws. Parents or grandparents may have converted before marrying other converts. Jews had lived in Germany for nearly 2,000 years and their degree of assimilation was such that perceived differences were only imaginary. Secular Jews could not comprehend the primitive concept of removing professionals from their positions because of the religion of their grandparents. Hans Gál, following his dismissal as director of Mainz's Music College, was convinced the situation would revert to normal as soon as institutions ceased being able to function. He took his family for a holiday in the Black Forest, blissfully ignorant of what horrors lay ahead.

Zionist and non-Zionist Jewish charities in Germany immediately began responding to events. Until Hitler's appointment as chancellor in January 1933, these Jewish charities had little in common and their views as to how to respond were different. Initially, the Nazi government simply put Zionist and non-Zionist charities together under an umbrella organisation called 'Aid and Development', later changed to 'The Central Office for Jewish Economic Aid'. By September 1933, regional chapters were included in the Reich's 'Representation of Jews in Germany'. The purpose of these organisational mutations was to give the outside world the impression that it was Jews who were excluding themselves in order to appeal for immigration sponsorship.

In the ensuing confusion several people came up with the idea of the Kulturbund at the same time. The twenty-six-year-old stage director Kurt Baumann seems to have been the first to have mapped out a coherent strategy. His cousin Julius Bab contacted the conductors Michael Taube and Joseph Rosenstock along with the hugely talented, multifaceted Kurt Singer, who was an accomplished networker and an indefatigable operator. Singer was ruthless and appears to have taken ownership of Baumann's concept. The reality, however, was that whoever ran such an organisation would need to interact with important people in the Nazi administration. Singer's seniority to Baumann, in addition to his clarity of vision and mixture of intellect and charm, made him the perfect frontman.

Nevertheless, Baumann had already done the groundwork and calculated that with Berlin's population of some 175,000 Jews, it was possible to commercially maintain a parallel cultural institution. The obvious thought at this early stage was to provide employment for thousands of Jews recently ejected from opera houses, theatres, ensembles and orchestras. The degree to which emigration was even a consideration can be debated. Zionist organisations in Berlin wanted a focus on emigration from Germany to Palestine and would have preferred events taking place in Yiddish or Hebrew, languages that most assimilated Berlin Jews did not speak or understand. An additional idea began to take shape, namely that plays, performances and concerts would actually eclipse those in Berlin's established non-Jewish institutions and venues. Certainly, in many cases the best and most famous musicians had been dismissed from orchestras, administrative offices and ensembles. In an article in the *Central-Verein-Zeitung*, Singer offered his own version of events:

> In those days during which we Jews had to put up with work restrictions, the young director Kurt Baumann came to see me at the beginning of April with a plan for the foundation of a theatre and members' organisation. I had already worked out a similar plan and passed both of them on to Rabbi Dr [Leo] Baeck for his consideration. With his support I invited leading representatives of Jewish organisations for preliminary consultations. [...] One working committee drew up the statutes, while another prepared the organisational aspects for recruitment evenings and yet another took on the artistic planning. I presented official requests for permission to set up the 'Cultural League of German Jews' to various government offices. The decision on the matter was handed over to the Prime Minister of the Ministry of Education and the

Arts, under whom was placed the President of the Prussian Theatre Committee and the State Commissioner Hinkel, who conducted the negotiations in part in person and in part through his representatives. At the same time, I continually kept police headquarters and the Ministry of Propaganda [...] informed of the progress of discussions.[2]

He went on to add:

Keeping outer politics at bay from our affairs and not mixing in the domestic affairs regarding Jewish policies, we nonetheless stand up more boldly than ever for our Jewish heritage and believe in drawing from that all that is specifically Jewish in drama, music and various intellectual fields. [This] is our uppermost duty and must ultimately be our greatest gain! That we are living proof of what has been nurtured by German culture and its great masters does not need to be repeated to any German Jew. So, is this a compromise? Yes! But it is one that is made in the conviction that there is a will to join German Jewry's diverse communities of ideas into a single unit![3]

By March 1933 a nascent Kulturbund orchestra and chorus were in operation in Berlin under the auspices of the 'Community of Jewish Musicians'. On 22 May, Kurt Singer conducted this loose confederation of performers in excerpts from Handel's *Judas Maccabaeus*, along with works by Haydn and Schubert. In June, Singer was able to persuade Hans Hinkel, the Special Commissioner of the Reichskulturkammer, or Ministry for Culture, to officially recognise and support the German Jewish Cultural League. Not all prominent Berlin Jews were in agreement with the League's stated purpose, and Martin Buber denounced it as a ghetto operating under another name. Singer argued that a ghetto offering the services of the best musicians, actors and administrators would only underline the self-harm perpetrated by the Nazis on Germany's principal cultural institutions. In addition, the Kulturbund was the only place where one could continue to hear Offenbach, Meyerbeer, Mendelssohn and Mahler, all composers who continued to enjoy enormous popularity in Berlin. Furthermore, the Kulturbund could perform any work by Austrian composers, leading to a performance of Mozart's *Don Giovanni* in November 1933.

Not only were some of Berlin's top administrators put in place to organise the Kulturbund's events, they were using set designers, carpenters, costumiers and noted scholars and academics for dramaturgical support, press and publicity. By the time Lessing's play *Nathan the Wise* was mounted in October 1933, directed by Karl Löwenberg, it offered a cast featuring some of the city's most famous performers, including Käthe Foerder, Lilly Kann, Jenny Schaffer, Fred Alexander, Martin Brandt, Klaus Brill, Max Koninski and Fritz Lion. With such high-profile performances on offer, it swiftly became apparent that access had to be controlled and limited only to Jews. A complicated subscription scheme was put in place involving photo-ID membership cards and offering a mixture of cultural activities, ranging from opera and concerts to plays, readings and lectures.

As already mentioned, the definition of who was Jewish and who was not differed radically between Nazi and Jewish religious laws. With the advent of the 'Nuremberg Race Laws' in 1935, the definition of how Jewish any individual was depended on the number of Jewish grandparents. Given the large numbers who had left the Jewish community either because they weren't religious or had married non-Jews, or were the children or grandchildren of converts, it was possible for the Kulturbund to call upon the talents of a far larger group of people than Baumann had originally calculated. The Kulturbund now consisted of a disparate coalition of Zionists intent on emigration, religious and secular Jews, along with former Jews or the offspring of converts who felt every entitlement to remain in the country of their birth. Only Nazi policies progressively ghettoising everyone remotely classed as Jewish managed to keep this shaky coalition together.

The Kulturbund was from the beginning a Berlin initiative, from whence it spread across the state of Prussia. Soon chapters were opening up all over Germany. The committee members of the Berlin Chapter represented the best that Berlin's Jewish intellectual and creative community could offer and consisted of such important figures as Leo Baeck, Martin Buber, Leonid Kreutzer, Max Liebermann and Jakob Wassermann. Despite its stated ambition, Berlin's Kulturbund could only provide permanent employment to some 200 individuals, covering the work of an orchestra, a theatrical troupe, dancers and assorted administrators. Other initiatives attempted to provide opportunities for those unable to find meaningful work with the Kulturbund. The composer and conductor Berthold Goldschmidt formed a complete orchestra in 1934 consisting of sacked orchestral members from other ensembles. In Frankfurt, there was an ensemble called the Jüdische Tonkünstler Frankfurts (Frankfurt's Jewish Musicians). There was even a touring opera that operated under similar conditions as the Kulturbund.

The local council made the Charlotte Street, 'Berliner Theater', available to the Kulturbund, and with subscriptions of some 12,000 members the opening season was seen as a success. By the winter of 1933, membership had grown to 20,000 out of the 180,000 Berlin citizens considered Jewish by Nazi race laws. (Some 160,000 were active members of the local community while 20,000 members were counted as Jews by race laws.)

Programming remained a difficult and rather subjective undertaking. What was considered Jewish and what was German were often mixed up and unclear. For example, Austrian composers were allowed until the *Anschluss* in March 1938, despite the fact that Schubert, Bruckner, Haydn and Mozart were 'racially' German. Even Beethoven was permitted until 1937. Handel was considered English and Gluck Italian, allowing further performances of Handel's

Old Testament oratorios. Nazi musicologists often referred to the 'depth' and 'profundity' of 'German music' while banning performances of Mendelssohn's best-known and most-loved works, while at the same time allowing Austro-German composers for Kulturbund performances. With so little consistency, it was obvious that most programmes had to be submitted well in advance and permission was granted according to the mood of the day, or the good working relations between Hinkel and Singer. Even these points could alter from one moment to the next.

With Hinkel in overall charge of the Kulturbund within the auspices of the Nazi Kulturkammer and Singer his intermediary, the organisation managed to spread to twenty-seven chapters across Germany. In 1935 the central offices for the network of Kulturbunds were located in Berlin. In spite of the ensuing 'Nuremberg Race Laws' resulting in large-scale emigration, Singer became obsessive about maintaining the organisation's high artistic standards and often intervened in members' decisions to leave. At this point, it was clear that there was to be no interaction between Jews and non-Jews in Nazi Germany, a situation that was untenable for the vast majority of German Jews. Following the race laws, countless petty laws and regulations were enacted restricting the ability of Jews to lead ordinary, productive and happy lives. These mean-spirited regulations have been well documented and extended from the removal of Jews from public spaces to forbidding them from owning pets. Those living in so-called 'mixed-race' marriages, where one spouse was Jewish and the other was not, were moved into buildings where only Jews were allowed to live. Eventually, laws were passed requiring both partners in a 'mixed-race' marriage to be treated as Jews. Those with children were given a so-called 'privileged' status, which was as good as meaningless. The Jewish parent/spouse could be rounded up in raids requiring weeks of negotiations and bribes before being freed from camps. Singer appeared to be blind to these developments in his attempts to hold on to the best-known actors and musicians.

Despite huge investments made by the Kulturbund in the renovation of the Berliner Theater, its lease was not extended and other venues were not made available. The Kulturbund was able to take up residence in Berlin's former Yiddish Gebrüder-Herrnfeld-Theater in Kommandanten Street. Funds were found so that by 1937 an additional 700-seat accommodation could be made for recitals and chamber performances.

Nazi cynicism extended to using the Kulturbund for international propaganda purposes during the 1936 Olympic Games in Berlin. The high standards of performances were publicised and performances were sold out. The Olympic Games offered only a brief respite. Hinkel became less and less accommodating while Singer began travelling to Amsterdam and Paris in attempts to persuade members of the Kulturbund to return. Singer had gained a considerable international profile and was invited to hold guest lectures at Harvard University. He was offered a teaching position in the United States, which he turned down in order to return to the Kulturbund. Upon his arrival in Amsterdam, it became clear even to him that a return to Germany was as good as a death sentence. With the fall of the Netherlands in 1940, Singer was deported to Westerbork concentration camp in 1943, before being moved to Theresienstadt where he died aged fifty-eight in 1944.

With the annexation of Austria and the establishment of the Bohemian and Moravian 'Protectorate', Nazi Germany found itself acquiring more Jews than it was shedding. More draconian measures were brought in, such as barring doctors and lawyers from working. Yet complicated, increasingly bureaucratic measures along with a so-called 'flight tax' that left would-be emigrants penniless hindered most ordinary Jews from leaving. Inevitably, the Kulturbund would also become vulnerable and attempts to move it to Palestine were thwarted by an embargo placed on taking musical instruments and Kulturbund material out of the country.

The November pogroms resulting from Germany's 'natural revulsion' of the murder of a German diplomat in Paris by a young Jew named Herschel Grynszpan were effectively the death knell of the Kulturbund. Singer was no longer in Berlin and management had moved to the Dutch citizen Werner Levie, with Rudolf Schwarz in charge of musical events and the Austrian Fritz Wisten as head of theatre productions. With the declaration of war in September 1939, Levie fled to the Netherlands, leaving Martin Barsch from Berlin's Jewish Community in charge. Somehow a much-reduced programme of film and music could still be managed in 1939 and 1940, with smaller events taking place in one or two of the villas remaining in Jewish ownership. An extraordinarily symbolic performance of Mahler's 'Resurrection' Symphony conducted by Rudolf Schwarz, with the soloists Henriette Huth (soprano) and Adelheid Müller (alto), took place on 27 February 1941. Afterwards, Schwarz escaped to England, but Henriette Huth was murdered by the Nazis eleven months later. Nobody knows what happened to Adelheid Müller. Micha Michalowitz wrote in the *Jüdisches Nachrichtenblatt*:

> As the sounds of this miracle of the Temple, its resonance of bracing harmonies reaching the highest spheres, began to fade, the people in the hall sat for a few seconds in tearful silence before spontaneously lifting themselves out of their seats, deeply moved beyond description, demonstrating their gratitude. Everyone felt that of all the arts, only music was capable of leading to enlightened salvation the doubting soul and its questions of existence.[4]

The Kulturbund's last concert consisted of Mendelssohn and Jaromír Weinberger in May, and its last theatrical production in August was Ferenc Molnár's *Spiel im Schloß* (*The Play's the Thing*).[5] In September it was officially closed down. Its remaining employees were arrested and deported and, with the exception of one small publishing arm, its various operations were 'Aryanised'.

Beyond Berlin: The Kulturbund, Karlsruhe and Richard Fuchs

Although the principal focus has normally been on the activities of the Berlin Chapter of the Kulturbund, the many provincial chapters were equally significant. The orchestra in Frankfurt was arguably one of the best ensembles within the Kulturbund network. For example, programmes for November 1934 and given at weekly intervals offered a chamber music recital with the violinist Stefan Frenkel and pianist Wilhelm Steinberg performing works by Beethoven, Schumann and Ernst Toch. This was followed a week later by a choral concert and a week after that a play by Stefan Zweig, and then an orchestral evening of Beethoven. An introduction to the programme was written by Bernhard Sekles who, like Gál, Braunfels and Schreker, had been relieved of his directorship at a German music college, which in Sekles's case was the Hoch'sche Konservatorium in Frankfurt. He was particularly hated by the Nazis for hiring the Hungarian Mátyás Seiber to run the country's only dedicated jazz department. Also in common with Schreker, he died in 1934, indeed shortly after writing the notes to the Kulturbund programme. Featured in the Frankfurt series of orchestral concerts in January 1935 was Ernst Toch's First Piano Concerto, conducted by Wilhelm Steinberg with soloist Heida Hermanns.

Karlsruhe is a significantly more provincial city than Frankfurt, yet the provenance of its Kulturbund Chapter, actually the chapter for the state of Baden-Württemberg, owed its existence to the efforts of a local architect named Richard Fuchs (1887–1947), who was also president of Karlsruhe's B'nai B'rith.[6] Fuchs was in fact a relatively prominent architect who eschewed modernism and maintained a sturdy Germanic building aesthetic that was not as austere as the Bauhaus, while also recognising that the ostentatiousness of the mercantile nineteenth century was no longer appropriate. As a result, his buildings were largely without extraneous ornaments while remaining elegant with a certain Teutonic dignity. Fuchs's buildings

4. The four Fuchs brothers ready to fight for the Kaiser in the First World War: Richard, Sigmund, Walter and Gottfried.

were praised by Nazis unaware that the architect had been put out of work by their policies. The buildings designed by Fuchs that remain standing today are landmark-protected, though the synagogue he designed and built in the Black Forest town of Gernsbach was destroyed during the *Kristallnacht* pogroms.

Fuchs studied and worked initially in Berlin before returning to his home town of Karlsruhe where he completed his doctorate and married Dora Stern. Fuchs came from a family that belonged to Karlsruhe's haute bourgeoisie. He was only one of four highly successful sons in the family. His younger brother Sigmund was a psychologist, while another younger brother Walter was a successful businessman. Gottfried, however, the youngest of the Fuchs boys, was the best known of all and was Germany's most successful soccer star, who from 1904 until 1920 was recognised as the best centre forward in the world. Gottfried Fuchs scored more goals and played more international games for the German national team than any other German player until his record was broken in 2001. The brothers escaped Hitler's mandated mass murder of the Jews. Their sister Senta was less fortunate. She and her non-Jewish husband were murdered by the Nazis. Before their arrest and deportation, they at least managed to have their two children Rolf and Beate brought to safety in Great Britain.

Richard Fuchs's talent as an artist meant he spent the years of the First World War as a correspondent on the front, winning an Iron Cross before embarking on a career as an architect. In notes he made in preparation for a lecture he was giving in Wellington, New Zealand, he offers only scant information about his musical development:

> At an early age I showed signs of a gift for music and also for the arts, drawing and painting. Since my father was an ardent music lover, the atmosphere of my youth was favourable for the development of my musical talents. I went through the usual school education, and was thoroughly schooled in music at the same time. I was a student of the musical high school of my home town (the Hochschule für Musik Karlsruhe). My special musical interest was at all times directed to the knowledge of harmony, counterpoint and instrumentation. After the final school examinations, I nevertheless decided to study architecture, which surely was a profession of more practical usefulness, and gave also scope for my creative inclinations.[7]

We don't know with whom Fuchs studied at Karlsruhe's Musik Hochschule. Its archives were destroyed in the war and he doesn't appear to have mentioned this crucial point to those around him. Like many naturally talented musicians, he was probably self-taught using the scores of past masters as well as those still living, such as Mahler and Strauss. It is clear that his musical references were based on foundations set by the previous generation. Other composers born in 1887 such as Ernst Toch, Heitor Villa-Lobos or Heinz Tiessen were more confident in freeing themselves from the influences of late Romanticism. As Fuchs was not a professional composer until forced from his profession as an architect by the Nazis, he avoided the hothouses of Germany's many new music festivals that might have drawn him closer to contemporary musical developments.

As with many German Jews, most particularly those in the south-west and the Rhine Valley, there was little to distinguish Fuchs and his family from their non-Jewish neighbours. The Jewish community was integrated, and in several of the independent south-west German states prior to Bismarck's unification, Jews had already achieved full emancipation. Cities such as Worms, Speyer and Mainz self-identified as 'Jerusalem on the Rhine' and had active Jewish communities from the tenth century, with earlier settlements dating from Roman times. The degree of integration was noticeable to Austrians such as Ernst Krenek. For the most part, Austria's Jews prior to the Constitution of 1867 had come from intermarried communities and ghettos in the eastern regions of the Habsburg Empire. They were often identified by accents, gestures, body language and even certain stereotypical physical features, all of which fed into greater degrees of antisemitism than in many German states where Jews had intermarried and integrated more fully within the wider community. This was the Fuchs biotope and it was natural that all four sons would serve as officers in the German army during the First World War.

Despite Fuchs coming into his own as a composer after 1933, when he could no longer work as an architect, he had already begun composing seriously in 1931. Indeed, we know he had been composing before his D major Piano Quintet from 1931, written when Fuchs was already forty-four. There are two surviving songs from 1904 and 1905, and Fuchs's daughter Soni Mulheron recalled him talking about an opera he wrote with his cousin. None of these earlier works has survived. After composing his D major Piano Quintet, he wrote a string quartet in D minor the following year. In 1933, the year that Hitler rose to power, Fuchs composed a work called *Heitere Musik für acht Blasinstrumente* (*Cheerful Music for Eight Woodwinds*). More impressive is his Symphony in C minor. Another large-scale work came in 1935 with his orchestral song cycle *Frühling* (*Spring*), based on texts from Arno Holz's poem *Buch der Zeit* (*Book of Time*).

By 1933, Fuchs felt confident enough to send a selection of his compositions to Wilhelm Furtwängler and Felix Weingartner. Evaluations from local Karlsruhe Kapellmeisters were clearly not of interest to Fuchs, who appeared to be supremely confident in his abilities. Furtwängler didn't ignore Fuchs, but requested a pause of a few months until the summer when he could look at the material more carefully. Weingartner wrote back that he was astonished at the technical accomplishment of someone who was to all intents and purposes an 'amateur'. Tellingly, Weingartner went on to write that Fuchs's work deserved recognition, but added 'now is not the right time'.

In the same year, Fuchs requested the certification of his Iron Cross won in the First World War. This was obviously a result of the 7 April 1933 Law for the Restoration of the Professional Civil Service, which stated that the only Jews on the public payroll allowed to continue in employment were those who could prove they had fought on the front in the previous war. Such exceptions proved useful to several musicians, most notably Leo Blech who was principal conductor of Berlin's opera house Unter den Linden until 1937 when stricter measures were brought in, forcing Blech to move first to Riga, then Stockholm. Given Fuchs's almost immediate loss of work – whether private or public – it does not appear to have benefited him. After the *Kristallnacht* pogroms landed him in Dachau, he threw his Iron Cross in the river.

Loss of work as an architect allowed Fuchs to devote himself to running the local Kulturbund chapter and to composition. Ever since his D major Piano Quintet, he had continued writing Lieder. One of the most striking works from these early Kulturbund years was his *Hymnus für Gott* (*Hymn to God*), subtitled *Chassidic Song*, for tenor, organ and full orchestra. Equally well received was his orchestral song cycle *Frühling* (*Spring*), performed in November 1935 by the Frankfurt Orchestra under Wilhelm Steinberg with soprano Emmy Joseph. Lieder continued to dominate Fuchs's output until 1936 when he composed his Symphony in A minor and his large oratorio *Vom jüdischen Schicksal* (*Of Jewish Destiny*), set to militantly Zionist texts by Karl Wolfskehl as well as to a text by the Jewish Minnesinger, Süßkind von Trimberg.[8]

In the same year, 1936, Hans Hinkel began to purge the Kulturbund of German composers and writers and set out the Kulturbund as an opportunity for Jews to develop 'their own creative boundaries'.[9] What this actually meant was the source of great debate inside the Kulturbund and among Jewish musicians in general. Attempts to excavate a specifically Jewish musical characteristic had been a subject of discussion and concert planning with the founding of the Jewish Art Music Movement in Russia in 1908 by Joel Engel, Alexander Krein, Mikhail Gnessin and Joseph Achron, among others. The movement spread from St Petersburg to Austria where the cellist Joachim Stutschewsky established a similar organisation. All of these initiatives were growing out of the general nationalist movements that had started in the late nineteenth century. If Hungarians, Russians, Czechs and even the British had their own music, reaching back into the traditions of folk music, why not Jews? This seemed a relevant question to Zionists as well as European antisemites, who hated the idea of 'cultural appropriation' by Jews of what was deemed 'Germany's music'.

As in the case of Erich Zeisl following his arrival in Paris, what a nationalist musical idiom for Jews might sound like was a puzzle to German Jews who had lived in Germany for over 1,000 years. It was arguably less daunting for Central European Jewish musicians from Austria or Russia as Jews had been isolated and confined to ghettos where they had developed their own compositional folk-song modes and liturgical melismata for the synagogue. At the same time, liturgical music for the synagogue was also changing and becoming more 'Protestant' in character with works by Salomon Sulzer and, above all, Louis Lewandowski. Organs had also started to make an appearance in more progressive congregations, resulting in two developments happening at the same time. As the Zionist movement grew, there evolved a need for a nationalist musical idiom that was close, but not too close, to a Western European *melos*, while in liturgy every imaginable attempt was being made to sound more like the music heard and sung in German churches.

Fuchs had a very different approach and saw 'Jewish character' revealed through text rather than the use of non-diatonic modes. He believed in keeping the musical language Germanic while using it to set distinctively Jewish texts, and by doing so he was more than accommodating Hinkel's instruction to develop Jewish 'creative boundaries'. Indeed, the texts for nearly everything Fuchs composed in the early 1930s were by Jewish writers with the singular exception of *Frühling*, based on Arno Holz's *Buch der Zeit, Lieder eines Modernen* (*Book of the Time, Songs of a Modernist*), published in 1885.

The culmination of Fuchs's synthesis of German and Jew was his setting of Karl Wolfskehl and Süßkind von Trimberg in his oratorio *Vom jüdischen Schicksal*. The work was composed as an entry for a competition held by all of Germany's Kulturbund chapters. Entries were submitted in several categories, such as composition of a festive overture, a large choral work, or *a cappella* chorus. The results of the competition were announced in April 1937: Fuchs won in the 'large choral work' category with more points awarded to him than other winners in other categories. In describing the purpose of the competition, Kurt Singer wrote in the *Central-Verein-Zeitung* on 4 May:

The competition of the Kulturbund should combine the practical with the ideal. We wanted to encourage Jewish composers to write works that reflected contemporary Judaism, its spiritual condition-ality while at the same time enriching Kulturbund programming. [...] Dr (of engineering) Richard Fuchs, head of the Karlsruhe Kulturbund, won the absolute largest number of jury points in the category Choral Work with Orchestra for his *Vom jüdischen Schicksal*, set to texts by Karl Wolfskehl and Süßkind von Trimberg. Fuchs has entered the public limelight only in recent years with exceptional Lieder and indeed two symphonies for large orchestra. The oratorio is heroic, full of strength, power and occasionally monumental, but a work that stylishly unifies both form and content into a commonality.[10]

Singer then went on to announce which works would be publicly performed. *Vom jüdischen Schicksal* was conspicuous by its absence.

From their correspondence, it appears that Fuchs set Wolfskehl's poems before consulting him. The first letter from Fuchs to Wolfskehl is dated 2 January 1937. Fuchs seems most concerned about his justi-fication of setting Trimberg along with Wolfskehl and explains:

Süßkind's work spiritually bridges several centuries and joins the powerful resonance of your poems, whereby certain quotes in the music find an inner meaning that no person could have devised ... Süßkind's works come across as the evocation of a medieval spirit, and for me (perhaps also for you?) a melancholic appeal, something like a handshake across the ages ...[11]

Wolfskehl, who at this point had left Germany for Italy, not only approved of Fuchs's texts and their sequencing, but also approved and agreed with the use of Trimberg's works as a bridge across the centu-ries. He responded to Fuchs (addressing him as 'Dear Composer') in such musical terms that Fuchs deduced that Wolfskehl understood exactly what he intended. Fuchs then admitted that he had submitted the work to a competition, so he was unable publicly to reveal himself as the composer. Wolfskehl was nonetheless sent a piano vocal score and a full score from which he was able to see how the texts were set.

Following Fuchs's competition award, he concluded in a letter to Wolfskehl on 10 May 1937:

I'm compelled to thank you for the inspiring strength of your forceful verses, and I believe that with the accompanying music we have both created a work that does not bear a poor witness to the heroic spirit that empowers us to withstand our monstrous destiny.[12]

The presentation of the prize would, however, be only the beginning of Fuchs's troubled relationship with the Kulturbund, Germany, and the work itself, which he would never live to hear.[13]

The month following his award, Fuchs wrote to the committee of the Zionist weekly newspaper in Berlin, *Jüdische Rundschau*, and explained that he understood Singer's reluctance to promote the work. Indeed, he even understood that Singer had at that point not even showed the text to Hans Hinkel, fearing its defiance might create difficulties for the Kulturbund. Fuchs went on to describe his work as a 'cry from the soul of German Jews' and asked for the contact details of Bronisław Huberman in the hope that his oratorio might be performed in Palestine or America.[14]

Within a couple of weeks, Singer replied to Fuchs and requested study material in order to perform the work.[15] Fuchs supplied Singer with an initial fifteen chorus parts but mentioned the enormous costs of forwarding more material. He made some casting suggestions and demanded the top chorus in Berlin. Fuchs also mentioned that he hoped to have the work performed in Karlsruhe. He went on to add that the Karlsruhe performance would require input from Berlin, perhaps with Singer or Rudolf Schwarz as conductor.

Singer wrote back in September, wishing Fuchs the best for the Jewish New Year before recommending that the performance of his oratorio start without the opening and Wolfskehl's text – beginning instead with Trimberg, an arrangement Singer believed would be acceptable to the Nazi overlords. Singer informed Fuchs that should the work be rejected by Hinkel and his advisors, it could not be resubmitted. The text Singer felt would be rejected outright was the poem 'Und dennoch' ('And yet'):

Ever driven forth and scourged with hate
What fearful right have ye to take our tears?
Crouching all day to prey upon our fears?
And watch us scowling by night always terror torn!
To wailing, oath and prayers, ye, ye gave us only scorn:
Nothing we heard but hatred, shrieking cry –
And [yet,] we do not die![16]

As can be imagined, Fuchs was not happy with this suggestion and even went so far as to express his concern that Singer could potentially lose his important position within the Kulturbund as a result of the Wolfskehl text; nevertheless, *Vom jüdischen Schicksal* could under no circumstances be allowed to lose its opening – indeed the most defiant text of the work and in light of the 'Final Solution' a brave shot across the Nazi bow. Fuchs pleaded that he be allowed to speak to Hinkel himself and suggested taking his brother Gottfried, who lived in Berlin and had won the highest of all war decorations, the medal of the Hohenzollern Order. Fuchs wanted at least to find which words were the most objectionable and hoped Wolfskehl could be persuaded to find gentler synonyms. Fuchs then demanded that *Vom jüdischen Schicksal* be performed together with his recently completed symphony, which he intended to dedicate to the 'courageous' Dr Singer. The obvious flattery and bribe of dedication only pointed to the hopelessness and desperation of the situation.

Six weeks later, Fuchs's letter remained unanswered, and he wrote again explaining the need for clarification and also the requirement to settle arrangements for a performance in Karlsruhe, something only possible with subsidies and the use of the orchestra based with the Frankfurt Kulturbund. This last plea ended with a letter co-signed by Kurt Singer and his deputy, Werner Levie, confirming the application for the performance of *Vom jüdischen Schicksal* had been rejected. The letter is formal and bureaucratic.

Fuchs was clearly disappointed. The letter he returned is equally formal and expresses at least a hope that the work could be performed in Palestine or America, which he hoped the Berlin Kulturbund would help with. This too was rejected by Singer in his letter to Fuchs on 8 November 1937, though he offered to try and facilitate a performance in Karlsruhe, speculating that Hinkel's authority might not reach that far outside of Berlin. Given the tone and careful wording of the correspondence, a more likely scenario can be deduced, and in all probability Singer and Levie decided that even showing the text to Hinkel was too risky. That being the case, it was easier for a performance to take place in faraway Karlsruhe than in Berlin: something that might escape Hinkel's notice.

In December, Fuchs sent the score to a contact in London, Mrs Laurie Rosenfeld in Elsworthy Road, St John's Wood. The letter is interesting as he sets out the situation as he saw it at the time and also allows us to evaluate his command of English before moving to New Zealand, where it would no doubt improve considerably:

Dear Mrs Rosenfeld

I owe your address to Mrs Franklin-Kohn at Bournemouth as you know. I am very happy indeed to find by your goodwill an occasion to send my work to some musical circle in England. – I have posted the score by enregistered letter on you today. The work itself is named 'Vom jüdischen Schicksal' (Jewish fate) and written for mixed chorus, solo-singers, and orchestra. The words

are partly of Wolfskehl a living german (jewish) poet partly of
'Süßkind of Trimberg' who was a ministrel in early middle-age
living in Germany. The work has won the first prize of the competition arranged by the League of Jewish organisations for art
and culture. (Perhaps you know that in this league all musical
and artistic life is concentrated.) Of course it was thought to
perform the work at Berlin and other places but the censuring
authorities don't allow any performance in Germany. – I am now
in that tragical position not to be heard by those who would
understand me with all their heart and feeling. You ask me, to
try a performance in England let me answer that I know to have
written a work which is worth to be saved from falling into
oblivion, but letting alone this I have also personally the ardent
desire to be saved and to find a country to be at home again,
and I hope to find once friends to help me and my family. – Of
course I know that it will be difficult to find a circle to which this
work especially would speak and of which it would be echoed.
It is too hard for men living in safety to imagine the position of
us, who are stired up and made homeless in our own country.
Nevertheless it is to be hoped that there will be found men,
human beings, who will understand. And I don't merely think of
jewish men.

I have put into the score the whole text by tipewriter because
I know the difficulties for Englishmen to read our letters. If you
believe it to be better, I could also send a translation, I have treid
myself, but I must confess that it is too difficult for a foreigner to
find poetical words. I can send the piano-arrangement too, if that
is needed and I beg you kindly to tell me if you think so. I hope
not to have made too much mistakes in writing english. I would
like to come to London if i can do something useful, having my
brother [Gottfried] there it wouldn't be too difficult for me and
besides I would have the pleasure to visit my daughter living at
school in England.

I hope to hear soon some words, begging you to receive my heartfelt thanks by anticipation.

yours very truly[17]

The work is in four sections with sections one, three and four set to texts by Wolfskehl and section two by Süßkind von Trimberg. The work opens with the poem 'Und dennoch' ('And yet'), quoted above. The rapid dotted accompaniment interspersed with short fanfares with side drum and piccolo is militaristically defiant. Fuchs does not see Germany's Jews simply allowing themselves to be annihilated, or at least not without resistance. It is surprising that Singer had become so intimidated by Hinkel that any anger resulting from Nazi policies excluding Jews from German life should never be suggested. With the militant character of the opening, this anger is not whispered or implied; it is openly stated and clearly meant to be understood as a call to arms.

Part Two, titled 'Stimme der Vorzeit' ('Voice from Before Time'), for baritone and orchestra, is set to a text by Trimberg. It too starts and ends with a bugle call, though its central section expands into a Brucknerian lyricism, openly laying claim to music traditions that Fuchs believed to be universal.

Part Three is titled 'Aufbruch! Aufbruch!' The term is difficult to translate as no English word exactly fits its dual meanings in German, which principally covers 'departure' while also suggesting 'arrival' (as in 'a new era' and 'Anbruch'). 'Striking' as in 'Striking camp' comes closest. In this section, we have obvious references to both Wagner and Richard Strauss, again expressing entitlement to a legacy from which Germany's Jews refused to be excluded. The soprano opens with a wondrous solo interrupted at its climax by Richard Strauss's *Elektra* motif. It concludes with a hymn sung reverently by the chorus while Wagner's Rhine motifs from *Das Rheingold* swirl underneath.

Part Four, 'Vor Ausfahrt' ('Before Departure'), is purely choral and largely homophonic, again with militaristic gestures expressed by trumpets interjecting bugle calls to action.

**Reichsverband
der Jüdischen Kulturbünde in Deutschland**

Berlin SW19
Stallschreiberstraße 44
Fernsprecher: A 7 Dönhoff 3712
Postscheck: Berlin 3648
„   (Stagma) Berlin 163832

Herrn
Dr.Richard F u c h s
Kriegsstr.120
K a r l s r u h e
==================

UNSER ZEICHEN:	IHR ZEICHEN:	IHR SCHREIBEN VOM:	DATUM:
			28.Oktober 1937

Sehr geehrter Herr Doktor,

zu unserem grössten Bedauern müssen wir Ihnen heute die
traurige Mitteilung machen, dass unser Genehmigungsantrag
für Ihr Werk "Vom jüdischen Schicksal" mit dem Vermerk
"Abgelehnt" von der Reichskulturkammer zurückgekommen ist.

So sehr es uns auch schmerzt, dass sich nun nicht die
Möglichkeit ergibt, das preisgekrönte und wertvolle Werk
im jüdischen Bezirk in Deutschland aufgeführt zu sehen, müssen
wir uns doch mit diesem Bescheid begnügen.

Wir begrüssen Sie

mit vorzüglicher Hochachtung
REICHSVERBAND DER JÜDISCHEN KULTURBÜNDE
IN DEUTSCHLAND

Wir bitten, Briefe stets nur an den Reichsverband der Jüdischen Kulturbünde, Berlin, nicht aber an einzelne Personen zu richten.

5. The letter from the heads of the Kulturbund cancelling the intended performance of *Vom jüdischen Schicksal* (*Of Jewish Destiny*).

The Nazis notoriously took communist fight songs, removed their Marxist texts and replaced them with their own messages. The idea was that music itself was powerful enough to convey the necessary propaganda. Fuchs cleverly reverses this idea with a dialectic that potentially spat the *faux*-militarism back into the faces of his Nazi overlords. *Vom jüdischen Schicksal* expresses a defiant German Zionism that Fuchs believed the Nazis should take as a threat.

There were other composers in the Kulturbund who took a different approach from that of Fuchs: Arno Nadel, Julius Chajes and Oskar Guttmann saw the development of 'Jewish character' in composition as an opportunity to distance themselves from Germanic tropes – something the Nazis actually encouraged. Even Fuchs would use liturgical and Eastern modes as colour rather than as a harmonic fundament in works such as *Kaddisch*, while his *Hymnus für Gott*, subtitled *Chassidic Song*, is diatonic in its harmonic language.

Richard Fuchs and the young Viennese composer and conductor Georg Tintner (1917–99) would both arrive in New Zealand within weeks of each other in April 1939. Fuchs would view himself as an 'elder statesman' and was genuinely perplexed that New Zealanders did not turn to him as a missionary from the Old World to the New. Native-born musicians of those New World countries offering refuge took what they needed from the 'Old World' and used it for their own ends. Georg Tintner was from a different generation. He could have been Fuchs's son. Both European composers were bemused and challenged by their new homeland and indeed, towards the end of his life, Tintner stated it was perhaps the only place he felt at home. Paradoxically, it would be the young Georg Tintner who would befriend the poet Wolfskehl, also exiled in New Zealand, rather than Richard Fuchs. Tintner and Wolfskehl lived in Auckland while Fuchs lived in Wellington and interaction between the two cities was fairly limited. Nevertheless, and in conclusion, the enforced ghetto of the Kulturbund brought about in Fuchs a condition that is entirely in keeping with the concept of 'internal exile'. This sense of exile in

one's own homeland resulted in a defiant claim to the cultural entitlement his birthright as a patriotic German demanded. We know
from conversations reported between Tintner and Wolfskehl that
both of them felt the same. The younger Tintner was clearly in a
better position to turn his adversity and many subsequent disap-
pointments into opportunities.[18]

3

Exile in Germany
Inner Emigration

In kleinen Städten war es wahrscheinlich schwerer, unbehelligt zu leben, und auf dem Lande besonders. Man wusste genau es gab in Deutschland Gegenden die waren sehr stark nazi und andere nicht, und das wieder auf verschiedene Weise und, wie ich später merkte, auch in Hamburg gab es noch sehr stark den 'Weimarer Geist', den Geist der liberalen, halblinken, deutsch-jüdischen Kultur. Anderswo gab es auch eine Art von Anti-Nazismus, aber wieder ganz anders, das war auf den hinterpommerschen Rittergütern, wo man sich sagte, diese Rabauken, diese Proleten. Andere Gegenden waren sehr nazi, nach Süddeutschland hin wurde es zum Beispiel schlimmer.

In smaller towns, it was probably more difficult to live without being affected, and in the country it was even worse. We were well aware that in Germany there were places that were passionately supportive of the Nazis while in other regions, less so, and these situations were also quite diverse. And as I later noted, in Hamburg, one still encountered the strong spirit of Weimar, the spirit of liberalism, left-of-centre, believers in German-Jewish culture. In other places, there was a kind of anti-Nazi feeling that was markedly different, such as the Pomeranian hinterlands in the homes of squires and landed gentry, which dismissed [Hitler's] ruffians and proletarians. Other regions of Germany were very supportive of the Nazis, for example, the further south one went in Germany, the worse it got.

Sebastian Haffner, *Geschichte eines Deutschen: Die Erinnerungen 1914–1933*[1]

Not all musicians and composers were in danger from Hitler's policies, but this does not mean they actively supported the NSDAP. Musicians often moved in progressive circles, and Jewish colleagues were crucial to musical life, with only the fanatically antisemitic believing otherwise. Yet antisemitism had many permutations. There were progressives such as the violinist Gustav Havemann, who led the purge in Berlin's Music Academy of the half-Jewish director Franz Schreker and fellow professor of violin Carl Flesch. Yet Havemann was a member of the left-wing Novembergruppe, a progressive organisation that named itself after the German Revolution in 1918. Other members of the Novembergruppe were Max Butting, Hanns Eisler, Jascha Horenstein, Philipp Jarnach, Felix Petyrek, Hans Heinz Stuckenschmidt, Heinz Tiessen, Kurt Weill and Stefan Wolpe. The Novembergruppe also included the American George Antheil and the Russian Wladimir Vogel. From this group of artistic and social progressives only Eisler, Horenstein, Vogel, Wolpe and Weill went into exile, while Antheil retuned to America. Also remarkable is the fact that Butting, Petyrek and Havemann joined the NSDAP. Havemann was the only outspoken antisemite, while Butting and Petyrek represented the dilemma of many who could not, or would not, emigrate and joined the Nazi Party because it was the only means of maintaining their positions as teachers or performers. After the war, they would continue to claim that their own compositions were frequently dropped from performances during the years of Nazi rule, despite their perceived sympathies and party membership.

Most successful non-Jewish soloists were too international to spend much time fretting about domestic politics unless they were directly affected. It left them naïve and unable to see clearly where a Hitler regime might lead. This apparent wilful ignorance is reflected in the violinist Alma Moodie's letter to her Swiss patron Werner Reinhardt, written on the eve of Hitler's appointment as chancellor on 29 January 1933:

These days in Germany one needs a lot of tact. Tempers are very heated and this Hitler business is very strange. This month I was together with various friends in Silesia who are mad Hitlerites. They are very cultured, infinitely refined people of unquestionable views, and I spoke with them for many hours. It seems to me that he is causing the greatest mischief (and this explains his success) by appealing to and operating with this somewhat fuzzy German concept of the 'emotions'. The whole thing seems to be about a 'feeling' that can't be explained, and that I don't yet understand – although I have made an effort. The whole thing is very woolly, within the Party they are not unanimous and if he comes to power now it will certainly depend on chance as to which way he will go. For us, much would depend on it. But it is a pity that friendships are being destroyed over it.[2]

To add perspective, in the next paragraph she mentions to Reinhardt that she is performing a Beethoven cycle with the pianist Artur Schnabel and the Brahms Violin Concerto under Otto Klemperer. Within months, both Schnabel and Klemperer had left Germany along with her beloved teacher Carl Flesch. Joining them in exile were a number of composers such as Ernst Krenek, Egon Wellesz and Paul Hindemith, whose works she had premiered, as well as her close friend, the poet Rainer Maria Rilke. Her replacement pianist for Schnabel, Eduard Erdmann, was another composer-pianist who was no friend of the Hitler regime but, like Moodie, joined the Nazi Party in order to continue working.

In light of what we now know, it seems incredible that such people would remain; every one of them came with issues that meant emigration was not an option. As they were not on a political black-list and were not Jewish, it was nearly impossible to convince family members to strike out into the unknown. One needed affidavits, and for affidavits one needed contacts abroad. After the Évian Conference of July 1938, it was clear that there was only a finite number of options. Jews and those who had been visibly opposed to the Hitler regime had a greater urgency to emigrate than non-Jewish musicians who had been largely unaffected by political developments. If the enormous number of letters to and from Alma Moodie are an indication, then it appears they watched in bewilderment as colleagues and friends were persecuted and forced to flee. Every visa issued under a quota system for someone who was not a Jew, a Social Democrat, a Communist, a homosexual, or some other persecuted minority, was one such visa less for someone who was.

As a result, there were several variants of 'inner emigration', or as it was also often referred to, 'inner exile'. For composers who remained, yet 'emigrated inwardly' while physically remaining in Nazi Germany, it meant they could write what they wished without censure, but also without resonance. Their works remained in desk drawers or were shared among a small group of friends.

The first type of 'inner emigrant' was the musician who had never attracted the malevolent eye of Hitler's cultural arbiters, but could not stand the thought of being performed in, or associated with, his regime. They saw performances as a form of acquiescence. I only know of one example of this first type of 'inner emigrant': Karl Amadeus Hartmann. Perhaps there are others, but so far none has come to the same prominence. Hartmann was in all likelihood a unique example who had the good fortune of being supported by his wife's family, thus allowing him the 'luxury' of following his conscience. There were other composers and musicians who were equally opposed to Hitler and, like Hartmann, were openly courted by the Nazi regime. That they came to an accommodation with Germany's new rulers was mostly a question of survival, trumping possible questions of ethics. Hartmann was fortunate, but it does not presuppose others would not have been equally 'heroic' had they been offered the same opportunities. Nearly every composer who found their true voice in the silence of a desk drawer was forced into moral compromises. Even Hartmann joined the Reichsmusikkammer (Reich Chamber of Music) and presumably went through the indignity of having his ancestry traced for any hint of 'non-Aryan' lineage. After the war, and employed by the American occupation forces, he was excessively eager to disclaim his earlier pro-communist sympathies. Thus, ethical positions evaporated when it came down to the merciless question of professional survival.

Another category consisted of 'non-Aryan' composers or performers who were in so-called 'mixed-race' marriages. They remained in danger of raids on the street that could result in them being interned in concentration camps until money for bribes to free them could be accessed. Towards the end of the war, their 'protected' status was lifted and their 'Aryan' spouses were arrested with them. The composers Walter Braunfels and Günter Raphael both lived under dangerous conditions but miraculously survived. Hans Winterberg, a Czech composer, also lived in the relative safety of a 'mixed-race' marriage and composed his only two symphonies during a period when there was no chance of performances and his own life teetered on a knife-edge. The operetta composer Edmund Eysler was such a well-known figure in Vienna that he did not dare leave the house for fear of being identified and 'rounded up'. The so-called 'privileged' status of 'mixed-race' marriages was insecure and did not guarantee protection. Richard Fuchs's sister and her non-Jewish husband were both murdered in Auschwitz.

The third, and in many ways the most interesting, category is the group of 'grey-zone' composers mentioned previously as part of the

Novembergruppe, or other well-known progressives such as Eduard Erdmann and Boris Blacher. Each of their stories is different and it would be impossible to find a common element except for the fact that they could not or would not leave Germany following Hitler's appointment as chancellor. These are the composers who most likely would have joined Hartmann in complete withdrawal if only they had been offered the same degree of support.

The fourth group is made up of a selection of important composers who outwardly sided with Hitler's regime while writing music they knew might never be performed. In most cases, they supported aspects of Nazi ideology while never knowing from one performance to the next if their works would be accepted by local promoters. This precarious situation resulted in a fascinating variant of 'inner emigration'. Most of them found they needed to forfeit aspects of their musical individuality, at best in order to maintain a presence within Germany's musical life and at worst to guarantee their own safety. As composers, they were sufficiently embedded within a contemporary aesthetic that allowed the NSDAP to show them off as examples of progressive artistic developments within Hitler's Germany. Yet at the same time, other Nazi Party elements in different regions of the country prohibited performances, denouncing the performers or composers as 'Cultural Bolsheviks'.

By manipulating these conflicting elements within the Nazi regime, they were able to avoid the fate of Paul Hindemith's total ban and exile. Hindemith was possibly the most prominent composer of his generation and was eager to come to an accommodation with Hitler's regime. Hitler's personal dislike of Hindemith sealed his fate, leaving other composers without Hindemith's recognition exposed. If someone as established as Hindemith could be thrown out of Germany despite pleading to remain, what chances did they have? After the war, in the course of their denazification hearings, they continued to evade culpability by citing the precariousness of their situation, either in reference to the modernist characteristics of their music or even by referencing Arnold Schoenberg or Franz Schreker as their teachers. They were mostly given light sentences and occasionally let off altogether, with membership of the NSDAP being a more determining factor than their actual support of the Nazi regime in the course of their musical lives. During the confused days following the defeat of Nazism, such works and explanations were enough to satisfy harried members of denazification panels, who had more to worry about than the possible culpability of musicians. With files of denazification hearings lost or destroyed, it is impossible to know the extent of their true compliance. In the decades following Hitler's defeat, they began a process of rewriting their past. The dilemma then, as well as for us today, is these were not insignificant composers and there is little to be gained by silencing them. As a result, after the war, it was often more convenient to accept their version of events.

The Opportunists

In the interest of perspective, it is this complex fourth group with which I wish to begin, and work backwards, finishing with Karl Amadeus Hartmann. By working in reverse order, it becomes easier to understand the ethical and practical implications of remaining in Nazi Germany while attempting to maintain a semblance of artistic integrity and autonomy.

This group includes Hermann Heiß, or Heiss (1897–1966), Hugo Herrmann (1896–1967), Johann Nepomuk David (1895–1977), Paul Höffer (1895–1949), Fried Walter (1907–96) and Wolfgang Fortner (1907–87). Some of the above-mentioned even landed on Hitler's exclusive list of *Gottbegnadeten*, a designation meant to convey a select group of composers whose gifts were uniquely bestowed by God. Being placed on this list meant they were spared military service, while all of them could prove during denazification sessions that they were actually in constant danger of falling from grace. What these composers have in common is their musical individuality and undoubted placement within the trajectory of twentieth-century music. They were not musical reactionaries or even proven antisemites such as Hans Pfitzner, Max Trapp or Paul Graener.

The overriding commonality in all of these very different composers is the artistic effect that living in the 'Third Reich' had on their output. This matter is made more difficult to calibrate as the Nazi regime was not in agreement as to what the cultural image of the Reich should be. Joseph Goebbels, as Chief of Propaganda, wished to promote a progressive international view of National Socialism, whereas Hitler himself, along with Alfred Rosenberg as Chief of Dogma, were inclined to a *Deutschtümelei* (jingoistic) view. They preferred the arts reflecting German stereotypes of national costumes, folksong and dance, with new compositions serving the same propagandistic role as Socialist Realism in the Soviet Union. In other words, they wanted the arts to be non-elitist and offer food for the soul to be consumed by the fundamentally good but unquestioning citizens of the Reich.

This meant that some composers were disliked by Hitler yet still managed to land on the coveted *Gottbegnadeten* list. It gave composers such as Paul Höffer a means of absolving themselves from complicity, since Hitler had made no secret of his dislike of Höffer's music. It is questionable, therefore, how far their 'resistance' to the regime was believable. If they composed music that was disliked by Hitler, this did not stop Goebbels from regarding them as proof offered to the international community that National Socialism was not backward-looking.

Even if National Socialism, Communism and Fascism wished to create new orders rather than restore old orders, it did not alter the fact that heading these movements were men who were fundamentally conservative. Conservative totalitarian governments such as military or clerical dictatorships in Spain, Portugal, Austria, Poland

and Hungary made no secret of seeing themselves as transitional regimes until the old order could feasibly be restored. As such, it is important to understand that European dictatorships were not identical. They did not share identical goals or shared values. What they had in common was a concentration of power centralised in an executive free from checks and balances. Yet this conflict between the self-perception of fascists, National Socialists and communists as modern while being led by dictators who were conservative would continue to cause confusion in the cultural politics of the Hitler years and afterwards. Denazification soon became a question of proving that a composer wrote music that Hitler would not have liked. It allowed such composers as Heiss, David, Herrmann, Höffer and others to prove they had worked and lived in 'inner exile', thereby facilitating their transition to being post-war arbiters, leading and framing musical life after Hitler.

For this reason, it's important to have an idea of what was being promoted as the acceptable face of modernism within Nazi Germany, before being able to establish the credibility of modernist composers who maintained they were forced into 'inner exile'. There were modernist trends that not only existed during the Nazi years but were promoted by leagues in support of 'German Culture', as well as many critics and numerous individuals working in ministries who could assure the safety of composers who dared to compose works they knew would not be tolerated by Hitler and the Rosenberg wing of the party. There are only marginal differences between these composers who worked with relative artistic freedom (though after the war, circumstances forced them to maintain otherwise) and those who maintained that their personal style was so contrary to the values of the Nazi Party that they had little choice but to compose propaganda works to assure their own safety, or to change their style to suit the mood of the time. Evaluating the credibility of the composers who claimed they were forced into 'inner exile' makes it necessary to have a brief look at three modernist composers who prospered under the 'Third Reich'.

The following three composers worked with few restrictions while writing music that continued along modernist developments already in train in Germany and Austria before the Nazis came to power. These composers enjoyed some of the highest-profile performances in many of Germany's most important houses and concert halls. Carl Orff and Werner Egk are not included because their profile was more in keeping with what was typified as a Nazi 'modernist' aesthetic. Flying against this acceptable variant of modernism were Rudolf Wagner-Régeny (1903–69), who composed in a style that to some extent recalled Kurt Weill; the Schoenberg pupil Winfried Zillig (1905–63); and Paul von Klenau (1883–1946). Both Zillig and von Klenau composed twelve-tone operas that were not only premiered in Nazi Germany but received genuine recognition within the Nazi cultural hierarchy.

Serialism, however, was not just a musical idea that Hitler and Rosenberg personally rejected as 'Jewish'; it was disliked by the broader German public as well. If their operas were seen by the international press as examples of artistic freedom in Nazi Germany, their removal after short runs had more to do with a lack of public interest than Nazi proscription. Yet, the mere fact that both von Klenau and Zillig felt they could work freely in Hitler's Reich demands some attention, as indeed do the successes of Rudolf Wagner-Régeny.

Although von Klenau, Wagner-Régeny and Zillig were not NSDAP members, they were all promoted within the Nazi regime and were never formally compelled to make compromises within their musical language. Indeed, von Klenau attempted to broaden the understanding of twelve-tone composition to make it compatible with Nazi ideology. All of them were in the fortunate position of being progressive voices within German music, largely protected and conceivably useful as propaganda to answer the charge that National Socialism was culturally regressive.

It is worth reading the defence of twelve-tone composition brought by Zillig and von Klenau as they tried to make the technique acceptable in the eyes of sceptical Nazi cultural arbiters who saw serialism as Schoenbergian and therefore 'Jewish'. In an interview about his twelve-tone opera, *Die Windsbraut* (*The Whirlwind*), published in 1941, Zillig twists and turns to avoid using the terminology of his teacher Arnold Schoenberg, and neither the words 'twelve' nor 'tone' appear. Nor is Schoenberg mentioned:

> Regarding the music, I only wish to state that I've been able to create a grand opera using strict construction principles that I've been able to develop over the years through numerous other works. These principles are so strict that every tone, every melody can be used as a starting point. Yet, on the other hand, it's so freely employed that it serves in facilitating classical and variation principles, such that much appears improvised, while other sections come across as strictly constructed along classical lines, for example, the form of the classical Lied takes the place of the aria.[3]

This is in stark contrast to Paul von Klenau, who in 1934 made no secret of his use of twelve-tone rows. Perhaps as the older and more fêted master with unquestionable 'Nordic' credentials, he could be more explicit. In any case, his arguments in defence of his twelve-tone opera *Michael Kohlhaas* were made in 1934 when he could successfully place his version of twelve-tone composition as a Nazi alternative to Schoenberg's. It allowed von Klenau to establish himself as one of Nazi Germany's most respected modernist masters, culminating in his final opera, also composed in his hybrid 'twelve-tone' language, *Elisabeth von England*, premiered in Kassel on 29 March 1939.

Von Klenau was more than compliant in matters arising from Nazi antisemitism. In 1935 he admitted in a letter to the music critic Friedrich W. Herzog to having divorced his Jewish wife in 1926. He went on to write that he 'maintained no further relationship with her or her family'.[4] In trying to promote his own works, despite being published by the 'Jewish publishing house Universal Music', located in still-independent Austria, he sent positive reviews of his *Gudrun auf Island* (premiered in 1918 in Mannheim) to the Hitler-supporting Friedrich W. Herzog, adding that he avoided quoting anything from the 'Jewish Press':[5]

> In my view, there are differing types of twelve-tone composition. I would refer to my version as a tonal variant of the twelve-tone theory. I organise my tone rows in such a manner that we have harmony, and disharmony and polyphony that also comes across as tonal. [...] My opera *Michael Kohlhaas* is the first work in which tonality-defined harmony and disharmony using the twelve-tone method is used. This is the reason that so many critics have not spotted that the work is written twelve-tone. [...] For the music of our day, we need the legitimacy of ethical order. This is because music that looks to a future in a National Socialistic world demands both proximity to the people as well as the technical expertise that [continuous] work as a musician affords.[6]

Although von Klenau lived in Vienna until 1940 when he returned to his native Denmark, he remained ever-present in Germany during the years of National Socialism, supported by the Militant League for German Culture, or Nationalsozialistische Kulturgemeinde, otherwise known as the Kampfbund für deutsche Kultur (Battle League for German Culture), and its associated critics such as Fritz Stege and Friedrich Herzog. In 1941 the Nazi Ministry of Culture even intended to place von Klenau in its projected Europe-wide International Cultural Ministry, a plan halted by the war.

Winfried Zillig, a far more daring and inventive composer than von Klenau, put his creative freedom down to Gerhard Scherler in the Nazi Ministry for Propaganda.[7] Nevertheless, he, like von Klenau, found a good deal of support within such publications as *Die neue Zeitschrift für Musik* – or *Signale*. Like Wagner-Régeny, he was happy in 1939 to compose a replacement score for Mendelssohn's banned *A Midsummer Night's Dream*, for a performance in Essen. The score was reviewed as:

[Zillig] offers a new score to this phantasmagorical play that suits the production, with its melodic development and colourful orchestration capturing the play's ever-changing romantic elements. [. . .] Visitors shouldn't only take pleasure in the performance [of the play, but] keep an ear open to the music as well.[8]

Rudolf Wagner-Régeny also composed a score for Shakespeare's *Midsummer Night's Dream*, and from all entries of the Ministry for Culture's competition in 1934 produced what was considered the best replacement for Mendelssohn's now unacceptable score. It was premiered as a concert work in Düsseldorf on 6 June 1935 at a convention for the *Nationalsozialistische Kulturgemeinde*, with its premiere as part of a stage production in Harburg-Wilhelmsburg on 1 October 1935.

The critic of the *Kölnische Zeitung Abendblatt* reviewed Wagner-Régeny's music on 7 June 1935, following the concert performance:

In theory, it was right that Rudolf Wagner-Régeny would attempt to steer the music for *Midsummer Night's Dream* away from its Romantic direction. His music is deliberately coarse and extremely rhythmic, like chopped wood, with simple, thick melodies. The gentle colours of moonlight and the poetry are all missing and everything comes across as something more appropriate for a puppet show than for Shakespeare's verse. As a result, the work remains in the most part dry without lasting charms.

The premiere of the music in the context of the play, performed on 1 October 1935, was reviewed the next day in the *Hamburger Anzeiger und Nachrichten*:

In place of the earlier and famous score we had a score presented by Rudolf Wagner-Régeny, one of at least five composers who have submitted substitutes. Under the baton of Josef Hager-Hajdú, the music was welded into the central ideas and nature of the work with occasional quite lyrical details that, as required, accompanied the lively flow of the play in both its gentle and vivacious moments.

All of this placed Wagner-Régeny in a favourable light with the ruling Nazi Party, a position that only increased following the success of his highly political opera *Die Bürger von Calais* (*The Citizens of Calais*), with a libretto by the Brecht and Weill stage designer Caspar Neher. Interestingly, Neher had also written the libretto for Weill's opera *Die Bürgschaft* (*The Pledge*), and he would go on to supply Wagner-Régeny with the libretto to his opera *Johanna Balk*, premiered in Vienna in 1941 and angering Goebbels to the point of lifting Wagner-Régeny's exemption from military service. His music to *Das Opfer* (*The Sacrifice*), written in commemoration of the Sudetenland's annexation, was well received and Wagner-Régeny's military service consisted of a desk job. After the war, Wagner-Régeny remained in the Soviet Sector where he, along with Hanns Eisler and Paul Dessau, made up a cadre of anti-fascist composers, despite the fact that both Eisler and Dessau had been driven into exile.

Why Wagner-Régeny, or indeed Caspar Neher, remained in Nazi Germany was down to the opportunities they were afforded. Wagner-Régeny was supported by Vienna's Gauleiter Baldur von Schirach, but as a showcase modernist there was support from other quarters as well. Wagner-Régeny came from the German-speaking province of Siebenbürgen in Transylvania and he acquired German citizenship in 1932. It might be argued that it was more his sense of German identity than any genuine sympathy for the Nazi cause that planted him so enthusiastically within the cultural life of Hitler's Germany.

These three composers are briefly outlined because it is important to know what was being composed openly when considering the claim of 'inner exile'. The following composers who maintained that they were forced into some type of 'inner emigration' are instructive because they claimed they were in constant danger. They believed that compliance was their only option. Yet von Klenau and Zillig composed without so much as a furtive glance over the shoulder, whereas Wagner-Régeny's misstep with *Johanna Balk* only landed him a desk job in the Wehrmacht. Clearly, without the protection of those in various ministries there was a danger of crossing a line, but it begs the question of whether evasion necessitated composing active propaganda for the Nazi cause. It was convenient for those musicians who chose to live in communist East Germany after the war that the Nazi genocide of Jews, Roma and Sinti was rarely if ever mentioned and the only victims who were remembered were 'anti-fascists'.

Hermann Heiß, for example, studied with Bernhard Sekles, who was condemned as 'entartet' by the Nazis because he was Jewish and because he had opened a jazz degree course at Frankfurt's Music Academy, where Heiß went on to teach in 1941. After the war, Heiß was declared 'unbelastet' or 'uncompromised' during the Nazi years and would go on to become a leading figure in Darmstadt's Summer Courses, seen today as one of the main progenitors of the European avant-garde. He composed twelve-tone music until 1934. Afterwards, he delivered a number of works on behalf of the Nazi regime, such as *Festmusik* and *Festliches Konzert* in 1935 for a party conference of the Hitler Youth. In 1936 Heiß composed *Das Jahresrad* (*The Wheel of the Year*) for the Berlin Olympic Games. In 1938 he composed the fight song *Auf! Steh auf!*, adding further songs and marches for the Luftwaffe. He published his thoughts on writing militaristic music with the title *Vom Schlachtruf zum Soldatenlied* (*From Battle Cry to the Soldier's Song*). Heiß composed a cantata for the birth of Goering's daughter Edda, called *Wiegenlied für ein deutsches Jägerkind* (*Lullaby for the Daughter of a German Hunter*), along with a number of other propagandistic 'cantatas'. In 1940 he published an article on the use of music in war. Perhaps most incriminating was his article in the *Deutsche Bühnenkorrespondent* (*German Stage Correspondent*) on 24 March 1934 when he wrote: 'The Jew Schoenberg and his atonal music has been uniformly rejected by National Socialist Germany. The Führer has decreed that this kind of degeneracy and corruption has no place in our New Germany.'[9]

Perhaps it was Heiß's good fortune that most of his original material was destroyed in an air raid in Darmstadt in 1944. Only a few years later, he was promoting, writing and teaching electronic music in the Darmstadt Summer Courses, an important influence on the Stockhausen and Boulez generation of young composers. Heiß was undoubtedly a music progressive and an avant-gardist pre- and post-Hitler. Before the arrival of the Nazi dictatorship, he studied twelve-tone composition with Josef Matthias Hauer. His development into the outer reaches of the musical avant-garde after the war offers psychological speculation derived from observations. It might have been the natural evolution of a modernist whose trajectory was interrupted by Hitler, or it might have been a focus on a musical aesthetic that distanced Heiß as far from the twelve years of the Nazi regime as possible. His reputation rests largely on Darmstadt's *Studio for Electronic Composition Hermann Heiß*. It is this jump from military marches and works evoking the German countryside, such as his *Heide, Moor und Waterkant* (*Heath, Moor and the North Sea Shore*) for wind ensemble, to the propagation of a musical avant-garde that alienated all but the most determined post-war audiences, that begs questions. It offers a singular example of an important composer outwardly compensating for his participation during more than a decade of nationalistic, racist and murderous madness, in which Heiß was a full, active and willing participant. Perhaps he even saw his active participation in a post-war aesthetic he knew would have been detested by Hitler as a means of atonement. Whatever his

6. Hermann Heiß as a post-war pioneer of new and electronic music in Darmstadt.

motivations after the defeat of the Nazis, it does not diminish Heiß's genuine significance and belief in Europe's post-war avant-garde.

In contrast to Heiß, who appears to have been ready to provide whatever propaganda the Hitler Reich requested, Johann Nepomuk David comes across as a passive naïf. Like Heiß, he didn't join the NSDAP or appears not even to have considered joining until it became apparent that his appointment as Director of the Leipzig Music Academy was dependent on party membership. His inability or apparent unwillingness to join the Nazi Party is mentioned in reports that claim he must be 'politically sound' or he would not have moved from his native Austria to Nazi Germany in 1937, or converted from Catholicism to Protestantism. David appears to have joined a 'pro-family' organisation instead, possibly in the belief that it might compensate for not being an NSDAP member. His works were frequently performed across Germany and even at official functions. His musical language was progressive but closer to New Objectivity and neo-classicism than departures from tonality or Schoenbergian serialism. He was prolific during the Nazi years with his symphonies no. 2 (1938), no. 3 (1940), no. 4 (1945), a *Divertimento after Old Folk Songs* (1939) and an orchestral *Partita no. 2* (1939), along with two sets of orchestral variations: one on a theme by Bach and another on one by Heinrich Schütz. David's musical centre of gravity appears to have been liturgical. He composed prolific quantities of church music before moving to Nazi Germany and again after the war. During the Nazi years he composed, in addition to chamber works, *a cappella* motets, a cantata for small chorus, oboe and organ, and some liturgical *Minnelieder* (*Minstrel Songs*) based on texts by Mechthild von Magdeburg.

David was from Upper Austria, a region sharing a border with Bavaria that was more sensitive to being excluded from Bismarck's unification of German states than other Austrian regions further east. Hitler was also from Upper Austria, and culturally there is little distinction between its regional dialect, local customs or religion and that of neighbouring Bavaria. David seems to have been attracted to the idea of pan-German unification more than the ideology of Nazism itself. One ostensible declaration of pan-German fidelity was that he converted from traditional Austrian Catholicism to Protestantism. This was despite the fact that Bavaria and the Rhineland were predominantly Roman Catholic. So intoxicating was the pan-German movement in the German-speaking regions of what, pre-1918, was 'Greater Austria', particularly in those regions bordering Germany itself, that conversion to Lutheranism seemed the ultimate declaration of German identity. David's music from this period represents this fundamental 'Teutonic' musical identity. There is monumentalism, pathos and an adept use of fugue and counterpoint, all of which were seen as distinctively 'German' and 'Nordic'. His symphonic works are effective and powerful, so it is perhaps based on these factors that he, unlike Heiß, was found to be compromised by complicity with Nazism and placed on the American blacklist of musicians embargoed from further employment. It did not prevent David's move to his native Austria in 1945, where in Salzburg he became a professor of composition. In 1948 he was allowed to return and work in Germany.

During his denazification inquiry, David attempted to present his promotion of Stravinsky's *Symphony of Psalms* in Leipzig as proof that he resisted Nazi proscriptions. As Stravinsky himself was ambivalent about Fascism, and was viewed in many quarters favourably by the Nazi hierarchy, David's claim was dismissed. More convincing would have been the fact that he was not allowed to become Director of the Leipzig Music Academy because he was not a party member. The selection committee even went so far as to suggest waiting until the war was over before making the appointment, when a returning soldier from the front with sounder politics might instead be engaged. David was spared military service by virtue of being on Hitler's *Gottbegnadeten* list. He went on to compose another four symphonies, but the sheer quantity of his church and organ music composed after the war, and indeed before his emigration from Austria to Nazi Germany, more than suggests that this is where his fundamental creativity lay.

Fried Walter was primarily a composer of music that suggested a closer affinity with his near-contemporary Jean Françaix than his teacher Arnold Schoenberg. Walter was in any case more interested in writing for cinema and much of his career was spent playing and composing *variété* and cabaret. During the Nazi years he composed the opera *Königin Elisabeth* (*Queen Elizabeth*), which was successfully premiered in Stockholm. Heinz Tietjen, the wily director of Berlin's State Opera Unter den Linden and survivor of the eras before, during and after the Nazis, invited him to compose an opera, a commission that kept Walter from having to serve in the military. *Andreas Wolfius*, based on E.T.A. Hoffmann's story of Cardillac, was premiered in

Berlin's State Opera in 1940, followed by a ballet, *Kleopatra*, that premiered in Prague in 1943. Although he was not a party member, but possibly because he was on Hitler's list of *Gottbegnadeten*, Walter was placed on the American blacklist. Despite this, he managed to find work as a répétiteur in the Soviet Sector in Leipzig from 1945 to 1947.

Walter's apparent exoneration proves that naked opportunism was essentially dependent on who was carrying out the denazification hearings and who was seated on the panels. He was not a member of the party, but enjoyed considerable success and high-profile premieres. Walter wrote a bit of military music during the Nazi years, but his general output was lightweight. The Soviet Sector had taken the position that a reinstatement of musical life was crucial to the restoration of normality. The Americans took a view that denazification was more important than any other factor, while the French considered that German audiences needed to be educated away from their monumentalist tastes. The British felt re-education or even denazification to be largely pointless, holding to their historic views of national stereotypes as irredeemable and unchangeable.[10] If Walter managed to evade post-war proscription, it was in all probability because he was not a party member and had won a scholarship to study composition with Schoenberg. After the war, any affiliation with Schoenberg, no matter how tenuous, sufficed to exonerate someone. Walter had little interest in serialism and there is no trace of it in his own work. His post-war evasion of landing on an American blacklist demonstrated how easy it was to find work in another sector, or even, as in the case of David, to leave Germany altogether and work in Austria.

More compelling as a composer was Wolfgang Fortner, who made no secret of his interest in new music, even to the point of being labelled a 'Cultural Bolshevist' by the more conservative elements in the NSDAP. Fortner was clearly of the view that progressive ideas of music had a place in Nazi Germany, and as a composer with an individual voice he was among the strongest and most distinctive of young progressives. After the war, he would play an important role in bringing new music to wider audiences. He was president of the German sector of the ISCM (International Society for Contemporary Music) and took over Karl Amadeus Hartmann's *Musica Viva* series in 1964. There are few awards and honours that Fortner did not receive post-war, though he landed on the denazification blacklist, unable to work until 1947. Fortner was a prominent composer of liturgical music, but like David, was happy to project church music into the twentieth century, flirting with atonality, dodecaphony and Expressionism. In 1935 Gerhart Göhler, writing in *Die neue Zeitschrift für Musik*, made the intriguing comment, 'Though Fortner is not the most modern composer – since "modern" is luckily no longer the means by which a work's value is assessed – but the most untamed of newly performed church music composers ...'[11]

Fortner's music for Nazi events provided far more than empty gestures, but offered a modernist credibility that compensated to some extent for Germany's loss of Paul Hindemith. Fortner was certainly admired by the more progressive and open elements of the Nazi press, who viewed his work as exciting and headstrong. He also saw himself as an educator, and took on the Hitler Youth Orchestra in Heidelberg from 1936 to 1939. With the start of the war, he was a willing provider of propaganda vocal works with titles such as *Wer zur Fahne rennt* (*He Who Runs to the Flag*) or *Setzt ihr euren Helden Steine* (*Build Your Heroes Monuments*).

Fortner clearly composed in a manner that was not always compatible with Nazi sensibilities and he appears to have enjoyed the recklessness his distinctive talent afforded. Nevertheless, in an article about Fortner in 1982, Gerhard Schumacher referred to his composing in a manner unacceptable to the NSDAP and having to enter 'inner emigration' as a means of artistic survival.[12] Fortner joined the NSDAP on 1 January 1940. He clearly believed in the idea of German renewal under Hitler and made no secret of his ambition to flourish under the regime. In 1941 he wrote that Schoenberg's belief in the direction of musical progress was an indication of his 'rootlessness' and proof that such views could only lead to nihilism.[13] As early as 1933, Fortner was ingratiating himself with the new regime by openly denouncing the music policies of Prussia's Social Democrat Leo Kestenberg, and poking fun at Anton Webern.[14] In 1934 Fortner composed a Concerto for String Orchestra as part of the Kampfbund für deutsche Kultur. He also composed a *Workers' Cantata* for the First of May, called *Arbeit ist Ruhm* (*Work is Glory*). Throughout the following years, works by Fortner were played and promoted by Nazi Germany's musicians and cultural arbiters. His works were performed at political events and festive occasions, though to what extent this was down to Fortner's passive opportunism or to the support and promotion of his publisher is unclear. For example, his *Feierkantate* (*Festive Cantata*) was composed for the 200th anniversary of the founding of Göttingen University. That it was performed at an event celebrating Hitler's rise to power was not something Fortner appears to have intended, though obviously if he had objections they were not profound enough to prohibit the performance altogether.

Fortner undoubtedly spoke for many fellow musicians and composers compromised by their active participation within the musical life of Nazi Germany, when in conversation with the historian Fred Prieberg he said:

> But do we have to bring all of that up again? Of course I could spend an evening telling you about disagreements and difficulties [...] but to put it all on record would be difficult and only opens an angry can of worms. If we just compare the famous '1000 years' with all of these things, then I have to count myself fortunate in having been granted a few extra years where I could work in freedom and substantiate myself. Please, just allow these matters to remain in the past . . .[15]

Prieberg went on to write that Fortner didn't allow 'these matters to remain in the past', but did everything he could to present himself as a victim, indeed as someone whose 'inner emigration' was the only means to express his true self.

Hugo Herrmann was another composer of exceptional gifts, with a distinctively individual voice. He was a pupil of Franz Schreker in Berlin and was close to Paul Hindemith. If he is remembered at all today, it's through Hindemith's contact, which resulted in Herrmann's composing concert literature for the accordion (*Sieben neue Spielmusiken für Akkordeon*) (*Seven New Pieces to Play for the Accordion*), op. 57, composed in 1927. As with Fortner and David, Herrmann attempted to modernise German church music. His legacy, however, is difficult to judge, which is why he's included in the group of musical progressives who appeared to experience both highs and lows during the Nazi years, often forcing periods of camouflage. He, like the other composers mentioned in this context, was proof that Nazi Germany could still offer a platform for exceptional individuality. It was how these composers dealt ethically with the hands fate dealt them that makes it unusually difficult to pass more than a moral judgement made more damning in light of Nazi crimes. Musically, much of these composers' output is strong and the best pieces deserve their place in Germany's twentieth-century canon. In describing his own compositional style in 1944, Herrmann wrote the following:

In my work, I've always striven towards a totality in all musical fields and over time have focused more on choral and folk music. My pedagogic work within the wider population has propelled me into the most compelling assignments. I see my artistic calling within the synthesis of folk music's expressiveness and German monumentalism.[16]

It is a description that fits many of his post-war works as well. Herrmann, however, was clearly taken with Nazi ideology from early on. His interest in composing for the accordion and later for the hand-harmonica was almost the perfect means by which to write contemporary marches, modern folk songs and choral works that accentuated the sort of German tribalism promoted by the Nazis. Titles of fight songs and folk songs include *Die deutsche Straße* (*The German Street*); *Deutsches Bekenntnis* (*German Avowal*); *Potsdam, 21. März 1933* (*Potsdam, 21 March 1933*); an arrangement of the notorious Nazi anthem *Horst Wessel Lied* for the 'chromatic handheld harmonica'; and so on. In 1934 Herrmann initiated a folk-music section within the Donaueschingen Festival, which until 1933 had been one of Germany's foremost centres for new music. In 1936 he composed a work called *Kantate auf einen großen Mann* (*Cantata to a Great Man*), which is obviously meant to signify Hitler, while not mentioning him by name. And yet Herrmann found himself included in various proscription lists as 'entartet' or 'degenerate'. He maintained that in light of these attacks, and in the interest of his own safety, he needed to ingratiate himself visibly with the Nazi regime by joining the party in 1939. During the first year of the war in 1940, he was composing straightforward Nazi propaganda with titles such as *Ich bin des Führers Frontsoldat* (*I'm the Führer's Front Soldier*); in 1941, *Die toten Brüder* (*The Dead Brothers*) and a motet called *Die Stimme des Volkes* (*The Voice of the People*); in 1942, *Weckruf* (*Reveille*); in 1943, *Marsch nach Osten* (*March to the East*) and *Der Kamerad* (*The Comrade*).

The official line in Herrmann's biography is that he joined the NSDAP because cultural arbiters within National Socialism had condemned him for writing in a style denounced as 'Cultural Bolshevism'. The biography also states that he left the NSDAP in 1944, though Fred Prieberg's meticulous research does not mention this point. His file lodged with the State Archive of Baden-Württemberg, in a civilian court in Tuttlingen in September 1948, merely confirms that Herrmann had declared he left the NSDAP in July 1944. Given the late date and with the war going badly for the

Germans, there is probably little documentary evidence beyond Herrmann's own claim to the Tuttlingen civilian court to back this up. Clearly, he was blacklisted and only allowed to return to work in 1948. If Herrmann did indeed undergo a form of 'inner emigration', it was in order to offer his undoubted talent, imagination and creative gifts to the service of Hitler's government for his own protection. That his symphonic, church and chamber music was not accepted in many quarters within the NSDAP, thus forcing a sacrifice of his personal style and integrity, does, however, suggest some form of subconscious inner emigration. A composer with lesser gifts would merely have been denounced as nakedly opportunistic. Do Herrmann's marches and fight songs in cringing support of the Nazi dictatorship outweigh the undoubted quality of his best works? Ultimately, only the latter remain and time will tell.

The Compromised

If the composers in the fourth category experienced a form of 'inner emigration' while outwardly supporting the Nazi regime, the following composers belonged to a group of musicians who had little sympathy for Hitler or his ambitions. They also remained in Nazi Germany and in many cases even joined the NSDAP in order to maintain their positions as teachers or performers. As seen in the case of Johann Nepomuk David, party membership was required for many official positions, and for lowly, jobbing performers unable to emigrate, party membership was the only means whereby enough work could be found to support families and pay bills. From their circle of friends to the political beliefs they held prior to Hitler and, most tellingly, to the degree their creativity was negatively affected during the Nazi years, it is evident that the 'inner emigration' experienced by the following composers was of quite a different order to that experienced by those described above. They are the composers who have been referred to over the years as inhabiting a 'grey zone'.

Boris Blacher (1903–75) straddles any number of ambiguities. He was fêted by Carl Schuricht, who brought Blacher to prominence by premiering his *Concertante Musik für Orchester* with the Berlin Philharmonic in December 1937. The work was so well received it was performed a second time in the same concert. Blacher's style recalled the 'New Objectivity' of Ernst Toch and Paul Hindemith, juxtaposing rhythmic energy with often long melodic lines while never yielding to bathos or sentimentality. He made little secret of his interest in jazz – already a black mark with many Nazis – yet continued to be one of the most frequently performed composers during the Nazi years, despite the tightrope he found himself having to walk once it emerged that he had a Jewish grandparent. Critics who earlier had been heartened at his daring modernism, such as Fritz Stege, started to express ideological and political doubts. Blacher was openly attacked by Herbert Gerigk who headed the music office in Alfred Rosenberg's department. Blacher's colleague, the equally fêted young composer Werner Egk, was responsible for passing on confidential correspondence in order to expose others who, like Blacher, were tolerated by the NSDAP despite being quarter-Jewish.

Performances of Blacher's works were sometimes footnoted with the comment that he was not a pure Aryan. He was already considered suspicious because he was born in China to German Estonian parents. His father was a banker from Tallinn and until Blacher's move to Berlin at the age of nineteen he had lived in a number of countries, including China, Siberia and Manchuria, and learned their languages; he also spoke Estonian, German and English. In 1942 he reminded the composer Werner Egk that he was officially stateless, and tried to defend his status as 'quarter-Jew' by mentioning others in prominent positions, information Egk promptly passed on to the appropriate authorities. Karl Böhm managed to procure a position for him at Dresden's Conservatory in 1938, only for Blacher to lose it the following year. The combination of his musical personality, his background and his one Jewish grandparent left him professionally isolated, though paradoxically his *Concertante Musik für Orchester* continued to be performed until 1942. This was the year when Blacher began his oratorio *Der Großinquisitor* (*The Grand Inquisitor*) based on Dostoyevsky's *The Brothers Karamazov* with added passages from the New Testament.

Blacher was a highly prolific composer. His musical style was energetic and, though dissonant, it was always immediate and accessible to audiences. Just as von Klenau claimed to have created a tonally based twelve-tone system, so Blacher's atonality never sounded unmoored from tonality. It was in a sense tonal-atonality and held the fascination of listeners and musicians because of his individual sense of structure, rhythmic energy, sparkling orchestrations and conciseness. In addition, Blacher knew how to integrate lines of tonal lyricism onto fundamentally atonal canvases, creating an often exhilarating effect, as can be heard in the final movement of his *Concertante Musik für Orchester*.

Nevertheless, few of these characteristics are found in Blacher's *Der Großinquisitor*, a work that often feels closer to Hindemith's American works, most notably his Walt Whitman *When Lilacs Last in the Dooryard Bloom'd: A Requiem for Those we Love*, which was written around the same time. Hindemith was in any case a composer to whom Blacher felt the closest aesthetic affinity, though Blacher always maintained a rhythmic tension and instrumental sparkle often missing in Hindemith's American years. An uncharacteristic darkness tends to permeate elements within *Der Großinquisitor*, despite moments of Blacher's syncopation and rhythmic verve in his choral sections. The work takes its cue from Bach's Passions, with the chorus both relating the narrative and representing the mob. The Grand Inquisitor's massive soliloquy, written after the war, is hectoring and heavy, representing something more dramatically trenchant than mere recitative and often veering close to *Sprechgesang*. Written in 1942, the year when Blacher's professional isolation was at its darkest, the text of *Der Großinquisitor* reflects his sense of injustice as innocence is placed at the deadly mercy of authority. It cannot be a coincidence that Blacher decided to set this particular passage from *The Brothers Karamazov* at the height of the Nazi genocide of Jews, Roma and Sinti.

In Dostoyevsky's account of the 'Grand Inquisitor' taken from *The Brothers Karamazov*, Jesus returns to earth a second time, arriving in Seville in the midst of the Inquisition, where he encounters the ninety-year-old Cardinal, Grand Inquisitor, who 'for the glory of God' burns at the stake all enemies of the Church. The Cardinal, who is dressed in the simple garb of a monk, watches as Christ repeats the miracles from the New Testament on the streets of Seville. He orders Jesus' immediate arrest. Despite the rapture of the crowd, their fear of the Cardinal is greater than their sense of wonder at Christ's miracles. When the Grand Inquisitor, his 'desiccated face and sunken eyes inflamed with hatred', confronts Jesus, he tries to provoke him by referring to temptations offered by the Devil in the desert. This is the part that Blacher took from the Book of Matthew and treats in such a manner that implies that the temptations Christ refused had been greedily accepted by Germany's rulers. The figure of Christ will not be provoked and refuses to answer any of the accusations. At the climax of their encounter, Jesus places a kiss on the Inquisitor's 'ninety-year-old bloodless lips', whereupon the Inquisitor orders that the jail be opened while demanding that Christ leave and never return.

The symbolism resonates unmistakably, and the work would have been too provocative to perform during the Nazi years. As the war continued, Blacher became progressively disheartened, even suicidal, and left the oratorio incomplete until Blacher's pupil, Gottfried von Einem, persuaded him it could be performed after Hitler's defeat. It is only in the final third of the two-part oratorio that the Inquisitor, sung by a dramatic baritone, is heard. It is where Blacher picked up the work again after putting it to one side. The tone of the Inquisitor is despotic, self-righteous, and unmistakably meant to stand in for Blacher's own accusers.

Blacher remained popular after the war, able to profit from his own persecution by the Nazis with thankfully few questions asked about his years of success under the same regime. Yet he remains important for different reasons as well. Blacher was undoubtedly an important pre-Darmstadt modernist and represented one of the most viable directions music could have taken after the war. His sense of structure and the rhythmic tension he injected into most of his works set him apart from contemporaries. Perhaps his fundamental aesthetic point of departure remained that of pre-war New Objectivity, but uniquely, his sense of emotional detachment did not come across as arid or merely utilitarian.

Max Butting (1888–1976) is another case of a major talent being shut down by the very agencies that should have been promoting him. The Nazis' black marks against Butting were inconsistent. He joined the radical left-wing Novembergruppe in 1921, but then, so did Gustav Havemann who nonetheless went on to be an active member in the Nazi Kampfbund für deutsche Kultur. Butting, however, would never have considered such incompatible allegiances. He ran the music events for the Novembergruppe until 1927. He also contributed to Social Democratic publications and was on the board of the German chapter of the ISCM from 1925 to 1933. He was promoted and recognised as an important German composer, and was the co-chair of the board of Germany's Guild of Composers. His Third Symphony was performed by Hermann Scherchen in Geneva in 1929.

Butting may be remembered as a pioneer in the development of music for broadcast. Radio was in its infancy and broadcasts of classical concerts were far from satisfactory. It was believed in light of the cloudy wash offered by traditional orchestral concerts that new works explicitly composed for radio were needed. A number of composers wrote specific works for broadcast, such as Kurt Weill's Violin Concerto, in which the only strings in the orchestra are the soloist and a contrabass. It was believed the winds and brass were more compatible with radio technology than strings. Complex harmonies and counterpoint were also avoided. Hindemith and Weill composed an oratorio about Charles Lindbergh's 1927 solo flight across the Atlantic and, in the same vein, Schoenberg and Schreker wrote music for films – not feature films, but visuals that were meant to accompany their music rather than the other way around. Butting was a close friend and associate of the cinematographer Walter Ruttmann, who is today principally remembered as the director of the silent-film Berlin portrait, *Symphonie der Großstadt*, with a score by Edmund Meisel. In 1920 Butting provided Ruttmann with a score for his film *Lichtspiel Opus I*.

With his experience in what at the time was considered 'new media', Butting was appointed to the consultation board of *Die Funkstunde* (*The Broadcast Hour*) in 1926 (until 1933), and from 1928 to 1933 he was head of the Studio for Broadcast Music Interpretation at the Klindworth-Scharwenka Conservatory in Berlin, while teaching Music for Broadcast in Berlin's Hochschule für Musik's experimental studio. Butting was, in short, a product of Social Democratic Berlin and the Weimar Republic. Like the director of Berlin's Musik Hochschule, Franz Schreker, he was linked to Berlin's Cultural Advisor Leo Kestenberg, one of the Nazis' most hated establishment figures. In 1934 Butting was resoundingly denounced in the Nazi music journal *Die Musik*:

> What did Max Butting hope to find in this circle of young academics? Admittedly, he was called to the Academy under the old Kestenberg system. But on what basis of music accomplishments? What he accomplished in Donaueschingen as the leader of a left-wing internationally oriented group of composers is of no use in today's New Germany. He has to put forward a work that we may take seriously, something that until today he still has not managed.[17]

Another denunciation was in a memo regarding 'Cultural Bolshevism' written by none other than the notorious Dr Herbert

Gerigk, co-author of the *Lexikon der Juden in der Musik* (*Dictionary of Jews in Music*), a Nazi blacklist of performers, composers, academics and agents. In a memorandum in which Gerigk lists 'Cultural Bolsheviks' from 1939, he wrote:

> [...] please note that the composer Max Butting remains off-limits. As a participant during the years of cultural decay [a Nazi description of the Weimar Republic years] he was one of the leaders in the putrefaction of German musical life.[18]

Yet as can be heard in his Third Symphony, Butting's compositions were anything but academic. Indeed, they shared many of the monu-mentalist characteristics of composers applauded by the Nazis. His former pupil Christian Darnton, in his review of a biography of Butting written by the East German musicologist Dietrich Brennecke in 1976, the year of Butting's death, wrote:

> As a composer, Butting greatly interested himself during the 1920s in music specially written for the radio. He also wrote *Gebrauchsmusik*, 'practical music', as a reaction to the virtuoso demands of the Romantic School [...] Slightly different was his *Hausmusik* for amateurs: fun to play, agreeable to listen to. [...]
>
> Apart from a few excursions into the 12-note method, Butting's harmonic thought throughout his life was basically triadic, with a well-defined tonal orientation. A characteristic of his music up to the 1930s is a spiky angularity of melodic line, the idiom showing influences of jazz (as, similarly, in the music of Weill, Hindemith, and Stravinsky) which overlay his early loves: Debussy and Reger. Yet the romantic tenderness of Butting's slow movements clearly reveals these two influences.
>
> Fundamentally, however, Butting was a contrapuntal thinker. Everything he wrote is *durchkomponiert* [through-composed]: The basic material is sustained throughout every movement – there is

a sense of direction, of inevitability that carries the listener along without faltering. [...]

Butting's fondness for unison and octave doubling might be criticized, but as far as his early music is concerned, this is partly explained by the fact that so much music of his was specifically composed for radio.[19]

Despite his works being blacklisted by the Nazis, Butting managed to hold onto a liaison position at STAGMA, the Nazi performing-rights management office. This ended in 1939 and he was forced to leave music altogether. He took over his father's hardware business, a situation requiring him to join the NSDAP. It begs many questions how someone who was roundly condemned by the Nazis was able to join the NSDAP in 1940, having been removed from the last vestiges of cultural life only the year before. He was clearly not remotely in agreement with the regime or its policies, something that Gerigk's memo had documented, and which was generally known. Notwithstanding, Butting continued to compose during this period, producing three large symphonies, his ops 42–44.

After the war, Butting settled in the German Democratic Republic, though in 1945 it was still the sector of defeated Germany occupied by the Soviet Union. These post-war years unleashed a period of productivity that lasted until his death in 1976. Much of the music from this period was of a practical nature in keeping with many of the didactic ideas of pre-war Germany. Nevertheless, Butting's general musical legacy is enormous, with ten symphonies and ten string quartets, a piano concerto and a flute concerto, along with a good deal of vocal music. His ban by the Nazis and his post-war output coming out of East Germany meant Butting was a composer who was kept out of the Western European mainstream. Despite this, he remains a significant figure.

Heinz Tiessen (1887–1971) was a composer whose cultural importance far outweighed the post-war allegations laid against him.

In correspondence with Fred Prieberg from 1963, he stated the following:

Whoever doesn't know me may wonder why I simply didn't emigrate. However, I was lacking in all the necessities that would have made that feasible. I had binding ties and needed to care for dependents. The only solution was for me to 'play dead' in order to stay alive. My fundamental characteristics as composer, the very reason I was called to teach composition at [Berlin's] Music Academy, had to remain hidden from students. Individual private performances at the Prussian Academy of Arts couldn't compensate for the total removal of the recognition I had won as a composer from 1914 to 1932. The few performances after 1939 were limited by the war, since my most important, larger works were never included. The resultant loss of paid extra work and lack of income meant I had to take out loans and pawn my piano while living off a minimal salary [partially from STAGMA, the performing rights organisation for Nazi Germany]. The repayments only ended in 1940.

Peter Raabe always tried to have me re-engaged somehow, and called for me to serve on the Olympia Jury in 1936. But it didn't stop further performances of my ADMV [Allgemeiner Deutscher Musikverein] commissioned organ work from being cancelled shortly after the start of the festival.

For once it is possible to believe that Tiessen's own assessment of his situation was accurate. He did not attempt to present himself as totally innocent, and yet he was far less compromised than nearly any of the other composers covered thus far. As with Max Butting, he was a member of the Novembergruppe with strong socialist convictions. He wrote music for performance by working men's choruses. Tiessen was the quintessential German Expressionist, making only marginal, limited and contained excursions into atonality. Expressionists and the Romantics shared many characteristics, chief among them being content determining form, and emotional energy taking priority over structural purity. His earlier works were promoted by Richard Strauss and, indeed, a more modernist Straussian language perhaps best describes Tiessen's first two symphonies.

From the early 1920s, upon joining the Novembergruppe, his language started to become more astringent, though never entirely entering the realms of arid New Objectivity. Tiessen was also a founding member of the IGNM, the German abbreviation for the ISCM, International Society for Contemporary Music. Nevertheless, the first work of his performed by the ISCM was at the 1928 Sienna Festival: his duo sonata for piano and violin, op. 35, composed in 1925. Later, he appeared as a jury member in Geneva in 1929 and in Vienna in 1932. Tiessen's musical voice differed from mainstream New Objectivity while being strong enough to stand as an example of the creative plurality that distinguished the interwar years. Even in works that move towards the dominant language of the time, there remains a feeling of controlled improvisation. Had his politics not been openly antagonistic to the NSDAP, even to the point of refusing to join the party, he might have been fêted by Nazis as just the sort of modernist voice to represent their 'Germany of today'.[20]

Tiessen's works were denounced and therefore were not taken up by Germany's orchestras. Fritz Stege in *Die neue Zeitschrift für Musik* wrote, 'Have we completely forgotten what role in the world of music Heinz Tiessen played during Marxist times?'[21] Yet apparently he was still seen as acceptable enough in 1940 to be commissioned to write battle songs for the Wehrmacht. His *Ernste Hymne* (*Serious Hymn*), op. 50, for wind ensemble was another work commissioned by the Department of War Propaganda. A review of the work stated that it '... remembers the fallen, and all heroes, with song-like invention; it moves from solos to full ensemble while painting triumphant sorrow in luminous colours ...'[22]

Although Tiessen was not seen as compromised after the war, his participation in a jury with Fritz Stein, Paul Graener, Richard Strauss, Georg Schumann and Gian Francesco Malipiero in charge of selecting music to accompany the 1936 Olympic Games in Berlin may have been viewed as ill-judged. Certainly, Fritz Stein and Paul Graener were closely associated with the NSDAP; Richard Strauss had been the head of the Reichsmusikkammer until 1935, when he was succeeded by Peter Raabe. Malipiero was a prominent Italian fascist. The position was offered to Tiessen by Peter Raabe. Tiessen was at the mercy of such gestures as he was virtually destitute. In addition, he was well recognised as a voice of dissent, and his appointment to the jury was meant to show the world that such a committee would not simply be rubber-stamping whatever the Nazi Party demanded. Although Tiessen was appointed as Director of Berlin's Conservatory after the war and later head of the Academy of Arts, his post-war absence from concert programming was due to twelve years of enforced silence. After the war, stylistic dictates found him out of step with new developments. For Tiessen, however, 'inner emigration' was silence. Unlike others, he did not compose for the desk drawer. The Nazi years left Tiessen, by any measure a significant composer, without a voice at all.

Tiessen's legacy may rest in his students, who included Joseph Tal, Sergiu Celibidache and the Latvian composer and pianist Eduard Erdmann (1896–1958). Erdmann, like his teacher, was drawn to the Expressionism of Alban Berg. Indeed, his First Symphony from 1919 was dedicated to Berg. Erdmann was an exceptional pianist whose performances included the entire German repertoire as well as Busoni and the compositions of his friend Artur Schnabel. From 1925 to 1935 he taught piano at Cologne's Music Academy until quitting in protest at the treatment of Jewish colleagues.

Post-war denazification hearings were soon to establish that membership in the NSDAP did not automatically mean complicity, and as a freelance performer and teacher it was a necessary factor in procuring engagements. Erdmann's teacher Heinz Tiessen, though allowed to continue teaching at Berlin's Music Academy, was reduced to penury because of his unwillingness to join the Nazi Party. By the time of Erdmann's departure from Cologne's Music Academy, his own works had been denounced and were tacitly removed from programming. By 1937 his only hope of employment rested on becoming a party member.

In a letter to Erdmann, the composer Hans Pfitzner is particularly harsh, while representing the view of Hitler's establishment:

> [. . .] against which, you performed every piece of atonal rubbish that happened to be in fashion at the time. And now that the German-speaking world has turned sharply right, your heart discovers the delights of my piano concerto. You must not judge me for seeing your sudden interest in my concerto in a sceptical light. Of course you're free to perform this work, which has been publicly available for a very long time, but you mustn't expect me to assume interest in your relationship with my music. I do not hand out artistic acknowledgements that are dependent on 'specific situations'.[23]

What makes Pfitzner's attack even more unpleasant was his admiration for Erdmann's violinist partner, the Australian-born Alma Moodie, who had premiered his Violin Concerto. There is copious correspondence between Moodie and Pfitzner, so he would have been aware of her relationship with Erdmann. Indeed, she too had performed what Pfitzner denounced as 'atonal rubbish' with works by Krenek (with whom she had an affair), Bartók, Egon Wellesz and others. Erdmann dedicated his solo violin sonata to Moodie. Erdmann and Schnabel had both been regular recital partners with Alma Moodie. Erdmann and Moodie had performed together as early as 1921, but with Schnabel's departure from Germany, Erdmann and Moodie became an important duo performing together until Moodie's presumed suicide in 1943.

Erdmann made his pianistic debut as part of Hermann Scherchen's 'Evenings of Contemporary Music', performing his own works as well as Arnold Schoenberg's op. 19 piano pieces and Alban Berg's Sonata. From 1921 to 1923 he was a member of the jury at the contemporary music festival in Donaueschingen. Erdmann played an opening concert for the Bauhaus in Dessau, a school of design and architecture that personified everything the Nazis hated about Weimar Constitution Germany. In 1929 Otto Klemperer conducted his First Piano Concerto.

Erdmann retreated to his home near the Danish border for the duration of the Nazi years. With Hitler's defeat, he performed a recital of works by Krenek, Hindemith, Schoenberg and Alban Berg, composers banned by the Nazis. He agreed to offer master-classes in Hamburg at the behest of his friend, the composer and former Novembergruppe member Philipp Jarnach, but refused other teaching positions offered to him in Berlin and Munich.

As with Tiessen, Erdmann's musical language is highly expressive, but it represents an Expressionism that is rooted in nineteenth-century Romanticism. Despite his admiration of Alban Berg, Erdmann's music is less tonally abstract. Dissonance is a feature that never obscures his clear melodic coherence. There is structure and form, plus a rhythmic urgency not often characteristic of other German composers of his generation. As with Tiessen, 'inner emigration' for Erdmann meant an enforced compositional silence, with his only notable work being a string quartet from 1937 dedicated to the Expressionist painter Emil Nolde. This is in itself a mystery, as Nolde was a passionate supporter of the Nazis and an ardent antisemite. Despite this, he was condemned as 'degenerate' in the 'Entartete Kunst' exhibition in 1937, the year of Erdmann's dedication.

Passive Resistance

The German musicologist and historian Albrecht Dümling mentions a number of additional important composers who found themselves in similar situations to Butting, Tiessen and Erdmann. He cites Philipp Jarnach in this context along with Wolfgang Jacobi, Robert Kahn, Heinrich Kaminski, Karl Klingler, Walter Kollo and Heinz Schubert.[24] Perhaps of greater musical significance and interest are the composers Ernst Pepping and Günter Raphael. Pepping was largely noted as a composer of Protestant church music, while Raphael, like Braunfels, was half-Jewish but remained in Germany in the safety of a so-called 'privileged marriage' with an 'Aryan' spouse.

The safety of these 'privileged marriages' was very much a question of luck. As already mentioned, the Viennese operetta composer Edmund Eysler refused to leave his home for fear of finding himself denounced and falling victim to a spontaneous round-up of Jews. He was well known in Vienna and highly recognisable. The diaries of the philologist Victor Klemperer offer a detailed account of living in a 'mixed-race' marriage. He and his wife were forced from their home into the common quarters of a 'Judenhaus'. Towards the end of the war, non-Jewish spouses were regarded as Jewish and shared the fate of their Jewish husbands and wives. The aforementioned Richard Fuchs's sister Senta and her non-Jewish husband were both murdered in a Nazi extermination camp. And yet, two remarkable composers dared Fate and survived while continuing to compose.

Günter Raphael (1903–60) was the precociously musical child of a scion of composers. His grandfather Georg Raphael married the salonnière and singer Julie Cohn. Their son Georg Raphael converted to Lutheranism and became a prominent church music composer. His maternal grandfather Albert Becker was head of music at Berlin's cathedral, a prominent teacher whose students included Georg Raphael. His daughter, Georg's future wife, Maria née Becker, was a professional violinist.

Günter Raphael's entrance into Berlin's Music Academy was funded by the Robert Schumann Leipzig Foundation scholarship. He studied with Robert Kahn and Max Trapp before coming under the tutelage of Karl Straube, the Thomaskirche Kantor in Leipzig. He continued his studies with Arnold Mendelssohn in Darmstadt. In 1925 his first quartet was performed by the Busch Quartet. Despite early reviews praising Raphael's technical skills, it was not until 1926 that Wilhelm Furtwängler and Leipzig's Gewandhaus Orchestra performed his First Symphony. His Divertimento, op. 33, was also taken up by Furtwängler and the Gewandhaus Orchestra for performance in February 1933.

In March 1931 Johann Weissenborn gave Raphael's *Te Deum* a lavish endorsement and referred to his ability to synthesise both the old and the new with 'daring harmonic changes, short, tangy themes, rhythmic verve and astonishing polyphonic virtuosity'.[25] In fact, *Die neue Zeitschrift für Musik* devotes nearly an entire volume to the promising young composer from Leipzig, with a fulsome biography and a copy of his *Geistliches Lied*. It is clear that although doubts had been expressed regarding Raphael's ability to get beyond his technical excellence, Breitkopf & Härtel had already decided he was a composer of the future.[26]

Despite Raphael's 'racial disadvantages', his works continued to enjoy occasional performances, with his *Smetana Suite for Orchestra* conducted by Eugen Jochum in Hamburg in 1938. Again, reviews admired his workmanship and skill while 'hoping for better things to emerge'.[27] The fact that Raphael was embargoed as a 'half-Jew' was known. In 1934 he lost his position in Leipzig and moved with his wife Pauline Jessen to Meiningen, where she held a teaching position. Despite exclusion, chronic tuberculosis acquired in 1934, and the constant threat of potential denunciation and deportation, Raphael's works were performed from time to time, though his *Smetana Suite for Orchestra* was clearly a work of light entertainment and perhaps permitted for this reason.

Given the exclusion of Boris Blacher who was quarter-Jewish and far more established by 1938, it is surprising that performances of any of Raphael's works took place at all. Yet he managed to compose a *Dance Suite for Small Orchestra* in 1934; an organ concerto in 1936; his *Smetana Suite* and a toccata for two pianos in 1937; two piano sonatas in 1939; his Third Symphony in 1942 and two sonatinas in 1944; a considerable amount of organ music based on various chorales; a number of works for various solo instruments; four trios; and a bewildering assortment of religious music for chorus both accompanied and *a cappella*, some of which was even performed in Dresden in 1937 and 1938.[28] From looking at Raphael's output during the Nazi years, it becomes clear he found security, and probably comfort, in writing liturgical music.

Immediately after the war, Raphael was in a no man's land, having been largely, but not completely, banned by the Nazis. As a result, he was not as compromised as other, more established, musicians, many of whom he positively endorsed during their denazification hearings. Raphael and his wife performed as a piano duo until he was offered a teaching position in Duisburg. He was not entirely forgotten, as attested by a performance on 7 December 1950 of his Fourth Symphony with the Berlin Philharmonic under Sergiu Celibidache.

In 1956 Raphael was offered the position of Kantor at the Thomaskirche in Leipzig, but a long-held rejection of Communism led him to a far less prestigious position at Cologne's University for Music. As he wrote to the composer Hans Gál in 1946:

I haven't dared venture into the Russian Zone yet, though my flat with two grand pianos, an upright and a Baroque organ is in Meiningen in Thüringen and therefore in the Soviet Sector. (The Russians seem keen to have me and have offered professorships in Leipzig, Halle and Weimar, but as long as they maintain their Zone frontiers, I shan't take a single step towards the East. I wish to remain free to go from one place to another.) [...]

[Hermann] Abendroth left Leipzig in a dreadful sulk and has become an alderman for the Weimar 'Thüringer' local council and head of all music provision. His swastika would not have gone down well in the West! But perhaps he carried the red flag long before it had a swastika in the middle! This is also why I don't return to Middle-Germany [the Soviet Sector]: Everywhere you go, you meet the same old 'good' friends (even still in their same old uniforms) who look down on you.[29]

Raphael's greatest tragedy was his early death at the age of only fifty-seven resulting from his long-standing fight with tuberculosis. With most of his important works sidelined during the Nazi years and a new aesthetic projected across Europe, he died before he could obtain the recognition he deserved and would doubtless have achieved. Yet he still leaves a legacy consisting of five symphonies, two remarkable violin concertos, along with a number of concertos for different instruments, and an impressive amount of chamber and liturgical music.

Walter Braunfels (1882–1954) is the most senior of all the composers mentioned thus far. He was also the only composer who made no secret of his aesthetic allegiance to the previous century. He was closely associated with both Hans Pfitzner and Hermann Abendroth who, with Walter Braunfels, was co-founder of Cologne's Music Academy. There were certainly no aesthetic questions surrounding Braunfels's work. His falling out with the Nazi regime had less to do with the degree to which his parents and grandparents were, or were not, practising Jews and more with the fact that he clearly did not like or agree with anyone remotely connected with the NSDAP. In an essay called *Das Judentum im Musikleben Kölns* (*Jews in Cologne's Musical Life*), Braunfels is denounced for 'stuffing the Music Academy with a veritable army of Jewish teachers' and accused of 'supporting a network of inform-ants, in a bitter fight against any- and everyone who supports Adolf

Hitler'.[30] In fact, his name is missing from a list of non-Aryan composers deemed unsuitable for performance that was compiled in 1935.[31] This in itself is surprising as the list names the non-Jewish composers Ernst Krenek and Alban Berg. The listed Jewish composers wrote works that flirted with jazz or were seen as otherwise musically, culturally and politically progressive. None of these characteristics applied to Braunfels. With his Iron Cross won in the First World War, he was convinced that his establishment credentials would ultimately be recognised and restored, a hope that was dashed with confirmation from the Reich's Chamber of Music dated 5 December 1938 stating, according to §10 of the Chamber of the Law Pertaining to Culture, that he was excluded from any further participation in musical life within the German Reich.[32]

Rather than emigrate, Braunfels decided to remain in Germany and after several relocations eventually withdrew to Überlingen on Lake Constance, near the Swiss border. In a post-war article for the *Bodensee-Zeitschrift* (*Lake Constance Magazine*), he wrote:

> My existence would be like that of a stone in a dam set against the flood of evil. But also, I felt that if I were to leave my homeland, I would be ripping out the most important roots feeding my talent. I was richly rewarded for keeping to this position: the years spent in contemplation allowed the source of creativity to well up fresh and clear.[33]

Like Hans Pfitzner, Thomas Mann, Wilhelm Furtwängler and others in Braunfels's immediate circle, the sense of German identity, the humanity of German culture and the fundamental sense of national belonging would have made Braunfels sympathetic to the promises of National Socialism and the idea of restoring Germany's honour. He was unable to comprehend the depth of belief that held any genealogical degree of Jewish parentage incompatible with the Nazi concept of being German.

Braunfels was certainly one of the most established composers of his generation. His operas such as *Die Vögel* (*The Birds*) had been premiered in Munich by Bruno Walter, but his other operas such as *Don Gil von den grünen Hosen* (*Don Gil of the Green Breeches*), or *Prinzessin Brambilla* (*Princess Brambilla*), or *Ulenspiegel* (*[Till] Eulenspiegel*), had also been championed by the likes of Hans Knappertsbusch and Max von Schillings. Braunfels's *Te Deum* enjoyed over 100 performances until 1933. His orchestral works had been conducted by Abendroth, Siegmund von Hausegger and Pfitzner, and his *Phantastische Erscheinungen eines Themas von Berlioz* (*Fantastic Apparitions on a Theme by Berlioz*) was an absolute hit of its day, conducted by the likes of Artur Nikisch, Furtwängler and Bruno Walter.

In 1909 Braunfels married Bertha (Bertele), the daughter of the German sculptor Adolf von Hildebrand, who, until her encounter with Braunfels, had been engaged to Wilhelm Furtwängler. Her brother, Dietrich von Hildebrand, a prominent professor of philosophy at Munich's university, rebelled against his atheistic upbringing and in 1914 converted to Catholicism. Indeed, he became something of a Catholic celebrity, with Pope Pius XII citing him as an important church scholar of the twentieth century. Bertele converted shortly afterwards and according to accounts, was close to being considered a religious fanatic. Braunfels was raised Protestant and his strong Protestant ethos provided the context for some of his earlier works such as his opera *Ulenspiegel*. Initially he was reluctant to join Bertele and Dietrich in their conversion but a combination of his wife's persuasiveness and his own experiences during the First World War moved him to convert in 1918. From this point, Braunfels's Catholic faith would be significant in his life and work. It is what sustained him during his twelve years of isolation following the fall of the Weimar Republic to Hitler's 'Third Reich'. More crucially, it defined nearly all of his subsequent work as a composer, especially those works composed from 1933 onwards.

An interesting connection in the Braunfels story is his relationship with the arts patrons Werner Reinhardt (1884–1951) and his brother Hans (1880–1963), sons of a wealthy Swiss businessman, Theodor Reinhardt. Their financial help, along with that of their younger brother Oskar (1885–1965), threaded through a large number of musicians, composers, painters and writers. Specifically with the brothers Werner and Hans, these included familiar names such as Stravinsky and Hindemith but also the poet Rainer Maria Rilke, and the composers Walter Braunfels, Heinrich Kaminski, Hans Pfitzner and, most especially, the violinist Alma Moodie, whose children Werner Reinhardt brought to his home in Winterthur following her death in 1943.

From 1920 onwards, it was clear that even the most successful musicians and composers in defeated Germany were existentially under threat. It was Reinhardt's help that kept many afloat, while he established a circle of interconnecting composers, musicians and writers.

After 1933, following Braunfels's dismissal as director of the Cologne Music Academy, he and Reinhardt appear to have cobbled together a 'Lake Constance' plan that brought Braunfels and his family as close to Winterthur in Switzerland as borders would allow. In a letter quoted in Ulrike Thiele's dissertation 'Musikleben und Mäzenatentum im 20. Jahrhundert: Werner Reinhardt', Braunfels mentions the distance of only twenty-eight kilometres plus ferry crossing, making them 'virtual neighbours'. In the same letter he wrote in further detail about why he could not emigrate:

> These last weeks were highly eventful and the fate of our Jewish friends causes great concern. Perhaps history will view things differently but for the present things are unspeakably awful. [. . .] The uncreative individual can extract himself, but an artist has his creativity deeply rooted in his people, and is helpless if he's unable to be their voice. This demands a huge amount of strength today!

One is constantly fighting against the currents and occasionally one feels pulled under ...[34]

In the same fortnight as the above letter, Alma Moodie also wrote to Reinhardt about Braunfels:

I get particularly homesick for you when I see people I can talk to about you & W'thur. Last night Braunfels, his wife & Erdmann were here – it was a very nice evening, he has turned so very much nicer. You must have written him a very kind letter recently, he couldn't say enough grateful things about you & it & he told me all about Ermatingen[35] & I had the feeling that it did him good to be in a house in Germany where nur menschlich gewertet wurde [people were judged humanely]. How did you like Erdmann, how did he play? He certainly is the most entertaining friend I have got, & is such a good friend.[36]

In any case Reinhardt was already closely following events concerning Braunfels. Both Alma Moodie and Braunfels were based in Cologne and as early as 2 February 1932, Moodie alerts Reinhardt to Braunfels's problems at the Music Academy:

The other 'news' that interests us is a terrible event that Braunfels experienced. Before Christmas, everybody in Köln, and actually as it turns out also in Kerstenberg [a suburb in Berlin], the various ministers and also Kappelmeisters [sic], received a disgusting anonymous letter, in the most evil tone, attacking Braunfels. Calling him a vain (especially), incapable and almost unfair person and, touching on a weak point, making great accusations that these days he's playing the complete Mozart concertos on the radio instead of letting the young ones have a go. Naturally his Jewishness and suchlike is also mentioned. In January, Braunfels played an evening [concert] in the musical society. A very difficult program, and unfortunately very bad. Because when he's troubled with nerves, he has no routine method by which to save himself, and it can be, and is, painful. After that he received a letter from the same anonymous people, who just wanted to make it impossible for him to perform in public. The whole thing is particularly nasty because it is not entirely unjustified, which apparently he senses himself – he's also strangely tactless and awkward and his unpopularity is enormous, although everyone recognises his good intentions, his passion, and the achievements of his well-run Hochschule. For the moment no one knows who the writer is. One presumes it's one of the lower-ranked teachers – it's done by a specialist – but for the time being we are searching hard without finding anything. Naturally it's the sensation of the day, because quite clearly it's a matter of making it so impossible for Braunfels that he has to leave. His unpopularity is quite remarkable. The students (I notice it with the ones who come to me every week) think he's ghastly, although he looks after them like a father and when they need something, or things are going badly, they immediately turn to him knowing that he will always help. It's very funny! and by the way, typical for Köln am/R! the good city that in our times has so much to think about and to do.[37]

Safely out of Hitler's direct line of fire, and comfortably close to the Swiss border, freed from the administrative duties of running a music college, Braunfels could begin to take control over his creative life and ponder his musical priorities. Put succinctly in a letter after the war to Gilbert Schuchter: 'I see my mission as the consummation of the Christian opera.'[38] Over the next twelve years he composed three large stage works that veered between opera and oratorio. *Der Traum ein Leben* (*A Dream is Life*) is based on the Austrian playwright Grillparzer, who in turn based his play on Calderón. Although the action is based in a fantastical Persia, the theme of the play is that egotistical actions inevitably lead to catastrophe. Neither the play nor the opera is expressly Christian in the sense of the next stage works that Braunfels wrote. *Der Traum ein Leben* was composed during the years 1934 to 1937 and represents a continuity with his previous musical language. As with *Don Gil von den grünen Hosen*, it offers a return to the richness of Spanish literature, which Braunfels would have encountered in his youth. His father, Ludwig Braunfels, was famous as a translator of Cervantes's *Don Quixote* and other works by Spanish playwrights. The morality of the work is arguably Christian, but more arguably humanist.

This is in contrast with the following two stage works: *Szenen aus dem Leben der Heiligen Johanna* (*Scenes from the Life of St Joan*), composed in 1938 and inspired by a performance of Hindemith's *Mathis der Maler*. As with *Der Traum ein Leben*, Braunfels wrote the libretto himself and used the original transcripts of the trial of Joan of Arc as a basis. If there is a notable change in Braunfels's musical language, it is an increasing tendency towards austerity. The work is impressive but less immediately lyrical or harmonically chromatic. The text dominates and the music often illustrates declamation. It is in any case distinct from the Humperdinck/Straussian qualities of his earlier works, *Prinzessin Brambilla*, *Ulenspiegel*, *Die Vögel* and *Don Gil*.

The last work in this triumvirate of operas/oratorios is *Verkündigung* (*The Annunciation*). In his essay on Braunfels and *Verkündigung*, Martin Wettges explains that Paul Claudel's text to *The Annunciation* was introduced to the Braunfels family in 1913 via Reynald de Simony, a friend of Bertele's nephew Harry Brewster who, following the loss of his parents, had effectively become an adopted son of Bertele's sister Elisabeth Brewster. De Simony was a devoted follower of Paul Claudel and even wrote to him how he had brought his *L'Annonce faite à Marie* to Braunfels. As the play was popular among church groups in France, de Simony suggested to Braunfels that a musical setting of the text would enjoy equal popularity, even if only in France. Claudel, like Braunfels, was a convert and the play's theme of innocence made to suffer resonated with Braunfels. He described *Verkündigung* as a musical testament. He considered it his most important work, written at a time when Hitler had tried to silence him and living in a world where 'horrible things were happening and even more horrible things were being imagined'.[39]

The musical language of *Verkündigung* initially comes across as fragmentary, with motifs fractured and gaining coherence through subconscious assimilation. There are moments that remind one of Pfitzner's *Palestrina*, as well as moments of Bruckner. The overall impression, however, is uniquely Braunfelsian. The work is 'through-composed', and is expressive without being maudlin, offering a spiritual austerity that demands 'through-listening'. It is not an opera of highlights; yet its power derives from its narrative flow and the receptiveness of the listener. In a letter to de Simony, Braunfels asked that it be explained to Claudel that the word was dominant and music would be used as reinforcement. The spirit that empowers Claudel's text would equally empower Braunfels' music.[40]

A series of misunderstandings led to Braunfels's assuming Claudel was not prepared to allow a German setting of his play. Claudel, on the other hand, assumed Braunfels was only setting various scenes, and mentioned that his friend Darius Milhaud had already written incidental music for the play. Braunfels's lack of sympathy for Milhaud led him to suspect that Claudel's musical expectations would be incompatible with what he intended to deliver. Notwithstanding the many misunderstandings, an agreement was reached. Claudel requested only that Braunfels, if unable or unprepared to set the original French text (which Braunfels had attempted but then aborted), should set a German text freely translated. Under no circumstances should Braunfels use the published German translation by Jakob Hegner. Ultimately, this was the only text that Braunfels felt able to set, finding the original French an impossible challenge. The opening of the opera is indeed written in both languages until a crucial point when the text continues only in German.

Bruno Walter was shown the score of *Verkündigung*, and given Walter's enthusiasm for *Die Vögel*, Braunfels was unsettled when the conductor found himself unable to understand the composer's musical intentions. Braunfels's musical journey had taken him further away from his beginnings than he had appreciated. The premiere of *Verkündigung* in Cologne in 1948 was met with everything from respect to enthusiasm. It would be forty years after Braunfels's death before it would be staged.

In Braunfels's music of inner exile he retreated deeper into his faith. In addition to the three stage works, he composed a *Passionskantate*, op. 54, and a song cycle called *Die Gott minnende Seele* (*The God-Courting Soul*), op. 53. He also composed two string quartets, op. 60 in A minor and op. 61 in F major, along with a string quintet in F-sharp minor, op. 63.

In truth, composers who were banned and exiled because of their Jewish parentage, regardless of whether they themselves were Jewish, often reflected and even returned to the legacy of their parents and grandparents. As Hitler had removed their national identity, they often arrived on strange shores lacking any identity at all. A return, or at least a revival, of Jewish self-identity was often the best they could achieve. In the cases of Raphael and Braunfels, we encounter two composers who were persecuted for a faith they did not follow, and for a 'race' that for them was meaningless. By remaining in their German homeland, they both drew strength from their profound depth of Christian belief, reflected in the music they produced without any hope of performance. For them, their retreat into an ever deeper Christian faith transcended Nazi dogma and the gross injustice to which they had been subjected.

Karl Amadeus Hartmann: Active Resistance

Karl Amadeus Hartmann (1905–63) has achieved near mythical status as the 'one good German musician' during the Hitler years. He not only refused to emigrate, but rejected performances of his works in Nazi Germany or anywhere in Nazi-occupied Europe. There is a good deal of truth in this myth, but it also leaves unanswered the observation that Hartmann was not well known enough at the time to have had performances to reject. Such myth-making leaves ethical questions begging consideration, even if they cannot be fully addressed. How did Hartmann manage to move about so freely? How could he travel outside of Germany without restrictions? Was he in secret agreement with the Reich's Chamber of Music? They certainly knew of his movements and that works of his were being performed at the International Society for Contemporary Music (ISCM) Festivals in Prague and London. Even Hermann Scherchen, Hartmann's erstwhile promoter and patron, went through a period of not trusting Hartmann, who appeared to be recognised, respected and established in Germany even if his works were unperformed.

It would be foolish to believe that any creative individual surviving in Hitler's Reich would not be forced into a complex moral maze. In the first instance, Hartmann was known and registered with the RMK (Reichsmusikkammer – The Reich's Chamber of Music), and cleared their genealogical barriers without issues. The file they kept on Hartmann is not critical. When he travelled to the ISCM festival in Prague in 1935, it would have been without the support of the RMK, which had started its own organisation as a counterweight to the far too 'Jewish and international' ISCM. His RMK file mentions that he should not have gone to Prague, but 'no further action was taken'. There was a report from his local Munich Chapter called *Siegestor* (Victory Gate) that in 1941 he had expressed interest in becoming a member of the NSDAP. He gave generously to NSDAP-sponsored charities and when attending local meetings, offered the 'Hitler salute'.

It should come as no surprise that Scherchen grew suspicious when Hartmann refused to emigrate. Yet it is in the context of these conflicting actions that one can start to see the ambiguity mere survival required. Not to have given to Nazi charities was already an indication of political dissidence and would have drawn unwelcome attention. The same would apply to withholding the Hitler salute. Hartmann's enquiry about party membership was in all probability meant as camouflage.

Hartmann was young, unpublished and despite being regarded as one of Munich's more promising talents, he was in the shadow of Werner Egk (1901–83) and Carl Orff (1895–1982), both of whom were more established and had already taken opportunistic advantage of Nazi patronage, even if they too never bothered to join the NSDAP. Egk and Orff also made it onto the Führer's *Gottbegnadeten* list of important German composers. Hartmann had to rely on a friendly doctor in his close-knit circle of Munich's dissidents for a military exemption.

Looking at the ages of the individuals discussed in this chapter, there has to be some understanding for young composers without international contacts and not in danger of Nazi persecution. For them there was only one means of survival and that was rapprochement. This would have been the case with composers who were of a similar age to Hartmann such as Boris Blacher, Wagner-Régeny, Wolfgang Fortner, Winfried Zillig, Paul Höffer and Ernst Pepping, all of whom were born within a few years of Hartmann. Older composers could risk more, whether it was Paul von Klenau, born in 1883, who wrote twelve-tone operas and argued the importance of serialism as part of Nazi dogma, or Walter Braunfels, born in 1882, who seemed fearless in his refusal to leave, even if it required relocating to the Swiss border. Composers in Hindemith's generation, in other words, those born during the last decade of the nineteenth century, were usually more established but with the exception of Hindemith no more connected internationally than their younger colleagues, and none was financially in a position to risk emigration with families and dependants to support. Even Hindemith was reluctant to leave Germany until it was made clear that he had fallen into such disfavour that remaining was no longer an option.

The familiar Hartmann story usually goes along the lines of the brave composer who continued to live in Nazi Germany, dependent on his father-in-law's benevolence and who radically distanced himself from Nazi ideology. In truth, he camouflaged himself as a young composer who had yet to make a mark in his native country. His deceit required caution. When his orchestral work *Miserae* was premiered to great success in the 1935 Prague ISCM festival, its controversial dedication was only visible to the conductor Hermann Scherchen. Given Hartmann's participation since 1928 in the Munich exhibition circle called *Juryfreien* (Jury Free), an artistic dissident group for which he provided the musical programming, had the dedication been publicised it could have led to Hartmann's being silenced for the duration: *Meinen Freunden, die hundertfach sterben mußten, die für die Ewigkeit schlafen – wir vergessen euch nicht. (Dachau 1933–1934) – To my friends who died in their hundreds and now sleep eternally, we won't forget you. (Dachau 1933–1934).*

Michael Kater's chapter on Hartmann in his book *Composers of the Nazi Era: Eight Portraits*,[41] offers a more equivocal view of Hartmann, while not underestimating the difficulties he faced. The relationship with Scherchen was dysfunctional, with both men attempting to exploit the advantages offered by the other, until Scherchen's suspicions over Hartmann's refusal to emigrate caused a rupture that was only repaired after the war. By that time, Hartmann was conspicuous as the most uncompromised composer left in the country.

Scherchen was a decade and a half older than Hartmann and already established as one of Germany's leading musicians. He was unsympathetic to Hartmann's personal circumstances.

Initially, the parents of Hartmann's wife Elisabeth Reußmann did not approve of their daughter's marriage, but subsequently they accepted and fully supported the young couple by providing accommodation and modest support. Alfred and Antoinette Reußmann were sympathetic to the political views of their daughter and Hartmann, whom they had met at a *Juryfreien* event in 1929 when Elisabeth was only sixteen. If they had doubts about their teenage daughter's attraction to the older composer, they had come to accept both as a couple by the time they were married in 1934. Reußmann was not wealthy, but as a manager in a local factory his well-paid position meant he could provide an apartment and keep the young couple nearby. By 1942, and in order to escape the bombing of Munich, the Hartmanns moved to the Reußmann summer house on Lake Starhemberg. Such dependency on his wife's family left Hartmann without the agency necessary to emigrate, a situation Scherchen appears to have been unwilling or unable to accept. This blindness to Hartmann's predicament led to Scherchen's eventual suspicion that Hartmann could have been set up to monitor political dissidents abroad.

The Hartmann scholar Hanns-Werner Heister has attempted to identify his subject's methods of musical resistance by noting his incorporation of elements that were conspicuously anathema to the Nazi authorities.[42] The first of these would have been references to Marxism (Hartmann set texts by Karl Marx and Johannes R. Becher, a prominent poet in what would later become the German Democratic Republic). It is this specific point that makes an assessment of Hartmann's music of 'inner emigration' difficult, as it underwent a degree of post-war 'retrofitting' in order to make himself more acceptable to his American employers who had little sympathy for Marxist dalliances – regardless of when or under what circumstances they were written. Works that were outwardly subversive or dedicated to socialist or communist fighters – such as Sergei Tretyakov and the Chinese revolutionary Den Shi-Hua in Hartmann's *Sinfoniae Dramaticae* (subtitled 'China Fights') – from 1941–43 were quietly changed post-war to less controversial individuals. Paradoxically, in neutralising his earlier defiance in order to accommodate his American post-war employers, Hartmann diluted the degree of his resistance to the Hitler regime.

The second element was his references to Jewishness, such as the Jewish melody *Eliyahu ha-navi* incorporated by Hartmann in his First String Quartet and his opera *Simplicius Simplicissimus*. The third element used by Hartmann as an obvious provocation was what had been condemned as 'Cultural Bolshevism', a portmanteau concept that meant anything dissonant, atonal or departing from the aesthetic parameters of conventional tastes.

Heister also refers to a 'reclamation of history', a term that more recently has been adapted into 'cultural appropriation'. In other words, taking musical gestures or traditions such as spoken choruses, or liturgical templates (such as the Baroque Lutheran cantata) and reclaiming these uniquely Germanic musical templates as active resistance. Hanns Eisler had already 'appropriated' the template of the Protestant cantata into which he set anti-Nazi, Marxist and socialist texts. Hartmann's 'appropriation' was his opera *Simplicius Simplicissimus*, based on Hans Jakob von Grimmelshausen's novel published in 1669 on the Thirty Years War, a period of scorched-earth conflict that had been utilised by the Nazis for propaganda purposes. In fact, texts from the Thirty Years War had also been set by prominent anti-Nazis, such as the exiled Austrian composers Ernst Krenek and Hans Gál. In making references to such nation-defining events as the Peasants' Revolt and the Thirty Years War, Hartmann used obvious folk songs and other parodic references to the Nazi appropriation of German cultural identity.

It would be contentious to suggest these 'between the lines' messages were obvious and understood by the initiated as a musical equivalent of the clenched fist against Fascism. The audiences who heard these works during the Nazi years were in any case open to new music and attending events that were taking place outside of Germany where National Socialist Germany was conspicuously absent. Certainly, Hartmann was not, *pace* Scherchen, the envoy to such events sent by German authorities.

Of Hartmann's first six symphonies, only the Second Symphony was a new work, with the others reworked using material composed during his years of inner exile. His First Symphony was based on his cantata from 1936 with words by Walt Whitman. In 1938 he added the title *Unser Leben: Symphonisches Fragment* (*Our Life: Symphonic Fragment*) with the idea of demonstrating life under the Nazi regime. It was ultimately premiered in 1948, conducted by Hans Rosbaud in Frankfurt under the new title of *Versuch eines Requiems* (*Attempt at a Requiem*). Until 1955, Hartmann had designated his *Miserae* as his 'First Symphony'. After extensive reworking, the *Miserae* was withdrawn and the new work was officially designated Symphony no. 1 upon its premiere in 1957 with contralto Hilde Rössel-Majdan and the Vienna Symphony Orchestra under Nino Sanzogno.

Hartmann's Third Symphony from 1948 was based on his *Sinfonia Tragica* from 1940 and his *Klagesang* from 1944, dedicated to Robert Havemann who was imprisoned by the Nazis. The work incorporated quotes from composers deemed 'entartet' by the Hitler regime. His Fourth Symphony is a reworking of his Symphonic Concerto for Strings and Soprano, composed in 1938; his Fifth Symphony used his Concertino for Trumpet from 1932; and his Sixth Symphony was a reworking of his *Symphony 'L'oeuvre'* from 1937 and 1938.

Notwithstanding any post-war retrofitting that may or may not have been intended to suit those in charge of the American Sector in Munich, Hartmann's works during the Nazi years expressed genuine defiance and were far braver than anything attempted by his colleagues. It is also arguable that with greater exposure and prominence, Hartmann felt his earlier works needed adjustment for a non-Hitler, post-war Germany. Nevertheless, there were numerous works by Hartmann that would have resulted in persecution had they been noted by the political toadies of the RKM. Such unequivocal examples would be his two-movement Cantata from 1933 for *a cappella* male-voice choir based on texts by Johannes R. Becher, *Kohlenbrot*

(*Coal Bread*), and by Karl Marx, *Wir haben eine Welt zu gewinnen* (*We Have a World to Win*), composed the same year as his *Miserae* with its provocative dedication to murdered political dissidents. In 1934 he set three scenes from the youth of the eponymous character, *Simplicius Simplicissimus* with a libretto by himself with Hermann Scherchen, Wolfgang Petzet and based on Grimmelshausen. Hartmann's *Cantate* and *Symphonic Fragment* based on the poems of Walt Whitman were from 1935–36 before being reworked as his Symphony no. 1. The following year he composed his cantata for soprano, four-part mixed chorus and piano, *Friede Anno '48*, based on texts by Gryphius and dedicated to the memory of Alban Berg. His *Concerto Funebre* – perhaps the work of Hartmann most frequently performed – was composed in 1939 and originally called *Musik der Trauer* (*Music of Mourning*), and written in response to the fall of Prague to the Nazis. These, along with other works such as his *Klagegesang* from 1944–45, were defiant. Others that were composed during the years of 'inner exile' may have been less provocative with titles and dedications, but remained far from the preferred musical language of the Nazi regime.

With the defeat of Hitler, Hartmann stood alone and personified both a myth and a reality that post-war Germany badly needed. Given the paucity of performances during the Nazi years, it is difficult to state how much of his work was openly defiant and how much was claimed as defiant after the dangers had passed. His widow Elisabeth maintained he was always on the lookout for texts that rejected Nazi ideology. It is clear that Hartmann wanted and needed performances, just not performances in Nazi Germany. As a result, the extent to which he self-embargoed his own works remains unclear. He was, as Fred Prieberg points out, not seen as a major figure by German authorities at the time.[43] Nevertheless, he did enjoy a fair number of moderately high-profile performances abroad, including in Prague, Strasbourg, Liège, London, Brussels and St Gallen. As Kater points out, Hartmann would spend the rest of his life doing an inordinate amount of good for new music, promoting composers as diverse as Hans Werner Henze and Karlheinz Stockhausen. His *Musica Viva* concert cycle was provocative and challenged audiences in the former Nazi bastion of Munich. As he wrote to Egon Wellesz on 2 January 1948:

> Sadly, new music is not much appreciated. The public thinks back with longing to the past twelve years: Art for the people! How nice that was: the tastes of the average Joe were well catered for. It is because of this that someone with absolutely no artistic quali-ties such as Carl Orff was heaped with honours. Believe me, observing such things makes one despair at having to live amongst such people. We can only slowly build up circles and groups. At the moment, I have one that consists of only 250 people, but they're loyal and attend all events. It is for this group that I would ask permission to perform your [latest] quartet.[44]

In the end, when confronted with opportunities to work in the Soviet or the American sector, Hartmann remained in the American sector. His sympathies during the Nazi years leaned towards Marxist ideals, and any number of like-minded colleagues opted for a future in what would become East Germany. Others would point to Hartmann's belief in democracy and the promise of new institutions as his reason for remaining in West Germany. A more realistic assessment comes down to the same reason he chose not to emigrate: he and his wife's family were citizens of Munich and had no desire to leave their home town.

Hartmann need not have fretted about the honours being heaped on fellow Bavarian Carl Orff, as noted in the above letter. From 1948 onwards, hardly a year went by when Hartmann was not presented with one prize or another, or appointed as fellow of one of Germany's Academy of Arts institutions. In retrospect, it would be easy to be cynical and dismiss Hartmann as the 'good German' all Germans needed in 1945, thereby making him into a better German than he actually was. Yet standing in the way of this assessment, and despite whatever myth-making and retrofitting that took place, there can be no denying the substance, power and quality of Hartmann's music. His decisions and dilemmas merely place the decisions and dilemmas of all the other composers in this chapter into perspective.

4

The Music of Resistance

Es ist eine erstaunliche Zeit gewesen, eine widerspruchsvolle Zeit. Und ich kann mir gar nicht vorstellen etwas Schöneres. Mit all den Schrecken und auch der Kümmerlichkeit und den Schwierigkeiten, die wir hatten – es war fabelhaft. Also ich wünsche jedem jungen Künstler so was Produktives. Es wurde produziert! Wir waren nämlich sehr fleißig. [...] Und unser echter Glaube, daß, was wir für den Schreibtisch schreiben, das nie Aufführbare, ganz groß einmal aufgeführt werden wird. [...] Nicht den Glauben in sich, sondern den Glauben an die Nützlichkeit einer Arbeit. Wir schreiben nützliche Dinge, und deswegen machen wir es.

It was an astonishing time of contradictions and I simply cannot imagine anything more agreeable. Despite all the horrors, the worries and the difficulties we suffered, it was fabulous. In fact, I would wish that every young artist has a chance to experience such a productive period. We were productive! We were actually industrious [...] and our deep belief that what we wrote for the desk drawer, having no prospect of performance, would one day experience a truly great performance. [...] It wasn't empty faith, but the belief in the usefulness of our work. We wrote useful things, and that was why we did it.

Hanns Eisler in conversation with Hans Bunge[1]

Resistance has already been addressed if only as acts of defiance: Richard Fuchs and his refusal to abdicate his German identity, or Hartmann and his refusal to compromise on the critical works he had performed outside of his homeland while actively embargoing performances, or at least not pursuing opportunities for performance in Germany. Those who were astute recognised these actions as representing resistance. They were not alone. Their Nazi overlords also recognised resistance.

The German historian Wolfgang Benz defines 'resistance' as an 'umbrella term of different perspectives, actions and types of behaviour aimed against the ideology and tyranny of National Socialism'. He then goes on to state that it 'must be a conscious effort to change immediate circumstances'.[2] If this implies active resistance, it does not discount the camouflaged acts of resistance found in the Terezín Ghetto by musicians and composers who refused to let internment deprive them of their humanity. As such, carrying on as normal was an act of striking back. The same might be said of composers in hiding who carried on writing music despite cramped conditions in attics, basements, large cupboards or as 'submarines' – a term given to people who regularly changed their location from one safe house to the next.

Nevertheless, music as *active* resistance is an oxymoron. Music has no physical power and can only inspire and influence. It is in a different category from partisans hiding in the forest, a sniper in a church tower or a homemade bomb. 'Music as a political weapon' was at one point a common metaphor. However, to have any effect, such 'weapons' needed to be used where the enemy was found. Covert BBC broadcasts of Mahler and Offenbach could, for example, be seen as taking resistance to the enemy. It is questionable what effect agitprop and fight songs might have had in rallies held outside of occupied Europe. They stiffened the spines of those who were already anti-Nazi, and largely out of harm's way.

Yet the music of defiance did not need to be a fight song to be political. It is surprising how many composers reached for templates from the past to remind themselves and others of the grandeur and humanity of German culture, a culture they now viewed as betrayed. Hanns Eisler's *Deutsche Sinfonie* is a work that recalls Bach's Passions, while Paul Dessau's *Deutsches Miserere* takes a liturgical concept to represent Germany's ultimate tragedy. Equally, Hans Gál's *De Profundis* from 1936 based on poems by Gryphius and other poets from the Thirty Years War recalls the devastation of German warfare from past centuries using the template of oratorio. Perhaps the most notable, if at the same time contentious, work in this category would be Paul Hindemith's *Mathis der Maler*, a story set during the Peasants' Revolt (1524–25), and the artist's attempts at securing the right to creativity even under the most difficult of political circumstances. It was seen as both a work of resistance and a work of appeasement. When the Nazis rejected everything Hindemith could offer, his attempt at appealing to the nobility of Germany's past became his gauntlet, thrown down as a challenge to barbarity.

As a result, the wide variety of works that conceivably count as 'resistance' to Hitler's regime start to fall into very general categories. The first of these would be music as 'political weapon': agitprop and fight songs. The second would be works composed in camps as an attempt to create normality in the environment of chaos. The third group would be works by those composers who in hiding continued to write music. The final and fourth category of compositions evoke a better, nobler Germany than the one promised by Hitler.

Resistance to What?

It is very difficult from today's perspective to understand the European biotope in the first half of the twentieth century. A World War blew apart a continent of empires and monarchies where the aristocracy continued to have a say in the lives of ordinary men and women. Even France had gone from republic to monarchy to republic, suggesting that a republic was not the 'default' setting of governance. Only the United States of America had successfully retained its balance between federated states and a central, democratically elected government. It had in-built checks and balances in its judiciary and its Constitution and Bill of Rights. It was the obvious model for the new republics emerging out of the network of empires and monarchies post-1918.

Europe, however, was not the United States. It was not a 'new' country populated by people fleeing monarchies and despotism, but of people who had managed to find some degree of accommodation with such regimes. The concept of elected heads of state and fully enfranchised voting was bewildering to many, perhaps even to most of the common people who had never been able to imagine any other way of organising their societies. When empires and monarchies were swept away, they were not automatically replaced by fully functioning, democratically mandated republics.

Even the relatively progressive Weimar Constitution would subtly morph into an older, more familiar system. The president was granted enormous power, almost as a replacement for the Kaiser. By the time Paul von Hindenburg was elected President of Germany in 1925, a post he held until his death in 1934, he had become something akin to a regent, holding onto power until a king or emperor could return. The Republic was further hampered by its 'Article 48' that allowed the Constitution to be suspended on little more than a whim of the president. During the fifteen years of the Weimar Republic, Article 48 was implemented on countless occasions that, viewed from today, appear to have been hysterical over-reaction.

Over the following two decades, the newly created democracies evolved into various totalitarian systems, some of which were seen as progressive, while others were reactionary. A line was drawn between systems that believed the people needed what a strong central state unhampered by parliaments could provide, and systems that saw themselves as the first steps towards restoring previous hereditary models. By 1938, only Czechoslovakia, out of all the newly formed nation states following the dissolution of Europe's empires, remained a democracy. It too fell, following the Munich accord in 1938 leading to Hitler's proclamation of Bohemia and Moravia as a German 'protectorate' in March 1939.

Communism, National Socialism and Fascism were three systems that saw themselves as progressive, offering a strong collectivist state working on behalf of the common citizen: building roads, schools and hospitals; making trains run on time; nationalising large industries and carrying out the collectivisation of agriculture. These three systems headed the states in the Soviet Union, Nazi Germany and Fascist Italy. To outsiders, there appeared to be little difference between them. Such obvious similarities allowed them to form pacts and alliances at various points during the 1930s and 1940s. At other times, their differences made them the deadliest of enemies. In other European states such as Poland, Austria, Spain, Portugal, Hungary, the Baltic Republics and Romania, regents, military and/or clerical dictatorships took over. These declared an intention to restore formerly deposed monarchies when the time was ripe. Such dictators saw themselves as temporary, only remaining until kings, emperors or other absolute rulers could return. All of the states, whether reactive or collectivist, were authoritarian, employing disentitlement and confiscation; operating with informers, spies and secret police forces; maintaining large prison populations and suppressing individual rights.

The ever-changing nature of Communism, Fascism and National Socialism can be seen through the lens of shifting alliances. In 1933 Communism was National Socialism's biggest enemy, yet Hitler signed a pact with Stalin in 1939 and started the Second World War. Italian Fascism had begun as a socialist movement before becoming militantly nationalist. In 1934 it forced Hitler to withdraw from his attempted coup in Austria. By 1938 Italian Fascism and German

Nazism had become an alliance and the annexation of Austria that year took place without Italian interference. General Franco's efforts to topple the democratically elected government of Spain's Republic were fundamentally reactionary with a view of restoring the authority of the monarch and the Catholic Church. Yet both Fascist Italy and Nazi Germany came to Franco's aid while the communists caused divisions and intra-civil wars within the anti-Franco forces.

Authoritarian nationalism was common to all of these systems of totalitarianism, and there was considerable cross-fertilisation. Nazism and Italian Fascism soon threw in their lot with private industrialists and big money, a characteristic of reactionary systems intent on restoring the privileges of the aristocracy. For this reason, in retrospect, there seems to be little difference between these authoritarian regimes, yet at the time, great and even deadly differences were perceived. Thus, a fight song in the Spanish Civil War was usable as a song of the resistance in Nazi Germany or occupied France.

The United States Holocaust Museum in Washington, DC, lists different types of songs of resistance. These include, among others, songs from concentration camps; songs from the ghetto; the music of Terezín; the music of protest; and partisan songs. They also include songs written in hiding. The remit is broad, but it is worth isolating several of these specifics, starting with concentration-camp anthems, dialectically transformed into songs of resistance.

The Camps

There is already an enormous amount of literature on music in concentration camps and ghettos in Nazi-occupied Poland, where there was a wealth of Yiddish and Polish fight and resistance songs. This section focuses more specifically on the *idea* of resistance. This idea of resistance is taken out of the broader environment of musical life in the camps, which indeed included orchestras, choruses and ensembles, varying considerably from camp to camp. Ghettos and concentration camps were not the same thing, and no two camps were alike; nor were any two ghettos alike. Most of the fight and resistance music from ghettos and camps was spontaneous, based on well-known folk tunes, movie chansons or local hit songs. They were usually conceived and sung by amateurs. All were valid expressions of resistance. Limitations of scope and length restrict this section to the music produced by professional musicians and composers writing in the language of the oppressor, in other words, German.

The first National Socialist mention of a 'concentration camp' can be found as early as 1921, taken from the Nazi propaganda publication *Völkischer Beobachter*: 'One can prevent the Jewish hollowing-out of our people by, if necessary, isolating those responsible in concentration camps.'[3] At this point, a concentration camp was seen as a means of isolating undesirable elements from general society. The idea that these might become death camps did not develop until later, and then officially, following the Wannsee Conference in January 1942. Ultimately, there would be fifteen different types of camp, extending from re-education camps to labour camps to death camps to ghettos. This resulted in camps holding different people, often with different languages, held for different reasons. Singing became both a means of defiance as carried out by inmates as well as a means of persecution as carried out by camp management and personnel during roll call or forced marches. Most music was utilitarian, often popular songs with changed lyrics, but perhaps the most utilitarian of all was the camp anthem.

The earliest of these, serving as a model for later songs, was the *Moorsoldatenlied* (*Song of the Peat Bog Soldiers*). It referred to prisoners consigned to digging peat, who marched holding shovels like rifles giving them the appearance of soldiers. Two of the most famous subsequent songs were the *Dachaulied* and the *Buchenwaldlied*. The *Moorsoldatenlied* was written in the Borgermoor concentration camp on the Dutch border to a text by the poet Johann Esser and the actor Wolfgang Langhoff, with a melody composed by Rudi (Rudolf)

Goguel. The *Moorsoldatenlied* pre-dates the other songs by some five years and its rapid spread beyond Borgermoor to other camps, including concentration, penal and detention camps, offered a template that can be heard in the *Dachau* and *Buchenwald* songs. Goguel, who composed the melody, was a political activist and not a musician. Unlike the composers and lyricists of the *Dachau* and *Buchenwald* songs, none of the authors of the *Moorsoldatenlied* was Jewish. Indeed, Esser, following his release, went on to write verses in praise of Hitler and the 'Third Reich', though this was arguably out of fear of being rearrested as a dissident. The earlier composition date and the fact that the writers of the *Moorsoldatenlied* were political rather than 'racial' prisoners, catapulted the song firmly into the realms of agitprop, eventually becoming paradigmatic of all the anthems commissioned by Nazi camp administrators that were seditiously turned into fight songs by the prisoners forced to sing them. It was later adapted by Hanns Eisler and recorded by Ernst Busch, a singer of political chansons known as 'The Tauber of the Barricades', a name that played on the fame of the opera star Richard Tauber. Despite the text reference to the specific work and location carried out by inmates, the message was deemed broad enough for Busch to perform it in an anti-fascist event during the Spanish Civil War:

Wohin auch das Auge blicket,	Wherever the eye may wander,
Moor und Heide nur ringsum.	All around only moor and heath.
Vogelsang uns nicht erquicket,	No singing of the birds to raise our spirits,
Eichen stehen kahl und krumm.	Oak trees stand bleak and crooked.
Refrain:	Refrain:
Wir sind die Moorsoldaten	*We are the peat bog soldiers*
und ziehen mit dem Spaten	*And travel spade in hand*
ins Moor!	*Into the moor!*

Hier in dieser öden Heide	Here in this bleak heath
ist das Lager aufgebaut,	The camp was built,
wo wir fern von jeder Freude	Far from any joy
hinter Stacheldraht	We lie hidden away behind
verstaut.	barbed wire.

Refrain: *Wir sind die*   Refrain: *We are the peat bog*
    Moorsoldaten ...   *soldiers ...*

Morgens ziehen die   Work columns leave in the
    Kolonnen   morning

in das Moor zur Arbeit hin. To go into the moor.
Graben bei dem Brand der We dig while the sun burns
    Sonne,   down on us,
doch zur Heimat steht But our thoughts remain with
    der Sinn.   home.

Refrain: *Wir sind die*   Refrain: *We are the peat bog*
    Moorsoldaten ...   *soldiers ...*

Heimwärts, heimwärts jeder Homewards, homewards, each
    sehnet,   of us longs
zu den Eltern, Weib und For our parents, wives and
    Kind.   children.
Manche Brust ein Seufzer A sigh stretches many of our
    dehnet,   chests,
weil wir hier gefangen sind. Because we are caught here.

Refrain: *Wir sind die*   Refrain: *We are the peat bog*
    Moorsoldaten ...   *soldiers ...*

Auf und nieder gehn die Posten,	The guards walk back and forth,
keiner, keiner kann hindurch.	No one, no one can get through.
Flucht wird nur das Leben kosten,	Escape will only cost you your life,
vierfach ist umzäunt die Burg.	The fort is fenced four times around.
Refrain: *Wir sind die Moorsoldaten ...*	Refrain: *We are the peat bog soldiers ...*
Doch für uns gibt es kein Klagen,	But for us there are no complaints,
ewig kann's nicht Winter sein.	Because it cannot be winter forever.
Einmal werden froh wir sagen:	Someday we will happily say:
Heimat, du bist wieder mein.	Home, you are mine again.
Dann zieh'n die Moorsoldaten	Then the peat bog soldiers
nicht mehr mit dem Spaten	Will no longer travel spade in hand
ins Moor!	Into the moor![4]

The song's ultimate popularity and seminal status as anthem of the fighting proletariat was due, according to its lyricist Wolfgang Langhoff, to copies being smuggled out in huge numbers prior to its first performance in August 1933. Its wider dissemination even resulted in a mini-genre of Peat Bog Soldier songs, some of which kept close to the original while others deviated.

One of those to deviate from the original was Hanns Eisler's subsequent adaptation. Busch related the account of first hearing the work while recording in London in January 1935. It was sung by someone they assumed to have been a prisoner. In fact, the singer was an undercover German informant who could not recall the melody and altered it with every repetition. Eisler adapted the work along the lines he presumed it had been composed, later re-composing the song in its entirety while only keeping a few elements of the presumed original.

The *Dachaulied* was composed by the Austrian Herbert Zipper (1904–97) with a text by Jura Soyfer (1912–39), a Russian refugee who arrived in Vienna as a young child in 1921. Both Zipper and Soyfer were Jewish, though Soyfer had been a Marxist activist since his schooldays and was already well known as a provocative writer of political cabaret. He was arrested by the Austro-Fascist Schuschnigg government in 1937 but released following a general amnesty only a month before Hitler's annexation of Austria, which in turn led to the arrest of both Soyfer and Zipper as Jews. They were both deported to Dachau where they composed a song along the lines of the *Moorsoldaten* song: a song to be sung by inmates while on work duty. The text is more clearly defiant than the subtly implied text of the *Moorsoldaten*. Despite its obviously sarcastic reference to the slogan at the entry of the concentration camp, *Arbeit macht frei* (Work sets you free) in its often-repeated refrain, it was sung not only by the work crews but also by guards who joined in the catchy refrain. In Dachau, prisoners were made to pull waggonloads of heavy stones:

Stacheldraht, mit Tod geladen,	Barbed wire heavy with death
ist um uns're Welt gespannt.	Is what surrounds our world.
D'rauf ein Himmel ohne Gnaden	Above, a pitiless heaven
sendet Frost und Sonnenbrand.	Sends frost and sunburn.
Fern von uns sind alle Freuden,	Far from us are all delights,
fern die Heimat, fern die Frau'n,	Far from home and wives,
wenn wir stumm zur Arbeit schreiten,	As we silent in our thousands
Tausende im Morgengrau'n.	March to work.

Refrain:

Doch wir haben die Losung von Dachau gelernt	*Yet we learned Dachau's slogan*
und wurden stahlhart dabei.	*Which made us hard as steel.*
Sei ein Mann, Kamerad.	*Be a man, comrade.*
Bleib ein Mensch, Kamerad.	*Stay a human, comrade.*
Mach ganze Arbeit, pack an Kamerad.	*Finish work, pitch in comrade.*
Denn Arbeit, Arbeit macht frei.	*Because work,* Work sets you Free.

Both Zipper and Soyfer would gain release and emigration papers from Buchenwald, where they had been transferred in the autumn of 1938. Tragically, in February 1939, Soyfer died of typhus at the age of twenty-six while still in Buchenwald. Zipper immigrated first to Guatemala then to the Philippines. The remaining three verses demonstrate Soyfer's brilliance as a political cabarettist and are more confrontational while holding to the general model of the *Moorsoldatenlied*, with its depiction of work and life. With the exception of Zipper's catchy refrain, the subsequent verses were deliberately tricky to learn. Zipper and Soyfer believed it was a means of keeping prison labourers mentally engaged. Such pedagogical concepts were typical of Zipper, who devoted most of his post-war life to the musical education of young people.

The *Buchenwaldlied* was by Austria's most famous composer of cabaret songs, Hermann Leopoldi (1888–1959). It was set to a text by Fritz Löhner-Beda (1883–1942), who was one of Franz Lehár's librettists (*Das Land des Lächelns* – [*The Land of Smiles*] and *Giuditta*) as well as the author of Paul Abraham's popular operetta hits *Viktoria und ihr Husar, Ball im Savoy, Die Blume von Hawaii* and Joseph Beer's *Polnische Hochzeit*. With the exception of Beer's operetta, which was only gaining popularity at the time of Hitler's arrival, Löhner-Beda's operetta collaborations were the successes of the day. He was a household name and arguably the most popular lyricist of his generation. Following his arrest after the annexation of Austria, he was deported to Dachau on 1 April 1938 before being moved to Buchenwald in September. In 1942 he was sent to Auschwitz as a slave labourer at the IG Farben factory where he was murdered by the henchmen of the factory directors:

Wenn der Tag erwacht, eh' die Sonne lacht,	When the day awakes, before the sun laughs,
die Kolonnen ziehn zu des Tages Mühn hinein in den grauenden Morgen.	the crews embark for the toils of the day, into the dawn.
Und der Wald ist schwarz und der Himmel rot, und wir tragen im Brotsack ein Stückchen Brot und im Herzen, im Herzen die Sorgen.	And the forest is black and the sky red, we carry a small piece of bread in our bags and in our hearts, in our hearts our sorrows.

Refrain:

O Buchenwald, ich kann dich nicht vergessen, weil du mein Schicksal bist.
Wer dich verließ, der kann es erst ermessen, wie wundervoll die Freiheit ist!
O Buchenwald, wir jammern nicht und klagen, und was auch unsre Zukunft sei –
wir wollen trotzdem "ja" zum Leben sagen,
denn einmal kommt der Tag dann sind wir frei!

Refrain:

Oh Buchenwald, I cannot forget you, because you are my fate.
Only one who has left you, can measure, how wonderful freedom is!
Oh Buchenwald, we neither lament, nor complain, and whatever our future may hold –
we still want to say 'yes' to life,
because one day the time will come – then we will be free!

Und das Blut ist heiß und das Mädel fern,
und der Wind singt leis, und ich hab' sie so gern,
wenn treu sie, ja, treu sie nur bliebe!
Und die Steine sind hart, aber fest unser Tritt, und wir tragen die Picken und Spaten mit
und im Herzen, im Herzen die Liebe.

O Buchenwald, ich kann dich nicht vergessen . . .

Und die Nacht ist kurz, und der Tag ist so lang, doch ein Lied erklingt, das die Heimat sang:
wir lassen den Mut uns nicht rauben.
Halte Schritt, Kamerad, und verlier nicht den Mut, denn wir tragen den Willen zum Leben im Blut und im Herzen, im Herzen den Glauben.

O Buchenwald, ich kann dich nicht vergessen . . .

Our blood runs hot and our girls are far,
And the wind sings softly, I love her so much,
if only she stays true – only stays true!
And the stones are hard, but sure our steps, and we carry our picks and spades with
love in our hearts, in our hearts.

Oh Buchenwald, I cannot forgot you . . .

And the night is short and the day so long, though a song sounds that the homeland sang:
We won't have our courage stolen.
Keep in step, comrade, and don't lose courage, since we keep the will to live in our blood, and faith in our hearts, in our hearts.

Oh Buchenwald, I cannot forget you . . .

Leopoldi was a composer of popular songs, cabaret and chansons that were so well known and loved it would be almost impossible to overstate his prominence within the German-speaking world. The *Buchenwaldlied* is more modest in its defiance, expressing instead a longing for home and family, typical of operetta and popular songs of the day and keeping to the idea of an 'anthem' for the camp. The reframing is an obvious exhortation to stay strong and survive. Nevertheless, in common with the *Moorsoldatenlied*, both the *Buchenwaldlied* and the *Dachaulied* are marching songs and offer the strong suggestion of compliance through clenched teeth.

All the songs were sung openly, with even the guards chiming in, either unable or unwilling to recognise coded references. Indeed, these were often so oblique as to be obvious only after the war. Nevertheless, the last verse of the *Moorsoldatenlied*, with its 'winter not lasting forever', remained just ambiguous enough to thwart potential suspicion of active resistance.

In fact, many other camps had 'anthems', some of which were clandestine while others were official. Many of the earliest, such as those for the camps at Lichtenburg and Esterwegen, were mere adaptations of existing well-known soldier songs – in this case, *Ich bin ein Bub vom Elstertal* (*I'm a Boy from Elstertal*). Others were adapted from agitprop or folk songs. More compelling were the 'official' anthems as commissioned by camp commands. Such was the above-mentioned *Buchenwaldlied*, commissioned by the detention camp leader Arthur Rödl and composed by Hermann Leopoldi. Its provenance as officially commissioned explains its intrinsic qualities as a popular song or operetta melody. Contrafacts of the *Buchenwaldlied* were sung in both Wewelsburg and Treblinka. These 'anthems' were sung at roll call and on marching duty, and even if commissioned by camp command, the prisoners would soon take ownership of the songs, altering melodies or words as they were moved from one camp to another.[5]

The *Dachaulied*, on the other hand, was obviously subversive with its play on *Arbeit macht frei*. Another obvious song of resistance was the *Auschwitzlied*, based on a popular song by Friedrich Fischer-Friesenhausen in 1922 called *Wo die Nordseewellen* (*Where the Waves of the North Sea*), but set to a text by Camille Spielbichler, Camilla Mohaupt and Margot Bachner:

Zwischen Weichsel und der Sola schön verstaut	Wedged between the marshes of the Weichsel and
Zwischen Sümpfen Postenketten, Drahtverhau	Sola [rivers] are watchtowers and wire,
Liegt das KL-Auschwitz, das verfluchte Nest,	It's the concentration camp of Auschwitz,
das der Häftling hasset, wie die böse Pest.	The cursed nest that inmates hate like the plague.
Wo Malaria, Typhus und auch andres ist,	It's where you find things like typhoid and malaria,
wo dir große Seelennot am Herzen frisst,	And one's heart eaten by spiritual deprivation,
wo so viele Tausend hier gefangen sind	Where so many thousands are locked away
fern von ihrer Heimat, fern von Weib und Kind.	far from their homeland, far from wife and child.
Häuserreihen steh'n gebaut von Häftlingshand,	Rows of domiciles built by work detachments,
bei Sturm und Regen musst du tragen Ziegeln, Sand,	Carrying bricks and sand in wind and rain,
Block um Block entstehen für viele tausend Mann,	As block after block is built for thousands of men,
Alles ist für diese, die noch kommen dran.	All for those who have yet to arrive.

There was also a *Ravensbrücklied* based on a Russian folk song with lyrics by Soviet prisoners. What becomes apparent in looking at these songs is their light music, or indeed, amateur provenance. Like much cabaret that was current at the time, political texts were set to well-known melodies from a film or operetta, thus saving the effort of learning or writing a new tune. As Zipper and Soyfer demonstrated, however, the creation of a new melody regularly punctuated by a memorable refrain could also offer an opportunity of engaging prisoners and taking them out of the drudgery of their workday.

Terezín

Art was a part of the structure of daily life in the sense that it contributed substantially to form human personality into the spirit of humanitarian ideals – it was an element of the daily life's structure, the challenges of life, the confirmation of life in the service of humanity . . . Art was Resistance in the deepest sense of the word; it was Resistance to defeat by barbarity.[6]

These are the words of Wilhelm Girnus at the start of a conference in 1979 exploring the role of art in concentration-camp life. Music also had the purpose of taking prisoners out of their daily existence. This was consistently seen as being the case, whether reading accounts of individual members of camp orchestras or reading the memoirs of the Austrian composer Hans Gál and his experiences in a British internment camp as an 'enemy alien' in 1940. His *Huyton Suite* for flute and two violins was utilitarian in as much as these were the instruments he had with competent players, and the work stands in some contrast to his darker output during the war years. It is light and fanciful, even thumbing its nose at the misery of morning roll call. To read Gál's memoirs is to be reminded that internment was dehumanising regardless of who was carrying it out.[7]

The musical life of Theresienstadt, or Terezín, has been well documented, though new material is always coming to light.[8] We shall return to the concept of 'Jewish identity' by inmates who were condemned as 'non-Aryan' despite being practising Christians. Of interest were concerts in Terezín where works that were generally banned were performed, and of course the propaganda value of music as exploited by the Nazis as part of the 'Potemkin village' charade for the Red Cross and an accompanying propaganda film, *Der Führer schenkt den Juden eine Stadt* (*The Führer Bestows a Town on the Jews*).

Terezín was the penultimate station for a generation of Czech composers, whose roots lay more with Janáček and arguably Bartók than Hindemith or Schoenberg. They made up a generation that broke with the Austro-German traditions of Czech composers such as Smetana, Dvořák and Josef Suk, and struck out confidently synthesising Janáčekian polyrhythms and fractured lyricism with French neo-classicism and Bartókian dissonance. Arguably the only survivors of this generation were Bohuslav Martinů and Hans Winterberg.

Yet there was more to Czech identity than the jagged lyricism of Janáček. In common with the literature of the time, there was a tilt towards surrealism and the phantasmagorical. The 'magic realism' of the artistic association of Devětsil, founded in 1920, set a uniquely Czech tone that stood in opposition to the contemporaneous 'New Objectivity' of Weimar Germany, where music, art and architecture were reduced to utilitarian fundamentals. The opera output of a Devětsil-influenced generation of Czech composers tells its own story: Erwin Schulhoff's Dadaistic take on *Don Juan* with *Flammen* (*Flames*); Pavel Haas's opera *The Charlatan*; Hans Krása's *Betrothal in a Dream*; Martinů's *Julietta*; and Viktor Ullmann's *The Fall of the Anti-Christ*. If anything, Czech aesthetics were producing a movement of 'New Subjectivity'.

Hans Krása's opera *Brundibár* is a children's opera. Musically, it is hardly representative of Krása's importance as a composer, and the work's popularity has overshadowed his more significant output.

Brundibár's message of friendship and solidarity defeating cruel avarice, however, continues to resonate. It was originally written in 1938 by Krása and his librettist Adolf Hoffmeister as part of a government competition. With the Nazi proclamation of Bohemia and Moravia as a 'protectorate' in March 1939, the opera's performance took place in 1941 at Prague's Jewish orphanage. When the children and faculty were transferred to Terezín, Krása managed to cobble together a new version, re-orchestrating on the basis of his piano score and using the instruments available. The plot of the opera is simple: Brundibár is an evil organ grinder who chases away children trying to earn money by singing on his patch. The children need to purchase milk for their sick mother and ultimately turn to the animal world and a sense of fairness to defeat the evil organ grinder. Whether the intention was to use Brundibár as a symbol for Hitler cannot be known, but circumstances at the time made the comparison obvious to those living in the ghetto. The children outsmarting Brundibár in the name of natural justice carried a defiant symbolism unrecognised by the ghetto's Nazi command. According to Joža Karas's *Music in Terezín 1941–1945*, one line of the opera was changed by the poet Emil Saudek as an open act of resistance, altering the anodyne line of 'he who loves his mother and father and homeland is our friend' to 'he who loves justice and will abide by it'.[9]

To the children performing the work, it was a means of retrieving a childhood that had been taken away. Anna Flachová, a survivor who sang in the production, described it as follows:

We loved that opera ... our childhood had been stolen from us ... we were forced to mature more quickly and we missed our lost childhood. In this opera, we could play and pretend to be children. At that point, we felt liberated. In reality, we couldn't fight against injustice, but in the opera we could fight and punish the unjust Brundibár who had stolen our money. That gave us hope.[10]

The significance of *Brundibár* also lies in the fact that it was actually performed in Terezín, which was not the case with Viktor Ullmann's far more profound cabaret operetta, *Der Kaiser von Atlantis* (*The Emperor of Atlantis*). Ullmann felt that life was a mission and every element was to be seen as part of an individual path. His manifesto *Goethe and Ghetto* was a cry of passive resistance and defiance by acceptance:

> The role models, whom we take as examples, influence our 'habitus' by reaching into the very way-of-life of subsequent generations. And it seems to me that cultivated Europeans have over the previous 150 years had their behaviour and thoughts, world view, language, relationship to life and art, determined by Goethe. A symptom of this is the way people refer to Goethe, regardless of how different the dialectical ideologies may fundamentally be. (The second great influence being the 'antithesis', the 'counter-stream', which came from Darwin and Nietzsche.)
>
> For that reason, Goethe's maxim 'Live in the moment, live in Eternity' always seemed to me to reveal the puzzling nature of art. Painting captures the ephemeral, making it permanent, such as the still life with its flowers that then go on to wilt, or its landscapes that change, the faces and statues of people who later grow old, or capturing the fleeting historical event. Music does the same for the spiritual, for the emotions and passions of people, for the 'libido' in its broadest sense including Eros and Thanatos. It is from this point that 'form', as understood by Goethe and Schiller, must be conquered by 'substance'.
>
> Theresienstadt was and remains for me a school that teaches form. Previously, it was easy to create the beautifully structured work of art when one was no longer compelled to experience the force and cruelty of material survival. These had been subdued, thanks to the magic of civilisation and the comforts it provided. Here, where the substance of existence is subdued to daily

structure, where artistic inspiration stands as a total contrast to our surroundings, is where one finds the masterclass in what Schiller called the 'secret' of art: 'substance must be overwhelmed by form'. This indeed is presumably the mission of mankind, and not just aesthetic mankind, but ethical mankind as well.

I have composed quite a lot of new music here in Theresienstadt, mostly at the request of conductors, stage directors, pianists, singers and according to the various requirements of the ghetto's periods of free time. It would be as irksome to count them as it would be to remark on the fact that in Theresienstadt it would be impossible to play a piano if there was none available. In addition, future generations may be interested in the sheer lack of manuscript paper that we presently experience. I emphasise only the fact that in my musical work at Theresienstadt, I have bloomed in musical growth and not felt myself at all inhibited: we simply did not sit and lament on the shores of the rivers of Babylon that our will for culture was not sufficient to our will to exist. And I am convinced that all who have worked in life and art to extract form from unyielding substance will say that I was right.[11]

Der Kaiser von Atlantis oder die Tod-Verweigerung (*The Emperor of Atlantis or The Refusal of Death*) was the final title, though the original subtitle was *Der Tod dankt ab* (*The Abdication of Death*). It's not clear when Viktor Ullmann and Peter Kien[12] began writing *Der Kaiser von Atlantis*, or even how its concept emerged. It would have been clear to even the most boneheaded that the Emperor of Atlantis, called Emperor Overall, was primarily a representation of Hitler. Nevertheless, both Ullmann and Kien, despite the difference in their ages, would have been cognisant of the fact that Hitler was only the latest in a line of deadly supreme leaders, lording it over vast stretches of Europe. Emperor Overall is arguably an amalgam of Hitler and a touch of Prussia's Kaiser Wilhelm. At a certain point in the work, Overall's full list of titles is announced with many referring to conquests by Hitler with additional added historic titles consistent with those held by the House of Habsburg. The concept of 'Atlantis', however, places the opera's narrative more firmly within Nazi party ideology and its view of a supreme Aryan race derived from mythological associations with the lost city of Atlantis.

Der Kaiser von Atlantis is difficult to classify as cabaret, revue or operetta, while at the same time synthesising all of these elements. Perhaps 'cabaret operetta' comes as close as possible, and places it with other difficult-to-define genres such as Kurt Weill's *Mahagonny Songspiel* (*Mahagonny: A Song-Play*) or Stefan Wolpe's *Zeus und Elida*. With its phantasmagorical, allegorical treatment of material, its Dadaistic amalgamation of styles, it remains closer to the dominant Devětsil aesthetic of Prague and neo-classical Paris than to Berlin New Objectivity, or Schoenbergian Vienna. At the same time, it makes use of the Brechtian concept of alienation – detaching actors from their characters and thereby allowing a parallel commentary to emerge in the minds of the audience. The very figure of the Loudspeaker is itself a stand-in for the idea of alienation.

The work can be performed with a minimum of five characters doubling roles, and in Terezín, Ullmann used six. Why he chose to use the English 'Overall' for the name of the Emperor is unclear. Probably in the same fashion as used by Brecht, with only a crude command of English meant to add a sense of exoticism for local audiences. He most certainly would not have been aware of 'Overall' as an article of clothing.

Loudspeaker announces the work and the protagonists: 'Emperor Overall hasn't been seen for years, hunkered down in his enormous palace living completely by himself, as this condition abets his despotism.' The Drummer is 'not quite a true apparition – more like a radio', but is understood to represent war or the voice of Emperor Overall. The Loudspeaker is 'heard but not seen'. A young soldier and a young girl who is also a soldier represent love; Death is shown as 'a decommissioned soldier in the tattered uniform of a Habsburg

The characters of *Der Kaiser von Atlantis* and their scene entrances, voice type and original Theresienstadt casting[13]

Character	Scene entrance	Voice type	Theresienstadt cast
Kaiser Overall (Emperor Overall)	Scenes 2 and 4	Baritone	Walter Windholz
Der Tod (Death)	Scenes 1 and 4	Bass	Karel Berman
Harlekin (Harlequin)	Scenes 1 and 4	Tenor	David Grünfeld
Der Lautsprecher (The Loudspeaker)	Prologue, Scenes 2 and 4	Bass	Bedřich Borges
Ein Soldat (A Soldier)	Scene 3	Tenor	David Grünfeld
Bubikopf – ein Soldat (Bobbed-haired girl – a Soldier)	Scene 3	Soprano	Marion Podolier
Der Trommler (The Drummer)	Scenes 1, 3 and 4	Alto/ Mezzo-soprano	Hilde Lindt-Aronson

regiment' and the Harlequin is understood to represent his counterpart: Life. In earlier versions of the opera, Harlequin is called 'Pierrot', a character who was already familiar from Schoenberg's *Pierrot Lunaire*, Korngold's *Die tote Stadt* (*The Dead City*) and Karol Rathaus's ballet *Der letzte Pierrot* (*The Last Pierrot*). In *Kaiser von Atlantis*, Pierrot, once young, innocent and naïve, has now aged into a cynical Harlequin who starts off by singing a vaguely ridiculous song about the moon, perhaps as a tip of the hat to Schoenberg's *Pierrot Lunaire* and a distant memory of youth:

Death and the Harlequin are sitting in old soldier retirement quarters. We see Life is no longer able to laugh and Death no longer able to weep in a world that is unable to delight in living, and unable to succumb to mortality. Death is annoyed at the speed and haste modernity has been forced upon him. Indeed, he is insulted, and smashing his sword determines to teach humanity a lesson. From that moment on, not another person will ever be allowed to die.[14]

Clearly, not having Death onside when fighting a war rather defeats the purpose of war altogether. Emperor Overall initially tries to square the situation by promising eternal life to his brave fighters. The work throws up situations whereby executions are futile and soldiers who cannot kill each other choose instead to fall in love. To love rather than kill is a clear act of resistance in Hitler's (Overall's) fevered concept of 'total war'. The Drummer's call to arms is a dissonant and distorted rendition of the German national anthem. The soldiers in love ignore him.

The Harlequin, the Drummer and Emperor are together in the fourth scene. Without the aid of Death, Overall is being defeated on all fronts and from the radio, unaccompanied by music, an announcement is made about the blindness of a nation being healed so that the enormity of its sins can be seen and its punishments anticipated. Overall's enemies threaten to tear down the fortress of evil and remove the weeds that grow into hate. The Emperor in his final rage sings a trio with the Harlequin and the Drummer:

Five, six, seven, eight, nine, ten, hundred, thousand bombs, a million cannons. I've put myself within windowless walls. Even that was taken into consideration! What does a person look like? Am I even still a person or just God's calculator? (He rips the covering off a mirror and in its framed reflection sees Death. He tries to cover it up again.)

As a segue from the idea of 'ripping out the weeds of hate', Death presents himself to Emperor Overall as 'the Gardener Death'. Overall begs Death to return: 'People cannot live without dying!' Death agrees only to return if Overall submits to being the first.

The work is enormously powerful, sarcastic, and full of references such as quotations from a Polish Christmas song; *Deutschland über alles*; Suk's *Asrael* along with Dvořák's *Requiem* and a direct quotation from a popular *Des Knaben Wunderhorn* lullaby, '*Schlaf, Kindlein, schlaf*' ('*Sleep, Little Child, Sleep*'). The opera ends with a variant of the Lutheran chorale, '*Ein' feste Burg ist unser Gott*' ('*A Mighty Fortress is our God*'). If Death presents himself to Overall as a comforting release, he follows the chorale with a sobering promise of wars still to come.

It can hardly come as a surprise that *Der Kaiser von Atlantis* would never be performed in Terezín, though it did make it to a dress rehearsal. Ullmann's concept was not always in accord with the librettist Peter Kien. Ullmann was a believer in anthroposophy; Kien, in contrast, was an angry young man who was less accepting of death's place in life than Ullmann. In a poem from his time in Terezín he prophetically wrote:

I'm frightened
by the immense blue darkness
of death
I'm seized by horror
to think of him, who deviously waits
I'd rather not.[15]

It is possible that disagreements as to how confrontational the text should be was what held up performances. It could be that guards hearing the distorted version of the German National Anthem halted performances, or perhaps everyone was simply placed on the deportation list to Auschwitz without regard to the pros or cons of the work. In October 1944, Kien and Ullmann were both transported to Auschwitz where Ullmann was murdered and Kien would die of sepsis. The existing text and editions of *Kaiser von Atlantis* are a hybrid, reconstructed from the orchestral score (written on the back of lists of prisoners to be deported to other camps, including Auschwitz); the piano score of Karel Berman, who sang the role of Death, and conjectures made by the Ullmann scholar Ingo Schultz, subsequently published by Schott in an edition prepared by Andreas Krause and Henning Brauel in 1992.

Peter Kien, like Gideon Klein, was born in 1919 and died in 1944 (Klein died in January 1945). Kien was not just a sharp-eyed writer and poet; he was an exceptional portraitist and left hundreds of charcoal and pencil sketches of fellow inmates behind. There were also numerous oil portraits; as his friend Peter Weiss wrote, 'It was as if he kept them alive by drawing their images.'[16] The sketches and drawings were given to his lover Helga Wolfenstein. Kien was already an established writer in Terezín with his plays *Marionetten* (*Marionettes*) performed twenty-five times; his poem *Peststadt* (*Plague City*) was set by Gideon Klein. Other plays written by Kien in Terezín (but never performed) included *Medea*, *An der Grenze* (*On the Border*) and *Der böse Traum* (*The Evil Dream*). Ullmann's score and material to *Kaiser von Atlantis* were given to the Terezín librarian Emil Utitz before they were passed on to the poet Hans Günther Adler, later known as H.G. Adler, who himself would write the definitive account of life in Terezín.[17]

Ullmann's score of *Der Kaiser von Atlantis* offers a sampling of both Austrian and Czech musical traditions, synthesised into a personal language. Janáčekian polyrhythms and broken melodies lurk in the background rather than foreground. His association with Schoenberg is barely present and neither is a similarity to Kurt Weill particularly obvious, though it has been claimed frequently in reference to this specific work. Ullmann's early years in Vienna and association within Schoenberg's circle, along with his *Variations and*

Double Fugue on a Theme by Schoenberg, would suggest a strong musical alliance with Vienna. Subjectively viewed, the Czech character of the work overwhelms the German by its use of dissonance and surrealism while never quite departing from tonality for longer than expressively required. The Germanic is militaristic, which changes into a surreal lyricism in the scene with the soldier and the young girl.

Ullmann was ultimately an Austrian composer. He was born in what is today Poland in 1898, but from 1909 he lived in Vienna. At the Rasumowsky-Gymnasium he became friends with future Schoenberg pupils Hanns Eisler, Josef Trávníček, known as Joseph Trauneck, and Erwin Ratz. Before enlisting in the Austrian army and fighting on the Italian Isonzo Front, Ullmann studied piano with Eduard Steuermann and theory with Josef Polnauer, both of whom were also Schoenberg students. A brief period of actual studies with Schoenberg confirmed Ullmann's position within the circle of Vienna's contemporary music scene. His move to Prague as a professional musician at the age of twenty-two, in order to join Zemlinsky at the German Opera, only continued this line of development, perhaps culminating in his 1925 *Variations and Double Fugue on a Theme by Schoenberg* based on the fourth work in Schoenberg's piano pieces, op. 19. This period of composition stretched from 1918 to 1920 when Ullmann left Prague for a short period to the Sudetenland district of Außig (today, Ústí nad Labem) then to Zurich in 1929, where he turned to anthroposophy, and in 1931 he left music altogether, moving to Stuttgart, where he ran a bookshop specialising in anthroposophical literature.

As an Austrian with Jewish ancestry, Ullmann left Germany in 1933 and returned to Prague. From 1933, he began his second and final period of composition, beginning with a reworking of his *Variations,* already reworked from twenty-one *Variations and Double Fugue on a Theme by Arnold Schoenberg,* to Five Variations and Double Fugue in 1929, to a newer version in 1933 dedicated to Polnauer, and finally in an orchestral version finished in 1939. In 1936 he won the publishing Hertzka Prize for his opera *Der Sturz des Antichrist* (*The Fall of the Anti-Christ*), with a text by Albert Steffen. Given the anti-semitism in Europe's largest market for new music, there was no hope of his works being published or performed. Ullmann self-published the first four of his seven piano sonatas along with his two operas: the aforementioned *Fall of the Anti-Christ* and a one-act opera based on Heinrich von Kleist's *Der zerbrochene Krug* (*The Broken Jug*), completed in 1941. Most of Ullmann's works not self-published between 1933 and 1942 would be lost. Paradoxically, almost all of his works composed in Terezín have been preserved. It was a period of enormous productivity for Ullmann, as well as stylistic eclecticism.

Ullmann sits on a historic fence, unable to be claimed by any particular country, movement or tradition, and too individual in his musical expression to declare an unqualified personal allegiance to Vienna, Berlin, Paris or Prague. From 1933 until his deportation to Terezín in 1942, he would have been considered just one of the many German-speaking Czechs in Bohemia and Moravia. His musical language was often expressionistically abrasive, but also inclined towards a gentler Romanticism as heard in Richard Strauss or his post-Janáčekian Czech colleagues.

Not all German-speaking Czechs yearned to be drawn to the 'fatherland' of Nazi Germany. A British journalist reporting at the time, G.E.R. Gedye, maintained in his collection of articles from the period, published under the title *Fallen Bastions*, that most German-speaking Czechs were Czech patriots. They were proud of their democracy, which was still standing in 1938 when all the other countries to come out of the Habsburg Empire had fallen to various forms of totalitarian rule. There was still a feeling that a natural sense of liberalism and tolerance would allow the different linguistic and religious communities to coexist as proud Czech citizens.

It was a false hope, as the case of Hans Winterberg would demonstrate. We shall return to Winterberg again, but his three-movement

Theresienstadt Suite for piano composed in the winter and early spring of 1945 while imprisoned in Terezín is a representation of music as escape, or diversion from the grim reality of the ghetto's surroundings. It carries the same sense of utilitarian purpose as Hans Gál's *Huyton Suite*, composed in the Isle of Man Internment Camp. Nevertheless, not only is the work darker than *Huyton Suite*, there is implied resistance in simply continuing as normal. For musicians and composers, that meant making music. It is interesting that Winterberg would not include the *Theresienstadt Suite* in any of his later compiled worklists.

The Hidden Resistance of Wilhelm Rettich

A few notable composers managed to offer musical resistance from hiding, while living at the mercy of neighbours, friends or strangers as they moved from one hiding place to another. Wilhelm Rettich (1892–1988), born in Leipzig, is perhaps one of the most remarkable. Even before leaving Berlin for the Netherlands with Hitler's appointment as Germany's chancellor in 1933, his life had been something of an adventure. In 1914 he was taken as a prisoner of war and held in West Siberia. With the poet Franz Lestan he composed an opera called *König Tod* (*King Death*), the first performance of which did not take place until 1928 in the north German city of Stettin (now Szczecin in Poland). He managed to survive in a prisoner-of-war camp until freed by the Russian Revolution in 1917; he then taught music in Tschita in Eastern Siberia, became a fluent Russian-speaker, and returned to Germany via Shanghai, Trieste and Vienna.

The success of *König Tod* in 1928 led to Rettich's appointment at the newly founded Leipzig broadcaster, Middle German Radio (MDR). In 1931 he moved to Berlin where he became music director of the Schiller Theater and Berlin's Radio Orchestra. In 1932 he proclaimed his pacifist views in an oratorio called *Fluch des Krieges*

(*The Curse of War*), set to texts by the Chinese poet Li-Tai-Pe, and in a set of Lieder with texts by Else Lasker-Schüler, works that would be singled out for attack by the Nazis.

Following Hitler's appointment as chancellor, he fled Berlin via Prague and ended up in the Netherlands where he made many friends and felt safe enough to remain, despite earlier intentions to immigrate to America. He changed the spelling of his name from Wilhelm to Willem and became a Dutch citizen. From 1934, he settled in Haarlem where he taught, worked for Dutch Radio, VARA, and founded the Haarlem Symphony Orchestra. With the German occupation of Holland from 1940, it was only a question of time before Rettich would lose his paid position at VARA. In 1942 he went into hiding at the home of a pupil in Blaricum close to the musicologist Casper Höweler, whose music library he continued to consult in secret.

Formative in Rettich's musical developments and self-identification as a Jew were his parents. His mother came from Riga and was related to the Jewish music historian Abraham Zevi Idelsohn, often referred to as the 'father' of modern Jewish musicology. His father was an Orthodox Jew originally from Tarnów in Polish Galicia and formerly part of the Austrian Habsburg realm. At the age of seventeen, Rettich studied composition with Max Reger in Leipzig, and upon graduation began work as a répétiteur at the Leipzig Opera, while conducting performances at the opera in Wilhelmshaven.

During his years of hiding in Blaricum starting in 1942, Rettich would return to Idelsohn's legacy and compose *Symphonic Variations for Piano and Orchestra on a Hebrew theme* from Idelsohn's collection. He dedicated it to his mother who, along with his brother, had been betrayed in Haarlem, deported and murdered. Another work from this period was his Third Symphony, titled *Sinfonia Giudaica – in memoriam fratrum*, a work for large orchestra and lasting over an hour. The *Symphonic Variations* are remarkable and despite remaining in a style still redolent of German Late Romanticism, offer a seamless synthesis of German and Jewish tonalities. The Jewish theme sounds Germanic, and the Germanic treatment of the theme sounds modal, offering an exoticism that sounds perfectly natural and in context. The *Sinfonia Giudaica* is more identifiably Jewish in character, with a slow-movement quotation of the *Kol Nidre* and the *Hatikvah* quoted in the finale. It is dedicated to the victims of war. Remarkable is the enormous pianism demanded in the *Symphonic Variations*, which, together with other works, was composed in a cupboard by candle-light without a piano. Also from this period was his *Hebraic Rhapsody* for cello and piano given the opus number 53A, making it an offshoot of his op. 53 *Sinfonia Giudaica*. Yet even before going into hiding his Violin Concerto, op. 51, offers more than a hint of the same seamless linking of both German and Jewish modes. Another work from this period is his op. 52A, *Rembrandt's Portrait of a Rabbi* for voice and piano, which shares an opus number with his second symphony for chorus, soloists and orchestra called *Sinfonia Olandese*.

Rettich survived the war, unlike the rest of his family. Afterwards, he swore never to return to Germany, an oath he later broke in 1964. Musical values had altered and even before the war Rettich was conservative and dismissed as conventional. Post-war cynics would have sneered that had he not been Jewish, he was writing the sort of music the Nazi hierarchy would have loved. He joined a long list of Jewish composers who were similarly disregarded by new generations of music managers, performers and composers eager to put as much aesthetic distance between themselves and their collective pasts as possible.

Nevertheless, Rettich composed a great deal, indeed over one hundred and fifty opus numbers, and would frequently return to Jewish subjects. His music was most definitely conservative but not conventional, despite post-war charge sheets. If anything, Rettich, like many other persecuted Jewish composers such as Richard Fuchs, held tenaciously to their Germanic musical self-identifications, into which they had perfectly merged their Jewish musical traditions.

Fight Songs and the Memory of a Better Germany

Hanns Eisler could be called the musical father of German agitprop. His adaptation of the *Moorsoldatenlied* was only a single point in a continuum of writing the music of protest and political instruction. By 1919, his elder sister Elfriede Eisler, who soon became famous/ notorious under the name of Ruth Fischer, and his elder brother Gerhart Eisler had already become political activists in Berlin. At the same time, Hanns Eisler, living in barracks for soldiers returning from defeat with the likes of George Lukács, directed the workers' chorus of the Siemens-Schuckert factory in Vienna's working-class district of Floridsdorf.

From 1920 to 1925, Eisler remained in Vienna and enjoyed early success as an avant-garde composer. He signed a five-year contract with Universal Edition and relocated to Berlin, leaving his wife Charlotte behind to care for his ailing mother. In any case, the political scene was far more turbulent and confrontational in the Weimar Republic's capital than in Austria's Vienna. It was not until 1927 that Eisler would start writing political music himself in collaboration with Erwin Piscator's theatre for a work by Franz Jung called *Heimweh* (*Homesickness*). In 1928 he wrote music for the agitprop street theatre *Das rote Sprachrohr* (*The Red Megaphone*), and it was also the year in which his first collaboration with Bertolt Brecht took place with *Ballade vom Soldaten* (*The Ballad of the Soldier*). In the following year he was already involved in the ISCM festival's project *Music for Workers*. He also met Ernst Busch. In 1931 he was directing an association with the politically heavy-handed name of *Dialectical Materialism and Music*. From 1932, he was making regular visits to the USSR and emerging as the music collaborator of choice for Bertolt Brecht, first with a play that would undergo transformations into an oratorio called *The Mother* followed by the political film *Kuhle Wampe, oder Wem gehört die Welt?* (*Kuhle Wampe or Who Owns the World?*).[18]

By the time Hitler had made himself Germany's dictator, Eisler was already notorious as a political agitator, with his Jewish father only adding fuel to the Nazi antisemitic fire. One of his fight songs, *Roter Wedding* (*Red Wedding*) – Wedding being a working-class district in Berlin – was so well known, it was usurped into a song for the Hitler Youth called *Unsere Fahne flattert uns voran* (*Our Flag Waves Ahead*). His anthem, *Solidaritätslied* (*Song of Solidarity*), made famous in the film *Kuhle Wampe*, was savaged in the 1937 Düsseldorf Nazi exhibition *Entartete Musik* (*Degenerate Music*). In 1932 he and Brecht wrote a Hitler parody to the tune of *It's a Long Way to Tipperary* called *Der Marsch ins Dritte Reich* (*The March into the Third Reich*). Written a year before the 'Third Reich' became a reality, both Brecht and Eisler regretted the trivialisation of Hitler. Already by 1933 he was no longer a laughing matter. A year later, they wrote another song intended to puncture a hole into the inflated public perception of Adolf Hitler called *Das Lied vom Anstreicher Hitler* (*The Song of House-Painter Hitler*). Others followed, such as *Das Lied vom Baum und den Ästen* (*The Song of the Tree and the Branches*). In 1934 Brecht and Eisler were at it again with a song for the Saarland referendum called the *Saarlied*.

Eisler was in Vienna with Anton Webern when Hitler took power in Berlin. He returned to Berlin to close down his apartment and start a life of travelling from one safe haven to the next. The very peripatetic nature of his exile became a form of propaganda in its own right. Convinced that Hitler's Reich couldn't last, Eisler began working with a coalition of anti-fascist, social democratic and communist movements called the Unity Front (*Einheitsfront*), with music his own area of responsibility within its cultural remit. Following a request from Erwin Piscator in 1935, he and Brecht wrote an anthem called the *Einheitsfront Lied* (*Unity Front Song*). Eisler went on to take over the International Music Office at Comintern and even tried, unsuccessfully, to establish a collaboration with the fiercely apolitical ISCM. Over the next years,

Brecht and Eisler would continue to write fight songs aimed at Hitler and his 'Third Reich'. With the outbreak of the Spanish Civil War in 1936, this expanded into fight songs against Fascism in general with renditions of ¡No Pasarán! and Marcha del 5. Regimiento. Eisler was also visibly engaged in various workers' music festivals and events such as an 'Olympics' of Workers' Music in Strasbourg in 1935, as well as a similar jamboree of workers' music in Reichenberg (today Liberec) in northern Bohemia. Such events placed Eisler in the middle of stadia surrounded by tens of thousands of participants.

As such, it is difficult to see how protest, defiance and resistance propaganda songs take on a separate identity in the context of exile. Nevertheless, Eisler wrote and spoke extensively on aspects of exile and its effects on his composition. In 1938 he even wrote a song called Über die Dauer des Exils (On the Duration of Exile), and his song Der Kälbermarsch (The March of the Calves) was Brecht and Eisler's 1943 attempt to parody the Nazi Horst Wessel Song.

For Eisler, as we shall see later, exile's effect on composition was eventually to take him away from the role of agitator, even if his works remained politically engaged. They began to lose their four-square anthem characteristics and moved towards more subtle methods such as subverting the structures of Bach Passions as expressions of political despair. He had already begun experimenting with this pseudo-liturgical model in his politically didactic stage work, Die Maßnahme (The Measure Taken), from 1930, which takes an outward form reminiscent of an Alpine village Easter pageant.

A sequence of secular cantatas would find their way into a larger work he called Deutsche Symphonie (German Symphony) in the same manner that Bach cantatas made up oratorios and passions. As he mentioned in his interviews with the East German dramaturg and stage director Hans Bunge years later:

Perhaps great works spring from a mood. I recall quite clearly being tired during a tour of America – every evening telling the

Americans about the cultural barbarism of Germany – I simply got tired, since it was monotonous always giving the same talk with few variations. I decided in order to get back to doing some work, even on a dreary autumn evening in a Chicago Hotel, to compose the *Deutsche Symphonie*. The source of the work was a mood, a mood that would carry on for another five years.[19]

In a letter to Brecht dated July 1935 he went on to explain his intentions even further:

> I want to write a large symphony that will have the subtitle 'Concentration Camp Symphony'. In some passages a chorus will be used as well, although it is basically an orchestral work. And I certainly want to use your two poems 'Burial of the agitator in a zinc coffin' (this will become the middle section of a large-scale funeral march) and 'To the prisoners in the concentration camps'.

Even in a work as powerful as Eisler's *Deutsche Symphonie*, the inclination towards agitprop would remain, as evident in his original intention to title the work *Concentration Camp Symphony*, and setting exclusively political texts. Like a musical magpie, Eisler attempted to find a place for every element in his creative toolbox. The work is serial, with twelve-tone rows that sound like street ballads. He put in copious quotations from, for example, *The Internationale* and *Unsterbliche Opfer* (*Immortal Victims*) and even his own *Song of Solidarity*. Despite the attempts to spin the work as Marxist political instruction, its fundamental hallmarks are loss and hope. It is ultimately not a work of agitprop but a statement coming out of exile itself. Decades later, it would fall short of any hopes he may have harboured of presenting the work as enlightened Marxism. The East German Communist Party rejected his settings of texts by the Italian renegade Ignazio Silone. The *Symphonie* is a massive synthesis of melancholy, despair, pessimism and hope, while including inevitable political sloganeering. It forms a multifaceted, twentieth-century Passion in which the subject is not Christ but Germany. His own intentions were 'to express sadness without sentimentality and struggle without militarism'.[20]

Begun in 1935, it would be twenty-four years before it was first heard in its final version. Of the eleven movements, Eisler began with what would ultimately become the third movement with his *Etüde für Orchester* (*Etude for Orchestra*), which started life as part of his Orchestral Suite no. 1 from 1930. In 1936 and 1937 he went on to compose movements 1, 2, 4, 5, 7, 8 and 9, with the orchestral movements 6 and 10 composed in 1939 and 1947 respectively. The core of the work is made up by the seventh movement called *Begräbnis des Hetzers im Zinksarg* (*Burial of the Agitator in a Zinc Coffin*) along with the two 'secular cantatas' in movements 8 and 9, called *Bauernkantate* (*Peasants' Cantata*), and *Arbeiterkantate* (*Workers' Cantata*) which uses Brecht's *Das Lied vom Klassenfeind* (*The Song of the Class Enemy*). The last movement, *Epilog* (*Epilogue*), was composed in time for the long-delayed 1959 East German premiere and originated from his *Kriegsfibel* (*War Primer*). This final movement is meant to present the returning immigrant's challenges of living with those who only a short time before were mortal enemies. It was a sense of uneasiness that was present even when living in a Marxist state that was avowedly 'anti-fascist'. In retrospect, it can be argued that the true conditions of life in the German Democratic Republic were the underlying motivations for its last-minute inclusion, and an additional reason for its subsequent rejection by the East German music establishment.[21]

The titles of the movements definitely suggest calls to action, typical of agitprop and fight songs: the second movement carries the title *To the Fighters in the Concentration Camps*, and a Brechtian dialectic proclaims the prisoners in the camps as Germany's real 'Führer'. The fourth movement is another setting of Brecht's *Zu Potsdam unter den Eichen* (*In Potsdam Under the Oak Trees*), in addition to the better-known version by Kurt Weill. It refers to the violent breaking-up of an anti-war demonstration. The fifth movement is called *Sonnenburg*, named after a camp used for political prisoners. There follows an *Orchestral Intermezzo*, leading to the core of the work with the aforementioned movements 7, 8 and 9.

The selection of movements and their position within the dramaturgy of the work was not pre-defined and despite a sense of balanced architecture and a clear narrative, it was by no means pre-ordained; with additions and alterations made throughout the decades the work remained unperformed. Initially, the opening movements were seen as one of the best new music submissions 'ever made' to an ISCM festival in 1936. The enthusiastic response was dampened by German pressure, ultimately ending with Jacques Ibert's suggestion that the text – too obviously political for the Paris ISCM Festival – be replaced with saxophones. Eisler, unsurprisingly, refused.

There have been other suggestions that the 'symphony' is itself found within the orchestral movements: no. 3 (*Etüde*), no. 6 (*Intermezzo*), no. 10 (*Allegro for Orchestra*) and no. 11 (*Epilogue*) – a symphony tucked away in a large cantata. The work is epic in the Brechtian sense and catapults the listener in and out of the narrative using the same means of alienation as Brecht employed in straight drama. For example, the *Arbeiterkantate* offers whispered dialogue with a wordless chorus in the background, while the *Potsdam* movement and funeral march of the *Agitator in a Zinc Coffin* burst the restrictions of symphonic or choral structure with cinematic elements. The *Bauernkantate* uses texts from Ignazio Silone's novel *Bread and Wine*. Silone, like other important writers and intellectuals such as Manès Sperber and Arthur Koestler, publicly attacked the Stalinist show trials in the 1930s and found himself denounced as a renegade. Eisler's use of a Silone text was unacceptable to East German communist cultural arbiters and his name is missing from earlier publications of the score.

Eisler's twelve-tone-row constructions offer serial composition in an altogether more digestible form. The rows are created in such a fashion as to be compatible with melodic comprehension and even offer a passacaglia that carries through with variations. Rows are rarely transposed and when they are, they move up or down a fifth, a more normal transposition and easier on the ear. In such a manner, it's possible for diatonic quotations to come through as totally recognisable, if ever so slightly skewed.

Eisler's ultimate artistic goal was accessibility. His falling-out with his teacher Arnold Schoenberg was based on his view that Schoenberg's ideas perplexed rather than engaged the listener. Schoenberg, however, was convinced he could create a new sound world, a new way of perceiving tonality where dissonance and wide intervals formed coherent patterns in the brains and ears of listeners. It imposed order on the disorder of atonal Expressionism. By doing so, new expressive opportunities would come forward and music could strike out unbound by the shackles of previous centuries. Eisler agreed with many of these ideals while wishing always to remain comprehensible to the listener. To Eisler, 'communication' and 'Communism' open with the same combination of letters. Schoenberg was never a communist and made no secret of the challenges encountered in attempting to comprehend his most complex music. Eisler believed that synthesising contrasts created new experiences and expressive opportunities. Such contrasts were made with parallel representations of power and repression; perpetrator and victim; tonality and atonality; folksiness vs Formalism and popular music vs classical music; or, ultimately, difficult and easy. For this reason, despite the many twists, turns and occasionally rambling episodes, there remains something fundamentally simple and approachable about Eisler's grandest, most Mahlerian work.

Paul Dessau (1894–1979) wrote a work also based on Brecht's texts that mirrors many of Eisler's intentions. Indeed, it was written in parallel, composed in 1943 and 1944 and completed in 1947, but not heard until 1966, ten years after Brecht's death. The similarities of the two works are often remarkable. Dessau, who met Brecht in New York in March 1943, showed him his settings of *Kampflied der schwarzen Strohhüte* (*Fight Song of the Black Straw Hats*), taken from Brecht's play, *Die heilige Johanna der Schlachthöfe* (*St Joan of the Slaughterhouses*). Dessau and Brecht continued to meet in New York. In one of these meetings, Dessau relates a conversation in which he said:

> You know, Brecht, I want to tell you about something. I really very much want to write a work that's a kind of *German Requiem*. But not like Brahms's – quite the opposite; more like a large-scale *Miserere* – a German work that relates the enormous tragedy of our Fatherland.[22]

This suggestion appears to have engaged Brecht and he started to hunt for material; he was clearly not averse to handing over the same poems to Dessau that Eisler had already set in 1936. Indeed, both works open with *O Deutschland, bleiche Mutter* (*Oh Germany, Pale Mother*). Both works take liturgical templates and subvert them for secular use. Even concepts such as 'Symphony' or 'Requiem', renamed 'Miserere', merely take familiar concepts as accessible entry points for works of grandiose secularism. Dessau is overt in his employment of liturgical references; Eisler, on the other hand, is covert. Eisler inserts his secular cantatas in his *Deutsche Symphonie*, but Dessau directly quotes Brechtian religious references such as 'Ewigkeit' (eternity) or his *Lullaby*, in which a pregnant mother addresses her unborn child as the coming redeemer. There are also oblique biblical references such as *Für sieben Jahre aßen wir das Brot des Schlächters* (*For seven years we ate the bread of the knacker man*). It is not biblical, but it was meant to sound as such.

The title *Miserere* itself is taken from Psalm 50 and sung on Good Friday: *miserere mei Deus secundum magnam misericordiam tuam et secundum multitudinem miserationum tuarum dele iniquitatem meam*, the King James Bible translation of which is, 'Have mercy upon me, O God, according to thy loving kindness: according unto the multitude of thy tender mercies blot out my transgressions.' With its effectiveness in conveying the sufferings of Jesus, it has become a much-exploited passage by composers across the centuries. What the works by Eisler and Dessau share is the view that Germany was not just a perpetrator but a victim, a country where mothers were losing sons to war. The loss of a child was still a loss regardless of the side on which her son fought. The triumvirate of Dessau, Brecht and Eisler had experienced first-hand the helplessness of cannon fodder, commanded by people over whom one had no control. They saw only lives wasted by leaders who had no entitlement other than that accorded by an unjust authority.

The differences between the two works, however, are of an aesthetic nature, consistent with the differences in the individual musical languages of Eisler and Dessau. Added to this was a certain tension between Eisler and Dessau, with Dessau never quite achieving the prominence within the East German cultural hierarchy as Eisler. Brecht seemed to enjoy exploiting such tensions, perhaps out of irritation at Eisler's ebullient arrogance in his alteration of texts to suit his musical structures, and Dessau's compliance in adjusting his structures to Brecht's texts. Although both works exploit concepts that were already familiar, such as the 'idea' of a symphony in the case of Eisler and the model of Brahms's *German Requiem* in Dessau's *Miserere*, they offer differing degrees of anger, sadness and exhortation. The Brecht texts in Dessau are more prominent and monumental, even four-square in a way that Eisler avoids. Dessau's work is less subtle and more agitated in its messaging. It is theatrical and dependent on outside visuals in its second section, with photos beamed onto screens while various extracts from Brecht's *Kriegsfibel* (*War Primer*) are sung. Both works are epic in the Brechtian sense with tendencies to cinematic, extra-musical devices that alienate but also make the line between performer and listener less distinct. Put more simply, Eisler sees his music as the conveyor of Brecht's message; Dessau, on the other hand, sees Brecht's message as the conveyor of his music. Dessau's music is forceful and gives us anger in sadness. Eisler conveys sadness in anger. Both works are meant to envelop the listener with an experience that today might be described as 'interactive'. The listener is not allowed to remain passive but must be drawn into the theatrics of both works.

Both works require enormous resources for performance, with Dessau demanding the addition of visual projections, along with quintuple winds, six horns, four trumpets, four trombones, bass and contrabass tuba along with two harps, Trautonium, an organ, two pianos, ranks of percussion, an army of string players, a large mixed chorus, a children's choir and soloists. Eisler's requirements appear almost modest by comparison, with double winds, quadruple brass, timpani, percussion, chorus and soloists. Dessau's twenty-seven movements are too numerous and complex to list, but part III stands in simple opposition to the block-like dimensions of parts I and II. It consists of a simple lullaby, *Als ich dich in meinem Leib trug* (*When I carried you in my womb*).

Do the Eisler and Dessau works stand as equals to Britten's *War Requiem*? Perhaps, but what separates both from Britten's oratorio is their provenance as works of exile even if later completed in East Germany. They are both nostalgically, unapologetically Germanic while Britten reaches across borders towards reconciliation. Indeed, there is something defiant in Dessau's outright rejection of appeasement by musical means or beauty. Even Eisler saw these as important elements if only as dialectical instruments in order to draw attention to their opposites as a form of expressive counterpoint. Dessau had no time for Eisler's over-intellectualising of contrasts and offered a war oratorio written in desperate times, and though written far from danger, it was also written far from his family. His parents would die in Terezín. Neither work is easy to like, but neither requests such a reaction from listeners. Instead, they give us despair and anger at their lack of redemption. Dessau, however, ends his oratorio with a simple lullaby, a mother who sings to her unborn child in the hope that through future generations, redemption might still be possible.

5

Kurt Weill and the Music of Integration

Es ist, wie Sie ja wissen, ein sehr schwerer Boden hier, besonders für jemand, der eine eigene musikalische Sprache spricht, aber die Situation des Theaters ist hier immer noch besser und gesunder als irgendwo sonst, und ich glaube, dass ich hier soweit kommen kann, das fortzusetzen, was ich in Europe begonnen hatte.

As you know, this is a hard place to make a mark, especially for someone who speaks a very individual musical language; but the situation with theatres is still the best and healthier than elsewhere, and I believe I can make it to the point that I continue here what I started in Europe.
Kurt Weill writing from New York to Alfred Kalmus,
28 July 1937[1]

In February 1949 the Arts Council of England announced a competition for a new opera in English. The understanding was the winning submission (or, should the quality warrant, winning submissions) would be staged and performed as part of the United Kingdom's post-war jamboree, the Festival of Britain, in 1951. To make the selection process impartial, submissions were made anonymously using code names. Some 117 operas were put forward and included such well-established British composers as Malcolm Arnold, Albert Coates, Cyril Scott and Bernard Stevens. The standard did indeed prove to be high, and in the end three operas were chosen. The first two were composed by the German refugee Berthold Goldschmidt and the Austrian Karl Rankl. Goldschmidt's opera was called *Beatrice Cenci* and based on a historic poem by Percy Bysshe Shelley; Rankl's opera was called *Deirdre of the Sorrows*, based on the Irish play by John Millington Synge and W.B. Yeats. The third was by an Australian, who at the time was a resident of Canada, Arthur Benjamin, with *A Tale of Two Cities*.

That none of the top selections was composed by a British-born composer became a potential source of national embarrassment. The competition was extended in the hope that matters could be rectified. After all, the whole point of the Festival of Britain was to celebrate post-war recovery and British creativity. Mounting two English operas written by former 'enemy aliens' did not proclaim the desired message of triumph over adversity. Eventually, operas by Lennox Berkeley (*Nelson*) and Alan Bush (*Wat Tyler*) were included along with, grudgingly, a performance of *A Tale of Two Cities*. The operas by the German-speaking composers Goldschmidt and Rankl were pushed aside with all sorts of embarrassing excuses. It led to Rankl's imposing an embargo on his own music being performed in the United Kingdom and a twenty-five-year silence from Berthold Goldschmidt. Both composers had made enormous efforts to distance themselves from their musical personas in Weimar Germany while remaining true to the integrity of their artisanship. They accommodated the tastes and criteria of the British music establishment while maintaining their musical individuality. To listen to either opera, or Goldschmidt's orchestral song cycle composed around the same time, *Mediterranean Songs*, is to encounter works sharing the same sound world as Britten or Tippett. In the end, it was Britten's masterpiece *Billy Budd* that was premiered, however not in its present form, but in a version that received extensive criticism.

Goldschmidt had been an Anglophile even before discovering the BBC had broadcast *Wozzeck* in 1932. In 1925 he had been Erich Kleiber's assistant and keyboard player for the world premiere of the opera in Berlin. Goldschmidt was already fluent in English when he arrived in 1935. In 1946 Rankl was appointed as principal music director and conductor at the Royal Opera House in Covent Garden and given the task of rebuilding its ensemble and orchestra following its lengthy wartime closure. It would be difficult to imagine two more grateful and patriotic Britons, especially given the sacrifices they had made in fleeing their homelands and the gratitude they felt in being taken in. The creative silencing of both by excluding them on the basis of where they were born would probably not have been the case had they found refuge in the United States, which tended to view refugee musicians as a bonus rather than a threat.

Arriving in a new homeland, serious music composers viewed the landscape and wondered if they could fit in. If they felt there was a chance, the next question only a few composers asked themselves was what stylistic changes would be required. More often it was a case of composers arriving in new homelands believing they were bringing centuries-old musical traditions to relatively under-cultivated but eager-to-learn locals. This was especially true of composers arriving in the United States. Serious music composers and performers who found refuge in the New World tended to see themselves as cultural missionaries, rather than providers of agreeable performances of whatever might please the native-born. Despite the multinational interconnections of the ISCM, most serious music composers arriving in the New World viewed local efforts as naïve, unchallenging and shallow. Performers were fêted as offering an idiomatic authority of the European canon. Few orchestras needed to bother with home-grown talent with so many geniuses landing on their doorsteps. Even second- and third-tier cities such as St Louis, Cincinnati, Salt Lake City, Minneapolis and Detroit instantly acquired kudos with appointments of refugee *bona fide* European music directors. Performers who had previously championed new music in Europe such as Fritz Stiedry, Otto Klemperer, Eduard (Edward) Steuermann, Georg(e) Szell, Rudolf Kolisch, Artur Schnabel and Felix Galimir found themselves celebrated as authorities on the Austro-German repertoire of the eighteenth and nineteenth centuries.

Things were somewhat different with popular music. These were composers who believed that they could not only fit in, they could establish themselves with greater hits than any of the locals. With America being more of a European melting pot, with more Jewish popular musicians and composers than anywhere, those composers who had written *Schlager* and film chansons in Europe saw a great future for themselves in America. Oddly, few of the truly successful musicians in Europe would manage to achieve the same degree of recognition in America, even if their hits in Europe had been best-sellers. Times had changed, and the idea that operetta and cinema could fuse had stopped appealing to younger audiences, though Nelson Eddy, Jeanette MacDonald, Sigmund Romberg and Jerome Kern still had considerable pulling power until the late 1930s.

Even in Germany and Austria, times had started to change, though Jan Kiepura and Marta Eggerth remained the dream operatic couple who would bring some of their magic to Hollywood. Nevertheless, despite the recognition and wealth enjoyed in Europe by the likes of Kiepura and Eggerth, Werner Richard Heymann, Friedrich Hollaender, Emmerich Kálmán, Ralph Benatzky, Paul Abraham and Jaromír Weinberger, they would never enjoy the same success as before. Some ended up writing for television, others returned to Europe as soon as permissible; Weinberger committed suicide and Paul Abraham suffered a mental breakdown.

Popular music was always transitory and local. With new countries and their different customs, languages and social structures thrown into the mix, most popular composers and performers could not keep up. Success depended on more than just taking a popular tango from an UFA-made movie in Berlin and giving it a new text, such as Wilhelm Grosz had done (under the name of Hugh Williams) with his American hit *Along the Santa Fe Trail*.[2] Grosz died in 1939, at a point when films still saw a 'hit song' as essential to their possible success. It was probably the last time a European hit could be repackaged as American and become a success. Indeed, paradoxically, *Nach dem Tango, vergiß mich nicht* (*Don't Forget Me After the Tango*), as performed by Joseph Schmidt, never achieved the same success as *Along the Santa Fe Trail*. It was, however, the exception that would prove the rule, though Grosz never lived to see these developments take place, having died unexpectedly in New York before setting off to Hollywood.

To make a success locally, it clearly required something much more than taking an old formula and applying it to new markets. Kurt Weill was arguably the composer who realised this fact soonest. He was also the most successful in creating something new on Broadway, growing out of a fusion of European musical confidence and American tunefulness with the addition of the wittiest, cleverest writers in the business. Arguably, even his opposite number in Hollywood, Erich Wolfgang Korngold, made fewer concessions and simply placed his musical imagination and mastery unquestioned in the service of Warner Bros. There was even an anecdote that Korngold claimed to have stopped writing for Warner Bros when his English had improved to the point he could understand what the films were about.[3] Weill and his estranged yet devoted, unfaithful wife and companion, Lotte Lenya, simply reinvented themselves as Americans, albeit Americans with thick accents and an eccentric command of American syntax, as demonstrated in the oft-told anecdote of Lenya relating, 'Vhen Vee arriff't in Amerika, Kurt (deep breath) WH-AY-L and I ...' It is funny, but betrays the frame of mind that was necessary to make a success. Unlike Brecht, Eisler or any of the far more important grandees, Weill did not arrive in America believing himself to be the missionary of European sophistication with which to convert the heathen.

A European Idea of America

The Americanisation of music in Germany and Austria in the 1920s and 1930s was viewed initially with an almost equal mixture of admiration and ridicule. Both elements are abundantly present in Elisabeth Hauptmann/Bertolt Brecht and Weill's *Happy End*; Brecht and Weill's *Aufstieg und Fall der Stadt Mahagonny* (*The Rise and Fall of the City of Mahagonny*) and its original concept, *Mahagonny Songspiel*, along with their *Sieben Todsünden* (*Seven Deadly Sins*). Brecht's English song texts are little more than a jumble of German schoolboy words selected to sound American. The impression he was seeking was more important than any attempt at authenticity. It could be argued that Brecht and Weill were presenting a satirical view of how Germans themselves viewed America. Syncopations and the inclusion of a banjo did little to alter the beer-tent character of the music and this was arguably the impression both were attempting. It was German music with a fake American accent. It was a parody of operetta's presentation of America as a country of boundless wealth, dearth of sophistication and supposedly limitless opportunities for those prepared to walk over dead bodies. It comes up in Leo Fall's 1907 operetta *Die Dollarprinzessin* and reappears after the First World War in many popular operettas, using a makeshift jazz as a convenient symbol for all things American. Such shorthand indications of Americana are found in works by composers such as Emmerich Kálmán, Paul Abraham, Ralph Benatzky and Robert Stolz. Even Korngold had a go at 'American jazz' in his last grand opera, *Die Kathrin*.

By the late 1920s and 1930s, authentic American jazz can be heard can be heard in items such as the Black Bottom's number in Max Brand's *Maschinst Hopkins* (*Mechanic Hopkins*) from 1929, or a Dixieland number in Erwin Schulhoff's opera *Flammen* from 1932. Ernst Krenek's notorious success with his so-called jazz opera *Jonny spielt auf* (*Jonny Strikes Up*) from 1927 had, despite delusions to the contrary, more in common with the Brecht/Weill parody of American

8. The Korngolds safely arrived in Los Angeles in October 1930. From left to right, Ernst, Erich Wolfgang, Luzi and the young son Georg standing in front of them.

jazz. It may have sounded genuine enough to European audiences, but fell flat once it reached New York. Pseudo-American jazz could also be found in works by Stefan Wolpe, Wilhelm Grosz, Walter Gronostay and even Ernst Toch and Paul Hindemith. However, with the exception of the diegetic numbers in the Brand and Schulhoff operas, these efforts largely remained American music with an accent as noticeably German as Ravel's French accent in his American-hued piano concertos. The important development for composers arriving in the New World was how quickly they could lose these European accents when composing music for local audiences.

Korngold was more compliant, composing in his own style whatever was demanded and delivering sweeping musical scenarios that more than compensated for the limitations of the cinematography of the time. With mostly European storylines to set, he could remain comfort-ably un-American. One work that feels more overtly American, though not particularly jazzy, was his score for the film *Between Two Worlds* from 1944. With its subject of Europeans escaping Hitler and finding themselves between the world of the living and dead, it must have dealt with complex emotions Korngold would have experienced. For Korngold, America was more about its distinctive harmonic language than its syncopations. His one deeply 'American' movie, *Kings Row*, owed the provenance of its magisterial opening theme to the fact that Korngold apparently thought it was another film about England or its swashbuckling seafarers, following *Captain Blood*, *The Adventures of Robin Hood*, *The Sea Hawk*, *The Prince and the Pauper* and *The Private Lives of Elizabeth and Essex*.

Kurt Weill's Americanisation in Britain

Kurt Weill's loss of European accent was more clearly quantifiable. His first encounter with the English language was disheartening. His revision of his German operetta *Der Kuhhandel*[4] with a text by Robert Vambery was reworked into a three-act operetta for London audiences in 1935 with the title *A Kingdom for a Cow*, using a book by Reginald Arkell and lyrics by Desmond Carter. If *Kuhhandel* was biting and political in its representation of American big business in the affairs of neighbouring nations, the reworked version for London offered more than a nod towards Gilbert and Sullivan (Vambery had translated *The Pirates of Penzance* for the Schiffbauerdamm Theater in Berlin) and, along with the German original version, confirmed Weill as following in Offenbach's footsteps. It was not necessarily a comparison Weill would have welcomed. It was also a comparison Theodor W. Adorno pejoratively made in his less than flattering obituary of Weill in the *Frankfurter Allgemeine* on 15 April 1950.[5] *Kuhhandel* and its London incarnation *A Kingdom for a Cow* was Weill's attempt to write the sort of light music the man in the street would have appreciated. It was neither arch nor knowing, both qualities that dominated the musical theatre of London's Ivor Novello and Noël Coward. The work spins American dance numbers, with added marches, waltzes and tangos.

The Weill scholar David Drew makes the point that the Offenbach Weill may have accepted as a possible model was the variant presented through the prism of the Viennese satirist Karl Kraus, who performed Offenbach 'readings' enhanced by his own raspy sung renditions.[6] Such political sniping is still obvious in *A Kingdom for a Cow*, with its pillorying of the armaments industries. It even appeared particularly 'of the moment' following the highly publicised sales by American arms dealers to the two belligerents Bolivia and Paraguay in their Gran Chaco dispute, taking place in 1934. This miscalculation of mixing what Drew refers to as 'socio-political journalism'[7] with light musical comedy would end in a rare box-office failure for Weill following its opening at the Savoy Theatre on 28 June 1935, and most probably halted any ideas (if indeed any were ever seriously harboured) of remaining in England.

Weill expanded his American jazz input from the German *Kuhhandel* for the English version by adding one or two individual numbers. David Drew also saw this operetta as a turning point in Weill's output and representing a step beyond his German works towards a more populist language. He also writes that *A Kingdom for a Cow* was 'the unhappy result of an attempt to superpose the conventions of modern musical comedy on an incomplete formal structure that had been designed according to the quite distinct if related conventions of operetta'. Put more simply, by trying to stretch the conventions of a musical onto the moribund structure of operetta, the work succeeded as neither one nor the other. In addition, the 'society musicals' of London's West End offered a bourgeois detachment from the vulgarity of current politics, something that must have perplexed Weill, having recently arrived from Berlin and Paris. Thoughts of reworking the operetta for an American public came to nothing, but he did return to *A Kingdom for a Cow* in order to use various numbers in some of his later works such as *Knickerbocker Holiday*, *Lady in the Dark*, *Johnny Johnson*, *Railroads on Parade*, *The Firebrand of Florence* and *One Touch of Venus*.

Johnny Johnson

In a letter to Weill's sister Rita in Mannheim written by Lotte Lenya on 5 June 1936, she describes how they had rented a house by a lake with a producer and a writer for Weill's first American collaboration: a 'play with music', *Johnny Johnson*.[8] The fascinating point in this letter is its reference to the specifically American input of the producer Cheryl Crawford who, together with Lee Strasberg and Harold Clurman, was in charge of the Group Theatre, a political theatre initiative. Paul Green, a writer who today is probably best known for his long-running pageant on the North Carolina Outer Banks called *The Lost Colony*, was brought in to supply the book and lyrics. Weill's recent creative collaborators to this point had been Georg Kaiser, Bertolt Brecht, the Hungarian Robert Vambery and the Austrians Franz Werfel and Max Reinhardt. Despite this, even

Johnny Johnson must be seen as Weill still in transition from European to American. Green had spent the late 1920s in Europe, where he was influenced by Russian Expressionist theatre and Brechtian ideas of epic, non-realistic political theatre. Following his return from Berlin, he chose to mount his next plays in the provincial North Carolina university town of Chapel Hill. *Johnny Johnson* was to mark his return to New York but even this was only after hefty persuasion from Crawford. Weill, who followed her to Chapel Hill to meet Green, was not convinced, describing him as 'an odd boy . . . I'm not convinced he's up to it'.[9] His 1926 play *In Abraham's Bosom* had won a Pulitzer Prize and his successive plays had dealt with incendiary civil rights issues in the American South. Political theatre dominated Green's output, though *Johnny Johnson* could also be seen as the start of his high-profile approach to epic theatre in critically representing American historical drama. *Johnny Johnson* would be Green's only Broadway musical.

Johnny Johnson – the name that most often appeared on the lists of American servicemen – opened on 19 November 1936 at the Group Theatre's 44th St Theater, directed by Lee Strasberg, who dropped some of Weill's music in order to focus more on the drama. Nevertheless, the work did, according to a letter written by Weill to his Viennese publisher Alfred Kalmus, win 'the Drama Prize' of 1937 and make it into a list of the ten best new plays of the year.[10] It was by any means a good start, though it only ran for sixty-eight performances. In reality, it was acknowledged that Strasberg's changes had resulted in a confused revision of the original, only partially remedied when the work was revised again by Green for Los Angeles later the same year.

Johnny Johnson's provenance as an Americanisation of Jaroslav Hašek's *The Good Soldier Švejk* was apparently Weill's suggestion and it was an idea that was clearly in the air at the time. Brecht and Eisler would turn to the same material for an update to the Second World War in 1943. Europe was turning both fascist and militaristic: the

Second Abyssinian War began in 1935 and ended just as the Spanish Civil War began in 1936. The new European order, as envisioned after the First World War, was clearly not going to plan, and a political, anti-war work was timely.

In preparing *Johnny Johnson*, Weill used the creative period set aside for rehearsals and development in July 1937 to discuss the philosophy of musical theatre and to teach the actors songs from *Die Dreigroschenoper* (*The Threepenny Opera*). The grit of Berlin's theatre is still apparent in many *Johnny Johnson* numbers, such as 'Aggie's Sewing Machine Song', 'Mon Ami (My Friend)', 'Capt. Valentine's Tango', 'The Psychiatry Song' and even 'Johnny's Melody'.

Perhaps the most defining comment on *Johnny Johnson*'s European provenance appeared in an article on 17 October in the *Midweek Pictorial* describing the work as follows:

> While the play is studded with songs, it is not a musical show in the traditional sense. The lyrics written by Green, and scored by Weill, flow naturally as an opera aria from the situations in which the characters find themselves. They are written with the directness and casualness of prose speech, and attain a tuneful, gay and mocking quality not usual in the tin pan alley songs America consumes.[11]

The opening night went better than expected but the reviews were ambivalent, with the *New York Herald Tribune* calling it '... a disturbing and often hilarious medley of caricature, satire, musical comedy, melodrama, farce, social polemic and parable',[12] while the *New York American* was more dismissive, describing it as 'a strange, brave, bungle'.[13] The *New York Post* may have come closest with its description of the work as a 'revue', meaning some bits were brilliant whereas others were forgettable. Marc Blitzstein contradicted this point when he mentioned that Weill's songs for *Johnny Johnson* were no longer in the music hall style of his Berlin years and categorically dismissed the view that the work was closer to 'revue' than any other genre. Blitzstein wondered rhetorically if critics would damn it for not being 'American or folksy' enough. Blitzstein admitted to being critical of Weill in the past, but was won over, seeing the work as a new form of musical theatre, 'not really opera', despite its possible perception as such.[14] Weill, had found his populist language, but it hadn't quite lost its German accent at this point.

Maxwell Anderson and *Knickerbocker Holiday*

Erich Wolfgang Korngold and Kurt Weill both owe their American rescue from the Nazis to Max Reinhardt. Korngold came to America initially to arrange Mendelssohn's score for Reinhardt's 1935 version of *A Midsummer Night's Dream*. Korngold then began an irregular commute between Austria and Hollywood until finally returning to Warner Bros for *The Adventures of Robin Hood* in 1938, thus saving him and his family from the Nazi occupation of Austria. Weill first came to America in 1935 for his collaboration with Reinhardt and Franz Werfel on *The Eternal Road*. Yet another common denominator was Maxwell Anderson, who had penned the play *Elizabeth the Queen*, the movie version of which was *The Private Lives of Elizabeth and Essex*, with a score by Korngold. Anderson would also be Weill's collaborator for his next Broadway opening, *Knickerbocker Holiday*, billed as a 'musical comedy'.

In an article for *The American Hebrew* from 8 January 1937 titled 'Protagonist of Music in the Theater', Kurt Weill made an interesting point by explaining that the nature of music-theatre is predominantly 'epic'. He went on to explain that the function of music is not to represent an inner narrative, or provide continuity or facilitate processes or even to inflame passions, but be present as an element that goes its own way, inserting itself in the action's static moments. He continued that this was only possible if the action was presented as an epic narrative, which allowed the audience to follow

9. Arriving in America, October 1935. From left to right, Francesco von Mendelssohn and his sister Eleanor, Kurt Weill, Lotte Lenya and Meyer Weisgal.

clearly the events on the stage. The music, in the framework of this more organic development, could maintain its concert-like character and achieve its maximum effects.[15] The article was published following interest in *Johnny Johnson*, but at the time he was in the middle of working on *The Eternal Road*, to which it obviously applied even more, and to which we shall return later.

In any case, it also could have applied to Weill's next Broadway opening, the 'musical comedy' *Knickerbocker Holiday*. It was Maxwell Anderson's first musical and for both of them their first financial success, with the hit songs 'September Song' and to a lesser degree 'It Never Was You'. *Knickerbocker Holiday* itself represents a certain paradigm change. The satire in *Knickerbocker Holiday* is uniquely

American, with Maxwell Anderson making fun of Franklin Roosevelt and his New Deal. Although Anderson toned it down to some extent, the satire remained obvious and apparently Roosevelt had the grace to laugh at all the right places when he saw the show. Unlike *Johnny Johnson*, which was a would-be Americanisation of *The Good Soldier Švejk*, the political messaging in *Knickerbocker Holiday* made no attempt at universality and was self-referentially American to a degree that must have made Weill believe he had not only arrived, but he had assimilated.

In 1939 he wrote a concept for a film version of *Knickerbocker Holiday* in which he emphasises several crucial points: the main character is to be a young man who refuses to take orders. Peter Stuyvesant is a man who only gives orders and the central theme is the clash that results. Weill went on to state that Stuyvesant was to be modelled on the 'modern dictator' such as Mussolini. The film rights were purchased by United Artists in 1939 and Weill's treatment was ignored when the movie, directed by Harry J. Brown, came out in 1944. Nevertheless, the Weill treatment underlines a juxtaposition of the European confronting a new life in an America where the citizen is not someone who has to take orders from his superior. It denotes a definite shift in mentality and an Americanisation of Weill's *Weltanschauung*.[16]

The music in *Knickerbocker Holiday* is conspicuously lacking the rat-a-tat-tat, clank and grind of Weill's Berlin Brechtian collaborations. Weill appreciated the lack of artifice in American musical theatre, something that emphasised the difference between the genres of musical and operetta. He and Brecht had aspired to something similar in Berlin and had stated their preference for the natural singing of actors to that of opera singers. Weill believed this aspect automatically brought the dramatic narrative closer to the public, thus providing the 'epic' qualities that modern drama required.

An uncharacteristic smoothness of rhythm, harmony and melodic development in *Knickerbocker Holiday* shows that Weill had moved on from where he was with *Johnny Johnson*. Indeed, between the two works there were many opportunities to adapt his style. Apart from changing *Der Weg der Verheißung* into *The Eternal Road*, he delivered a Hollywood film score in August 1937 for something called *The River is Blue*. In the end, the producers rejected his score, though this disappointment was balanced by Weill's application the same month to become an American citizen. In 1938 he also began work on another musical called *Davy Crockett* as well as a further collaboration, with Paul Green, called *The Common Glory* that remained unfinished. He returned to Hollywood with a score for a film directed by Fritz Lang called *You and Me*. It was not a musical, and much of the material was ultimately reworked by Paramount's in-house music department. In the spring of 1938, Weill started work on a pageant he referred to as 'a fantasia on Rail Transport' called *Railroads on Parade*, significant for his first high-profile use of American folk music.

The paradigm change may have come, however, with a project that is now lost, called *The Opera in Mannheim*. Until the Nazi takeover, the opera house in the city of Mannheim, along with the Kroll Opera in Berlin and the Opera in Leipzig, was one of the leading houses in Germany for experimental productions of new works. The New Objectivity movement had started in Mannheim in 1925, during a time when Ernst Toch had initiated a new music group along with an accompanying publication also based in Mannheim.[17] Berthold Goldschmidt's opera *Der gewaltige Hahnrei* (*The Magnificent Cuckold*) had been premiered in Mannheim in 1932. There was an agreement that it be performed in Berlin in 1933 following performances of Weill's own opera *Die Bürgschaft* (*The Pledge*), which itself was meant to transfer to Mannheim. The plot of *The Opera in Mannheim* would have been the most autobiographical of any of Weill's works, and involved Jewish musicians, driven out of Germany, arriving in America. Correspondence confirming the completion of five numbers is all that survives. Finance for the production could never be found and it was questionable whether the genuine plight of Jewish musicians in Germany was suitable material for light musical entertainment.

There were other proto-European returns composed during this time in addition to *The Eternal Road*, such as two songs for Yvette Gilbert for inclusion in *L'Opéra de quat'sous* in Paris, as well as an unpublished work for piano called *Albumblatt für Erika*. In the end, the application for American citizenship and the chance to write American music for a play about American politics resulted in a new sound, even as Weill's ideals and musical integrity remained unchanged. Indeed, as an indication of the fluidity of before and after the watershed of *Knickerbocker Holiday*, the major hit tune, 'September Song', already existed, at least in part, in *Der Kuhhandel* (*A Kingdom for a Cow*).

Knickerbocker Holiday opened at the Ethel Barrymore Theater on 19 October 1938 and ran for six months and 168 performances. 'September Song' is perhaps the only number to survive in the collective consciousness thanks to covers by Bing Crosby, Frank Sinatra, Maurice Chevalier and countless others. Yet *Knickerbocker Holiday* is a veritable treasure trove of musical parody carried out with wit and profound understanding. Weill recognised that to send up pomposity, you needed first to understand it. In this, he and Maxwell Anderson were soulmates and remained close friends for the rest of Weill's life.

The two years between *Knickerbocker Holiday* and Weill's greatest Broadway hit, the 'musical play' *Lady in the Dark*, were hardly his most productive, but again they offer a wormhole into the way his mind was assimilating his new identity. Of interest was an unfinished and misguided attempt to address American racism with another Maxwell Anderson collaboration in 1939 called *Ulysses Africanus*. Weill was not the first nor only émigré to the United States to be appalled at segregation. Korngold penned several numbers without a fee for the film *The Green Pastures* in 1936, a visualisation of biblical stories as seen through the eyes of African Americans. Like many such attempts at addressing racial injustice, it was patronising. As Anderson put it to Paul Robeson in a letter intended to win his participation in the project:

> Although I haven't worked out the plot in detail, it's my intention to make it the story of a man who was born a slave and had never been obliged or encouraged to make an ethical decision for himself. Finding himself free but entrusted with valuable property, which was placed in his hands for safekeeping by a master to whom he owes no duty save that imposed by loyalty and friendship, he is tempted to consider the property his own. [...] He sets out in his search again, having discovered his freedom brings with it responsibilities as a person, which he had never to worry about before.[18]

It comes as no surprise to contemporary readers that despite Anderson's best intentions, *Ulysses Africanus* was dismissed by Paul Robeson as 'condescending'. The project was dropped, but then some of the material was reused in the adaptation of Alan Paton's novel *Cry the Beloved Country*, Weill's last staged work, the 'musical tragedy' *Lost in the Stars*.

Another Maxwell Anderson collaboration was *The Ballad of Magna Carta*, a cantata for narrator, tenor and bass soloists, chorus and orchestra. It, along with his music for Brecht's *Nannas Lied*, appears to have catapulted Weill stylistically back into the musical language of *Sieben Todsünden* and *Silbersee*. *The Ballad of Magna Carta* was a CBS commission and David Drew surmises that Weill composed the full score in only a fortnight. His reconnection with Brecht would inevitably have revived his former Berlin lyricism. Nevertheless, *The Ballad of Magna Carta*, despite sounding like Weill's musical return to Berlin, deals again with the question of tyranny and, intriguingly, includes references to the treatment of Jews.

The Big Successes: *Lady in the Dark* and *One Touch of Venus*

Weill's next two Broadway shows could hardly be more different from what had gone before, and are considered together because they are stylistically similar in tone, manner and expression. The 'musical play' *Lady in the Dark* composed in 1940 with its Broadway opening at the Alvin Theater on 23 January 1941 and his 'musical comedy' *One Touch of Venus*, which opened at New York's Imperial Theater on 7 October 1943, confirmed Weill as an important voice within American musical theatre. Both works offered one hit after another, with Weill's skill as melodist completely acclimatised to his new American home. In the case of *Lady in the Dark*, the more innovative of the two works, it comes down to the sophistication of Moss Hart's book and Ira Gershwin's lyrics. The setting is drop-dead glamorous Manhattan and involves a successful career woman undergoing psychoanalysis in order to help her make decisions about life and love. Arguably, Freud's influence could still be classed as 'European' but its American manifestation in *Lady in the Dark* is pure New York. Weill wrote the music originally as through-composed 'dream sequences' that emerged during therapy sessions. The hits were embedded, though ultimately extracted in later versions of the play and the subsequent Paramount film with Ginger Rogers, which ditched most of the original music altogether.

It is difficult to overstate the significance of *Lady in the Dark*. It was in some ways America's answer to Krenek's *Jonny spielt auf.* What New Yorkers saw on stage was themselves, or at least portrayals of their aspirational selves. It was sophisticated, chic and up-to-the-minute topical to Manhattan's worldly inhabitants. More to the point, it portrayed New York in just the manner New York wanted to be seen. Ira Gershwin's lyrics were snappy and funny; Gertrude Lawrence was elegant, smart, tough and vulnerable at the same time and so outstanding in the role that she ended up on the cover of *Time* magazine. Danny Kaye became a star and Weill was confirmed as guaranteed box-office. It ran for 467 performances with hits such as 'My Ship', 'Tchaikovsky', 'The Saga of Jenny', 'This is New' and 'One Life to Live' able to strike out on their own as sheet music for fans and amateurs.

That *Lady in the Dark* came at the right time financially for Kurt Weill was confirmed in a letter to his parents in which he informed them he could now afford to pay for their affidavits.[19] It was a situation repeated in the correspondence of Hollywood's refugee composers who felt they needed studio work, no matter how demeaning, in order to save relatives and friends from danger. Yet in a later letter dated 24 June 1942, Weill explained to his parents, Albert and Emma, his hesitation on moving too quickly to the next play, conscious of the fact that a success followed too soon may end up a flop. He was still waiting for material that was 'good enough' for him to accept.[20]

The bombing of Pearl Harbor and America's entry into the Second World War in December 1941 would come between the January opening of *Lady in the Dark* and the opening of *One Touch of Venus* in October 1943. A number of propaganda songs, events and pageants with titles such as *Fun to be Free*, *Your Navy*, *Mine Eyes Have Seen the Glory* and *We Shall Never Die* followed the success of *Lady in the Dark*. We shall return to the Zionist- and Jewish-themed pageants later. The nine American songs for the war effort composed in 1942 are an intriguing mix of Berlinesque declamatory ('Song of the Free') and Anglo-American music hall ('Schickelgruber'). Their innate American sensibility veers demonstrably away from the in-your-face agitprop of Hanns Eisler.

In fact, the differences between Eisler and Weill become apparent when comparing the two Brecht texts Weill set in America, *Nannas Lied* and *Und was bekam des Soldaten Weib?* (*And What Was Left for the Soldier's Wife?*). Weill's versions of both are more lyrical and play less with Eisler's emotional dialectics. *Nannas Lied*, or *Lied der Nanna* as it's called in Brecht's 1938 play *Die Rundköpfe und Spitzköpfe*

(*Roundheads and Pointed Heads*), is similar in many ways to both composers, despite Eisler's signature march-like chordal accompaniment. Both Weill and Eisler offer contrasting lyrical treatments of a refrain that expresses unobtainable yearning. Eisler's unremitting chordal accompaniment seems to suggest a musical representation of the world's oldest profession, while Weill's from 1939 goes out of his way to avoid vulgarity.

If Weill saw tragedy in *Und was bekam des Soldaten Weib?*, Eisler saw anger that he accentuates by setting the text to a jig-like melody that trivialises the excitement of war, thereby eliciting heightened emotional response from the listener and creating a shocking contrast with the song's final verse. The Weill scholar Nils Grosch in his essay on various settings of the Brecht text highlights Weill's version as a synthesis of the structure of American music-theatre songs (AAB) and the strophic nature of Brecht's poem, adding a 'C' section at the end of the song for dramaturgical effect.[21] Brecht and Weill had originally seen the song as part of a future reworking of *Švejk* material, conceivably even as a musical. Lotte Lenya was intended as the original interpreter. Brecht's update of *Švejk* to the Second World War was never realised during his lifetime and Eisler's settings of the relevant texts were written between 1957 and 1961. As a result, Weill's version carries Brecht's stamp with Lenya's deadpan delivery offering a strong anti-Nazi punch at the end. Eisler's treatment is harder-hitting and more shocking in its post-war application as East German, anti-fascist messaging. Thus, Weill's nine all-American songs for the war effort retain lyric elements that confirm his inability or unwillingness to demand the calls to action that characterised Eislerian agitprop. What they do, however, is offer Weill a platform to proclaim his newfound allegiance to the country that gave him refuge and opportunities.

If it was not possible for various reasons to engage Moss Hart and Ira Gershwin again for *One Touch of Venus*, S.J. Perelman and Ogden Nash were more than adequate substitutes. The storyline is not as smart as *Lady in the Dark*, and in the wrong hands would even come across as naïve: A love-struck barber puts the engagement ring intended for his fiancée onto the finger of a statue of Venus, bringing her to life in a classic fable of suffering the consequences of wishing for the unobtainable. Ogden Nash was absolutely the right man to add racy humour to an otherwise predictable morality tale. Indeed, the danger of sentimentality was so turned onto its erotic head that Marlene Dietrich rejected the role as too steamy. Dietrich's refusal to take the part of Venus was an enormous disappointment to Weill, who had penned *Speak Low* with her in mind. Dietrich's loss was Mary Martin's gain and, as with Danny Kaye, Weill's show made her a star. More to the point, with *One Touch of Venus*, Weill determined the 'sound' of contemporary Broadway to the same degree that Korngold was setting the tone for escapist Hollywood.

Mark N. Grant, writing on the work on the Kurt Weill Foundation website, notes that Weill's mastery of the American orchestral pop music vernacular in *One Touch of Venus* even outdid *Lady in the Dark*. The orchestra contractor Morris Stonzek took Weill around New York and 'educated' him into American swing orchestral writing.[22] The result was a band of twenty-eight players, large by Broadway standards, resulting in a virtuoso display of American popular music styles of the day: ragtime, swing, blues and even a barbershop quartet. In addition to direction by Elia Kazan and choreography by Agnes de Mille, the relatively unknown Mary Martin playing an insatiable sex-kitten in pursuit of Rodney, a nondescript barber already engaged to someone else, assured the show's appeal and made it Weill's longest-running Broadway musical. Although 'Speak Low' is the principal hit that remains current, other numbers are no less memorable: 'I'm a Stranger here Myself', 'West Wind', 'Foolish Heart' and 'That's Him' all deserve greater familiarity.

A potential issue for Weill was that neither *Lady in the Dark* nor *One Touch of Venus* were 'progressive' in the didactic manner of his past stage collaborations. Broadway was a platform for progress, with even *Show Boat* provoking new positions on racial equality. Running at the same time as *One Touch of Venus* was Hammerstein's Bizet update *Carmen Jones*, about African-American soldiers. It addressed social issues of disadvantaged Americans more profoundly than either of Weill's biggest Broadway successes. *Lady in the Dark* and *One Touch of Venus* addressed issues that were central to New York's affluent professional classes, such as sexual hypocrisy, psychotherapy and even modern art. If these works are seen today as proto-feminist, it is questionable whether Weill would have recognised this as necessarily positive, or indeed pivotal. His was of a generation still influenced by Otto Weininger's negative view of the predatory, hyper-sexual female.[23] In *Lady in the Dark*, Liza, thanks to psychoanalysis, is finally able to decide which man she wishes to marry, somewhat debasing the idea of female empowerment, while *Venus* represented exactly the stalking she-monster Weininger believed would destroy masculine purity.

Johnny Johnson by contrast was unapologetically political with its anti-war polemic and offered a bridge between the ethics of Berlin and Broadway theatre. Unlike *Lady in the Dark* and *One Touch of Venus*, it was not particularly successful. *Knickerbocker Holiday* took America as its subject and showed that it too could fall to Fascism under the right circumstances. Neither work would provide Weill with the same degree of success as his two biggest hits. It must have been dawning on Weill that didactic theatre needed a totally different treatment in America than it did in Germany: the more heavily laden the 'instruction', the less successful the show.

Socially Didactic Theatre in America vs the Lehrstück in Berlin

Kurt Weill was a child of Germany's Weimar Republic, and losing a monarchy and aristocracy demanded a new type of politically engaged citizen. The concept of an elected president was foreign to most Europeans, apart from the French, and the Germans arguably played safe by electing a new emperor in the guise of the First World War general, Paul von Hindenburg. As president, he continued to suspend the constitution whenever he felt the need, invoking its emergency 'Article 48'. During the years of the Weimar Republic, this exceptional measure was used some fifty times.[24] It was self-evident to progressives that the masses, most of whom had little more than elementary education, needed political instruction. The interwar years were the perfect time for socialists and communists to move towards a fairer post-imperial society. Brecht and Weill provided this instruction via didactic theatrics such as *Der Jasager* (*He who Says Yes*) as did later Brecht and Eisler in *Die Maßnahme* (*The Measure Taken*). Even within the context of epic theatre, the idea of political instruction dominated, such as the scenes in *Aufstieg und Fall der Stadt Mahagonny* where excesses of American dystopian capitalism are pilloried. Weill's European works, including *Die Bürgschaft* (*The Pledge*), *Die Sieben Todsünden* (*The Seven Deadly Sins*) and *Der Silbersee* (*The Silver Lake*), continued with the socio-political narrative, something that is conspicuous by its absence in both *Lady in the Dark* and *One Touch of Venus*. As early as 1929, Weill had stated his belief that the great works for the stage had always been socio-critical and not only addressed contemporary issues but also issues that would arise in the near future.[25] It is obvious, and possibly disturbing, that both of his big successes at best skated over any suggestion of provocative social polemic.

Weill critics such as Theodor W. Adorno, Ernst Krenek and more recently David Drew and Claudia Maurer Zenck took issue with Weill's apparent departure from interwar European modernism, while neglecting the fact that he was at best a fair-weather follower of New Objectivity and had no time at all for Schoenberg's twelve-tone school or its aesthetic of wide, dissonant intervals.[26] If Weill's genius for melody was arguably more sophisticated than Hanns Eisler's, it did not mean his ability to employ it towards creating a better society was any less persuasive. Weill's dialectics were more subtle, even in Germany while working with Brecht. Yet Weill also realised that the society in his new American homeland was different from that in Germany and the means of creating a better society involved emotional approaches rather than political sloganeering. In America, Weill could confidently state: 'I write only to express human emotions. If music is really human, it doesn't make much difference how it is conveyed.'[27] For a generation of interwar New Objectivists, appealing to emotions was taboo as it detracted from the need for responsible, civic, sober detachment.

It was clear, however, that Jews who made it to America had a greater burden to bear than non-Jewish political exiles. They needed to get family members and friends to safety. The only way to do this was to earn as much money as possible. If it meant lowering standards and going 'downmarket' then so be it. Hollywood was full of Europe's brightest and most innovative composers prepared to write whatever was required in order to guarantee passage out of Berlin and Vienna for parents, grandparents and cousins. It was far easier for Hindemith, Stravinsky and Krenek to hold themselves to loftier standards than Ernst Toch or Kurt Weill. Even Schoenberg struggled to provide guarantees for his daughter, son-in-law and their two children by having to state to authorities that in addition to his university salary, he also taught private pupils.[28]

No doubt, if offered the choice, Jewish composers would have preferred remaining in Europe with its many new music festivals, where ideas, philosophies, social ethics and the interaction of culture and society could be discussed and projected through new works. Although Korngold's stylistic changes in Hollywood were not as obvious as those made by Kurt Weill, the snobbery and derision directed towards his success were the same. Korngold left Warner Bros as soon as the war was over. Weill was determined to continue his work on Broadway. Like Eisler in Hollywood before his deportation in 1948, Weill was convinced there was ample creative scope within the limitations of populist culture for bettering society and making good, if not lasting art: 'I write for today. I don't give a damn about writing for posterity.'[29]

Weill's American 'Flop': *The Firebrand of Florence*

Inevitably after the successes of *Lady in the Dark* and *One Touch of Venus*, flops for Weill would follow. These were partly due to a miscalculation on the direction of musical theatre with his 'Broadway operetta', *The Firebrand of Florence*. They were also in part due to his operetta film *Where Do We Go from Here?* not being released until after the war, when public tastes had moved on. Both works reflected a view that operetta was still a viable genre and with sufficient innovation could coexist with the American musical. The premise was proven wrong, though the technical brilliance of Weill's scores remained consistently high. If *Where Do We Go from Here?* was meant to offer a comic speed date through American history, at the very least allowing Weill to feel comfortable in his newly acquired American citizenship, *The Firebrand of Florence* was unapologetically European in its concept, even if the music itself was pure Broadway. Weill had decided this synthesis of operetta with Broadway was exactly what he was put on earth to achieve. Unfortunately for him, Richard Rodgers not only got there first, he bettered Weill with *Carousel*, along with his fusion of book and musical numbers in *Oklahoma!*, which opened six months before *One Touch of Venus* and went on to run for 2,212 performances against just 567 for *One Touch of Venus*.

Paradoxically, *Carousel* was based on a story from Budapest that Rodgers and Hammerstein had wisely relocated to Maine for American audiences. Weill, who had been an American citizen since August 1943, took the story of the sculptor Benvenuto Cellini in *The Firebrand of Florence* in an attempt to move away from American themes. Cellini was in any case a character type who was already familiar to Weill, sharing the charm of the anti-hero Mack the Knife from *Die Dreigroschenoper*. He was the loveable rogue who was redeemed at the end. The problem with *The Firebrand of Florence* was simply the fact that American self-confidence after the war meant it no longer felt beholden to European culture. *Carousel* had calculated more wisely by its repositioning to America's New England. *The Firebrand of Florence* ran for a mere forty-three performances. Ira Gershwin had provided zingingly contemporary lyrics for both *Where Do We Go from Here?* and *The Firebrand of Florence*, and Weill's music more than set off his punchiest lines. The humour was in using wise-cracking New York slang and relocating it back into history. American audiences, however, were after something else and Weill never managed to compete with the emotional pull of Richard Rodgers's greatest hits. Weill's innovations would have to avoid direct competition with Rodgers and move towards other developments within American musical theatre.

Weill's 'Folk Operas' *Down in the Valley* and *Street Scene*

The concept of 'folk' was strong in Weill's Germany and conveyed more than traditions of music, singular mythology and religious confession. By the time of Hitler's arrival, it represented a certain tribal, even biological element that resonated strongly in Europe. Although German-speaking Europe had been largely united into a single nation state since 1871, it was still split by differences between Catholic and Protestant, north and south, wine regions and beer regions, dialects, accents and even the gender of nouns and syntax in speech. Italy, during its fight for unification, had sought to smooth its own regional and linguistic differences via the concept of 'the village' representing 'true Italy'. So Germany too turned to the idea of a countryside of forests, mountains and rivers as the unifying element within a still disparate nation. This rural idyll with its legends of Christian knights and castles, exploited by Mahler in his songs of

Des Knaben Wunderhorn, morphed into the untranslatable nationalist concept of *Völkisch* – a description of ethnic identity united by a common folklore of 'blood', music and religion. It was defined as much by those who belonged, such as German-speaking Catholics and Protestants, as it was by those who were excluded: Jews, Slavs, Roma, Sinti and anyone with a different skin colour. As a result, Weill arrived in America with a good idea of the power of 'folk' as a mythologising yet unifying and, for himself, assimilating agent. As with the best verismo elements of Italian opera during the *Risorgimento*, 'folk' as a genre had the capacity to argue for social justice and change. Where Weill's concept of 'folk' differed from European concepts was his belief that the salt of the nation's 'true people' was found in urban as well as rural communities. His next two stage works reflected both elements: the short one-act opera originally for radio, then reworked for students, the 'folk opera' *Down in the Valley*, and his lengthy grand-opera representation of life in a neighbourhood of New York tenements, *Street Scene*.

In number of performances, nothing Weill composed outsold *Down in the Valley*. The idea of a show used as instruction for American actors and singers in the very specific genre of American musical theatre took off. By 1950, Hans Heinsheimer of Schirmer Music publishers claimed the work had been performed 800 times in churches, schools and colleges.[30] In the nine years of its existence, it received 1,600 productions and 6,000 performances.[31] Apart from *Der Jasager*, it was the closest Weill came to *Gebrauchsmusik* – music for the amateur, the dilettante, the enthusiast and the student. Stylistically, *Down in the Valley* was drawn from Americana and folk music, while the socio-political message again argued that even miscreants and outcasts were part of humanity, a common theme in *Oklahoma!*, *Carousel* and later in *Street Scene*.

Originally, a collaboration for *Down in the Valley* had been initiated by the *New York Times* music critic Olin Downes, who had co-authored an anthology in 1943 called *A Treasury of American*

Song. The idea was to build a series of radio dramas, each based on the text of an American folk song. None of Weill's previous collaborators was particularly interested in the project and the playwright Arnold Sundgaard was brought in to provide a dramatisation. His choice was initially the folk song 'Down in the Valley', which was about a murderer just before execution and his hope that someone, somewhere still loved him. Ultimately, following the change from radio opera to school opera, Weill used a number of American folk songs and composed additional material which sounded so authentic that it supported Harold Clurman's observation that Weill's adaptability as a composer meant that if he were forced to live among the Khoekhoe, he would in no time at all have become their leading composer.[32] In any case, building a dramatic narrative around the text of the song was a challenge. Weill himself wrote in correspondence:

> [...] in connection with the words, the idea behind it, just the hillbilly connections [...] seemed to me perfectly suited to the purpose. Sure, it is somewhat more 'corny' than other folk tunes (it seems to me a sort of German-type tune) and it is certainly not a first-class melody, but its very limitations as musical material seemed attractive to me for this piece.[33]

He thereby underlined Langston Hughes's view that 'Kurt Weill did not scorn even the least of these songs, for he knew that the least might well be the most.'[34]

It can be argued that the sheer technical brilliance of German- and Austrian-trained composers gave them the flexibility to write in whatever style was required. Wilhelm Grosz's Tin Pan Alley songs 'Isle of Capri', 'Red Sails in the Sunset', 'Harbor Lights' and others do not betray his provenance as a pupil of Franz Schreker. Nor does Joseph Kosma, the godfather of post-war French chanson, with 'Les Feuilles mortes', 'Barbara' or 'Sur la Rue de la Seine', betray his studies with Hanns Eisler. Assimilation was a necessity for composers and perhaps after the disappointment of *The Firebrand of Florence*, Weill's hyper-assimilation via the means of American folk music was as much about substantiating his new identity as it was about exploring ways of popularising opera.

Today, the Kurt Weill stage work that receives the most revivals is his opera *Street Scene*. In its way, it is the perfect American folk opera. It stands in stark contrast to Aaron Copland's *The Tender Land* and anticipated Leonard Bernstein's *West Side Story*. With *Knickerbocker Holiday*, *Railroads on Parade* and *Where Do We Go from Here?*, Weill had actively participated in American colonial mythology. With *Street Scene*, he was able to break with the notion that America had grown out of its Pilgrim legacy. Weill correctly identified contemporary and future Americans as largely emerging from the tenements of New York City. American operas such as *The Tender Land* or *Porgy and Bess* had almost wilfully excluded the Jewish experience from America and its self-identity, despite both Copland and Gershwin being Jews. Weill incorporated the Jewish experience within the American opera in *Street Scene*, thereby confirming Jewish Americans as part of America's 'folk' heritage. Newly arrived Americans first had to survive confronting roads paved with asphalt rather than gold. As an émigré, and one who had landed on his feet better than most, Weill was aware of how important this step up from Ellis Island was to the story the nation told itself.

In looking at previous attempts to write an opera for Broadway, it was inevitable that Weill's template would to some extent be *Porgy and Bess*. One of the paradoxes that characterise *Street Scene* was his request that Langston Hughes, an African American poet, write the lyrics sung by immigrants, including the Jewish family of Abraham, Sam and Shirley Kaplan. This mirrored Ira Gershwin, a Jewish American, who had written the lyrics for the African Americans in *Porgy and Bess*. And it was Hughes's genius that he was able to project exclusion, disappointment, aspiration and hope into all of the disparate immigrant communities living side by side.

Weill always considered himself a theatrical innovator, and he designated different genres for many of his various works. He called his school opera *Der Jasager* a 'didactic opera', *Das kleine Mahagonny* (*The Little Mahagonny*)[35] was called a 'Songspiel', whereas *Aufstieg und Fall der Stadt Mahagonny* was called an 'epic opera': in this sense, 'epic' was a term used by Erwin Piscator and Bertolt Brecht to designate something that offered more than a straightforward dramatic narrative. It was almost a fusion of revue and play with songs interrupting actions, actors stepping outside of character, and even including a certain degree of audience-to-stage interaction. Weill went on to try and classify his Broadway compositions by calling *Lady in the Dark* a 'musical play', *One Touch of Venus* a 'musical comedy' and *Lost in the Stars* a 'musical tragedy'. *Street Scene* was variously referred to as a 'dramatic musical' and 'Broadway opera'. The competition on Broadway to expand its dramatic and musical remit without scaring away the punters became a competition between Richard Rodgers and Kurt Weill, with Weill very much the underdog. Rodgers and Hammerstein ultimately must be declared victors in trying to steer a course between something that was too operatic, such as *Porgy and Bess*, and something that was merely a lightweight play with musical numbers inserted.

Depending on the glass half-full or half-empty principle, it can be argued that Weill either succeeded, or alternatively, created something of a dog's breakfast, leaving *Street Scene* neither a musical nor an opera. Yet for the purpose of this chapter, *Street Scene* offered something more important than its success or otherwise in the canon of American musical theatre. Its significance lies in its representation of Weill's American musical assimilation. It also gave him an opportunity to portray America critically as well as positively. The central story of the Maurrant family is virtually lost in the clutter of musical vignettes and concessions to the boilerplate Broadway musical. Yet it is specifically in these distracting concessions to Broadway that Weill is able to make his points about American assimilation. It is not only a stage work that allowed Weill to demonstrate his own degree of musical assimilation by offering virtuoso accounts of America's popular music of the moment, but it allowed other immigrants to give voice to their own assimilation. This is occasionally done with humour, such as a debate between Swedes and Italians as to who was first to discover America, or pathos, as when a young girl in the tenement has managed to graduate from high school just as the family is evicted for not being able to pay the rent. Hopes of self-improvement through hard work and education are dashed by being thrown onto the street. There is a 'unifying' moment when all of the immigrants come together to sing the praises of ice cream. This unifying moment comes despite the cruel nativism of Mr Maurrant, the frustrated Mrs Maurrant, the German wife of the Italian ice-cream vendor or Kaplan's ageing Jewish revolutionary and the cruelly hypocritical Mrs Jones, whom playwright Elmer Rice decided was Irish, though with a name like Jones was most likely Welsh. All of them considered themselves better Americans than their neighbours while at the same time fixating on their own ethnic superiority.

Among the mix of immigrants from Europe we also have the African American janitor, whose role was originally more important but was latterly reduced to a single aria (sung twice) in Act 1. Weill's representation of him as the dog everyone could kick and his good-natured tolerance of his place in the tenement hierarchy feels patronising after the removal of his second-act aria 'Great Big Sky', in which he sings that the sky is big enough for everyone. By Act 2, the focus had moved on to the Maurrant family, and the dramatic narrative could not withstand the detour an interpolated character number would have brought, despite such numbers and ensembles dominating most of Act 1. Following *Carmen Jones*, and his own failed *Ulysses Africanus*, Weill was determined to give the African American a voice – even if in *Street Scene* it would remain pitiful until Weill's final Broadway show, *Lost in the Stars*.

The central 'opera' within this 'Broadway opera' is the story of Mrs Maurrant, who is bullied by her husband. She finds a new sense of self-worth in an affair with the milkman. When Mr Maurrant comes home early from a shift, he shoots both of them. The harm from Mrs Maurrant's infidelity is paradoxically neutralised when the cruellest gossips are reminded by the young romantic, Sam Kaplan, that she has no agency, an argument dismissed by Mrs Jones who believes once married, a woman must accept whatever she's given. In the aftermath of the tragedy, the budding love-interest between Sam Kaplan and the Maurrants' daughter Rose falls apart. Rose comes away with the observation that it is wrong for one person to think he or she owns another. It is a moment of social enlightenment that is so unexpected that it almost falls short of making its mark. There is no build-up other than the shock of seeing what happens when jealousy results in murder. Until this point, and against the odds and objections of Sam's own family, romance was blooming. Rose had already rejected her confidence-trickster boss, who promised to put her on Broadway and make her a star. It is soberingly clear that Rose is ultimately the strongest character in the opera. Sam Kaplan, who has one of the most important arias with 'Lonely House', is left lonely in the end as the curtain closes. The work represents critical assimilation. It goes against the wholesome suburban Americana template with its contented housewife, happy kids and working husband. It demonstrates how far this American dream is for most of the people who have come looking for it.

Musically, the 'opera' segments of *Street Scene* offer some of Weill's most profoundly beautiful moments, with genuinely complex structures and proof that the music only sets in when the words need to take flight. It was his ambition that music and book be so integrated that songs didn't become standout numbers but were seamlessly integrated into the action. Yet against this ideal, the 'Broadway' segments of *Street Scene* do indeed offer generic standout show-biz numbers. If these segments, beyond the superficial brilliance of their construction, are distracting and interrupt the 'opera', they nonetheless present their own narrative of the aspiring American. For those who simply could not bear the thought of Weill selling out to 'downmarket America', there is the potentially redeeming orchestral prelude to Act 2, which is nearly identical to his music for Erwin Piscator's *Konjunktur*, its English title being *Oil Boom*, from 1928. David Drew suggests this may have been an unconscious borrowing, while pointing out that Weill and Piscator were in contact during their New York years.[36]

Weill mentions in his notes to a recording of extracts from *Street Scene* that his ambition had been to write 'the American opera' while settling on the 'Broadway opera' designation as ultimately printed in the score. His original idea of calling it a 'dramatic musical' was probably an attempt to placate Cheryl Crawford, the producer who felt the word 'opera' was commercial poison. Yet the ambition to write an 'American opera', something American composers had, until *Porgy and Bess*, been attempting with only local, rather than international success, is comparable with Berthold Goldschmidt's and Karl Rankl's desire to write an 'English' opera, thereby underlining the assimilation pull on refugee composers arriving in new homelands.

Weill would have been familiar with Marc Blitzstein's opera *Regina*, if only because Maurice Abravanel, conductor of *Street Scene's* 148 performances at the Adelphi Theater following its opening on 9 January 1947, went on to conduct *Regina* at the 46th St Theater at the end of October 1949, a run that, as with *Street Scene*, lasted only six weeks. Yet in the 1950s, a number of 'American' operas were performed: Aaron Copland's *The Tender Land* in 1954; Carlisle Floyd's American representation of the biblical *Susannah* in 1955; and Douglas Moore's *The Ballad of Baby Doe* in 1956. All of these operas, in common with the verismo idea, project a rural image of a nation as the true ideal. Weill, and latterly Bernstein with *West Side Story*, saw America as urban, and not always ideal.

The Prototype of the 'Concept Musical': Kurt Weill's *Love Life*

Opening in October 1948, Weill's next stage work, *Love Life*, a collaboration with Alan Jay Lerner, was another critical look at American life and offered more of a synthesis of his previous developments than *Street Scene*. The Weill scholar Kim Kowalke maintains that *Love Life* was the prototype of the 'concept musical', thus setting the stage (literally) for Stephen Sondheim, John Kander and Fred Ebb.[37] He adds:

> ... many theater historians now consider it the prototype for the 'concept musicals' of the 1960s and 70s, a succession of shows, beginning on most lists with *Cabaret*, which tend to be non-linear in structure and unconventional in their use of diegetic musical numbers, rely on the cumulative effect of vignettes rather than plot, concern themselves with social or political issues, and revolve around a central concept or metaphor that informs virtually every aspect of content and presentation.[38]

Yet the idea of integrating vaudeville, an American version of *variété* or revue, can also be found in Richard Strauss's *Ariadne auf Naxos*, Erich Wolfgang Korngold's *Die tote Stadt* or even Alban Berg's *Lulu*. *Love Life*, like many of Weill's works, creates a narrative by contrasting apparently incompatible elements. In *Street Scene* it was the contrast between Broadway and opera. The musicologist and Weill historian Stephen Hinton goes on to explain that there was also the contrast of a surreal ballet and film sequence in Weill's *Royal Palace*; a diegetic gramophone tango in *Der Zar läßt sich photographieren* (*The Czar Has His Photograph Taken*); the boxing arena in *Mahagonny-Songspiel*, also known as *Das kleine Mahagonny*; the straight play with musical dream sequences in *Lady in the Dark* and so on.[39] The idea of presenting a play in a non-linear fashion, or in a manner that objectified the story, was not new. Even in *Aufstieg und Fall der Stadt Mahagonny*, there are banners that detract from the

storyline, or actors who go in and out of character in order to provide
commentary. One is meant to observe the characters on stage as a
scientist would a laboratory rat. There was never any intention of
permitting empathy.

In examining *Love Life* as a work of exile, several issues emerge.
One is Weill's use of Americana in the opening sequences and even
its generic designation as 'vaudeville', starting with a magician in the
manner of a circus ringmaster similar to *Lulu* or the conférencier in
Cabaret. Alan Jay Lerner described it as follows:

> Kurt Weill and I discussed the basic story idea first. We knew
> what we wanted to say. Now and then we talked and talked – for
> about two months before we figured out the form our story would
> take. That, from the writing standpoint, was the most important
> problem we had with *Love Life* – finding a way to tell our story.
> Finally, after discussing hundreds of notions, the idea of doing the
> show as a vaudeville found its way into our misty heads. We
> decided on it for a host of reasons. To begin with, we were telling
> a basically American story and we felt that vaudeville is a basically
> American form. Secondly, the form was loose enough to allow for
> any kind of invention.[40]

The story of *Love Life* is an examination of marriage in an ever-
changing America. It charts a couple, Sam and Susan, through their
marriage and, using a touch of 'epic' in its non-Brechtian sense, the
couple do not age but go through stages starting in America in 1791,
1821, 1857, 1890, 1920 and finally, in Part 2, 1948 (the present) in
New York. Although neither the couple nor their children Johnny
and Elizabeth age, they move into their respective roles with every
epical transition, each preceded by an illuminating vaudeville act. The
narrative is linear inasmuch as it has a beginning, middle and end, but
this narrative is stretched over 157 years in order more easily to 'objec-
tify' the study of the American marriage as it forms, establishes itself,

and starts to fall apart as the world around it changes. The play ends with the couple approaching each other precariously on a tightrope, leaving the audience unsure of whether they can re-establish contact. This was apparently Lerner's autobiographical input using his own failed relationships as reference, similar to Moss Hart's incorporating his psychotherapy into *Lady in the Dark*. Yet, the ambiguity of the so-called 'happy marriage' could equally have applied to Kurt Weill and Lotte Lenya.

Weill's critical look at American marriage could not have been welcome in an age of bobby socks and American apple-pie perfection. The 1950s were an awakening of American cultural hegemony, and negative representation was simply not on the agenda. It was an age of returning soldiers who wanted tranquillity and aspired to big cars, lawns stretching down to the sidewalks in front of ranch houses, perfect marriages and perfect children. This was the picture America was exporting, and in war-torn Europe it was a fantasy that was easy to sell.

A variety of industrial disputes kept *Love Life* from having any post-run afterlife. Scores were not printed, material was not made available, and only a few of its presumed 'hits' were published separately as sheet music. The work was admired by those whose craft was musical theatre, but sadly not by the public. The important reviews were also fairly negative, resulting in Lerner and Weill agreeing to forgo royalties after January just to keep the show running. It came to an end after 252 performances. Revivals were further thwarted by Lerner who, after seven marriages, had decided its negative presentation of American marriage was too close for comfort, or as he put it: 'I can never allow that show to be revived. I've turned into everything I satirized in that show.'[41]

Musically, *Love Life* is a case of form determining content. Weill delivers a panoply of American pop music styles from ragtime to hillbilly, yet most of it sounding generic and providing little more than an earworm to go with the words, but none of the depth he achieves in *Street Scene*. But this was, of course, not the purpose of *Love Life*. It wasn't conceived as a traditional musical, or even a 'Broadway opera'. It synthesised Brechtian ideas and translated them into American stagecraft. Great music would merely have got in the way. In that respect, it also provided a model for many of Stephen Sondheim's 'concept musicals'.

Most of Weill's stage works for Broadway were socially and politically critical, but the trajectory is clearly defined when looking at these works as a singularity. *Johnny Johnson* was verging on agit-prop in its anti-war message. *Knickerbocker Holiday* offers a friendly warning that tyranny is never far away, even in democracies. *Lady in the Dark* was New York's *Zeitoper* and it, along with *One Touch of Venus*, rejoices in the fun and zaniness of American musical theatre with little room left for polemics on social injustice. Following Weill's acquisition of American citizenship and his operetta *The Firebrand of Florence*, he as good as leaves American social commentary altogether with a hybrid work set in Renaissance Italy. Its juxtaposition of wisecracking text and American popular music was intended as light entertainment, and it is significant that it was Weill's least successful work. With *Down in the Valley* and *Street Scene*, we come to unapologetically critical 'folk' works, with one placing America's 'folk' in a rural environment and the other in an urban landscape. *Love Life* punctured the American dream just as Americans were starting to dream big. The war was over and everyone in the world wanted to be American. *Love Life* placed a question mark after that assumption.

Lost in the Stars – Weill's Last Musical

Weill's initial attempt to create a polemic for American racial equality, *Ulysses Africanus*, had not anticipated the delicacy of public sensitivities. It was one thing for entitled citizens of white European extraction to campaign on behalf of African Americans, but they needed to avoid *de haut en bas* when doing so. *Porgy and Bess* had preserved DuBose Heyward's original novel and play about African Americans in South Carolina, and though today it appears to present them stereotypically, at the time the contrasting social elements within the material gave even their singular dialect an aura of nobility. It presented the rural, Southern African American community as it was, though critics have since claimed it offered no direct appeal to improve their lives. To argue thus is to misunderstand the dynamics of how Heyward created his characters and their environment. It would be a mistake to apply today's views on a novel called *Porgy*, published in 1925. Edna Ferber's novel *Show Boat* would follow in 1926 and the musical in 1927. The film *Guess Who's Coming to Dinner*, released in 1967, highlighted the slowness of change in the lives of African Americans. By then, the subject of the movie was how prejudiced even progressive white Americans still were forty years after the opening of *Show Boat*.

With such obvious sensitivities over how Americans of white European extraction should portray African Americans, one possible solution seemed to be to relocate the injustices of segregation to South Africa and hope audiences understood the similarities. Alan Paton's novel *Cry, the Beloved Country*, published in 1948, seemed perfect. After the confused and equivocal response to *Love Life*, *Lost in the Stars* enjoyed a genuinely positive reception. In a letter dated 5 November 1949 to his parents, Weill wrote the following:

> As I telegrammed, my new play is a big success, and this time too it seems like it's not just an artistic success but it might even be a commercial success as well. That would be even more astonishing given the fact that we're dealing with a tragedy that's presented in quite a new way. The work is beautiful and deeply moving, totally interwoven with music, so that some people have been referring to it as a kind of opera. The music is possibly the best and most mature of anything I've written so far, and as you might imagine

it gives me great satisfaction to see it recognized as such. A good deal of the music is sung by a Negro chorus and the combination of this exceptional sound along with a chamber orchestra of only 12 instruments, I've achieved something that creates a new effect, never experienced before in the theatre. The audience is held under the spell of the music and the story from the very opening note to the last. This time, I've been able to work with people who match my own standards: Maxwell Anderson who has undoubtedly written one of his best plays along with Rouben Mamoulian, the best theatre director in America. The three of us have spent the last 5 months working together in total harmony and friendship. It was hard work because in a play such as this, there can be no let-up of intensity and all theatrical elements, word, music and movement must merge into a unity. This was more the case with this work than with anything I've done before.[42]

Jewish sensitivities to American race issues were particularly acute following the revelations of Nazi atrocities. Nevertheless, Anderson and Weill emphasised the underlying human tragedy rather than present an obvious anti-segregationist polemic. The location of South Africa did not come across as a metaphor for the situation in America. This, together with the shift to presenting a universal rather than specifically African focus, resulted in Alan Paton's less than enthusiastic view of the adaptation:

It was an unnerving and at times painful experience. It was my story indeed, but the idiom was strange, except for those parts which reproduced the actual language of the book. [...] I may say that this terrible evening was made more endurable by the beauty of the singing and by Kurt Weill's music. The chorus of 'Cry, the Beloved Country' was powerful and beautiful and moved me deeply, but these were not the words of a stranger, these were my own.[43]

He was further quoted as saying the show 'didn't have a big Black audience' because '[American] Blacks had so many problems that they didn't relate to Africa'.[44]

Weill rejected going down the road of ethnic Zulu music, though Paton had sent him examples. Instead, he chose a musical language with pentatonic and modal elements as a general stand-in for something that sounded exotic. The principal role of an Anglican priest and an ever-present chorus providing commentary suggested a biblical treatment that recalls Weill's Zionist pageants (something we shall return to), and as Naomi Graber, author of *Kurt Weill's America*, points out, Weill even adapted certain passages from *The Eternal Road* for *Lost in the Stars*.[45] The music is uniquely Weillian but moves in new expressive directions. There are certain 'New Objective' elements in his use of rhythm and lack of polyphony, along with violins missing from his orchestration: these are more than balanced by a deep sense of tragedy that is empathetically expressed rather than objectified, thus leaving it for individuals in the audience to draw their own conclusions. Weill uses his craft to the full in order to place the audience into a unifying emotional response. When asked once in an interview, 'What brings out the Weill in Weill?', he answered, 'Looking back on many of my compositions, I find that I seem to have a very strong reaction in the awareness of the suffering of underprivileged people – the oppressed, the persecuted.'[46] If *Lost in the Stars* failed in its intention of highlighting the evils of racism, it prompted Maxwell Anderson and Weill to move to their next, unfinished, collaboration, a musical adaptation of Mark Twain's *The Adventures of Huckleberry Finn*. *Lost in the Stars* closed after 281 performances. It was still running after Weill's unexpected death at the age of fifty on 3 April 1950.

This short survey of Weill's English-language/American stage works is intended to project a trajectory of adaptation to a new environment by one particular composer who was to all appearances very successful. His success was due to his ability and willingness to adapt to a new homeland rather than arriving with the conviction that he was bringing high European culture to the great, and grateful, unwashed. He was also lucky in that Americans responded positively to his efforts. Between his Broadway works there was a good deal of occasional work, some of which was at best applied music for particular commissions or events. His work in Hollywood was largely limited to truncated and bastardised adaptations of his musicals for cinema. The Americanisation of Kurt Weill took place uniquely on Broadway. His Jewish/Zionist works offer a very different view of music in exile.

Weill's success in America stands in contrast to Goldschmidt and Rankl with whom we started this chapter. They were not alone: Egon Wellesz also presented an opera called *Incognita*, based on William Congreve. Wellesz's work never even made it to the final round of the Arts Council of England's opera competition, though it achieved a short run in Oxford. Those composers fleeing Hitler who found a new homes in Great Britain and eventually proved successful were those who arrived as children or young students, or were still relatively unknown.

Alexander Goehr and Joseph Horovitz would never have considered themselves as anything other than British composers who happened to have been born in Germany and Austria respectively. Franz Reizenstein, who studied with Hindemith and then Ralph Vaughan Williams, shows influences of both composers in his works, such as the Violin Concerto, op. 31, from 1954. He would move effortlessly from arid New Objectivity to opera and lush orchestral works, though today he is mostly remembered as the composer of *Concerto Popolare* written for the satirical Gerald Hoffnung concerts, as well as his score for the Hammer horror film *The Mummy*. In America, André Previn, Lukas Foss and Walter Arlen considered themselves Americans, though we shall return to Walter Arlen whose compositions frequently grew out of his experience of exile. What can be concluded is that the success of composers in new homelands depended on landing in the New World, as opposed to the Old World, and the attitudes and adaptability of émigrés.

Franz Waxman

With the exception of Kurt Weill, few composers who already had established names in their European homelands were able to enjoy the same degree of success in new homelands. Erich Korngold, as previously noted, was another, though his stylistic changes were less than those Weill was prepared to make. The one composer who did make the transition from local fame in Berlin to international fame in Hollywood was Franz Waxman. His cabaret and *faux*-American jazz combos with the Weintraub Syncopators under his original name of Franz Wachsmann, along with some beautiful individual songs such as *Allein in einer großen Stadt* ('Alone in a Big City'), could never have predicted his virtuoso adaptability as Hollywood composer. He moved effortlessly from the late Romanticism of *Captains Courageous* (1937) and *Prince Valiant* (1954) to the astonishing inventiveness of *The Bride of Frankenstein* (1935). His Americanisation, however, is most apparent in works ranging from the Gershwinesque *Philadelphia Story* (1937) and small-town Americana of *Peyton Place* (1957) to the ultimate in cool sophistication in *A Place in the Sun* (1951) and *Sunset Boulevard* (1950).

Indeed, Waxman's versatility went well beyond that of most of his colleagues. If Korngold always delivered a Korngold score that rarely sounded far removed from *Die tote Stadt* or *Das Wunder der Heliane*, Waxman managed to deliver a custom-made score for each film, delivering not just appropriate music but also the appropriate style. His 'adaptability' in adjusting to America and the demands of Hollywood could arguably have made him the most successful of all the Hitler music-émigrés. Only after the war and the terrible realisation of the Holocaust did Waxman begin composing concert works of Jewish avowal, such as his oratorio *Joshua* in 1959, the symphonic suite *Ruth* in 1960 and the orchestral song cycle *Song of Terezín* in 1965.

Weill's accommodation with America and the enthusiasm he had for all things American are differentiated. There were, as with Waxman, in effect two composers residing in a single person: the composer who could deliver what the American market wanted and the composer who was profoundly aware of the persecution of Jews and a recognition that, confessional questions aside, these were his people and even a new life in America could not change that. With Weill's death in 1950 he avoided the McCarthy witch-hunts, though he must have been aware of the fanaticism of the House Committee on Un-American Activities that resulted in colleagues in California being deported or returning to Europe before they were forced to leave. As Thomas Mann explained, he had already been accused of being 'un-German'. He decided to leave the United States when accusations began of being 'un-American'.

The daughter of the composer Walter Goehr, Lydia Goehr, professor of philosophy at Columbia University, in her essay *Amerikamüde/Europamüde* refers to Adorno in examining a complex question confronting European composers, artists, writers and intellectuals in America:

> When Adorno insisted that life can no longer be lived in truth in a world that is untrue, was he thinking more about Germany than America or more about America than Germany? Was he contrasting a rotten German past with a better American present or a rotten American present with a better German or European past? I think he was doing both equally [...]. For, in the general discourse, it was claimed with one voice that what occurred in Germany or Europe hadn't yet occurred in the United States, and with another voice that Germany or Europe was becoming what America already stood for.[47]

214

This push-me, pull-you ricochet of life and culture continues today but was very much the conflicted mindset of European exiles in America. It describes the context in which Weill strove to assimilate and bring his American works into some degree of continuity with his European proto-American works such as *Aufstieg und Fall der Stadt Mahagonny*, *Happy End* and *Sieben Todsünden*.

6

The Music of Inner Return

Wenn ich komponiere, bin ich wieder in Wien.

When I compose, I'm back in Vienna.

Robert Fürstenthal[1]

In mentioning the concept of 'inner emigration' in the Introduction I cited its inverse as 'immigration'. Yet equally valid as a possible inverse to 'inner emigration' would be 'inner return'. However, 'inner return' is not the same as 'inner remigration'. Composers are not trying to accommodate inwardly the culture of the home they were forced to leave, but find themselves returning inwardly to a homeland that may only have existed as a yearned-for ideal. The quote that heads this article is the answer to a question I posed to Robert Fürstenthal in a meeting at his home in San Diego a year before his death in 2016. Although I have already mentioned this encounter in the Foreword, explaining that it was in some ways a catalyst in helping me understand the question of exile, it is worth repeating the story of Fürstenthal in this chapter as he so completely represented the idea of 'return' when composing.

His answer in the above quote was to a question that had been on my mind since first hearing of him while working as music curator at Vienna's Jewish Museum in 2009. The head of the Hugo Wolf Society sent some scores to me, stating they came from 'a Jewish composer from Vienna who had ended up in American exile'. As the scores showed an unmistakable thread from Wolf, Mahler and Richard Strauss, I assumed the composer to have come from the generation of exiled composers born between 1865 and 1880 such as Robert Kahn (1865–1951) and Richard Stöhr (1874–1967), both of whom seamlessly carried on within the aesthetic confines of late Romanticism. It came as a shock when I discovered the composer was actually a former accounts auditor from San Diego, born in Vienna in June 1920. He was self-taught, and because of Austria's *Anschluss* in March 1938 had missed the opportunity to study music in Vienna. He only returned to music in the mid-1970s. As accounts auditor for the US Navy based in San Diego, he was wealthy enough to purchase scores from his most admired composers and use them as teaching aids. He wrote hundreds of songs and chamber works and as an extremely capable self-taught pianist, performed everything with like-minded friends, amateurs and professional musicians, who finally persuaded him to send his scores to the Hugo Wolf Society in Vienna.

Robert Fürstenthal's Return to the Vienna That Never Was

Fürstenthal's best works betray little or no sign of the talented amateur and strike the listener as works by a consummate master. Among the hundreds of songs, almost all of which are in German, his musical journey is clearly charted, with attempts to develop certain musical ideas either being thwarted or jettisoned before completion. Occasionally there was a work where his thematic development took him too far from his starting point. Eventually, his Lieder reached a degree of technical assurance that placed him as the equal to a generation of composers who had largely gone out of style by the time he was born. If composing in the manner of Hugo Wolf brought him back to Vienna, it was not to the Vienna he had known, but to a very different city. Orson Welles remarks in his short film *Vienna* from 1968 about the greatest city in the world being the Vienna that never existed but everybody remembered. It was a place where Hitler remained an unimaginable nightmare and bourgeois Jews were instruments of enlightenment and progress, both socially and culturally. It was the Vienna of the salons of Eugenia Schwarzkopf and Berta Zuckerkandl, where the Secessionist movement was founded, where Alma Schindler met Gustav Mahler, where Max Reinhardt founded the Salzburg Festival (in the year of Fürstenthal's birth), and where Gustav Klimt, Egon Wellesz, Adolf Loos, Arnold Schoenberg and Oskar Kokoschka were regular salon guests.

Although composing 'returned' this enormously talented amateur to a vision of a past Vienna he could never have known, the concept of 'return' was itself powerful. If 'inner remigration' suggests an inner return to the reality of a former homeland, 'inner return' is a revisitation of an ideal. It emerges as an obvious thread through much that was written by exiled composers. In some instances, these were works meant for future performance, when the exiled could remind former homelands of what they once aspired to be. In other instances, they were works written solely for the desk drawer as a means of coming to terms with the abrupt changes of identity that exile imposed. For Fürstenthal, it allowed him to create his own Viennese biotope in distant San Diego, a city as foreign to Fürstenthal's Vienna as Shanghai or Caracas.

Robert Fürstenthal came from a Jewish family in Vienna's middle-class ninth district. It is one of the neighbourhoods that borders Leopoldstadt, which was the district with the largest concentration of Jews in the city. Most of the Leopoldstadt Jews were working-class, Orthodox or freshly arrived from the Eastern Habsburg provinces. The Jews in the ninth district were everything from academics (the university was nearby) to doctors (Freud lived and worked in the Berggasse, not far from Vienna's General Hospital, also in the ninth district) to middle management in private firms or mid-ranking civil servants. Fürstenthal's father Ludwig was an assessor at a bank, and his mother Gisella (née Weiß) came from the Hungarian part of the Habsburg monarchy. Fürstenthal's great-grandfather had made a name for himself as a Bible translator and poet.

When Fürstenthal's mother fell ill, he moved in with his uncle Arthur Trinczer, whose wife was Ludwig's younger sister. They lived in the same district, only a street or so apart. Robert's uncle Arthur was an amateur singer, whom he accompanied on the piano. Robert fell in love with his cousin Franziska. Neither family was religious – indeed, Ludwig took pride in being 'without religious confession', a status that in Austria was only acquired after officially leaving the Jewish community and obtaining a notarised confirmation that no other religious denomination had been joined. The Trinczers owned a small company that produced fine bed linen and hand-stitched ladies' wear. The annexation of Austria in March 1938 meant Robert and Franziska would be ejected from their schools. Robert was unable to complete his university entrance examination and any dreams of applying for the Conservatory or the Music Academy were dashed. The young couple was split up, with Robert heading to England for a year, where he worked as a gardener before leaving for America. Franziska's family escaped to Holland in 1938 where they managed to restart their business. Following the Nazi occupation in 1940, they were arrested, deported and murdered, a fate that also befell Ludwig Fürstenthal. Franziska herself escaped to Geneva in 1939, where she married, took the name Françoise Farron, and in 1956 continued her studies in microbiology in the United States, gaining her doctorate in 1969.

Robert was taken in by Jewish relief organisations in America in 1940, relocated to San Francisco, joined the American army, and after the war studied accountancy. His marriage of over twenty years was unhappy and it fell apart in the early 1970s. Françoise Farron's marriage also ended in divorce. She took a position as lecturer and researcher in microbiology at Harvard University. Following the break-up of his marriage, Fürstenthal (officially renamed 'Furstenthal' after 1945) became obsessive in his quest to find Franziska. With the help of a private detective, they were able to reconnect in 1973. When Robert phoned Franziska/Françoise, her first question upon hearing his voice was, 'Do you still compose?'

Françoise's question, followed by their marriage in 1974, led to an explosion of creativity that Robert had suppressed for thirty-five years. It was in this period, along with their joint relocation from San Francisco to San Diego, that led to years of composition by trial and error, though many of Fürstenthal's most beautiful and accomplished works had been composed when he was only sixteen.

Intriguingly, Fürstenthal set many of his songs to the poetry of Josef Weinheber, a staunch Nazi. Maybe Weinheber was also an antisemite, or possibly only an Austrian who saw in Hitler an opportunity for Austria to become part of the greater German nation and regain the dignity lost following defeat and the humiliation of the peace treaties of Versailles and Saint-Germain-en-Laye. In any case Weinheber, despite his possible pan-German aspirations, was a uniquely Austrian poet who expressed uniquely Austrian world views. Françoise admitted that Robert did not know anything about Weinheber's past, but she suspected that even if he had, it would never have made a difference since his poetry expressed so much that was intimate to both of them. She mentioned particularly Weinheber's poem 'Leitwort' ('Motto'), with the lines:

Nur jene [Liebe], die aus des Verzichtes Leid,	Only such love that blooms from the suffering
Aufblüht und sehnend wächst an ihrem Traum,	of denial, and from its dream of yearning grows,
Nur sie ist gnadenvoll und füllt den Raum	is merciful and fills space,
Und hört nicht auf in alle Ewigkeit.	never ceasing in eternity.

Just as the Vienna that Fürstenthal returned to in his music was the Vienna he could not have known, the verse explains that the most all-consuming love is the one that grows out of distance and denial.

More typical, and explicitly Austrian, is Fürstenthal's setting of Weinheber's poem 'Liebeslied' ('Love Song'):

Wenn nie mehr die Sonne wär	If the sun and springtime
und nie mehr Frühling	should cease forever
Und nie, nie Mond mehr	and the moon should never
über bleichen	shine again upon pale
Dächern,	rooftops,
wenn alle Farben tot, und alles	should all colours and
Helle;	brightness fade;
Ich würde trauern, aber nicht	I would be sad, but I would not
verderben [. . .]	perish [. . .]

The song is one of Fürstenthal's most beautiful and intimate, yet at the same time it adds a serene truth to the old joke about the difference between Germans and Austrians. For Germans, a situation is serious but not fatal, whereas for Austrians a situation is fatal but not serious. The Austrian sense of fatalism and morbidity of Weinheber's writing drew Fürstenthal in with an aesthetic of Vienna's *fin de siècle*, allowing him to 'return' to the Vienna that never existed but everybody remembered.

Walter Arlen: A Composer in Mourning

Walter Aptowitzer was a month younger than Robert Fürstenthal and living in the adjacent Viennese district of Ottakring. His grandfather, Leopold Dichter, like Georg Wertheim in Berlin and Théophile Bader in Paris, opened a department store, Warenhaus Dichter (Dichter Department Store), in the 1890s in working-class Ottakring with the intention it should offer the same services and quality of merchandise as the more prestigious stores in Vienna's inner districts. Eventually, Dichter's was so successful that a vast new building was commissioned, making it the only Art Deco building in Vienna. The top floor was turned into apartments for the Dichter and Aptowitzer families, and a large villa was acquired east of Vienna in Burgenland, a province that until 1918 had been part of Hungary.

Walter Aptowitzer's childhood was different from that of Fürstenthal. His family was Kosher and traditionally adherent. When Walter was six years old, his grandfather sensed he might be musical and took him to the Schubert scholar Otto Erich Deutsch. In later interviews, Arlen (formerly Aptowitzer) admitted that he had no idea how his grandfather even knew Deutsch, or why he believed him to be the appropriate person to assess his musical potential. Deutsch noted that Walter had absolute pitch and suggested he be given piano lessons. The lessons were apparently a waste of time and Arlen hated them; nevertheless, they did not dampen his fascination for music. As was common at the time, he was told he could study music but first he had to pass his Matura – the Austrian equivalent of the French baccalauréat – in order to enter university where he was expected to study something 'useful'. Often students could be inscribed in both the university and one of the city's many music colleges, the most prestigious of which were the Academy and the Conservatory.

The young Walter Aptowitzer did not attend exclusive private schools or the elite Akademisches Gymnasium in Vienna's first district, but was educated in a local Gymnasium, where he met Paul Hamburger, another young Jewish boy who was fanatical about music and already studying at Vienna's Music Academy.[2] Later, in English exile, Hamburger would become the pianist and coach for a generation of singers and instrumentalists, but Walter Arlen recalled them as boys poring over scores together. It was in this friendship that Walter Aptowitzer's musical foundations were established.

The annexation of Austria was a far more traumatic event for the Dichter/Aptowitzer families than for the Fürstenthals or Trinczers. As wealthy Viennese, they were vulnerable to the most criminal elements of Austrian Nazis. German National Socialism was a movement that had been suppressed by Austria's Schuschnigg dictatorship. With Hitler's arrival in Vienna, National Socialism exploded, alarming the rest of the world with its murderous antisemitism. Members of the Dichter family were beaten up while their apartments were plundered. Walter's father was taken to the Gestapo and later to Dachau. The business was 'Aryanised' and the family forced to move into rooms in a local pension. The villa in Burgenland was turned into local Nazi headquarters, which they burnt down in accordance with scorched-earth policy when Soviet troops approached in 1945. The day Walter's father was arrested, Walter composed a song set to Eichendorff's poem, 'Es geht wohl anders':

Es geht wohl anders, als du meinst,	Things don't end up as you fear,
Derweil du rot und fröhlich scheinst,	Yet while flushed and cheerful,
ist Lenz und Sonnenschein erflögen,	Spring and sunshine have passed,
Die liebe Gegend schwarz umzogen	The beloved region clouded black
Und kaum hast du dich ausgeweint	And when you finished weeping
Lacht alles wieder, die Sonne scheint,	Laughter and sunshine soon return,
Es geht wohl anders, anders, anders!	Things don't end up as you fear!
Es geht wohl anders als man meint.	They don't end up as you fear.

In fact, things ended up far worse than Walter Aptowitzer feared. Bribes were paid to free his father from Dachau only for him to be rearrested, with more bribes having to be paid to free him from Buchenwald. Fortunately for the Dichters and Aptowitzers, the Pritzker family in Chicago, related by marriage, provided affidavits. Only one Aptowitzer visa came through and Walter left to board the *Vulcania* in Trieste, not knowing when or if he would see his family again. Ultimately, they made it to England where Paul Hamburger helped them find accommodation. Walter was met in America by an uncle who told him to change his name to Arlen. The Pritzkers found him a job at a furrier, and with the outbreak of war he started work in a chemical factory.

Such trauma led to psychoanalysis, and to the conclusion that Arlen must return to music or suffer a total breakdown. The imposed lack of music had added to the chaos in his existence. Somehow he managed to be accepted as a student by Leo Sowerby, an American Pulitzer Prize-winning composer based in Chicago, who later became the organist at Washington, DC's National Cathedral. After the war, Arlen won a competition to live and work with the American symphonist Roy Harris, becoming Harris's amanuensis and copyist, living and travelling with the composer and his wife, the pianist Johana Harris. This arrangement lasted four years, during which he was able to meet everyone who was significant in American musical life.

Immediately following the war, with the whole family now reunited on America's West Coast, a letter arrived from the lawyer of Edmund Topolansky, owner of their 'Aryanised' department store, threatening that any attempt to have ownership of the department store restored would be met by police action and arrest should they attempt to return to Vienna. At the same time, the local council in Burgenland demanded that the site where the Dichter/Aptowitzer villa had previously stood be cleared within the following weeks or be requisitioned by the local council. This, along with the letter from

Topolansky's lawyer, left Arlen and his family feeling defeated by their former homeland and in any case, they did not have the funds to reclaim the land where the villa had stood, or fight actions by Topolansky's lawyers. In fact, Topolansky was by this time in jail (where he committed suicide), and the lawyer's letter was baseless. Arlen's mother, along with other members of his family, had despaired and taken their own lives; his best friend in Burgenland had vanished in a Nazi death camp and his grandmother had been shot in Treblinka. Walter told his father he had no wish to return to Vienna and wanted to remain in America and continue his music studies.

Arlen registered for a course in music criticism at UCLA run by *Los Angeles Times* music critic Albert Goldberg. One day, Goldberg announced that a work by Stravinsky was to be premiered that evening and assigned Arlen to cover it. Arlen worried that his written English would not be good enough. 'It will be,' said Goldberg, thus starting a career that would last for the next three decades.

With his work at the *Los Angeles Times*, Arlen came into contact with the international world of professional musicians and composers. He became part of the remains of the immigrant community in Los Angeles, which had arrived after 1933, though many returned to Europe after the war. He was friendly with Anna and Alma Mahler, the Zeisls, the Milhauds, Ernst Toch, Mario Castelnuovo-Tedesco, Korngold and others. Arlen was one of the few to attend Schoenberg's funeral and became a regular at the Monday Evening Concerts at the home of Peter Yates and Frances Mullen. Soon he was asked to establish and chair a music department at the Jesuit Loyola Marymount University in Los Angeles. His English was now perfect, showing no hint of an Austrian accent. Like his contemporary fellow émigrés Lukas Foss and André Previn, he had become unmistakably American.

Yet inside, things were not as they appeared outwardly. Inwardly, Arlen was profoundly wounded. He remained Austrian, with a love of the language, the people, the culture and the food, and continued

10. The twenty-five-year-old Walter Arlen in 1945 in Chicago next to his newly acquired Oldsmobile.

to speak his Viennese dialect with family members and other Austrians. The Vienna and homeland he remembered was not the one that never existed, but one he had lived in and recalled vividly. He continued to compose until 1952, when he decided it was incompatible with his profession as music journalist. In 1958 he met his lifelong companion and future husband, Howard Myers. In 1986 Myers presented Arlen with a set of poems by St John of the Cross he had translated into English. These were of interest to Arlen because St John of the Cross was originally from a family of Spanish Jews who had been forced to convert during the Inquisition. In addition, he had prayed to Jesus, writing his love poetry while wearing the mask of a woman. Such gender ambiguity resonated with both Arlen and Myers in the still homophobic climate of the time. His cycle *Five Songs of Love and Yearning* provided Arlen with the creative confidence to resume writing music.

From this point, composition became a regular part of Arlen's life, and in some respects there were similarities with Robert Fürstenthal. Neither composer bothered to include tempo indications, expression markings, dynamics or even phrasing. In the case of Fürstenthal, it was because he never believed that anyone other than himself would perform his works. In the case of Arlen, it was because he never intended the works to be performed at all and by and large, wrote them as a means of self-analysis. If Fürstenthal used music as a return to an idealised Vienna he could never have known, Arlen used music as a way of coming to terms with the Vienna he had known and lost. Fürstenthal was happiest adapting a style that reflected the Vienna of his imagination, whereas Arlen's musical education had developed in the United States and his musical language was as American as that of Copland and Barber. In fact, it is an even closer relative to that of fellow émigré composers Lukas Foss (with whom Arlen studied for a short period) and André Previn. There is often a hardness in his lyricism, and his choice of texts frequently betrays an inner anguish, such as his song cycle *The Poet in Exile*, set to poems by Czesław Miłosz, including 'For Jan Lebenstein', with its evocative references of growing up oblivious to the Baroque splendour of Central European cities.[3]

A concert at Vienna's Jewish Museum on 13 March 2008, in memory of the *Anschluss* tragedy seventy years earlier, finally brought a reluctant Walter Arlen and his music into the public arena. There followed recordings of songs and piano works, along with a recording of his oratorio *Song of Songs*. Arlen has remained equivocal about his recognition. Much of the music was deeply personal, such as the three-movement piano cycle *Arbeit macht frei*, with a second movement for solo metronome representing Auschwitz's gas chamber. Its final movement is a lullaby entitled 'Schlummerlied'.

Arlen's works for solo piano are often the most autobiographical, evoking personal memories of both places and people, such as a visit to Marienbad with his grandparents. These are pieces that are often difficult to approach, as their lyricism is intimate, dream-like, amorphous, and seems often to translate a meandering memory into sound. They recall feelings and sensations of places and people and lack a clear narrative arch, ebbing and flowing with little regard to structure.

Arlen set texts in English. His only German settings were prior to immigration, as with 'Es geht wohl anders', and later in America, a lullaby set to a text by Paul Heyse for his cousin Michi, another member of Arlen's family who committed suicide:

Singet leise, leise, leise,	Sing quietly, quietly,
Singt ein flüsternd Wiegenlied,	Sing a whispered lullaby,
Von dem Monde lernt die Weise,	Learn the melody from the moon
Der so still am Himmel zieht.	That so quietly draws across the sky.
Singt ein Lied so süß gelinde,	Sing a song so sweet and delicate,
Wie die Quellen, auf den Kieseln,	As the spring flows over stones,
Wie die Bienen, um die Linde,	As the bees in the lime,
Summen, murmeln, flüstern, rieseln.	Humming, murmuring, whispering, rippling.

Even Arlen's settings of the Austrian poet Rainer Maria Rilke were in English, he claimed because he could not find the original German version in Los Angeles. As he was a frequent guest at Lion and Marta Feuchtwanger's villa with its enormous library, this seems hardly credible. Yet Arlen's German settings depart from his American musical language and return to the Vienna that Robert Fürstenthal would recognise. Conversely, when Fürstenthal set English texts, such as those by James Joyce, he attempted to move into a more conventional twentieth-century idiom, as if English were somehow the conduit of displacement, and German a conduit to return.

Hanns Eisler: 'Art as Memory'

A little more than a generation lies between Hanns Eisler, Robert Fürstenthal and Walter Arlen, but this generational divide is itself important. The aspects the composers' outputs represent are Eisler's Lieder as Journal, Fürstenthal's Lieder as Return and Arlen's Lieder as Therapy. Arlen and Fürstenthal didn't consider themselves to be composers in the traditional sense, which offered them freedom not available to other former refugee colleagues working on America's West Coast. For all of them, art song was the means whereby they returned to their sense of a lost Elysium.

Eisler's songs of exile written in Los Angeles, latterly selected and collected as *Das Hollywooder Liederbuch* (*The Hollywood Songbook*), occasionally referred to by Eisler as *Das Hollywooder Liederbüchlein* (*The Hollywood Small Songbook*), are in fundamental ways quite different from those of Arlen and Fürstenthal. The principal difference lies in Eisler's idea of the songs' intentions and purpose. The similarity, however, is the broad adherence to a central European art-song aesthetic, marking a conspicuous step away from any obvious assimilation into American culture. Brecht went so far as to refer to the *Hollywooder Liederbuch* as Eisler's 'Brucknerian gesture'.[4] Eisler wrote for the desk drawer, again sharing a characteristic with his younger colleagues. Nevertheless, he wrote with the full intention of hearing his works performed at some point in the future. This is made obvious by his careful inclusion of very specific performance directives, elements that are glaringly absent from the songs by Arlen and Fürstenthal.

Brecht would comment in his diary that he rarely met such hardship as in the land of 'easy living' in Los Angeles, where the seasons never change and the only aesthetic unit of measure is commercial

11. Hanns Eisler's setting of Bertolt Brecht's *Über die Dauer des Exils* (*On the Duration of Exile*) from 1938.

consumption.[5] With recognition of Hollywood's artistic aspiration as offering whatever sells, while avoiding any hint of provocation, the idea of putting both 'Lieder' and 'Hollywood' into a single title offered an unmistakable clash of aesthetic values.

For Eisler, there was more than just 'placing tradition into a revolutionary context', as he once explained to Ernst Bloch.[6] It was also about reclaiming elements of German culture that were being forcibly requisitioned by the Nazis, for example, the poets Hölderlin or Eichendorff and the latter's settings by Robert Schumann. It was this type of juxtaposition that resulted in the *Hollywooder Liederbuch* evolving into a cultural memorial in the sense of offering memories of a homeland as seen from the perspective of exile. It was a perspective of both yearning and bitterness.[7]

Eisler himself did not view the collection of songs as cyclic, despite the presence of inner cycles within the volume of songs. Yet there is something cyclic in their supra-narrative that combines memories of childhood juxtaposed against events in the present. Some, including

Brecht, have referred to the collection of songs as a musical diary. The Brecht settings offer a degree of narrative cohesion in expressing his own, direct experience of 'exile'. Interspersed, however, are personal, more nostalgic references to a cultural homeland that Eisler saw as stolen and demanding restitution.

Unlike the songs of Arlen and Fürstenthal, all of which were written on America's West Coast, and to some extent wrestle with the same sense of displacement, a good number of Eisler's opening songs in the *Hollywooder Liederbuch* were set to texts written by Brecht while in exile in various Scandinavian locations between 1938 and 1940, before he arrived in Los Angeles. Indeed, some of these settings are the best-known songs of the collection, such as *An den kleinen Radioapparat* (*To the Little Transister Radio*), *In den Weiden* (*In the Pastures*), *Der Kirschdieb* (*The Cherry Thief*) and *Ostersonntag* (*Easter Sunday*). These were taken from Brecht's *Steffinische Sammlung* (*The Steffin Collection*) in memory of his former lover, Margarete Steffin, who had died of tuberculosis. Brecht wrote his impression of Eisler's musical treatments of these poems in his diary on 26 June 1942: 'For me, his settings are what performances of plays are: a test. [Eisler] reads with enormous exactitude.'[8]

The *Songbook* consists of Lieder composed by Eisler between May 1942 and December 1943. The first sixteen songs, in what was latterly compiled by Manfred Grabs from a potential collection of some two hundred, are set to texts by Brecht. With Brecht's departure to New York in February 1943 until his return in May, Eisler set other texts that expressed a similar context of loss, exile and nostalgia. This was his act of attempted restitution of poets confiscated by Nazi propagandists. This group included Mörike's translations of *Anacreon*, presented as 'Fragments'; *Erinnerung an Eichendorff und Schumann* (*Memories of Eichendorff and Schumann*), an undisguised attempt to reclaim both poet and composer from the clutches of Germany's cultural arbiters; Hölderlin fragments follow, along with a Bible text. In addition to these texts there was *L'Automne californien* (*Californian Autumn*) by

Berthold Viertel, another friend of Eisler's and the husband of the Santa Monica salonnière Salka Viertel.

Eisler often truncated texts or gave them new titles, manipulating their statements to fit within the general testimony of the collection. Initially, Brecht was surprised at the presumption but then declared Eisler's Hölderlin and Mörike/*Anacreon* cycles as 'wonderful'. Eisler began setting Brecht's texts again following his return to California in May 1943, though he mixed this final selection with poems by Blaise Pascal, Goethe, and even one by himself before bringing the collection to a close with Brecht's *Seventh Hollywood-Elegy*.

All of the *Hollywood Elegies* have a certain haiku quality and refer to the difficulties of Europeans trying to make a living in a country where the only requirement was commercial success. Brecht compared himself, no doubt with Eisler in mind, to Dante and Bach, having to prostitute themselves in order to earn enough to live. These were short, sharp texts written in German. The final Elegy is in Brecht's own twisted English, stripped down and simplified, but conveying the message of defeat. In this final Elegy, Brecht implies that the utilitarian need to earn money to rescue family and friends by guaranteeing affidavits has been turned into an end, rather than a means, and all have been caught in the 'swamp' of complacency, happy with the fortunes their prostitution has provided:

> I saw many friends, and the friends I loved the most among them
> Helplessly sunk into the swamp
> I pass by daily
>
> And a drowning was not over
> In the single morning
> This made it more terrible
> And the memory
> Of our long talks

About the swamp, which already
Held so many powerless

Now I watched him leaning back
Covered with leeches
In the shimmering
Softly moving slime:
Upon the sinking face,
The ghastly
Blissful smile

The forty-seven songs were never conceived as a unity and the entire *Songbook* was not performed as such until Roswitha Trexler's performance in 1982, twenty years after Eisler's death.

A Return to the Symphony

A return to the traditional art song, or Lied, was not the only means whereby composers in exile expressed their sense of European belonging. It was also found in a return to classical concepts, if not necessarily strict classical form. Even in American exile, Arnold Schoenberg composed a violin concerto in 1936 and a piano concerto in 1942. Karl Rankl, an Austrian Schoenberg pupil, began composing symphonies after fleeing the Nazis, with his first symphony composed in 1938 and premiered in Liverpool in 1953. He went on to compose another seven in 1941, 1944, 1953, 1954, 1961, 1962 and 1963. His musical language was nowhere near as uncompromising as that of his teacher. Indeed, his First Symphony received positive reviews from the British press, which at the time would suggest he had made considerable stylistic adaptations after leaving Germany. Certainly, his opera *Deirdre of the Sorrows* offers a tempered modernist voice capable of expressive lyricism and considerable beauty.

A more noticeable return to Viennese classicism took place after the defeat of the Nazis, as if their removal from Berlin and Vienna allowed the return of a stolen legacy. Although Korngold had composed sonatas and string quartets before the war, it was only with Hitler's defeat that he returned to classical composition with a string quartet presented to his wife on Christmas Day, 1945.[9] This was followed by a violin concerto in 1945 (revised from 1937–39). His *Symphonic Serenade*, composed in 1947, was arguably a homage to Robert Fuchs (1847–1927), a teacher he rarely acknowledged. Fuchs was well-regarded in Vienna for his five serenades for string orchestra, quite apart from having been the teacher of Gustav Mahler, Alexander Zemlinsky, Franz Schreker and Jean Sibelius. He was also the rarely acknowledged first composition teacher of the fourteen-year-old Ernst Toch.

Korngold's most important post-war work, however, was his Symphony in F-sharp, composed between 1947 and 1952. Although Korngold had charted out a plan for composing at least one symphony while still in his twenties, he only managed to complete this ambition after the stress and worry of war had passed. It is easy to presume that it became a very different work from the one he intended while still a young man in Vienna. By the early 1950s, he hoped the Symphony in F-sharp would hail his re-entry in Vienna. In fact, it had the opposite effect. Poor rehearsals, an unsympathetic conductor in the aforementioned Harold Byrns, and a feeling of antagonism from members of the orchestra confirmed to Korngold that he would never again be able to consider Vienna home. His hymn-like song *Sonett für Wien*, with a text by Hans Kaltneker, was his last attempt to express his love for a city that had resolutely decided it did not love him in return. Yet even earlier, with his *Die stumme Serenade* (*The Silent Serenade*), Korngold's compositions had started to retreat ever more into the 'Vienna everyone remembered but never existed'.[10] Today, the Symphony in F-sharp has staked its rightful place within the canon of twentieth-century symphonies.

Other composers such as Ernst Krenek and Karol Rathaus had composed symphonies and string quartets, sonatas and concertos before the war. The dates of Krenek's symphonies tell us something about his idea of cultural reclamation. His Symphony no. 3 was composed in 1922. He returned to write Symphony no. 4 in 1947 and Symphony no. 5 in 1949. His First Violin Concerto, written for Alma Moodie, dates from 1924. His Second Violin Concerto was composed in 1954. His First Piano Concerto was written in 1923, his Second in 1937 (which he admitted in his memoirs was composed with the intention of performing himself so that he could collect an additional fee); while his Third and Fourth Piano Concertos were from 1946 and 1950. Krenek's String Quartet no. 6 was composed in 1936, with his next quartet composed in 1944. Krenek had made no secret of his love of neo-classicism, yet it is possible to detect a gap in the war years, with his return to Viennese classical concepts as defeat for Hitler looked certain.

Karol Rathaus found himself confined largely to scoring films in Paris and London after 1933 and, as with Krenek, his First Symphony was a single-movement work from 1922. His Second Symphony dated from 1923, though he withdrew it presumably intending its revision. His Third Symphony would not be written until twenty years later, in 1943. There was also a ten-year gap between his Third and Fourth String Quartets. Whether it was due to his position as a teacher at Queens College in Queens, New York, or whether it was a natural development or conscious decision, his post-war works are more classically structured than those from before the war, where he had a tendency to improvisational rather than structured thematic development. His Third Symphony, however, comes across as more powerful, perhaps because of its strict classical four-movement architecture. The conductor Jascha Horenstein would continue to programme the work whenever he could, first in London then in Zurich, though his performance in Berlin in 1958 was met with some bewilderment and was criticised for its very qualities of form and balance. Rathaus was remembered as a young tearaway in the 1920s whose first works were conspicuously labelled 'modernist'. Returning post-war to Berlin with audience-friendly classicism suggested to Germany's music press that events, and life in America, had worn him down.[11] Rathaus's only comment regarding the work was in relation to a proposed performance in Berlin, in which he mentioned that '[the symphony] would not cause the audience any problems'.[12]

Bohuslav Martinů's six symphonies were also post-emigration works, written by a composer in his fifties. His First Symphony was composed in 1942 and performed by the Boston Symphony Orchestra under Serge Koussevitzky on 13 November that year. His Second Symphony was performed by Erich Leinsdorf in Cleveland on 28 October 1943; his Third, again premiered by Koussevitzky in Boston on 12 October 1945; his Fourth was premiered on 30 November 1945 under Eugene Ormandy in Philadelphia; his Fifth by fellow Czech Rafael Kubelík in Prague on 28 May 1947; and his Sixth, under Charles Munch and the Boston Symphony Orchestra, premiered on 7 January 1955. Despite the eight-year gap between symphonies Five and Six, it is clear that the energy to reclaim the symphony during his years as an immigrant was as strong for Martinů as it was for Ernst Toch and Egon Wellesz, both of whom turned to the symphony in exile and, like Martinů, continued to write symphonies in rapid succession.

Paul Hindemith is another composer who, in addition to his symphony *Mathis der Maler*, composed as an act of contrition in 1933, went on to compose another five symphonies in American exile: his Symphony in E-flat in 1940; *Symphonia Serena* in 1948; Sinfonietta in E major in 1949; *Symphonie 'Die Harmonie der Welt'* in 1951; and finally his *Pittsburgh Symphony* in 1958. This doesn't include his Symphony in B-flat major for concert band composed in 1951. Nevertheless, with his *Kammermusiken* composed in the mid-1920s, Hindemith had never wandered particularly far from the ideals of traditional classicism, even if he remade these ideals in his own image. The large American works, in contrast, have a seriousness about them that occasionally approaches world-weariness. The undoubted grandeur of works such as his symphony and, indeed, his opera *Die Harmonie der Welt*, may speak from the soul, but it is a sober soul who remains true to the aesthetic of New Objectivity. Hindemith's post-exile view echoes those expressed by his former New Objectivity co-advocate from Berlin days, Ernst Toch, in his *Glaubensbekenntnis eines Komponisten* (*Composer's Credo*) written in 1945, stating: '. . . if sentimentality has no place in true art, we should never forget that sentimentality should not be confused with emotion'.[13] World wars and the 'new sobriety' of the interwar years had already moved both composers away from any hint of sentimentality. The emotions injected into their post-war symphonies remain fundamentally serious.

The symphonies of Ernst Toch and Egon Wellesz are of particular interest because they both describe similar impulses at similar times to turn to the symphony as a means of cultural self-identification. The results are very different, as would be expected from two very individual composers, both of whom considered themselves interwar modernists. Toch admitted that he could 'only hear mistakes' in Mahler symphonies, yet it was most likely the shadow cast by the symphonies of Mahler and Bruckner that kept the generation of Toch and Wellesz from attempting symphonies themselves. Only the pan-German nationalist, Franz Schmidt, who welcomed Hitler's annexation of Austria, had taken up composing symphonies with any resolution. It suggested to a more progressive generation that the idea of the symphony as a musical form conveyed a conservative, nationalist sub-text. Yet, once these musicians were in exile, the symphony reappeared as a reminder of where they came from. The idea of composing a symphony shone to both Toch and Wellesz like a beacon from their former homeland. Of course, younger Viennese composers had approached the symphony during the interwar years, but both Karol Rathaus and Ernst Krenek wrote single-movement symphonies that seem stridently anti-Viennese, indeed, anti-Mahlerian.

Egon Wellesz and to a far lesser degree Ernst Toch considered themselves primarily as composers for the stage. With this in mind, they were as disinclined to turn to the symphony as a medium as were Verdi, Donizetti or Wagner (apart from his C major symphony). Alternatively, the symphonists Bruckner, Brahms and Mahler did not have a single opera or ballet between them (Mahler's reworking of Weber's *Die drei Pintos* apart). Exile instantly took away the possibility of future opera or ballet composition. Toch, though Austrian, did not return to Vienna post-1933 as did most Austrians working in Germany at the time, but went to Paris, then London, followed by America where he managed to establish himself as a film composer in order to earn money to rescue family and friends. Wellesz simply remained in Austria from 1933 until 1938, though he suffered the financial losses of Hitler's embargo against works by Jewish composers. In March 1938, the weekend of Hitler's triumphant entry into Vienna, Wellesz and Krenek journeyed to Amsterdam where Bruno Walter was conducting new works by Austrian composers, including Wellesz's symphonic poem based on Shakespeare's *The Tempest*, called *Prosperos Beschwörungen* (*The Incantations of Prospero*), and Krenek's Second Piano Concerto. Following the performances, Walter, Krenek and Wellesz did not return to Austria. Wellesz, at least, with his multi-movement symphonic treatment in *Prosperos Beschwörungen*, had established a certain foundation for symphonic composition. Similarly, Ernst Toch called his Second Piano Concerto *Symphony for Piano and Orchestra*, which, like Krenek in Amsterdam, he performed himself at the premiere at the London Promenade Concerts, conducted by Sir Henry Wood.[14] The seed had been planted in both composers, germinating during the chaos of exile, finally growing and bearing fruit following Hitler's defeat.

Both composers began writing symphonies with such enthusiasm that it would be possible to put the first four by Wellesz and first three by Toch into a single supra-cycle. Structurally, the first four by Wellesz are conceived as a homage to Vienna's symphonic tradition, melodically fluid, classically clear, with slow movements that recall Mahler. Toch, who until emigration had been a stickler for clarity and form, composed works that he admitted might baffle all attempts at music analysis. He added subtitles to the first three symphonies, while denying they betrayed anything programmatic. Against Wellesz's lyric clarity, Toch offers dissonant streams of musical consciousness, overflowing with ideas, often densely contrapuntal, uncontrolled and enormously expressive.

In the run-up to the premiere of Wellesz's First Symphony in 1948 with the Berlin Philharmonic under Sergiu Celibidache, the composer wrote the following explanation as to why he would attempt to compose a symphony at this late stage of his career just as he turned sixty:

> Having grown up in the Austrian traditions of music, I always saw the 'symphony' as music's highest possible statement. But I hadn't dared to approach this particular form since I had not achieved the necessary distance in order to contribute something that was individual.[15]

And in a letter to his Viennese publishers, Doblinger, from 27 June 1970, Wellesz went into slightly more detail:

> It was in the summer of 1945 when I was in my sixtieth year that I composed my First Symphony. Turning to this form, so well established within Austrian traditions, couldn't have happened any sooner. I had grown up under the overwhelming impression of Mahler's symphonies, which for our generation represented the crowning achievement of the form. As long as I lived in Vienna, I always saw myself as a composer of music-drama. Hence my only consequential orchestral work written in

Vienna, *Prosperos Beschwörungen,* which was based on Shakespeare's *The Tempest.*[16]

It was while on a walking holiday in England's Lake District, with its landscape similar to that of Styrian Austria, that the first thematic ideas occurred to Wellesz:

> The holiday was drawing to a close and I was walking along a path that followed a stream that reminded me of a path I used to walk in Styria at Altaussee and suddenly a theme occurred to me that I instantly recognised as the principal subject of the first movement of my symphony. The following day, the lyrical theme of the second subject came to me and it was obvious that it belonged to the first.[17]

Toch, by contrast, was still protesting any possible Mahlerian influences in his music as late as 1964. After reading an article in the German music lexicon *Die Musik in Geschichte und Gegenwart* (*Music in Past and Present*), he felt incensed enough to fire off a protest to its author Kurt Stone:

> [...] My doubts on the validity of [your] conclusion are based on my personal encounters with Mahler symphonies that have never been a model for me, indeed I only perceived [their] errors and felt a sense of strong rejection whenever I heard them. A factual reference to Mahler appears to me to be highly improbable.[18]

Wellesz was moved to write his symphony by his memories of Austria. Toch suffered a heart attack in 1948 and, confronted with his own mortality, left his teaching position at the University of Southern California. He had already given up on writing film scores the minute the war was over. In order to provide himself with the freedom and inspiration to compose a symphony, he returned to Vienna in 1949/50. Unlike other Viennese composers of his generation, he made no secret of his dislike of the city, distancing himself from all of its musical influences and eventually establishing himself as one of the leading exponents of German New Objectivity. Yet incredibly, at this crucial turning point in his creative life, he felt drawn to the city at the very point he felt motivated to compose a symphony.

He dedicated his First Symphony to his childhood friend Joseph Fuchs, who had unwittingly started Toch's career as a composer by secretly passing the manuscript of the schoolboy's First String Quartet to the Rosé Quartet, which they instantly took on for performance. Both Toch's first and second symphonies were written in such rapid succession that he admitted composing them more or less simultaneously. The First Symphony was premiered by the Vienna Symphony conducted by Herbert Häfner on 21 December 1950 in a gala concert attended by Austria's Chancellor. It was subsequently performed by Amsterdam's Concertgebouw Orchestra under Otto Klemperer and followed by performances in Cologne under Joseph Keilberth and Pittsburgh under William Steinberg.

The Second Symphony, also a product of post-war Vienna, was premiered on 11 January 1952, again with the Vienna Symphony under Herbert Häfner together with a repetition of the First Symphony. On this particular occasion, Toch provided a short note for the programme:

Shortly before my departure for Europe, my eyes alighted upon Luther's *A Mighty Fortress is our God*. As familiar as these short texts were, they struck me as particularly relevant to the events of the past decades and offered a new context to their meaning in the present. Despite this, my symphony, as in the case with all of my works, is free of any programme. Yet I'm confident that these words continued to resonate in me during the time of the symphony's composition. In confident gratitude thereof, I wrote out the poem on the last page of the score and with its publication, I took its opening verses as the work's heading:

Although the World with Devils filled should threaten to undo us, we will not fear, for God has willed his truth to triumph through us.

I was even more aware of the influences I was under during the composition of the Second Symphony than I was with the First. Over the years, I was inwardly taken by the presence of a man whom I respected more than all others alive today, or the handful of men I have respected from the past. I expressed this sense of devotion with the following dedication:

The Man who drew this work out of me
The only one who could see in a time of blindness
The only conqueror in a world of the defeated:
ALBERT SCHWEITZER

(I have never encountered Schweitzer personally. Nor have I had any correspondence with him.)

But the words from the Bible, 'I will not let you go unless you bless me' (Genesis 32:26–32) had a powerfully inspiring effect on me. I therefore took its vague significance and placed it at the beginning of the work as an epithet. At the same time, during the work's composition it took on a number of ever-changing meanings. The life of Schweitzer seemed to me to be the personification of the biblical quote, particularly after his return to Europe from Lambaréné, the place of his work and his sanctity. The quote represented for me my years of silent reverence for Schweitzer. And suddenly – this is something that occasionally happens to the creative artist – the ever-demanding call of the work reclaimed its own author from the foggy formlessness of its beginning to the last stroke of the pen: 'I will not let you go unless you – complete – bless me.'

We have to accept that we can't know if such personal complexities regarding the creation of something will bring the listener any closer. Perhaps it is only relevant to the artist and perhaps the listener would be better served to approach the work in all naivety. The one thing, however, that I'm convinced of, is that stylistic discussions or form analysis will not bring anyone to a point of understanding. Please forgive me if guidance is necessary, as I lead you through a different door.[19]

Despite Toch's apparent compositional surge, lacking self-editing and desperate to get notes onto manuscript paper, there is order in the apparent chaos. The works are largely tonal, though highly chromatic, and in the Second Symphony he exploits new orchestral colours by adding a piano played four-hands with harp and solo violin. His legacy from film music composition – bearing in mind that his contribution was mostly in the genres of science fiction and 'horror' – was to conceive of new colours and to create new soundscapes.

Toch's Third Symphony breaks with the four-movement, largely classically structured model, and reverts to three movements, the structure of which he described as 'none of the movements following traditional form. The only image that I might be able to use for this would be that of a ballistic curve. This applies to the individual movements as well as to the whole.'[20] Again, Toch attempted to create new sound effects and even invented instruments for the work, which he later discarded due to their lack of dynamic control. The added Hammond organ, however, remained. Nevertheless, the attempt to expand orchestral colours by using sounds from the environment would have been a legacy from Berlin days, with references to Ernst Krenek, Sergei Eisenstein's film composer Edmund Meisel and George Antheil. Toch, ever quick to distance himself from the all too obvious, instead chose to place his acoustic experimentation with Richard Strauss's *Alpine Symphony* and its use of cowbells. It is worth raising an eyebrow at his reference to Strauss rather than the cowbells of Mahler's Sixth Symphony. In any case, the work won Toch a Pulitzer Prize in 1956. His heading was taken from Goethe's epistolary novel, *The Sorrows of Young Werther*. Given the Third Symphony's commission by Chicago's American Jewish Tercentenary committee, the quote is conspicuously redolent of Ahasuerus, the 'Wandering Jew': *Indeed, I am a wanderer, a pilgrim on this earth – but what else are you?* The Third Symphony was premiered by William Steinberg conducting the Pittsburgh Symphony Orchestra on 2 December 1955. As with Toch's previous two symphonies, there is no suggestion that the work is a programmatic representation of its heading. Instead, the subtitles reflect the mood and mindset of the composer during composition.

The Fourth Symphony hints at Toch's emotional state in American life. He had rejected his Austrian homeland in favour of Germany as early as 1909 when he went to study at Frankfurt's Music Academy rather than remain in Vienna. Indeed, his year of entry into the Frankfurt Academy was the same as that of Paul Hindemith, with whom he stood shoulder to shoulder rejecting the notion that the arts should speak to emotions. New Objectivity was meant to offer something so new and compelling that these aspects alone would lead Germany's enlightened music lovers away from the constant need of Wagnerian emotional roller coasters. In his *Composer's Credo*, written in 1945, Toch as much as rejects everything he had stood for in interwar Germany:

Today there is a tendency to believe that science, in the fullness of time, will be able to explain everything. In the future, there will be no more mysteries – neither in nature nor within our inner lives. [...] Recognition of religion has almost nothing to do with a specific church. Instead, it comes closer to the devotion found within ancient cultures that saw every event, whether happy or sad, as being enigmatically linked with human destiny. It was called yielding up to life in the fullest sense of the word. And though science attempts to bore ever deeper while analysing the discoveries it makes, it is specifically within this border region of the human spirit that the arts thrive. And in this region, music thrives even more than the others. [...] In the past couple of decades, we have seen the production of much music that both excited our interests and stimulated our wits. We discovered and gained a great deal. But at the same time, we lost something. Perhaps it will be a while before we even notice that it's missing, but in due course it will become obvious. And this 'something' is simply too important to do without. As fed up with Romanticism as we eventually became, one should not forget the basic fact that music, in its innermost makeup, is de facto romantic. And if sentimentality has no place in true art, we should never forget that sentimentality should not be confused with emotion . . .[21]

Having rejected Austrian traditions for Germany, Toch was now rejecting German traditions for American ones and was clearly not afraid of the maudlin. He had found great peace and creative stimulus in the artists' colony run by the near-centenarian Marian MacDowell, widow of the American composer Edward MacDowell. Toch's Fourth Symphony is dedicated to her and, no doubt overcome by the emotional impact of her death shortly before its premiere, he wrote several celebratory texts to be read between its three movements. Unsurprisingly, these caused a good deal of concern and even mild embarrassment. Antal Doráti, who conducted the premiere with the Minneapolis Symphony Orchestra on 22 November 1957, on what would have been Marian MacDowell's 100th birthday, refused to include them. Toch objected and declared the symphony was not about Marian MacDowell but was dedicated to her, and for that reason alone the texts were significant and important. Apart from questions of taste, or literary value, the texts by Toch do indeed set up the individual movements. The opening is long and dominates the work. The text that would have followed ends with the words, 'and your joy-spreading laughter keeps dancing in my ear', leading into the symphony's short scherzo. The sombre mood returns in the final movement prefaced by a text ending with, 'So desperately striving – what you released in me must return to you!'

As with Wellesz's last four symphonies, the last three symphonies of Toch came almost in a single creative rush. His intention to write an opera based on Lion Feuchtwanger's last novel, *Jephtha and his Daughter*, was instead refashioned into a single-movement symphony, completed in May 1963 and premiered by Erich Leinsdorf and the Boston Symphony Orchestra on 13 March 1964. Following completion of the Fifth Symphony in May 1963, Toch finished his Sixth Symphony in November, after a period of only four months. His Seventh Symphony was begun in December 1963 and completed in March 1964. The three final symphonies were perhaps composed in the shadow of his own mortality. He had cancer, which he kept hidden from everyone until his final collapse and death on 1 October 1964. The final two symphonies are spontaneous outpourings, sometimes exuberant and often meandering as if every thought and idea had to be written down before it was too late. The Sixth Symphony was premiered by the Beromünster Radio Orchestra, conducted by Erich Schmidt, and the Seventh Symphony was premiered after Toch's death on 14 June 1967 by the Munich Philharmonic Orchestra under Rudolf Alberth. This rush of uncontrolled output was perhaps best summed up by Toch himself with the last lines he wrote in a poem to his wife Lilly: 'Ich schreibe nicht, ich werde geschrieben' ('I do not write, I am being written').

Wellesz's first four symphonies are more disciplined and contained. They are classically structured, though not always strictly so. They are diatonic, but without obvious tonal centres offering clear key designations, though his First Symphony is noted as being 'in C'. They have been described more accurately as 'neo-tonal'.[22] Wellesz was heavily influenced by Schoenberg's free atonality, starting in 1908 and 1909. As such, Wellesz created a system whereby tonal and chromatic sequences together with obvious neo-classical structures resulted in his first four symphonies having a very retrograde feel. Their obvious models are Bruckner and Mahler in mood, but Brahms, Mozart and Schubert in structure. His sense of contrasting subjects juxtaposed within individual movements remains constant even when he dramatically throws the stylistic constraints of his first symphonies overboard and strikes out in different directions.

His Fifth Symphony, which followed two years after completion of the Fourth Symphony, is a return to Schoenbergian twelve-tone composition, while his next four symphonies diverge even further from the gravitational pull of serial, modal or tonal centres. Yet amazingly, his sense of thematic balance informs the architecture of even these expressive and often abrasive-sounding works. The ear continues to latch onto motif and thematic narratives that can be followed. This is particularly the case with repeated listening in his later symphonies, though their obvious lack of immediate public appeal suggests that repeated listening can only be achieved with recordings. Notwithstanding, the opening four symphonies are as accessible and 'audience-friendly' as any work from the immediate post-war decades. Wellesz's signature use of wide intervals for expressive effect carries through all of his symphonies, including his first four. Indeed, particularly in the first symphonies they create a sense of profound yearning and poignancy.

Wellesz subtitled his Second Symphony 'The English'. The BBC commissioned the Third Symphony, which upon completion and submission was rejected by the BBC review panel for reasons unclear, unstated and never explained. It led to its performance being cancelled and left the conductor Adrian Boult in an awkward position, having commissioned the work in the first place. He clearly attempted to wriggle his way out of an embarrassing situation without compromising his standing within the BBC, while leaving Wellesz frustrated and exposed, with a feeling of the outsider unable to be accepted.[23] The BBC finally performed the Third Symphony in 2003, decades after Wellesz's death.[24] Karl Rankl conducted the premiere of the 'English' Second Symphony in Vienna. It is perhaps unsurprising that Wellesz would call his Fourth Symphony *Symphonia Austriaca*.

His Fifth Symphony would follow Schoenbergian principles more assiduously than his subsequent works. He justified such stylistic promiscuity by saying: 'If a contrasting musical idea occurs to me that follows different rules than those dictated by the tone row, then I have no hesitation in trusting my idea and composing a work that is tonal.'[25] Nevertheless, his drastic departure from the diatonicism and serialism of symphonies 1–5 can possibly be put down to his new relationship with the publishing house Doblinger and his deep friendship with and trust in its commissioning editor, Herbert Vogg, who appears to have encouraged Wellesz to adopt a more contemporaneous means of expression. Given Wellesz's age at the time (he was seventy-seven years old), it was something of a dare, with the results being a synthesis of abrasion, dissonance and finely chiselled thematic coherency. It meant there is a stylistic continuity in symphonies 6–9 that counterbalances the easier narrative cohesion of Wellesz's first four symphonies, with the Fifth Symphony acting as something of a pivot between them. They share their three-movement layout with Wellesz's First Symphony, with the *Adagio* as the third movement in symphonies 1–6. It is also the final (third) movement of his Ninth Symphony. The Seventh and Eighth Symphonies open with slow movements, a *Sostenuto* in number Seven and *Lento* in number Eight. The shadows of Mahler and Beethoven are again felt when Wellesz decided not to compose more than nine symphonies and to complete his cycle with a twelve-minute *Symphonic Epilogue* for large orchestra, finished in 1969. Of the later works, only the Seventh Symphony has a subtitle: *Contra torrentem* (*Against the Torrent*).

Austrian and German composers deemed 'non-Aryan', who were born at the end of the nineteenth century or early in the twentieth century, experienced a number of challenges to their sense of identity. It became necessary to establish a unique Austrian identity when institutions, treaties and sobering reality demanded that Austria remain a separate nation state from the dominant German nation state of the Weimar Republic in 1919. With the imposition of the theocratic dictatorships of Dollfuß and Schuschnigg after 1933, Austrian identity was grounded in its adherence to Roman Catholicism. The Austrian aristocracy that remained in the First Austrian Republic was only tangentially German, with most coming from Eastern and Southern Europe. This meant that Austria's historic identity was not exclusively German, but necessarily European.

With the antisemitism of neighbouring Germany becoming official policy after 1933, Jews in Austria were caught in an identity trap. Many like Hans Gál or Erich Zeisl decided that Catholic Austria was a made-up concept and personal identity rested in being Viennese, while being deeply steeped in the culture of Germany's Enlightenment, citing Goethe, Schiller and Kant as lodestars. This view of German culture was not recognised by the NSDAP. Such composers and musicians, similar to Richard Fuchs, believed that Adolf Hitler, an Austrian-born, pan-German fanatic, had no authority in deciding who was German and who was not. After removing German citizenship from Jews in 1935, Jewish composers and musicians were confronted with the dilemma of how they culturally self-identified. The choices were either holding steadfast to their own sense of self while refusing to acknowledge their imposed exclusion, or taking on the identity of new homelands, even if such a new homeland was part of a wider Zionist diaspora. It is a subject to which we shall return in a later chapter. It is in their music, however, where one hears most clearly how they saw themselves. The following case study on the composer Hans Winterberg demonstrates the complexity of such dilemmas brought by the trauma of dislocation.

7

Case Study
Hans Winterberg and his Musical Return to Bohemia

Da ich bis zu meinem 46sten Lebensjahre bis auf unwesentliche Ausnahmen in Prag, meiner Geburtsstadt verbrachte, wäre es natürlich sehr verwunderlich, wenn das slawische Element auf meine künstlerische Produktion nicht abgefärbt hätte. Dies zeigt sich neben Spuren ostischer Folklore vor allem in rhythmischen Momenten. Doch sind diese Elemente durchsetzt von einer Harmonik (besonders in meinen späteren Arbeiten) die durchaus westlischen Ursprungs ist, ich meine dies natürlich im weitestgehendsten Sinne.

Since I lived, with inconsequential exceptions, only in Prague, the city of my birth, until my 46th year, it would naturally be remarkable if Slavic elements had not coloured my artistic output. In addition to traces of Eastern folklore, this is apparent above all in rhythmic elements. But these are imbued with harmonic writing (particularly in my later works) that is completely West European in its provenance, and I mean this in its broadest possible sense.

Hans Winterberg in answer to a question posed by
Heinrich Simbriger, 10 January 1956[1]

The case of Hans Winterberg is a story of lost and assumed identities, mysteriously revealed in music written by a Jew who took refuge in a country that only a few years before had embarked on a policy intent on murdering every Jew in Europe. The multiple identities and lost homeland transcend questions of return, as return was impossible. Homeland as remembered no longer existed, and Winterberg's ultimate country of refuge demanded an allegiance to a new identity that he could only have agreed to out of fear. Few Jews would knowingly seek refuge in Germany immediately after the Nazi defeat in 1945, and yet opportunities and fate had forced just such a situation onto Hans Winterberg. His ability to 'return' to his Czech homeland was brazenly displayed in his music, while he appears to have played cat and mouse in the community that only reluctantly and with a good deal of scepticism agreed to accept him.

Hans Winterberg was born to Olga (née Popper) and Rudolf Winterberg in Prague on 23 March 1901. The Winterbergs were Jews and their roots in Prague went back some three hundred years. His paternal grandfather had been a cantor in Ústí nad Labem before becoming the Rabbi of Prague-Žižkov. Rudolf and his brother-in-law ran Fröhlich & Winterberg, a textile factory located in Rumburk in the north of the country, in a region that after 1918 would become the territorial association known as the Sudetenland. Hans Winterberg appears to have grown up in a comfortable, affluent home in Prague, where musical talent was not just noted but encouraged. While still a small child, he was deemed precocious enough to follow Hans Krása, another child displaying exceptional gifts, in the piano class of Terezie Goldschmidtová (born and more widely known as Thèrese Wallerstein) at Prague's Czech Conservatory.

At this point, Prague was a city in Austria's Crown Land of Bohemia. Before 1918, the Austria in which Winterberg was born was quite a different country to the small German-speaking Republic we know today. At the time of Winterberg's birth, Austria covered vast tracts of Central, Eastern and Southern Europe, and German was spoken by a minority of its citizens, with most speaking one of several Slavic languages, Hungarian, Yiddish, Romanian or Italian at home. German was the language of Austria's administration based in Vienna. The country was itself so un-German that Bismarck managed to have Austria ejected from the Confederation of German States in 1866, thereby facilitating the Confederation's first phase of unification under Prussia.

The Jews of Austria's Bohemian and Moravian Crown Lands tended to be German-speakers. It was also the principal language of the Jews in Prague and the Moravian regional capital of Brno (then known as Brünn). However, German as a language and German as an identity were two very different things in Austria prior to 1918. With the defeat of Austria in the First World War, it was decided to dismember the Habsburg behemoth and form a number of independent republics with distinct linguistic and cultural identities. Moravia, Bohemia, parts of Austrian-Silesia along with the former Hungarian territory of Slovakia were compressed into a new country called Czechoslovakia. The citizens who lived within the borders of this new constellation were offered the opportunity of retaining Austrian citizenship, or becoming Czech. The Winterbergs, along with most others, opted to become Czech.[2]

The victorious Allies of 1918 had not solved the linguistic and cultural issues that existed in former Austria, but merely transferred them to the new states of Czechoslovakia and Poland. Both countries had large German-speaking populations. They counted for nearly a quarter of the total population of Czechoslovakia, and more specifically, a third of the population in Bohemia and Silesia. In addition to German, Slovak and Czech, there were also many Ukrainian, Polish and Hungarian communities. To this end, a census was taken in 1930 to establish the exact ethnic make-up of the country, with each respondent classifying themselves as linguistically and culturally belonging to one of the above categories. The Winterberg family's census form was filled out by Rudolf, who marked the family as linguistically and culturally

Czech. This census is important, because it became the basis by which all German-speaking Czechs would be expelled in 1945.

Hans Winterberg attended German schools but no doubt spoke Czech as the ambient language within the city. He went on to study composition with Fidelio F. Finke and conducting with Alexander Zemlinsky at Prague's German Music College. Under the circumstances, it seems odd that Rudolf noted the family as culturally and linguistically Czech. During the years of Habsburg rule, the extrapolations of Darwinism that would result in eugenics and racist antisemitism had already taken hold in Austria, with Slavs seen as inferior to Germans. With the founding of the Republic of Czechoslovakia, an arrogant German-speaking minority found itself sorely disadvantaged, with prime appointments in the civil service, academia, the military, industry and politics no longer going to German-speakers but to Czechs. The Winterberg factory had public contracts and it might reasonably be assumed that Rudolf decided that noting the family as Czech was precautionary and meant to allow his sons to advance throughout the post-war ranks, while keeping his factory in favour with the Czech nationalist government. It is puzzling, however, why Rudolf would have filled in the census form on behalf of Hans, who in 1930 was already married to the composer and pianist Maria Maschat,[3] herself a German-speaking Czech from the Sudetenland.

Hans Winterberg must have had a promising future. There are high-quality publicity photographs taken of the twenty-year-old in 1921, which he signs using his Czech name 'Hanuš'. After graduation, he began working as a répétiteur in Brno and Jablonec nad Nisou. He was already noted as a composer in local German-language publications.[4] On 3 April 1935, Maria gave birth to their daughter Ruth in Prague.

The Munich Accord would change everything for the young family. Following the handover of the Sudetenland to Nazi Germany in 1938, an artificial perception of ethnic instability was propagated by the Nazis. Within months, the beleaguered

12. The twenty-year-old Hans Winterberg's publicity photo from 1921, signed 'Hanuš Winterberg'.

Czechoslovak president Emil Hácha was forced into accepting the status of 'Protectorate' for Bohemia and Moravia within the Nazi Reich. In all probability, as a Jew Hans would be expelled from any publicly subsidised position – a state of affairs that was already happening in Germany – meaning he could no longer work with orchestras or opera houses. It possibly explains the decision of the now thirty-eight-year-old Winterberg to join the composition class of the Czech microtone composer Alois Hába at Prague's Czech Music Academy. His fellow pupil was the twenty-year-old Gideon Klein.

In 1941 Winterberg's wife Maria took German citizenship, presumably because she was born in Teplitz-Schönau,[5] located in the Sudetenland, which was now officially part of the German Reich. From 1942, the couple ceased living together. Whether this was because Winterberg was forced into slave labour or because of marital incompatibility is unclear. The type of forced labour Winterberg had to carry out is also unknown. By late 1944, it was obvious that even the relative safety of marriage to a non-Jew could no longer protect him, his wife and daughter. They divorced in December 1944 along with many other so-called 'mixed-race' couples in Prague.[6]

Anyone who has read the diaries of Victor Klemperer will know how precarious such 'mixed-race' marriages were. As the war grew progressively worse for the Germans, they increased their efforts in 1944 to annihilate as many Jews as possible, removing the protection of Jewish partners within 'mixed-race' marriages. Where couples refused to divorce, both spouses were sent to the gas chambers. Winterberg and Maschat appear to have divorced on relatively cordial terms, as he handed various manuscripts to her and other friends for safekeeping before he was sent to Theresienstadt in January 1945. Another mystery that remains unresolved is the divorce certificate: Winterberg is listed as an insurance sales clerk and Maria, who was thirty-nine years old at this point, is listed as a piano student at the Czech Music Academy. This too seems unlikely, as Maria Maschat had made a name for herself as a pianistic child prodigy. As an adult, she was already an accomplished musician and composer.

By arriving in Theresienstadt as late as January 1945, Winterberg managed to avoid the notorious transport to Auschwitz in October 1944 resulting in the murder of his generation of Czech colleagues, including the much younger Gideon Klein.[7] Winterberg's mother and his first piano teacher, Thèrese Wallerstein, had both been shot in Maly Trostenets in 1942. His father had died before the Nazi declaration of the Protectorate; his uncle, however, died in Dachau shortly after Fröhlich & Winterberg's 1939 Aryanisation. While in Theresienstadt, Winterberg composed his three-movement work for piano entitled *Theresienstadt Suite*. The ghetto was liberated in May 1945 by Soviet forces. His Czech citizenship was restored to him and in June 1945 he was allowed to return to his apartment in Prague. His *Suite for Trumpet* is distinctly marked, 'completed 25. XII,'45 Prague'. His Wind Quintet from 1947 is also clearly marked as having been completed in Prague.

Earlier works that survive from Hans Winterberg's Czech years include a number of highly complex piano works and a First Symphony from 1936. They share characteristics that were common at the time with German New Objectivity while at the same time incorporating particularly distinctive post-Janáček features as found in the music of Hans Krása and Pavel Haas: subjects emerge from polyrhythms with clashes of bitonality and major against minor. The rhythmic energy of Winterberg's music, however, placed it well apart from the typical aesthetic characteristics associated with New Objectivity, while his avoidance of emotional lyricism suggests an attempt at synthesis. He admitted in an answer to a questionnaire sent by the composer and musicologist Heinrich Simbriger in 1956 that he was still trying out different ideas and styles during the pre-war years.[8]

In August 1945 the Potsdam Conference agreed to the removal of all German-speakers from the Soviet Union's buffer states from January 1946. This policy was already enacted in Czechoslovakia by

the so-called Beneš Decrees in September 1945. It has been estimated that between twelve and fourteen million German-speakers
in Eastern Europe were given hours to pack their belongings and
leave their homes, farms and properties. Some walked, others were
packed into cattle cars. Children were separated from parents and it
has been estimated that many thousands died en route.

Following his return to Prague in June 1945, it seems unlikely that
Winterberg, Maria and Ruth lived together as a family. In December
1945, Maria and Ruth left Prague for Bavaria. Czechs were convinced
they had been betrayed by their German-speaking fellow citizens,
even though German-speaking Czechs outside the Sudetenland were
largely supportive of an independent and democratic Czechoslovakia
and had little wish to be amalgamated into Hitler's Germany.[9]
Despite this, following the defeat of Germany, brutal anti-German
pogroms took place across Czechoslovakia with countless atrocities
committed by a gruesome coalition of victorious Allies, partisans,
revolutionaries and Czech nationalists. Anyone thought to be a
collaborator was in danger, and any Czech whose first language was
German was potentially seen as one. The murderous summer of 1945
would have been an incentive for the German-speaking Winterberg,
despite his official status as Czech, to consider relocation. Germany,
despite its position as enemy nation, was the only feasible option for
him. Winterberg was no Zionist and was unmotivated to learn a new
language and adjust to a different culture, or it would appear, to be
separated from Ruth and Maria. As a result, Israel and America do
not appear ever to have been considered by him as potential destinations for immigration, as was the case for most German-speaking
Czech Jews. Winterberg's German language was more important
than his Jewish identity, despite having lost friends and family to
Nazi atrocities.

In any case, Maria had German citizenship and was luckier than
other German-speaking Czechs, who were rendered essentially stateless or, more euphemistically, 'displaced'. German-speaking Czech

Jews who had been interned in concentration camps by the Nazis found themselves remaining in the same camps, which had been converted into camps for 'displaced persons'. Many German-speaking Czech Jews preferred to remain in Theresienstadt or other camps until visas to emigrate could be secured. Winterberg was safe. He was a Czech, saved by his father's answers to the census of 1930.

The following year, in 1946, Winterberg applied for a Czech passport. He explained to the authorities that, prior to internment in Theresienstadt, he had given his manuscripts to friends in Europe for 'safekeeping' and now needed to retrieve them. He received his passport and in 1947 he left for Munich. From there, he moved to Riederau in order to be closer to Maria and Ruth in Ammersee.

We do not have documentation that gives any indication as to whether Winterberg intended to remain in Germany from the outset. We have indications that he travelled to Austria on several occasions as early as 1946. It is conceivable that from there he went on to Bavaria to join Ruth and Maria. Prague had come out of the war fairly intact whereas Munich, where Maria was now working as a répétiteur at Bavarian Radio, had been severely damaged.

Ruth was in a home that was a quasi-retreat for traumatised children. Her education and life had been disrupted as a 'half-Jew' under the Nazis and then disrupted again with her departure to Germany. Hans did not return to live with Maria and Ruth, but remained nearby. Whether by coincidence or not, soon after the communist coup in Prague in February 1948, Winterberg took a job at Bavarian Radio as an editor, a position facilitated by Maria, along with another job, teaching at the Richard Strauss Conservatory. Whether it was due to the coup, or something he had planned all along, he decided from this point not to return to Czechoslovakia. His obvious problem was his Czech citizenship and documentation. In order to work in Germany, Winterberg firstly had to acquire the status of 'displaced person' to be eligible for German citizenship. But to obtain this status in post-war Germany, Winterberg had to find a means of convincing authorities that despite his legal arrival as a Czech citizen, he was in fact immigrating as a German-speaker who considered himself in danger if forced to remain in Czechoslovakia. In 1955 he admitted to German immigration officials that he had entered the country illegally in 1947, presumably in order to acquire refugee status. To German officials, such a position presented by a Czech Jew seemed difficult to believe, and would continue to result in issues of Winterberg's credibility.

On the face of it, Czechoslovakia had by 1946 become a homogeneous Czech- and Slovak-speaking country. Winterberg maintained in correspondence to Heinrich Simbriger that his command of the Czech language was poor.[10] It seems unlikely that this was the case given his earlier work in the Czech provinces, his childhood piano lessons at the Czech Conservatory, and later composition studies with the Czech nationalist Alois Hába.[11] In addition, Winterberg's publicity photos from 1921 were signed using his Czech name, as was all official documentation following his release from Theresienstadt. Winterberg had grown up in bourgeois German-speaking Prague. It was an environment he shared with Franz Kafka, Franz Werfel and the poet Rainer Maria Rilke. This world had been obliterated by both Hitler and the Beneš Decrees. Winterberg's mother and the rest of the family had been murdered; his brother had gone to Germany in a futile attempt to have the textile factory, Fröhlich & Winterberg, restored to the family. Following the communist coup, and viewed from the perspective of living in Bavaria, Winterberg may have decided there was no realistic future for him in Czechoslovakia. His self-declared lack of Czech and apparent declaration of German identity upon liberation from Theresienstadt suggest an attempt to acquire the status of 'displaced person' or political refugee in order to become a German citizen.

In the chaotic years immediately following the defeat of Hitler, it was easier to come up with an alternative version of events that few would doubt. German, rather than Czech, documentation exists stating that Winterberg informed the Czech authorities following the liberation of Theresienstadt that he was a proud German. It was then surmised that he was re-interned until he was allowed to emigrate in 1947.[12] Simbriger clearly knew of Winterberg's classification as Czech based on the 1930 census, since he demanded that Winterberg explain it. Winterberg offered the feeble excuse that his father had filled out the forms on his behalf and he had 'begged his father to put him down as German'.[13] This rings hollow when one recalls that Winterberg was already twenty-nine years old and married. Simbriger apparently remained sceptical, and Winterberg must have been only too aware of the number of displaced German-Czech musicians who knew him from earlier days. When Simbriger asked Winterberg about his command of Czech, Winterberg did not offer a clear answer, only writing in reply, 'Have you ever heard me speak Czech?'[14] Yet in later accounts of his arrival in Bavaria, Winterberg referred to 'emigration' rather than 'displacement'.

In any case, we know that the influx of millions of German-speakers from Eastern Europe was not welcomed by those living within the newly defined borders of defeated Germany. German-speakers from Eastern Europe were even seen as 'racially' different. Indeed, as reported in Harald Jähner's *Aftermath: Life in the Fallout of the Third Reich, 1945–1955*, it would be years before marriages between the communities would be accepted.[15] In short, there were no good solutions for Winterberg. To the locals, all of the German-speakers coming from Eastern Europe, including East Prussia, Poland and the Baltics, were 'Sudeten Germans'. The term no longer applied to those who came from the political enclave in the Sudetes Mountains called 'the Sudetenland', handed over to Hitler by Neville Chamberlain and Édouard Daladier in September 1938. On the other hand, nobody ever referred to Kafka, Werfel, Max Brod, Rainer Maria Rilke or Egon Erwin Kisch as 'Sudeten Germans'. Like Winterberg, they were simply German-speakers who came from the bilingual city of Prague. There is no documentation of Winterberg's ever referring to himself as a 'Sudeten German', though others had done so.

Simbriger's doubts about Winterberg and his credibility as a German-Czech remained. In January 1956 he asked Winterberg to fill in a questionnaire.[16] At this point, Simbriger was attempting to shore up the musical legacy of Sudeten Germans, and he broadened the definition to mean all 'Germans from Eastern Europe'. The fact remained that Simbriger was himself from the Sudetenland and knew Winterberg from their student days in Prague. Documentation and correspondence suggest that Winterberg felt himself to be vulnerable with Simbriger having the potential to denounce him as being Czech rather than a persecuted Sudeten German.

In the first question, Simbriger asked if the music of Germans from the East was different from those in the West. Winterberg remained cautious and believed that there were no fundamental differences, though by taking the examples of Felix Petyrek and Boris Blacher, both of whom had lived a good deal of time in the West, it was possible to note rhythmic characteristics that could be classified as 'Slavic'. He went on to write that if memory served him, all the Sudeten German composers held to models of contemporary music composed in the German Reich.[17]

In the next question, Simbriger asked about the characteristics of music being composed in his former homeland. Again, Winterberg's answers were vague, replying that he could only recall the music of Fidelio Finke (his teacher) who held to Viennese models starting with Richard Strauss but then continuing through Hindemith and Schoenberg, though Winterberg went on to state that the Sudeten German composers, he recalled, had largely rejected twelve-tone composition.[18]

In the third question, Simbriger asked how he evaluated his own music in the context of other German composers from the East. Winterberg answered that Finke saw himself as a bridge between the musical cultures of Austria and Germany; he had little information about the compositional styles of his colleagues but believed his own style might offer 'a bridge between East and West'.[19]

In question number four, Simbriger asked Winterberg to describe his own style and unique characteristics. Winterberg replied that having lived forty-six years of his life in Prague, it would be extraordinary if he were not influenced by 'the Slavic'. These characteristics became apparent in his use of folklore and rhythmic elements, while qualifying his rhythmic elements as existing in a harmonic context that was 'completely Western'. He also admitted to incorporating influences of Schoenberg and Hindemith and had a certain affinity with the idea of twelve-tone music without adhering to it dogmatically. More recently, fifths and fourths had started to influence his harmonic writing, a characteristic he stated as being more 'German'. He ended with a wry, 'Basically, you can find all of these elements in my music. I'm, so to say, a typical musician caught between two worlds.'[20]

The rest of the questionnaire is less personally revealing, though important points continue to come to light. Winterberg explained that he felt himself to be 'self-taught' and admired a wide variety of composers. He saw Hindemith as the most important German composer of his generation, but also admired Bartók and Blacher along with Frank Martin, Messiaen and, despite their chequered pasts, the Bavarian composers Werner Egk and Carl Orff, 'who also have legacies that simply cannot be ignored'.[21] He also answered questions regarding folk music, believing that the melodic in folk music should never be discounted in serious music.

In a question regarding Impressionism, Winterberg explained that he saw it as a development of Romanticism, and was unwilling to dismiss it. Romanticism and Impressionism, he answered, 'placed the individual with all of his senses in a metaphysical universe: this will remain a characteristic that will always continue to be "reactivated" in the arts. New Objectivity and twelve-tone composition with its serialism may attempt to drive Romanticism out of music, but who', he asks, 'would apodictically [*sic*] predict that these were not themselves paths that might return us to it?'[22]

After being asked about the composers Stravinsky, Schoenberg, Bartók and Hindemith, Winterberg explained in answer to another question that he wished to include 'everything' in his compositions, something he referred to as 'a certain universalism'.[23] Finally, when asked about the influence of his environment on his own music, he answered that he felt he had reduced his abundant inner sense of sound and become more economical, turning to 'inward values'. When asked if he felt at home in his environment, Winterberg answered that had political circumstances been different, he would have become a far more noted composer had he remained in his former homeland.[24]

Heinrich Simbriger became a shadow that followed Winterberg, watching every step and perhaps even hoping for a fall. Winterberg was aware that Simbriger knew more about him than he cared to have made public. In a letter from 1955, Winterberg begged Simbriger to step in and confirm to the authorities that he was indeed a refugee, so that he could obtain a loan.[25] German banking officials could not believe that a Czech Jew would choose to immigrate to Germany, thereby casting doubts on Winterberg's credibility.

In correspondence with Sir Cecil Parrott, Simbriger wrote more openly what he truly thought of Winterberg.[26] He described his music as 'late Romantic' and made no secret of the fact that he had little time for Winterberg as a person, finding him immoral and 'already on his fourth marriage'. He also goes on to state that he puts all of these flawed characteristics down to his 'lengthy time in Theresienstadt'. In fact, Winterberg was only in Theresienstadt for a few months, so 'lengthy time' suggests that he too believed that Winterberg had remained interned until 1947; this is stated again in an internal memo within the Bavarian Ministry of the Interior.[27] Of particular note in this memo is a reference to the fact that Winterberg was a Jew, something that surprised everyone who came into official contact with him. To some extent, this fact may even have been advantageous to Winterberg. As a Jew who deliberately chose to immigrate to Germany, he was indeed a rare and perplexing individual to post-war local officialdom.

The dislike that Simbriger so clearly expressed to Parrott may have been based on the fact that Winterberg had been taken up by the Sudeten German conductor Fritz Rieger.[28] Rieger, though nine years younger than Winterberg, had been a fellow pupil of Fidelio Finke. He had also been a former member of the NSDAP and since 1949, music director of the Munich Philharmonic, replacing the American appointment of Hans Rosbaud, whose musical programming had been too modernist for local audiences. Rieger was seen as a reliable conservative, so it comes as something of a surprise that he would be the conduit that ultimately led to Bavarian Radio's performing and recording three of Winterberg's four piano concertos, his two symphonies, much of his orchestral music including several ballets and two of his string quartets. Not all of the orchestral items were conducted by Rieger, but he obviously facilitated Winterberg's entry and acceptance with performances by both the Munich Philharmonic and the Bavarian Radio Orchestra along with Munich's best-known soloists. It possibly annoyed Simbriger that the one composer from Eastern Europe who should successfully be taken up by local institutions was potentially not exactly who he appeared to be.

Despite Simbriger's personal views, he was not averse to requesting Winterberg to leave his musical estate with his newly founded Artists' Guild of Esslingen, an archive that was ultimately combined with the Sudeten German Music Institute (SMI) in Regensburg following its founding in 1991.[29] Whatever Winterberg may have claimed, the truly disturbing element for Simbriger was the fact that Winterberg's music was unapologetically Czech, at least when compared with

German composers of his generation. His claims to Hindemith's influence are as questionable as his claims to Schoenberg's influence in, for example, his *Seven Neo-Impressionist Pieces in Twelve-Tone* for piano, works that offer the twelve tones of the chromatic scale without any trace of Schoenbergian sequencing. The post-Janáček characteristics heard in the music of the murdered composers Hans Krása, Pavel Haas and even Erwin Schulhoff, not to mention Bohuslav Martinů, are abundantly audible in the music of Hans Winterberg. It was not just the polyrhythms or the abrupt fracturing of melodic lines, but the unashamed use of folk music and the constant surrealist themes of his ballets and orchestral works. If German composers of Winterberg's generation tended towards 'New Objectivity', their Czech counterparts, as mentioned in Chapter Four, tended towards 'New Subjectivity'. Indeed, Winterberg arguably had more in common with contemporary Czech composers such as Viktor Kalabis, who was a generation younger, than he did with contemporary Sudeten Germans in Bavaria.

Winterberg appears to have maintained a friendly relationship with his first wife Maria, but there were terrible fallings-out with his daughter Ruth. She accused her father of womanising and he accused her of irresponsibility. Winterberg went on to marry younger women. His second and third marriages were brief affairs with former students, but his fourth marriage to Luise Maria Pfeifer, twenty-two years his junior, was long-lasting and appears to have been happy. Because of Winterberg's disagreements with Ruth, he agreed to adopt Christoph, the twenty-five-year-old son of Luise Maria, whose biological father was a former member of the SS. Luise Maria came from the Sudetenland and was made to join the long march on foot from her former home to Bavaria while heavily pregnant. Christoph was already a student in Munich when his mother and Winterberg married, and neither Winterberg nor Christoph had close or regular contact. Following their marriage, the Winterbergs moved to Bad Tölz, away from the surrounding communities of Sudeten Germans in Munich.

13. Hans Winterberg composing at home in the small town of Issing in 1964, prior to moving to Bad Tölz.

A tape recording made on Winterberg's seventy-sixth birthday in 1977 reveals a good deal of the family dynamic. Luise Maria is unhappy that Winterberg continued to allow the intrusion of his first wife and daughter. It was her lobbying that ultimately led to Christoph Winterberg's becoming the heir to the estate upon Winterberg's death in 1991. Equally revealing, however, was Luise Maria's expressed dislike of certain people in their circle who were antisemitic. Winterberg had never converted nor showed any intention of renouncing his Jewish identity.

It was during these years together with Luise Maria that Winterberg started to compose works with unequivocal references to a lost homeland, as distinct from mere stylistic references. In 1964 he composed a piano trio called *Sudeten Suite*. If the first movement sounds atypical and nostalgically lyrical for Winterberg, the subsequent movements are more representative, with a return to jagged rhythms and fractured melodic lines. Other works written specifically for Luise Maria remain undated, as if attempting to keep these as private correspondence. His

Impressionist Piano Suite offers cascades of *faux*-Debussy while incorporating distinctive Winterbergian touches. The two outer movements are full of light and air and the middle movement is a lovely barcarolle. Another undated piano cycle he entitled *Memories of Bohemia*. It represents the most overt departure from his normal style. He assigns key signatures to each work and creates audible and visual narratives through music that are not disrupted by complexity or fragmentation. Each movement creates images that are vibrant, descriptive and full of distantly recalled memories. Oddly, in a letter to the composer Wolfgang Fortner written in 1967, around the time of his marriage to Luise Maria, Winterberg wrote about his musical developments. As with his *Seven Neo-Impressionist Pieces in Twelve-Tone*, his understanding of 'serialism' is clearly very individual:

As a composer, I have to know, so to speak, all of the music developments of our century and have worked within each of them, starting with Impressionism or Expressionism from the 1920s, during a period when serial and atonal compositions from Schoenberg and his followers were also current. Later, and since my emigration from Prague (after the Second World War), I've intensively followed new music developments that have taken place specifically here in Germany. Nevertheless, after many long decades of musical roundabouts, I've finally found for myself, even if only in my more advanced years, a personal style. It is not just my own opinion, but it represents something akin to a free variation of serialism.

Winterberg and Luise Maria died within weeks of each other. Winterberg died two weeks shy of his ninetieth birthday on 10 March 1991. Luise Maria died on 30 March. Christoph Winterberg inherited the estate and their home in the small Bavarian town of Stepperg, not far from Ingolstadt. Winterberg requested that his estate go to the Artists' Guild in Esslingen, founded and formerly headed by Heinrich Simbriger. Simbriger had died in 1976 and his archive went to the SMI in Regensburg.

In 2002 Christoph Winterberg sold the estate to the SMI for the sum of 6,000 German Marks. The contract was disturbing on a number of points.[30] Most worrying was the condition that Winterberg was never to be referred to as a Jew, but must always be noted as a 'Sudeten German composer'. Indeed, any mention of Winterberg's Jewishness was to be met by a penalty of 10,000 Marks, a condition that was subsequently struck through, while remaining visible and uninitialled by the contracting parties. Equally disturbing was the condition that the musical estate be completely embargoed until 1 January 2031, in other words, forty years after his death and a loss of forty years of copyright protection. Nor was any family information to be made available to anyone either inside or outside the SMI. 'Any enquiries about Winterberg were to be answered in the negative.'

Fears about Ruth's reliability were well founded. She married in 1955 and gave birth to a son named Peter, only to abandon him and her husband months afterwards. Ruth's son, Peter Kreitmeir, would only start to hunt for his lost grandfather in his fifties, and it was encountering the brick wall of the Sudeten German Music Institute that ultimately led to the embargo being lifted and the music becoming available. Since performances began again in 2015, there have been numerous CDs. Winterberg is now published by Boosey & Hawkes, who describe Winterberg as one of the twentieth century's most important orchestral composers. The critical edition is being carried out under the supervision of Vienna's Exilarte Center.

The doubts that Luise Maria and indeed Hans Winterberg had regarding the reliability of his daughter Ruth were borne out. The story of Maria Maschat is if anything more tragic. She too was a recognised composer whose works were broadcast by Bavarian Radio, as were her performances of Hans Winterberg's piano pieces. With the exception of a few published works for recorder, her own legacy of more substantial compositions appears to have been destroyed. With Maschat's death in 1991, the musical estate was passed to Ruth, who left the manuscripts at the home of her then partner. Despite efforts made by Ruth's son Peter Kreitmeir, she refused all attempts at contact. As a result, Kreitmeir was unable to collect Maschat's manuscripts and Ruth's former companion disposed of the Maschat estate when Ruth was placed into long-term care prior to her death, aged eighty, in December 2015.[31]

The story of Hans Winterberg's inner return as expressed in his music is fascinating, as it was more obvious and in a way more daring. If 'inner return' had meant pursuing demons in works meant permanently to reside in desk drawers, Winterberg's return to Czech musical identity was brazen. Indeed, arguably, he never left it. He and Martinů represent the only surviving voices of a generation of Czech composers, most of whom were murdered. Winterberg survived, and in the teeth of prejudice, while living in the metaphorical lion's den of post-Hitler Germany, he composed music that told everyone who he was and where he was from.

8

'Hitler made us Jews'
Israel in Exile

In den Jugendjahren eines jeden deutschen Juden gibt es einen schmer-
zlichen Augenblick, an den er sich zeitlebens erinnert: wenn ihm zum
ersten Male voll bewusst wird, das er als Bürger zweiter Klasse in die
Welt getreten ist und keine Tüchtigkeit und kein Verdienst ihn aus
dieser Lage befreien kann.

In one's youth, there is always that painful, never forgotten moment for
every German Jew, when for the first time it is made clear that he was
born a second-class citizen and no amount of diligence or merit will
ever be able to free him from this state.
> Walter Rathenau (1867–1922), Foreign Minister in the
> Weimar Republic until his assassination by proto-Nazi
> extremists at the age of fifty-four[1]

Walter Bricht (1904–70) was one of the most visible and highly regarded Austrian composers and musicians of his generation. Hardly a month went by without Bricht appearing as conductor, composer, pianist, chorus director or even organist. His mother had been a prominent song recitalist and acquaintance of Johannes Brahms. His father was the cultural editor of *Volksblatt*, one of Austria's Catholic conservative newspapers. Walter Bricht was reputed to have been Franz Schmidt's favourite pupil. His orchestral works were conducted by the notorious antisemite Leopold Reichwein, who later committed suicide when it was clear Hitler had been defeated. In fact, Reichwein's antisemitism extended to a refusal to conduct Mendelssohn even before Hitler's appointment as chancellor. Bricht had also been taken up by the conductor Clemens Krauss, who was on the verge of conducting Bricht's symphony with the Vienna Philharmonic along with the premiere of his Second Piano Concerto. Bricht's symphony had already been premiered by the Vienna Symphony Orchestra in 1935, and was scheduled for further performances in Berlin and Dresden. Reichwein had premiered Bricht's First Piano Concerto with Bricht's wife, Ella Kugel, as soloist with the Vienna Philharmonic.

Following Austria's annexation by Nazi Germany in March 1938, RAVAG, Austria's national broadcaster, conducted genealogical research on its most prominent house artists, and in the process discovered that Bricht was three-quarters Jewish. Despite the fact that Bricht's grandparents had converted from Judaism, he was, according to the 1935 'Nuremberg Race Laws', a 'full Jew'. All of his RAVAG engagements were summarily cancelled. It is unknown whether Bricht was aware of his ancestry and simply did not mention it to powerful supporters such as Reichwein. Most likely, he was astonished to find himself compromised as a Jewish composer in Nazi Germany's new province of Ostmark – formerly known as the Republic of Austria.

Good words must have been put in by powerful supporters as Bricht was subsequently offered the status of 'Honorary Aryan', which would have allowed the concert with the Vienna Philharmonic to proceed as planned. Having witnessed the fate of Jewish musicians and composers in Germany since 1933 along with the pogrom that followed Hitler's entry into Vienna, Bricht rejected the offer, thereby losing the Philharmonic performances. He had friends at the American Embassy, who facilitated the immediate emigration of himself and his wife to the United States. Having arrived in a new homeland, Bricht managed to compose a few chamber works before being overwhelmed by changed circumstances. His marriage failed and his only means of earning an income was as a music teacher at a girls' school in West Virginia. Towards the end of his life, he took a position at Indiana State University in Bloomington and started to compose chamber works for Ella Kugel's flautist son.

Franz Schmidt was the clear influence on Bricht's musical language. Like another Viennese composer of his generation, Erich Zeisl, a pupil of Joseph Marx and Hugo Kauder, Bricht avoided trends set by Schoenberg and Hindemith and continued on a compositional path that conspicuously grew out of the transitional developments between Romanticism and modernism. His orchestral writing was often finely woven and miniaturist, occasionally even Impressionist in structure and harmony. His inability to remain as productive in exile hampered his compositional evolution. Like Zeisl, he was typical of the non-Schoenbergian Austrian composer who did not move to Berlin at the first opportunity. He sensed his aesthetic roots firmly in the Vienna of Brahms, Richard Strauss and Gustav Mahler. Bricht was a friend of the one-armed pianist Paul Wittgenstein, who also provided Bricht with the occasional commission. He performed the orchestral part of Ravel's Piano Concerto for the Left Hand on a second piano with Wittgenstein in a demonstration of the score to the composer. Ravel apparently praised Bricht and ignored Wittgenstein.

Bricht's story is an example of where Austrian and German Jews found themselves on the assimilation trajectory at the moment of Hitler's appointment as chancellor. It is a story that was repeated with variations among any number of composers. Some, like Bricht, were the children or grandchildren of converted Jews; others such as Egon Wellesz and Arnold Schoenberg were Jews who for various reasons had converted. In the case of Wellesz, he no longer considered himself a Jew after his conversion. In fact, he had converted to Catholicism before reconverting back to Judaism in order to marry

14. Portrait photo of the young Walter Bricht taken in Vienna, mid-1920s.

the noted art historian Emilie Stross. They both converted – she to Protestantism, he to Catholicism – nine years after their marriage and following the birth of their two daughters. Schoenberg converted to Protestantism in March 1898 at the age of twenty-three, but realised as early as 1921 following a humiliating visit to a favourite Alpine resort that refused to let rooms to Jews that conversion made no difference. Two years after this experience, he wrote to the artist Wassily Kandinsky:

> I've been forced over the last years to learn something that I've finally understood, and shall never forget. That is, I'm not German, not European and possibly not even human (Europeans showing a preference for even the very worst of their own race) since I am a Jew [...]. It was a dream. We are two different types. That is definitive![2]

The confrontation with being branded a Jew, and the negative consequences that followed, inevitably resulted in different reactions. Wellesz, for example, simply refused to acknowledge his Jewish birth and put his resultant Nazi persecution down to his monarchism. In letters to his wife following his escape to England and subsequent appointment as lecturer at Lincoln College at Oxford University, he refused to mention the Jewish purges taking place in Vienna and merely implored her to sell their villa as quickly as possible and come to England. Admitting to antisemitic persecution was not something he could concede even in the privacy of family discussions. The Nazis already knew of the Wellesz Jewish origins and had requisitioned royalties and bank accounts. Wellesz was simply not prepared to have the Nazis force him into admitting he was a Jew when he was a devout Austrian Catholic. He had converted out of religious conviction and not for perceived reasons of personal advancement.

Other noted academics who had probably not set foot in a synagogue but were denounced as Jews and forced to resign their posts were Franz Schreker, director of Berlin's Music Academy, and Walter Braunfels, director of the Music Academy in Cologne. Other Music Academy directors made to resign were Hans Gál, a non-religious Jew who was director of the Academy in Mainz, and Bernhard Sekles, who was director of the Hoch'sches Konservatorium in Frankfurt. Sekles, also in common with Franz Schreker, died in 1934 after being removed from public life, thereby leading to his music being all but forgotten, with only a few recent revivals. Sekles, like Schreker, was an important composition teacher, with students including Theodor Adorno, Paul Hindemith, Erich Itor Kahn, Hermann Heiß, Max Kowalski, Rudi Stephan and even Cyril Scott. His last work was a setting of Psalm 137, *By the Waters of Babylon*. Other works he composed with Jewish subjects included *Vater Noah* (*Father Noah*) for men's chorus and an orchestral prelude called *Der Dybuk*, both composed in 1928.

All of these music academy directors and teachers found themselves on different assimilation trajectories, with Schreker and Braunfels having being raised as Christians (indeed, Braunfels, as already explained, was a devout Catholic); Hans Gál was a non-observant Jew in whom one looks in vain for so much as the merest suggestion of Jewish self-identity, while Sekles began expressing his Jewish identity in music in the last decade of his life, before the rise of the Nazis. Schoenberg, as mentioned in Chapter One, took a very different position and became a militant Zionist, ultimately reconverting to Judaism in Paris in 1933 and attempting to establish a Jewish political party. He fully embraced his Jewish identity, if not necessarily Jewish confessional dogma and religious practices. His wife, Gertrude née Kolisch, a convert, raised their three children as Catholics.

Other composers expressed their imposed Jewish identity musically by trying to find a *melos* that was modal, but not conspicuously liturgical or folkloristic. It was a difficult challenge, and the degree of success could be debated. A near seamless synthesis of the diatonic with Jewish liturgical modes can be heard in the music of Erich Zeisl. His compatriot, Julius Chajes, following immigration to Palestine, would go further in the use of liturgical modes in secular music, eventually joining with Paul Ben-Haim (originally Paul Frankenburger from Munich) in establishing something later referred to as 'the Eastern Mediterranean School'. Until then, Jewish composers were not particularly interested in ethnically Jewish music but attempted to create a fusion of Western and 'Oriental' folkloristic modes, thereby establishing the integrity of Jewish music within Western European traditions. It was not that different from Bartók's and Vaughan Williams's attempts with Hungarian and English folk music earlier in the century.

Another reaction was to reinvent Jewish liturgical music in order to convey a Universalist message of hope, compassion, love and community. These were commissions by American rabbis and cantors who approached Jewish secular composers such as Ernst Toch, Arnold Schoenberg, Kurt Weill, Erich Korngold, Julius Bürger and others for works that spoke to wider communities than their congregations.

Such reactions and declarations of identity have been dealt with in earlier chapters, for example, the Jewish Cultural League or Wilhelm Rettich's composing his piano concerto based on variations on a Hebrew folk melody. In both cases, there was a defiant stand that insisted German music could also be Jewish music. If one could hear 'Jewish elements', as claimed by antisemites, in the music of Mendelssohn, Meyerbeer, Offenbach and, more conspicuously, in Goldmark's opera *Die Königin von Saba* (*The Queen of Sheba*), might there be an argument that these were as normal and acceptable within European music as any other national variation? As far as Richard Fuchs was concerned, Jewish music had every entitlement to co-existence in the same aesthetic sound space as Bruckner and Wagner.

Music and Political Judaism in Exile

On 24 May 1933, Arnold Schoenberg wrote the following letter to the stage director Max Reinhardt:

Dear Mr. Reinhart [*sic*]

In the 35 years that both of us have been in the public eye, it amazes and disappoints me that we have never had the opportunity for any kind of artistic cooperation.

I assume, however, that even if you do not love, you at least have some regard for what I have achieved.

But this is not the matter at hand. What I am writing to you about is more important. And as an indication of the seriousness with which I write, I would ask you to note my following recommendations:

The Jewish situation demands that everyone who is able does their duty with all of their strength, undertaking whatever is necessary for the survival of our people.

The status I have obtained thanks to my previous achievements persuades me to dedicate myself with all of my possible abilities to this duty.

For more than fourteen years [...] indeed, it was in 1924 that I took the decision to open up a propaganda campaign by writing a play. I carried this out in 1925 and 1926 [*Der biblische Weg – The Biblical Way*] but lost confidence due to lack of interest and, thus discouraged, I put my plans on hold. Today, I – and this includes all of us – am compelled to do nothing other than consider this question.

So let me commence!

At the moment, I do not wish to say more about my ways and means: I'm not allowed to!

But if you read my play, you will understand the most important element, despite much having to be expressed through theatrical symbolism. In spite of the fact that the play is only a concept, it is a sketch of that which must ultimately emerge.

But this too is secondary: regardless of the literary value of my play, I have at least put something together that potentially frames your talents, namely, propaganda that effectively speaks to a Jewish public.

You would have to stage productions in German, English and French, since it must include and inflame worldwide Jewry.

[Typed in red]: (I do not want to forget my assurance to you that there is nothing in my play that any government in the world could find offensive. It concerns itself with things about which everyone should be in agreement.)

I can let you know that my plans, despite my inability to say much about them at present, have found universal recognition, agreement and support. I find it greatly encouraging that so many see a significant chance of success, and that I should be the one to lead the way. (Though I have occasionally run successfully against walls that knock me back.) What a rare experience for Jewry to place trust in a single person.

At the same time, I am happy to inform you that I, along with many others, believe that you must join me in this first assault. You would mobilise a far greater public than even you have previously been able to reach. So, we must not forget: wherever there are Jews, non-Jews will always be able to find out what we are planning.[3]

The manic, messianic tone of Schoenberg's letter may suggest why Reinhardt's response would come four years later in collaboration with Franz Werfel and Kurt Weill. Indeed, Reinhardt agreed to direct what Lion Feuchtwanger later dismissed as a 'Jewish-American Oberammergau' in November 1933.[4] This followed a commission from the American promoter and producer Meyer Weisgal for a work originally conceived in German and called *Der Weg der Verheißung*, subsequently altered into an American version called *The Eternal Road*. It would be hard to identify three more secular and worldly Jews. As the son of Albert Weill, cantor at Dessau's Liberal synagogue, only Kurt Weill had a deeper understanding of Jewish liturgical traditions. Franz Werfel, despite the family's belonging to Prague's Maisel Synagogue, had effectively been raised a Catholic by his Czech nanny, with his early education carried out under the supervision of the Piarist Order of Catholic priests. Reinhardt, born Maximilian Goldmann, had refused the offer of 'Honorary Aryan' facilitated by the actor Werner Krauß in 1938 and had until then been largely indifferent to self-identifying as a Jew. Schoenberg was distracted enough by his political ambitions to put his opera *Moses und Aron* to one side, where it would remain a two-act torso.

Nevertheless, both works, *The Eternal Road* (or *Der Weg der Verheißung*) and *Moses und Aron* have a good deal in common. Unlike later agitprop pageants meant to raise awareness of Hitler's murderous policies against Jews, both works deal with biblical subjects and both concern Jews on a journey, in addition both deal with the ethical and moral questions of victimhood, persecution, flight and exile. In Schoenberg's opera, it is Moses leading the people to a new homeland and the question of what God is. In *The Eternal Road*, it concerns an Eastern European Jewish community hiding from a pogrom and comforting themselves with stories from the Bible. At the end, they too leave their homeland and strike out into the unknown. If *Moses und Aron* asks 'What is God?', *The Eternal Road* asks 'What is a Jew?' Both masterpieces would fall victim to the frailty of the creative ego.

If Schoenberg comes across as messianic, he was no less convinced of his own greatness than Max Reinhardt and Franz Werfel were of theirs, soon to have the ego of Norman Bel Geddes added to the mix. Kurt Weill, while modest by comparison, explained to Mosco Carner in an interview in London in 1935 that he was convinced he was writing something never before attempted. In order to position where Reinhardt, Werfel and Weill stood in the hierarchy, Carner appears to approach his questions from the point of view of Max Reinhardt's attempting to create a new form of musical theatre. He goes on to write a description of what this concept of new musical theatre is, quoting from directly and indirectly Kurt Weill:

This musical theatre maintains above all an epic character: it relates and narrates the paths taken by the individual and by humanity in its entirety. The broad stream of events and deeds are placed in the foreground, and not illuminated by psychological motivation. It follows from this, as Weill has previously explained, that the role music plays is 'not inwardly to propel forward the narrative, or to cement transitional moments together, or underscore events, or stir up emotions'. More crucially, music follows its own course and comes in during the action's moments of stasis. This is only made possible by an epic narration of the action that never permits the listener to lose the thread of scenic proceedings. The music, thus inserted during inactive moments, is allowed to retain its concertante character and be at its most effective without distractions. The objectively featured event within the action is not qualified by music, but rather accompanied in parallel by equally objective musical scoring. This is the point of 'New Musical Theatre'.[5]

Carner goes on to extrapolate from Weill's explanation that it is from this standpoint that the fusion of action and music in *Der Weg der Verheißung* is to be understood. He saw it as a formal synthesis of theatre, opera and scenic oratorio, which out of artistic necessity are organically brought together without sacrificing their distinctive individuality. He goes on to explain that it would be a mistake to assume that this is merely a play with music. The music in the work is comprehensive and offers such musical forms as extensive finales along with large-scale choral and solo passages. The finales coincide with dramatic climaxes such as the joyful reunification of Joseph and his father Jacob; the death of Moses; the consecration of Solomon's Temple followed by the destruction of the Temple and the appearance of the angel. Extended musical passages were also intended for the duet between Jacob and Rachel, or the Book of Ruth, which Carner describes as a mini-opera within the main work. It is clearly music that is intended for singers who can act rather than just actors. He goes on to describe the work as having 'covenant' as its fundamental musical theme, which with the consecration of the Temple becomes 'fulfilment'. In the same manner, Weill has composed a march that represents the fate of the perpetual wandering Jew.[6]

And there, the problems started. Werfel, whose poetry Weill had considered setting as a teenager, did assume *Der Weg der Verheißung* was a play. Indeed, perhaps with, or even without, music. Werfel attempted to have 'his' biblical drama put on by one of the Kulturbund theatres and in his correspondence failed to make a single mention of the fact that music was involved.[7] Reinhardt may not have conceived of *Der Weg der Verheißung* as a 'Jewish Oberammergau' (*pace* Feuchtwanger), but he most likely did see it as an answer to the deeply Catholic mystical plays of Hugo von Hofmannsthal such as *Jedermann* (*Everyman*), *Das Salzburger große Welttheater* (*The Salzburg Great Theatre of the World*), or *Das Mirakel* (*The Miracle*) by Karl Vollmöller. In that case, it would have been a play with songs and diegetic music for illustrating events. Reinhardt's concept would then have come close to what Werfel was writing and perhaps even aspiring to achieve.

Weill, however, had other ideas and had even contacted his father for copies of a number of specific liturgical works so that variants could be adapted for those moments when synagogue music was required. Werfel's admonitions that the play must not last more than three and a half, 'maximum four' hours, appeared to have shown little understanding of how the addition of even a little bit of music altered time-parameters. He delivered a text that on its own came close to exceeding his own limits. These problems may have been resolved had Werfel actually been in America with Reinhardt and Weill, but he sent his script piecemeal from his home in Vienna. There was no opportunity for dialogue or negotiation. Reinhardt could have intervened but, according to his son Gottfried, he had little appetite for the project and Gottfried even postulated that

Reinhardt either consciously or subconsciously sabotaged the work from the outset.[8]

Der Weg der Verheißung was always meant to be performed in an English version, but it was originally conceived in German as this was the language of its principal progenitors. Its initial English title was the literal translation, *The Road of Promise*. The work was conceived in four blocks, as Carner described in 1935, called *The Patriarchs*; *Moses*; *The Kings*; and *The Prophets*. The music on its own ran to 160 minutes, which already confounded Werfel's guidelines. With Ludwig Lewisohn's translation, the work became *The Eternal Road*, and with so many issues unresolved it ran until well past three in the morning on opening night. Obviously, cuts were necessary, but its length was not its only problem.

Reinhardt's original choice of set designer was Oskar Strnad, famous for his designs of Krenek's *Jonny spielt auf* with the locomotive and singing glaciers. Sadly, Strnad's health was poor and he died in September 1935. Reinhardt then turned to Norman Bel Geddes, with whom he had worked on an American production of Vollmöller's *The Miracle*. As Guy Stern explains in his excellent account 'The Road to *The Eternal Road*', Reinhardt and Bel Geddes simply brought out the worst megalomaniacal tendencies in each other. Set designs meant digging out floors, removing walls, reducing seats in the stalls, pre-recording orchestras against which actors had to synchronise, with individual musicians perched on precarious bits of scenery in order to function as a type of stage band. Reviews were good, but attendance, according to Weill, was less good, and the show closed after a relatively short run, leaving a number of bankruptcies in its wake.[9]

More recently, the American conductor John Mauceri has taken the view that the work exists in its entirety with all of its music in its original concept as *Der Weg der Verheißung*, which he has painstakingly pieced back together from its subsequent bastardisation as *The Eternal Road*. The American version had by necessity been shortened with much of the best music removed; the parts that were pre-recorded in New York's RCA studios had to be reconstructed, since they had gone missing over the intervening sixty-odd years. The fundamentals of the work, however, were available and merely required patience, diligence and intelligence. Following its reconstruction, it was mounted in Chemnitz in 1999, followed by performances in New York. Indeed, Mauceri managed to remain compliant with Werfel's wishes, bringing the running time to just over three hours, producing a viable and startlingly original work, unlike anything Weill had previously written.

Moses und Aron shares fundamental ethical questions with *Der Weg der Verheißung*. How can the inexpressible be expressed? Where and what is God and how is the Jew to live? The biblical stories related by the Rabbi in *Der Weg der Verheißung* are intended to provide comfort, while *Moses und Aron* challenges the ability to believe during dangerous times. Schoenberg did not live to see the opera performed. A segment of the work entitled 'The Dance around the Golden Calf' was played in Darmstadt on 2 July 1951, eleven days before Schoenberg's death. His unsuccessful attempts to finish the opera in Los Angeles have resulted in speculation and debate. Schoenberg definitely intended the work to be completed, as he wrote to René Leibowitz in 1948.[10] It has been suggested that his American compositional language had moved on, making it difficult to weld any newly composed act onto the existing torso, while others have suggested he could not solve the dilemma of Moses and his brother Aaron: Moses the true man of God who senses a presence that belies all representation and all explanation. Aaron, however, using miracles and magic, projected God into tangibles that people could see and understand. Yet God by its very nature, cannot, indeed, must not, be understood. Aaron represented the populist, who pandered to people's needs; Moses represented the Jew for whom belief was itself an expression of the inexpressible. For Moses: 'God is.' Indeed, the word for 'God' itself was too confining. One accepts that God exceeds comprehension and representation, either in words, miracles, magic or symbols.

And yet, people needed something in order to have the strength to continue; simply accepting the incomprehensible would not suffice and belief is a human necessity.

Perhaps the most likely reason the work remained unfinished was the contradiction that arose between the obvious grandeur of the first two acts and the reality of life in a city that must have seemed to Schoenberg like a different planet. In his American Elysium, there was no danger, no threat, and no compulsion to rise to the heights of what he had already composed. The creative environment that specifically resulted in the first two acts of *Moses und Aron* had disappeared. Exile in Los Angeles did not inhibit other powerful works from being composed, but whatever ignited his creative imagination from May 1930 to March 1932 had somehow vanished. Attempts to pick up again where he had left off in 1937 led only to a few sketches of ideas and a text that he suggested towards the end of his life could be spoken without music as a suitable conclusion.

If the torso of *Moses und Aron* would not see a staging until a performance in Zurich in 1957, Weill was able to recycle a good deal of his music from *The Eternal Road* into one of a series of consciousness-raising pageants meant to inform the world of the tragedy befalling Jews in Europe. *We Shall Never Die* was a spectacle put together by the American activist, journalist and writer Ben Hecht in 1943, along with another pageant called *A Flag is Born* in 1946. It would be a mistake to call these spectacles agitprop. The propaganda aspect is undisguised and open, but the agitation – call to action – is less militant and more a question of raising awareness in order to put pressure both domestically as well as internationally on governments persecuting and murdering Europe's Jews. It's worth noting that *We Shall Never Die* took place at a time when Hitler's genocide of Jews was only speculation, taking place in the fog of war. *A Flag is Born* from 1946 is a call for a Jewish homeland and is unapologetically Zionist.

Variety wrote up a performance of *We Shall Never Die* that took place in Hollywood on 27 July 1943:

> Solemnly conducted under starlet skies, 'We Shall Never Die', a memorial ceremony for the 2,000,000 [*sic*] Jewish martyrs of Nazi wrath in Europe, impressed a large audience in Hollywood Bowl, consisting of leaders in the fields of business, civics, drama and music and thousands of people from all walks of life. The theme of the ceremony, in which more than 1,000 took part, was not to weep for the massacred millions in the war-torn areas but to honor them as martyrs to the cause of humanity.
>
> Pageant, written by Ben Hecht, moved from the ancient greatness of Israel to the present day, recounting briefly the humanitarian works of its sons through the centuries. Under the executive direction of Jacob Ben-Ami, with staging by Herman Rotsen, direction by Moss Hart, musical score by Kurt Weill, orchestral conduction [*sic*] by Franz Waxman, production by Billy Rose and supervision by S. Syrjala.
>
> Jacob Ben-Ami enacted the Rabbi and the narrators were Edward G. Robinson, Edward Arnold, Paul Henreid, Katina Paxinou, John Garfield and Sam Levene. In the dramatic cast for the 'Remember Us' part of the spectacle were Edward J. Bromberg, Roman Bohnen, Shimen Ruskin, Art Smith, Akim Tamiroff, Leo Bulgakov, Helene Thimig, Blanche Yurka, Joan Leslie and Alexander Granach.[11]

A first-hand account of *We Shall Never Die* is provided by Luzi Korngold on 23 July 1943 in a letter to her husband Erich Korngold, who was working in New York at the time:

> I went to the big Jewish pageant at the Bowl armed with only a cheap seat in the best middle box, invited by a Greek actress named Paxaun[12] whom I had met and got to know and liked backstage.

She even studied music in Vienna. (The 'cheap' seat cost $3.30!) The impression of the first part was truly overwhelming. Two speakers sit right and left on the stage with a spotlight on each. The stage is totally dark. They start to tell the story of the Jews and what Judaism had contributed to mankind. They then list the names of prominent and famous Jews starting with Moses. With the mention of each name a little light goes on (the person who holds it remains invisible – it's a kind of torch with a long handle!). They go through ancient history, the Middle Ages up to the present in groups consisting of scientists, writers, composers. You get a mention as composer and Mr Weill 'un[named?] and un[surpassed?]'[13] had to write the music. Of today's (serious music) composers, they only list Ravel,[14] Schönberg, Bloch and you. Just after naming you (symbolically) a mention is made of Offenbach. This march through time, accompanied by the lights on the stage, was truly shattering, until the entire stage was a single ocean of light. I found the entire thing – by Ben Hecht – extremely serious and dignified. The performance on stage was not quite up to scratch and wasn't able to do true credit to the work itself. Nevertheless – it was a beautiful and noble beginning – just to get it written and performed. The music is in any case better than 'Lady in the dark'. Still, I can't help hearing snatches of [Berlin] street ballads at even the most sacred moments. Of course, it's difficult to judge after a single hearing. In any case, it's tuneful and very far from today's modern music – it's very simple, perhaps a bit too often deliberately simple. (You know what a plain girl I am at heart) [...] Helene – I forgot to mention – was sensational in the few words she had to say in the Jewish spectacle.[15] I found the following quite typical: during a prayer on stage, the entire Bowl stood up. Miss Lotte Walter[16] was also there and when asked if she had also stood, answered 'Oh – only the Jews stood up. I only stand for the American flag' – What a dirty mean Jew she is![17]

There was obvious antagonism felt between those refugees who had converted and those who had not, as can be deduced from Luzi Korngold's final comments regarding the daughter of Bruno Walter, who had converted to Catholicism.

After the war, a number of Zionist-themed events took place with Kurt Weill's *A Flag is Born*, a commission from the American League for a Free Palestine in which Weill incorporated bits from *The Eternal Road*, as well as *Kaddish Yiskadal*, a work he had already arranged. Later in 1947, Weill arranged *Hatikvah* for orchestra, following a commission from the American Committee for the Weizmann Institute. *A Flag is Born* presented a muscular, post-Holocaust vision of European Jewry with Marlon Brando as David, and with posters showing Soviet-style bare-chested workers with faces uplifted to a better future. Weill visited his parents who were living in Palestine in the spring of 1947 and wrote to Maxwell Anderson that this new homeland offered a fusion of 'the oriental', overlaid with 2,000 years of Christian civilisation.[18] *A Flag is Born* opened on 5 September 1946 with fifteen performances, before going on tour.

Equally interesting, and approaching the Jewish homeland question from another perspective, however, was *That We May Live*, with music by Erich Zeisl, in aid of the Palestine Emergency Fund and performed in New York's Madison Square Garden on 17 and 18 December 1946.[19] It was further billed as 'The British Colonial Policy on Trial' and announced upcoming performances in Washington and London. Zeisl, like Weill, also recycled previously composed works such as the overture to his opera *Hiob* (*Job*) and *Cossack Dance*. *That We May Live* featured Jan Kiepura (tenor), Marta Eggerth (coloratura soprano), Bela Lugosi (actor) and Jakob Gimpel (pianist), with Erich Korngold popping up as 'Guest Conductor'. It was in any case not just a Zionist work, it was a militantly anti-British production, with a script written by the screenwriter William Absalom Drake.[20]

The search for a post-Holocaust Jewish identity resulted in a deliberate suppression of any thought of Jews as victims. The crimes committed against Europe's Jews by Hitler were to be seen as the catalyst that allowed Jews to claim the right to a homeland. The concentration camps and the Holocaust would not become a subject until the trial of Adolf Eichmann in 1961 when the murder of millions of Jews was referred to symbolically as the *Shoah*. 'Holocaust' as a synonym for 'Shoah' appeared with an American television series in the 1970s. Neither term had currency in the immediate aftermath of the liberation of the camps. Indeed, many Zionist Jews believed it was shameful even to admit to surviving such conditions. Those who had, knew the costs that survival required and few were prepared to discuss their experiences. The world tried to move forward and forget Hitler's evil, replacing the painful past with a bright future and a new homeland. With every family affected by loss, few chose to dwell on it. As a result, Zionism had little or nothing to do with religious confession and everything to do with cultural identity. Consolidating this identity into a coherent legacy was complicated. Having been spat out by European antisemitism, the obvious embrace was to look for roots in the Middle East, while turning to 'two thousand years of living among European Christians' (to paraphrase Weill) as mitigation.

Karol Rathaus would write the music to several Zionist propaganda films: *Builders of a Nation* (1945) and *Gateway to Freedom* (1946), both commissioned by the National Labour Committee for Palestine. A third film dealing with the conflicts and hardships of the kibbutz was called *Out of Evil* and based on a book by Joseph Krumgold. According to Rathaus's biographer, Martin Schüßler, the film music composed by Rathaus was done out of financial necessity and not as a result of any deeper sense of Zionism.[21] Correspondence between Rathaus and his friend Soma Morgenstern underwent a cooling-off period in their debates about Jewish identity. In any case, it would appear that Rathaus provided the score as a favour to Paul Falkenberg, a member of the production team, 'Labour Committee for Palestine', and a colleague during Berlin days with their collaboration on the 1931 film *Die Koffer des Herrn O.F.* (*The Suitcases of Mr O.F.*). Nevertheless, the score is full of the all-important modal colours such post-war propaganda films required, with Rathaus's *Song of Israel* being printed separately as sheet music.

Such ambivalence must have continued with arrangements of Palestinian folk and dance music for the choreographer Corinne Chochem,[22] who persuaded composers such as Darius Milhaud, Mario Castelnuovo-Tedesco, Hanns Eisler (billed erroneously as 'Hans Eisler') and Ernst Toch to supply arrangements of traditional 'Hebrew' folk melodies and dances, subsequently recorded and released as a series of LPs. Despite such ventures in ethno-musicological exploration, uncertainty remained as most former refugees had been profoundly secular and still felt entitled to their Austro-German legacies. Max Reinhardt described *The Eternal Road* as being comparable with Bach's *St Matthew Passion*. If the Nazis saw Bach as the father of the 'Nordic' in German music, Weill responded by avoiding the obviously 'Oriental' in *Der Weg der Verheißung*. He claimed to have discovered that all such mannerisms as found in various liturgical collections were as artificially 'Jewish' as the songs of *Des Knaben Wunderhorn* were artificially Teutonic. They both emerged at a time of identity-seeking while part of supranational empires. The result is music that sounds as comfortably 'German' as Richard Fuchs's *Vom jüdischen Schicksal* composed for the Jewish Cultural League. Perhaps this characteristic was most clearly noted by John Rockwell, reviewing John Mauceri's revival of *Der Weg der Verheißung* in an article for the *New York Times* entitled 'In Endless Search of a Stage':

Curiously though, the music doesn't sound very Jewish, in the Eastern European-flavored modern American sense. The liturgical tradition Weill celebrated was that of German Jews, and the music sounds very German. This is almost a Jewish Passion, with the antecedents of Mendelssohn and Handel oratorios and especially

Bach Passions everywhere present, from organ-accompanied reci-
tatives like those of Bach's Evangelists to large fugues and double
choruses. It still sounds fascinatingly like Weill, either profitably
suspended between 'The Threepenny Opera' and 'Lost in the Stars'
or revealing the perhaps illusory nature of the gulf between the
German and the American Weill.[23]

The Prodigal Sons

Apart from the events in Europe, there was a feeling that Jewish
worship was in need of renewal, and different initiatives were started
almost around the same time. Two of the most fruitful would come
from the east and west coasts of America. The East Coast project
came out of the conservative Park Avenue Synagogue in New York,
begun by its resident cantor David Putterman. Rabbi Jacob Sonderling
at Santa Monica's liberal Fairfax Temple began an equally daring
initiative on the West Coast.[24] Putterman went further afield than
Sonderling and commissioned new liturgical works by non-Jews such
as Roy Harris and the African American composer William Grant
Still, while Sonderling went further than Putterman by commissioning works that were arguably more suited to the concert hall than
the temple.

Jacob Sonderling recounted his meeting with Ernst Toch, Boris
Morros and the actor and director Leopold Jessner along with the
story of Toch's setting of the Haggadah in his *Cantata of the Bitter
Herbs*, op. 65.[25] Toch picked up the story with his own account in
English, held among his personal papers at the UCLA Performing
Arts Library. As the first of the Sonderling commissions, it set the
tone for works that were 'non-denominational' and 'Universalist', a
model that was followed by Schoenberg, Korngold and Zeisl:

It was a chain of happening in my personal life which led me to
writing the Cantata of the Bitter Herbs. I learned about my

290

mother's sudden death in December 1937. My mother was a deeply religious being. She did not adhere to the full orthodoxy of the Jewish tradition but very strongly to some of its rites. The ordained prayers for the dead in the temple she would never miss. We were separated by 6000 miles when she died, all I could do was to dedicate myself to her way and spirit in reaction to my loss. I attended service and the prayers for the dead in a temple. After the service I spoke to the Rabbi of this temple, Dr. Jacob Sonderling, who mentioned a pending Chanukah celebration for children in which they would take part playfully and suggested that I bring my child. I did this, and between mother and child, for the sake of both of whom I had taken up [this] religious exercise known to me from my childhood, I remembered that, sometimes, somewhere it had occurred to me that the Haggadah, the scripture commemorating the Exodus of the Jews from Egypt and traditionally read at the family table at Passover addressing itself particularly to the children, might in an oratorio-like way well serve as a subject for music. I told Dr. Sonderling about the recurrence of this old thought of mine and he took it up with great enthusiasm and the resolve to make its realisation possible.

It was his idea to have it fused with the actual Seder-Evening service in the temple, permitting the wording of the story and the musical number to intertwine with the actions of the service. The attempt was made to bring into focus the requirement of the theologist and the musician. There were a few meetings with scholars of Jewish religious tradition, among them the venerable Rabbi Sonderling and one who was not a professional theologian but a prominent figure in the history of the German theatre, Leopold Jessner. Here Jessner officiated exclusively as the Jewish scholar and leader of the theological debate on permissible and impermissible texts, on permissible and impermissible freedom of departure or adherence to tradition and rites, and the discussion became so involved and topical that once, when I was asked what my opinion was on the debated subject, I could not help saying that I had none but was afraid that my music might evaporate in the heat of such discussions.

Very generously I was not taken to task for this revolt and a system was evolved by which I was presented with suggestions already clear with which to forge the frame for what I needed as a musician. Obviously it was implicitly assumed that I would turn to the store of existing, traditionally established music in the Passover services and integrate some [of them] into mine. Strangely enough, that thought never occurred to me. My conception of the tale told in the Haggadah was quite different, was non-denominational and broadly universal. It is the formula of the fate that men have inflicted on men time and again. Whenever it happens it causes sufferings told and untold and calls up powers of resistance, told and untold. It happened to the Jews and it has happened to others.

The simplicity of the Haggadah story as I experienced it as a child, not as part of a religious [sermon] but part of a festive occasion, the reading of the breathtaking account of history, the impact of the strong emotions it carried along, stayed with me and made me welcome the task to convey with corresponding simplicity how this story had moved me at a time when we were as yet blissfully unaware of its pending revival in the fate of our generation.

It appealed to me to address to children and to a community of religious people, whose privilege it is, as it is the privilege of all intrinsically religious men, to submit to, to accept, to reconcile the unfathomable with the assurance, the flooding, the ringing happiness of a faith.

At the first performance in the temple, our then 9-year-old daughter was one of the children who took active part in the stage service.[26]

The similarities between Jews escaping Hitler and the biblical book of *Exodus*, along with other divinely inspired reprieves, would continue to be referenced in Toch's output. The commission for the *Cantata of the Bitter Herbs* may have been the beginning, but one finds it again when he specifically chose 'The Covenant' when asked which part of Genesis he wished to represent in *Genesis Suite*, a work commissioned by the Hollywood composer and music director Nathaniel Shilkret to represent the eleven chapters in the Book of Genesis.[27] Shilkret approached a number of composers living in Los Angeles to contribute one or more chapters. In addition to Toch, Schoenberg (*In the Beginning* Prelude), Alexandre Tansman (*Adam and Eve*), Darius Milhaud (*Cain and Abel*), Mario Castelnuovo-Tedesco (*The Flood*), Igor Stravinsky (*Babel*) and Shilkret himself (*Creation*) were involved. Following a near-fatal heart attack in 1948, Toch underwent something he referred to as 'a religious epiphany'. This resulted in an outpouring of music full of symbolic, religious and Universalist references. It was the basis in his First Symphony for the heading with a quote by Luther; the dedication in his Second Symphony to Albert Schweitzer with the heading of Jacob fighting the angel, 'I will not let thee go except thou bless me'; and in his Third Symphony, Goethe's quote with its unmistakable reference to the 'Wandering Jew', *Indeed, it is true that I am only a wanderer, a pilgrim – but are you more?*' His Fifth Symphony was given the title *Jephtha*, and even Toch's one and only twelve-tone work, his String Quartet no. 13, op. 74, carries a heading of hope by Rainer Maria Rilke with obvious religious symbolism: 'Verstehst du auch den Strahl der Sonne, bricht er durch Wolken grau und trüb? – Er ist ein Gruß – ein Gruß voll Wonne, ein süßer Gruß – vom fernen Lieb!' ('Do you also understand the sun's ray, as it breaks through clouds grey and dull? – It is a greeting – a greeting full of joy, a sweet greeting – of distant love!').

In her oral history recordings, Toch's wife Lilly tended to dismiss any hint of her husband's Jewish identity. Her own sister had been murdered in the camps and yet her secular bourgeois upbringing had always represented a social chasm she found difficult to breach. Toch had grown up in a conservative Jewish family in Vienna's second district, Leopoldstadt. When the teenage Toch's First String Quartet was unexpectedly taken up by Vienna's Rosé Quartet, the city's most prestigious chamber ensemble, his parents refused to attend the performance simply because they had no idea how to behave in the social milieu that attended such events. Lilly née Zwack's family was originally Hungarian and they were wealthy producers of liquors and schnapps – indeed Zwack's Schnapps is still widely available in Central Europe. With wealth, social advancement and success, Lilly's family had 'outgrown' religion and it was expected that Lilly, a rather sturdy woman whom one would not readily describe as 'a great beauty', would marry a banker, lawyer or some other individual in the professions. When she fell for the handsome working-class composer from the 'Matzos Island' she undoubtedly had many inter-familial battles to win.

Toch, in contrast, had maintained a dream diary after the war, in which he recorded nightmare accounts of meeting the Rabbi from his Viennese childhood in Los Angeles and having to explain to him how different things were in America. In his private papers, such as the one quoted above, Toch practised his English and wrote articles that focused on the interrelationship between Jews and Germans, the subject of racism, and his own Jewish identity. Lilly was a tolerant stalwart yet remained a sober and often critical voice, frequently expressing quite negative opinions on her husband's work. She rightly thought his opera *Der Fächer* (*The Fan*), despite its undoubted qualities, had just missed the craze for contemporary, jazzy operas. She may have been right, but the real reason this work was lost to the world was the rising Nazi tide that resulted in protests every time it was mounted. Over the last years of his life, Toch found he needed to 'get away' in order to compose. His search for something spiritual was beyond Lilly's comprehension, and it suggests that there is no distance as great as that between people who were once close and whose lives are turned upside down by events beyond their control. Ultimately, Toch's return to his Jewish faith and identity would earn him an honorary doctorate in 1962 from Cincinnati's Hebrew Union College Jewish Institute of Religion.

Schoenberg, like Toch and Zeisl, was also a child of Vienna's 'Matzos Island' and his family was at least as traditional as theirs. His two large-scale works with Jewish subjects, *Die Jakobsleiter* (1917–22) and *Moses und Aron*, would both remain incomplete, despite their undoubted centrality to Schoenberg as artist and as a Jew. Towards the end of his life, he set Psalm 130, *De Profundis*, for six-voiced mixed choir, op. 50b, and left a fragment of a work called *Moderner Psalm für Sprecher, gemischten Chor und Orchester*, op. 50c. An idea to compose a large programmatic symphony in 1937, in which he wished to portray the current situation of European Jewry, amounted to no more than a few sketches. In any case, any work he could have composed that year would have been rendered meaningless by the time the full extent of Nazi crimes had become known. His work *A Survivor from Warsaw* would become the ultimate expression of defiance and rage and a strong musical response to the fate of family members of every refugee who had managed to get away.

It was the Russian composer and violinist Joseph Achron who initially introduced Schoenberg to Rabbi Sonderling. Following his successful commission from Ernst Toch, Sonderling lost no time in suggesting a commission to Schoenberg. The *Kol Nidre* (*All Vows*) is the prayer in which vows made to God but not kept are absolved. The prayer takes place on Yom Kippur, the Day of Atonement, the most important day in the Jewish calendar. It took some time to convince Schoenberg that the prayer was in fact appropriate – especially for him, given the fact that he had left his faith, been baptised, and had returned to his faith later. In a way, this was a demonstration of breaking vows and atoning for them. Sonderling was persuaded to write a more universal, contemporary text that Schoenberg could set, the thought being that it not be so worldly as to lose its place in the Jewish liturgy. Schoenberg was willing to compromise on a number of fronts, the most surprising being a setting of the prayer in G minor with an ending of repentance in a blazing chord of G major. The work required a speaker (rabbi), chorus and orchestra.

With its revised text, however, it was not taken up by other synagogues – quite apart from the practical issues involved in accommodating the forces Schoenberg required in the rather small building of Los Angeles's Fairfax Temple. Indeed, the premiere of *Kol Nidre* took place in the unlikely venue of the Coconut Grove nightclub at the Ambassador Hotel with members of the Twentieth Century Fox Film orchestra. Its text was too worldly for even the most reformed of synagogues. It nonetheless focused Schoenberg's thoughts on both his Jewish heritage and his new life in America and initiated a new chapter in his output, along with an expression of not just his identity as a Jew, but a confrontation with a religious faith resulting from the profound pain of European antisemitism.[28] There was, as we know, worse to come. The pogrom that followed Hitler's annexation of Austria in March 1938 showed what many believed to be the ugliest face of Nazism. The premiere of *Kol Nidre* took place on 4 October 1938, six months after the *Anschluss* and a little over a month before the deadly *Kristallnacht* pogroms that would start on 9 November. The full horror would not be known until after Hitler's defeat. Schoenberg responded with arguably the most powerful of Holocaust works, *A Survivor from Warsaw*.

Sonderling was very much the right man at the right time in the right place. He was based at the relatively small Fairfax Temple, which upon his arrival from New York in 1935 catered to a liberal Jewish congregation in Los Angeles. Perhaps presciently, he optimistically included 'Society for Jewish Culture' in the temple's name. In his article in the *Los Angeles Times*, he went on to explain his vision of worship renewal in the synagogue:

[This] relationship between the bible student and the composer of biblical musical texts dawned upon me while studying the composition by the grandfather of Friedrich Schorr, the famous Metropolitan baritone. The composition dealt with a prayer spoken on the Day of Atonement. The penitent sinner begs God to forgive, 'Turn from Thy fierce wrath' comes in a heavy bass voice. And, then, suddenly the tempo changes from Andantino to Allegretto. A soprano takes up the melody and repeats these words in a startling Scherzo. The composer, a cantor in Poland and a thorough student of the Bible, sought to interpret in this melody as the relationship between the Jew and God. It was to him the kinship of a father and an erring child. It is intensely human. The child, according to Schorr's conception, is horrified because of his sins and so he approaches his father in a repentant mood. But fearing the request for forgiveness will not be granted, he tries with all the winsome tricks of the child to make Him smile. Therefore, the female soprano voice comes trippingly out as though to say, 'You cannot punish me. See, I make you smile and since you smile, I know you will forgive.'[29]

Sonderling was a native German-speaker from the German-Silesian town of Lipiny (today Świętochłowice). He had a doctorate from Tübingen and a position as a rabbi in Hamburg following a chaplaincy in the Kaiser's army, before moving to the United States in 1923 where he settled in New York. Refugees from Austria and Germany arriving in Los Angeles, coincidentally at the same time Sonderling arrived from New York, established a link. Sonderling headed a liberal community, and the Jewish arrivals fleeing Hitler were largely 'liberal' to the point of being virtual non-believers. Many felt uncomfortable at returning to a religious confession that had been the source of their initial persecution. Sonderling appears to have eased this transition with tact, wisdom and understanding.

The next composer he met and commissioned was Erich Wolfgang Korngold who, unlike Schoenberg and Toch, came from a family that had turned their collective backs on religion in all forms. With Korngold, there were no childhood memories to conjure up, which might have offered a bridge into Sonderling's community. It is an indication of Sonderling's tact and tolerance that he managed to commission not only a large-scale *Passover Psalm* from Korngold but also a work called *Prayer*. Mindful of his secular upbringing, Korngold was equally mindful of the religious households in which his parents had been raised. Correspondence from Korngold's father Julius indicates that he and his wife had grown up in traditional Jewish homes, but affluence and social position had meant they had taken the decision not to impose religion on either of their two sons, Erich Wolfgang and Hans Robert. Luzi Korngold's family was even more illustrious in Vienna's Jewish community, with her paternal grandfather Adolf von Sonnenthal the leading actor of the day, a patron founder of Vienna's Jewish Museum in 1881, and one of the first Jews to be ennobled by the Emperor. The Sonnenthals, as with the Korngolds, had assumed a leading position within totally secular, bourgeois Viennese Jewry, a position that was common to their particular social circle. The move to Los Angeles by Korngold's parents when in their late seventies was traumatising. Perhaps understanding the comfort that such religious bridges offered, Erich took the manuscripts of both *Passover Psalm* and *Prayer*, along with his *Shakespeare Songs*, op. 29 and op. 31, and gave them as presents to his parents on their fiftieth wedding anniversary.

It is doubtful that Erich Korngold was completely ignorant on the subject, as he likely received some form of mandatory religious instruction at school. Not to have received any religious instruction would have required a notarised statement that the family was 'Konfessionslos', or without any religious confession. It was an almost unthinkable act in Habsburg Austria and probably, even for the free-thinking, secular Korngold family, a bureaucratic step too far. Erich Korngold and his wife Luzi, however, did take this step, raising their two sons without any religious instruction at all. Nevertheless, in Rudolf Stephan Hoffmann's 1922 biography of Korngold, written when the composer was only twenty-five years old, he devoted an entire chapter to Judaism with the intent of deflecting harmful antisemitic attacks on the still young composer.[30] Korngold would have been one of the Jewish refugees who would have declared that his Judaism had been imposed on him by Hitler. If anything, Korngold was much taken by the pageantry of the Catholic Church, which he incorporated in both of his major operas: overtly in *Die tote Stadt* and symbolically in *Das Wunder der Heliane*. It is the same sense of mystical pageantry that provides the aesthetic and musical language of his *Passover Psalm*.

Passover Psalm, op. 30, is for soprano soloist, mixed chorus, orchestra and organ. *Prayer*, op. 32, is for tenor solo, harp, organ and women's choir. Both works radiate an opulent devotional fervour, offering more than a passing acquaintance with the liturgical music of the synagogue. The *Passover Psalm* also reflects Korngold's attraction to Catholic mysticism with its lush ascending passages, which, subjectively at least, recall the closing moments of his opera *Das Wunder der Heliane*. The *Passover Psalm*'s grandeur was meant for the concert hall, and it was subsequently dedicated to the 'Society Friends of Music' at Vienna's Musikverein following a performance in April 1951. Sonderling compiled the Haggadah text for *Passover Psalm*, while Korngold chose *Adonai Eloheinu* by Franz Werfel in a version in both Hebrew and English for *Prayer*.

The *Passover Psalm* was premiered with Korngold conducting on 12 April 1941; *Prayer* followed on 1 October of the same year. Upon presenting them to his parents for their golden wedding anniversary on 27 September 1941 he included a humorous note suggesting these might be his 'Four Last Songs', or perhaps more optimistically, his Four *Latest* Songs.

The next works with Sonderling's input, either as commissioner or advisor, were expressions of sorrow or anger following the revelation of Nazi crimes against the Jews. These two works, Zeisl's *Requiem Ebraico* and Schoenberg's *A Survivor from Warsaw*, would represent the first reactions expressed musically to the murder of millions of Jews. The sorrow of Zeisl's *Requiem* and the anger of Schoenberg's *Survivor from Warsaw*, however, share defiant and ultimately victorious endings.

As the work's title implies, Zeisl's *Requiem Ebraico* was arguably the most Universalist of all of Sonderling's commissions. The premiere was part of an interfaith forum concert that took place in the First Methodist Church of Hollywood with the Santa Monica Symphony in 1945. Zeisl's designation of the work as 'Requiem' rather than 'Kaddish' already demonstrates its ecumenical outreach and his setting of the 92nd Psalm, with its joyous and uplifting paean of thanks, also surprises in this context, given the motivation to write the work followed the confirmation of the murder of his father and stepmother in Treblinka. Zeisl himself had the following explanation:

At that time war in Europe had just ended and I received the first news of the death of my father and many friends. The sadness of my mood went into my composition which became a Requiem, though I had not intended to write one and scarcely would have chosen the 92nd psalm for it. Yet the completed Requiem thus received a deeper meaning than I could have achieved by planning it that way.[31]

Its five parts are in both Hebrew and English and are, according to Kenneth Marcus, a representation of 'a profound attempt to achieve understanding and reconciliation with God, refusing to abandon one's faith in the face of extraordinary tragedy'.[32] Zeisl's biographer Karin Wagner describes the work as follows:

The expressive introductory theme, parts of which are in [a modal] 'gypsy-minor', is closely related to the theme of Menuhim's Song in *Hiob*. Augmented seconds also play an important and style-defining role in the Requiem and song-like melodies used in the past become ornamental cantilenas, recitative sequences and melismas in psalmodic rhetoric. Modal structures are of harmonic significance while archaic-sounding parallel chord shifts and the 6/4 time-signature – Zeisl's 'prayer meter' alongside 3/2 time – give the work its 'Jewish colouration'.[33]

Schoenberg jettisoned any awkward self-consciousness he might previously have had regarding his Jewish identity following the incident at the Alpine resort town of Mattsee in 1921, which refused lodgings to Jews. The fact that Schoenberg had been baptised in 1898 made no difference. The shock and anger some twenty-five years later at Nazi atrocities, let alone the personal tragedies each individual survivor now confronted, could never be expressed in any manner other than righteous fury. Unlike members of his family, he had not experienced the brutality against Jews with Hitler's annexation of Austria in March 1938, followed by the torching of the city's synagogues and murderous rampage eight months later in November. News of family members who were victims of Nazi mass murder began to trickle through. Schoenberg's brother Heinrich would be among them. Nearly every family would receive news of brothers, sisters, parents, relatives and friends lost to Nazi barbarity. Most were too stunned to respond. Composers and musicians who had lived fairly easy lives in Hollywood were sickened with guilt, and the number of musicians who left film work as soon as the war was over was significant. Others simply worked out their existing contracts, or reduced their work while they tried to re-establish ties.

How the concept of *A Survivor from Warsaw* came to Schoenberg remains unclear. Initially, it was a commission from the Koussevitzky Music Foundation in 1947. Explanations range from correspondence with Alma Mahler Werfel to a suggestion from the choreographer and dancer Corinne Chochem, who requested a commemorative work about the Nazi mass murder of Jews.[34] In any case, Schoenberg telescoped several events into one: the uprising in the Warsaw Ghetto on 19 April 1943 and the mathematics of counting off Jews being led to the gas chamber. It ends with a triumphal male chorus singing *Shema Yisrael* (*Hear, oh Israel*). If Christians believed in individual salvation, *Shema Yisrael* is a plea for the salvation of the Jews, 'God's chosen people'. Again, Rabbi Sonderling came to Schoenberg's assistance to help with the Hebrew text. In its eight minutes it incorporates melodrama, opera, barbarity and victory, starting out with a narrator in English recounting his experience in Warsaw in *Sprechgesang*. He quickly changes to German as he barks out the orders of a Nazi sergeant demanding the countdown of Jews being led to the gas chambers before being overwhelmed by the choral finale.

Despite the commission coming from the Boston-based Koussevitzky Foundation, the premiere took place with the consent of both Schoenberg and Koussevitzky under the baton of a former Kolisch Quartet violinist named Kurt Frederick in Albuquerque, New Mexico, on 4 November 1948. The chorus was made up of locals. When the performance was over, the audience of some 1,500 people sat stunned into silence. Only with an immediate repeat of the work was it received with the sort of applause ordinarily unknown to Schoenberg premieres.

Schoenberg's last work, *De Profundis*, completed in 1950, is a setting of Psalm 130: *From the depths, I cry out unto you, O Lord*. It was initially another Koussevitzky commission, but subsequently evolved as a suggestion from the choir conductor Chemjo Vinaver, who was compiling an anthology of Jewish Music, a collection commissioned by the Jewish Agency for Palestine. It is an unaccompanied work for six-part mixed chorus, featuring rhythmic speech throughout all parts and lasting under five minutes. Koussevitzky requested the work as part of the first King David Festival in Jerusalem in 1952. Schoenberg, now at the very end of his life, dedicated it to the State of Israel, thereby closing a circle that had started with his exclusion from the Mattsee resort in 1921 and continuing until his reconversion in 1933, a period when he decided to stop composing in order to dedicate himself to establishing a Jewish political party. It was a pledge he couldn't keep. Nevertheless, with his short *De Profundis* he was at least able, like Moses, to view the Promised Land from a distance.

Works memorialising the brutality of Nazi antisemitism by Jewish composers who as adults lived through these events, such as Schoenberg's *A Survivor from Warsaw*, Erich Zeisl's *Requiem Ebraico*, Viktor Ullmann's *Der Kaiser von Atlantis* or Mieczysław Weinberg's opera *The Passenger*, express a dignified lack of pathos. The generation of refugee Jewish composers born in the 1920s, with few exceptions, only addressed Jewish or Holocaust subjects when commissioned, and rarely as an act of memory. This self-imposed musical silence by those who survived is telling when contrasted with the plethora of often overwrought Holocaust works by composers who had no direct experience of Nazi persecution. It brings to mind the final sentence of Ludwig Wittgenstein's *Tractatus*: 'Wovon man nicht sprechen kann, darüber muß man schweigen' – 'Whereof one cannot speak, thereof one must be silent.'

Rabbi Sonderling's commissions exemplify the concept of 'return' to community, if not always a return to religious rites and dogma. It is striking that all of the composers he commissioned wished to expand their musical statements beyond the confines of the temple. Also striking is the overwhelming presence of triumphant endings in major keys, emphasising defiance and a look to a more productive and peaceful future.

Musical renewal in the synagogue was not limited to Rabbi Jacob Sonderling. Initiatives had sprung up from San Francisco to New York with approaches being made to secular and even non-Jewish composers. The most significant of these was undertaken by Cantor David Putterman of Park Avenue Synagogue in New York. As already mentioned, Putterman approached secular and non-Jewish composers such as Roy Harris and the African American composer William Grant Still for new liturgical works. Sonderling's willingness to move away from the confines of the religious service into more creative expressions contrasts with Putterman's more conventional efforts towards liturgical renewal. Where Putterman's and Sonderling's aspirations coincide was their desire that whatever works were commissioned, they should fully represent the musical language of the composer. Given Kurt Weill's epic musical treatment of his various Zionist pageants, including *Der Weg der Verheißung* or *The Eternal Road*, his *Kiddush*, composed for the Sabbath eve and commissioned by Putterman in 1946, is almost conventional, echoing only faintly its Berlin provenance. Weill's *Kiddush* is perhaps more literally a prodigal return to the cantorial traditions of his father and a marked departure from his overtly populist Berlin and Broadway works. Its premiere took place on 10 May 1946 and it was featured alongside liturgical works by fellow refugee composers. These included Alexandre Tansman's English version of the *Ma Tovu* prayer and a work called *May the Words of My Mouth* by Paul Pisk. Also performed that evening were earlier commissioned works by refugee composers Paul Dessau, Mario Castelnuovo-Tedesco and Heinrich Schalit.

Beyond the confines of temple and synagogue, other 'prodigal' composers even less connected to Judaism were forcibly brought closer to a community they had no idea they belonged to. This was quite literally the case with Viktor Ullmann, who was born into a family of converts to Christianity. Apart from his lost setting of *Psalm 130*, he demonstrated no indication of his Jewish heritage prior to internment in Theresienstadt. In any case, many non-Jewish composers, such as Orlando de Lassus and Heinrich Schütz and even Franz Liszt, had also set Psalm 130. Nevertheless, it is typically recited, sung or performed on the High Holidays of Rosh Hashanah and Yom Kippur. Over the course of Ullmann's life he had converted from parental Catholicism to Protestantism before finally settling on the Christian influences of Rudolf Steiner's anthroposophy, and in 1936 he reconverted to Catholicism. Whether as a commission or out of solidarity, while interned in Theresienstadt he composed a number of works with Zionist or Jewish folk elements. He incorporated a set of variations on *Rachel*, a Zionist song by Yehuda Sharett, in his Piano Sonata no. 7. Probably it was Rafael Schächter, or Siegmund Subak, or one of the conductors of Terezín's choruses, who gave Ullmann a copy of *Das jüdische Liederbuch* (*The Jewish Songbook*), from which his arrangements are taken. Prominent among Ullmann's Terezín vocal works are his three Yiddish Folk Songs, called *Březulinka* (a reference to the birch tree in the first song 'Berjoskele'), op. 58. The individual songs are entitled 'Berjoskele' ('The Birch Tree'), 'Margarithelech' ('Daisies') and 'A Mejdel in den Johren' ('A Girl Who is No Longer Young'). Ullmann took the basis for his arrangements from Menachem Kipnis's published volume of Yiddish folk songs. It appears that Ullmann probably assumed his fellow inmates knew all the verses to the songs and therefore only set the opening two. He also made voice and piano arrangements of them, most probably for a folk music concert held by Theresienstadt's Durra Choir. Nevertheless, the songs reflect Ullmann's personality and compositional style and are not mere transcriptions, instead representing a synthesis of Ullmann and the folkloric. Ullmann's numerous settings in Hebrew and Yiddish for mixed *a cappella* chorus along with his works for children's chorus suggest cultural re-identification with the community of Jewish internees if not a re-identification as a religious Jew. David Bloch, founder and director of the Terezín Music Memorial Project, addressed the point as follows:

Thus Ullmann, born Jewish, practitioner of several modes of Christian faith, ultimately confronted, if only in a functional, albeit in very artful, fashion, some vivid musical expressions of

Jewishness in shaping arrangements and variations of material of genuinely Jewish and Zionist character.[35]

It may be fatuous to suggest that arranging folk music was a means of tangential cultural re-identification when carried out by composers not born into Jewish traditions such as Viktor Ullmann. Yet it seems little different when even avowed secular international-ists such as Hanns Eisler joined Ernst Toch, Mario Castelnuovo-Tedesco and Darius Milhaud to arrange *Palestine Dances and Songs* for the Zionist choreographer Corinne Chochem. The music Karol Rathaus composed for Zionist films falls into the same category. It seems doubtful, no matter how financially stretched these composers might have been in the immediate post-war years, that the commissions paid might have tipped the balance had they not felt compelled by some acknowledgement of Jewish solidarity.

There were diverse reactions coming from other Jewish composers who found refuge in Hollywood. Korngold, Zeisl and Toch left the movie industry as soon as they could with the end of the war. Hanns Eisler was deported from America in 1948 following the hearings of the House Committee on Un-American Activities. Franz Waxman fits somewhere in between. Unlike Toch, Korngold or Zeisl, he was not a 'classical' composer, but one of Berlin's most successful popular song composers. He was also the pianist with Berlin's Weintraub Syncopators. The Weintraub Syncopators, according to the writer Yvan Goll in his scathing portrait of Berlin from 1930, *Sodom Berlin*, was the only jazz band to have if your event was to count for anything. Waxman went on to make his name in Berlin as Friedrich Hollaender's orchestrator for the film *The Blue Angel*, with a newly discovered Marlene Dietrich singing *Ich bin von Kopf bis Fuß auf Liebe eingestellt* – better known in English as *Falling in Love Again*. Waxman's Hollywood credits can easily stand alongside those of Korngold, Max Steiner, Alfred Newman, Miklós Rózsa, and are too numerous to mention.[36]

It was in the 1950s, when Waxman realised what had happened in Germany during his years in Hollywood, that he gradually turned away from film composition and focused on concert works. By the end of the decade, he had completed his oratorio *Joshua* for large orchestra, narrator and soloists. It was premiered to exceptional reviews by the Dallas Symphony Orchestra conducted by Samuel Adler in Dallas's Temple in May 1959. His 'Holocaust' work from 1964–65, *The Song of Terezín*, based on poems by children in the Theresienstadt ghetto, moves even further from his Hollywood language towards Stravinskian models of mid-twentieth-century modernism. Despite the tragic fate of the children in Theresienstadt, and the optimism of their poetry, Waxman maintained a rarefied seriousness that avoided gratuitous pathos.

Also in Hollywood at this time was the Italian composer Mario Castelnuovo-Tedesco who, like Toch, Zeisl, Korngold and Waxman, wrote film music for MGM during the war years; indeed, he was involved in some two hundred projects, though most of his work was uncredited.[37] Possibly his most famous film score came when Rita Hayworth commissioned him for *The Loves of Carmen* (1948). His overall output is enormous, with over two hundred opus numbers and half as many again unnumbered. Yet, unlike most of the other composers in this survey, he was continuously writing 'Jewish music'. One of his earliest is a vocalise from 1928 called *Chant Hébraïque*. There followed a commission for men's chorus from the Portuguese Synagogue in Amsterdam, *Lekha Dodi* in 1936 (reworked in 1943 for cantor and mixed choir); *Sacred Service* (1943); the 'small cantata' *Naomi and Ruth* (1947); a biblical oratorio, *The Book of Ruth* (1949); *Songs and Processionals for a Jewish Wedding* (1950); and the oratorio *The Book of Jonah* (1951). He continued from this point to compose an oratorio based on Hebrew scripture at regular intervals until his death in 1968 (the last being *The Book of Tobit*, dubbed a 'Scenic Oratorio', completed in 1965). For Castelnuovo-Tedesco, being

Jewish was not something he returned to but a central and continuous feature of his creative life.

With other composers writing occasional film scores, it's difficult to know what was commissioned, what was composed out of a sense of solidarity, and what was written in hindsight. Alexandre Tansman wrote a large *Rapsodie hébraïque* in 1933, the year the Nazis came to power in Germany.[38] Tansman was living in Paris at the time. But then again, he composed a *Rapsodie polonaise* in 1940 shortly after the invasion of Poland, thereby confirming his self-identification as a Polish Jew. As already mentioned, he contributed *Adam and Eve* in Shilkret's *Genesis Suite*, and in 1945 also wrote a *Kol Nidre*. This was followed by a symphonic oratorio for tenor, chorus and orchestra called *Isaïe, le prophète* in 1949 and 1950. He continued to write occasional Jewish-themed works, his last one being *Les Dix Commandements* for orchestra in 1978.

Similarly, Darius Milhaud, apart from early Psalm settings, did not turn to Jewish subjects until motivated by the ambient antisemitism of the day.[39] His David Putterman composition *Kaddish* was appropriately written in 1945, with his *Sacred Service* following in 1947. In 1948 he too composed a *Lekha Dodi*. Rather unpleasant correspondence between Putterman and Milhaud suggests the works, though 'written gladly and with all my heart', required payment, with Milhaud asking for $500 for publishing rights. There were other biblical settings and even a symphonic ballet called *Moïse* composed in 1940 and an opera called *David* premiered in 1954. As with Schoenberg's *De Profundis*, *David* was a Koussevitzky commission for the King David Festival in Jerusalem.[40] If Castelnuovo-Tedesco and, to some extent, Alexandre Tansman composed more and more music with Jewish subjects after the war and towards the end of their lives, Milhaud only did so following commissions. Given his enormous output, including a good deal of Christian liturgical music, his return to Jewish identity seems less compelling than that of his colleagues.

The Children of Exile

The next generation of Jewish-born composers, meaning those born primarily in the 1920s, were less focused on specific questions of Jewish identity, though several of them wrote commissions memorialising those lost in the Shoah. This generation arrived in new homelands as children or teenagers. They grew up with complex experiences, sensing hatred and exclusion at impressionable ages. Newly acquired identities were more important to them than the Jewish identity that Hitler had imposed upon their families. If their parents knew they themselves could never advance beyond the status of 'refugee' or 'immigrant', cursed to betray their non-native status in heavily accented, recently acquired languages, their children grew up with the full entitlement of their school friends, learning new languages without accent, and often reluctant to speak their parents' language at home. The composer Ursula Mamlok perhaps spoke for this entire generation when she mentioned she only became aware of her Jewish heritage when she relocated from the United States to Germany in 2006,[41] where she found herself speaking at lecture recitals and taking part as a 'witness to the times' in Germany's many memorial events.

Ursula Mamlok and Ruth Schonthal both ended up in the United States via Central and South America.[42] Schonthal studied at Yale University with Hindemith, while Mamlok studied with Roger Sessions, Stefan Wolpe and Eduard Steuermann. In numerous interviews and publications, no mention is made of any sense of their Jewish identity. Nevertheless, both composers were commissioned to write works memorialising the victims of Nazi persecution: Schonthal's Third String Quartet, 'In memoriam Holocaust', and Mamlok's *Rückblick: In Erinnerung an die Reichspogromnacht vom 9. November* (*Retrospective: In Memory of the Kristallnacht on 9 November*) for saxophone and piano. Both of these works were dated and premiered in 2002. Schonthal's output has several themed references to Judaism: *A Bird Over Jerusalem,* for flute, prepared piano and electronic tape (1987–92); and her *Fantasy – Variations on a Jewish Liturgical Theme* for electric guitar (1993–97).

Lukas Foss and Joseph Horovitz are examples of composers who did not consider themselves to be 'exile' composers or even German or Austrian composers.[43] Horovitz remained a member of the British music establishment, with only a single work recalling his experiences as a refugee: his String Quartet no. 5, about which he wrote the following:

> The emotional content of the music was deeply influenced by the fact that the commissioners [The Amadeus Quartet, who premiered the work in 1969], the dedicatee [Sir Ernst Gombrich, the noted art historian], three of the performers and I, the composer, were all Viennese refugees. We had made our home in England in 1938 after the surface Gemütlichkeit of Vienna cracked overnight from the pressure of the festering growth below. I was eleven then and this experience had not consciously influenced my music during the intervening thirty-one years. I believe that the long interval provided an essential perspective for a musical work to encompass extra-musical ideas; without such a digestive process, it might well become limited to mere reportage.[44]

Just as Horovitz saw himself as a British composer born in Vienna, Lukas Foss saw himself as quintessentially an American composer born in Berlin. Foss, unlike Horowitz, Schonthal and Mamlok, did compose a number of Jewish-themed works, including a setting of *Song of Songs* in 1946 and before that, *Song of Anguish* from 1945. Other Jewish-themed works by Foss have been recorded by the Milken Archive of Jewish Music ('The American Experience'). His own comment on the subject was: 'I am very conscious of my place in the world as a Jew, but I never ask myself if I write as a Jew.'[45] It is an observation that possibly stands for a generation of Jewish composers born in the 1920s, made to flee their homelands after 1933. New homelands defined their identity far more than the persecution of their Jewish parents. When asked on a visit to Berlin how it felt to be 'back home', Foss answered that he was looking forward to returning to New York.

Émigré Hollywood composers of this generation, such as André Previn (1929–2019), born as Andreas Priwin in Berlin, or Ernest Gold, born Ernst Goldner in Vienna in 1921, had become so assimilated that with the exception of Gold's score of the film adaptation of the Leon Uris novel, *Exodus*, no further reference to Jewish identity was made in their non-Hollywood film compositions.[46]

When we turn to Walter Arlen and Robert Fürstenthal,[47] the two West Coast American composers born in Vienna in 1920 who composed either for the desk drawer or for friends, we encounter a very different perspective. Neither composer sought to have their music more widely known, which arguably allowed them to be more personal in their statements. Fürstenthal's widow assures us that his family considered themselves 'enlightened' and Robert's father was proud of leaving Vienna's Jewish community as a gesture of rejecting all religious confessions. It therefore seems surprising that Fürstenthal managed to compose a number of song cycles with obvious biblical subjects such as *Die Geschichte Jakobs* (*The Story of Jacob*), composed, as he noted on the work's title page, 'In Grateful memory of Thomas Mann'. He also went on to set a number of Psalms and a cycle called *Die ersten sieben Tage* (*The First Seven Days*), set to a text by Hans W. Klopp. Fürstenthal's wife, Françoise Farron, mentioned in this context: 'Looking back over Robert's life, I believe very strongly that Robert would have been better off had he had a meaningful connection to the Jewish faith and community.'[48]

By contrast, Arlen's compositions focused on the trauma of displacement and alienation, none more so than his setting of Czesław Miłosz's cycle *The Poet in Exile*. Arlen's music is inward-looking and often brooding. These were not works meant for publication or public performance but experiences relived. Few were ever performed, with only the soprano Marni Nixon, former wife of fellow Viennese composer Ernest Gold, taking some of Arlen's songs for inclusion in a recital. Despite the frequent abstraction of form, there was always atmosphere with every note etched into Arlen's memory. Later in recordings, blind and unable to follow scores, he could still spot individual notes he recalled writing, but missed out, or wrongly inserted during the transcription process. As already mentioned in Chapter Six ('The Music of Inner Return'), Arlen wrote as a form of therapy, meaning he left out performance, tempo, dynamic or interpretive indications. His scores were notes on staff paper with bar lines meant for his inner ear only. The same was largely true of Fürstenthal's works, but this was because he assumed that nobody other than himself would ever perform them.

Other than his *a cappella* work *Three Dead Sea Scroll Fragments* from 1989, the closest Arlen came to admitting to a Jewish setting was his cycle *Five Songs of Love and Yearning*, set to poems written by St John of the Cross. As Arlen explained in an interview for the Irish broadcaster RTÉ:

I'm Jewish and St John of the Cross was really a Jew. His parents were Marranos. The Marranos were Jews in Spain in 1492 when the Jews were being exterminated. [As the Catholic rulers of Spain] tried to get rid of all of the Jews [...] they went into hiding, underground, and they were called Marranos, which means 'the pigs' because they agreed to pretend to be non-Jews [...]. So, these songs I found extremely attractive and moving and St. John of the Cross was a son of this Jewish family that went into hiding. And he actually fell in love with Jesus, and he went underground in Toledo in some cell that was just big enough to hold his body. [There] he fasted and [placed] a mask on his face, he had a mask made that made him look like the character he wanted to become, which was actually a woman's mask, [...] and he was there on penance, and really it's a very moving story, and he fell in love with Jesus in a way, that when he put on this woman's mask he imagined himself to have relations with Jesus as a woman. That was his inner religious attitude. I'm fascinated by the story and chose to use those words, which I called *Songs of Love and Yearning*.[49]

What is clear from this statement, along with that made by Fürstenthal's wife, is that neither composer felt sufficiently motivated to write a work that was conspicuously 'Jewish', or at least to be understood as a work that could be performed in a synagogue. Their Jewish identity was cloaked in code and steeped in literature. Subjects in Arlen's music such as 'exile' and 'loss' are referentially Jewish, but not exclusively so. Nor was his setting of Psalms by any means uniquely Jewish. In addition, despite Toch describing his Second Symphony as 'Jacob and the Angel' – a reference Mahler also made when describing his own Second Symphony dubbed 'Resurrection' – Fürstenthal makes it clear that his 'Jakob' triptych was inspired by Thomas Mann's novel based on the Old Testament account of *Josef und seine Brüder* (*Joseph and His Brothers*).

It becomes all the more curious, therefore, to discover that both composers at different points in their creative lives turned to *The Song of Songs*, or *Das Hohe Lied*. Arlen took Leroy Waterman's translation of *Song of Songs*, whereas Fürstenthal used a translation by the Austrian poet Josef Weinheber written in 1916. Françoise Fürstenthal felt her husband was most likely attracted to the eroticism of the text rather than any sense of Jewish self-identity. Interestingly, Arlen takes the opposite view, as he explained in the same RTÉ interview quoted above:

Basically, I found something that in some way gave me a sense of belonging, that I'm not a 'Dreckjud', 'Saujud' ['dirty Jew'] but that I belong to a people that have created the Ten Commandments, and whose religion is based on the Ten Commandments that eventually went into Catholicism and the New Testament. The subject itself influenced me, it interested me because I recognised then that it was the first example of poetry in the history of mankind. [...] This was poetry that was the beginning of an intellectual and emotional attitude expressed in language; it was the first of something that's still valid today. We write poetry, and throughout history, people wrote poetry [...]. I looked at it as the example of progress from polygamy [a harem is mentioned in the Song of Songs]: Solomon had 800 wives or concubines and there is this girl who's in love with a boy and there's this boy who's in love with a girl and she doesn't want to be part of the harem. She wants to have the kind of love that now is accepted as a way of life – you marry, you have one husband, you have one wife. It's an evolution from polygamy to monogamy. Because she refuses to go, she cries [...] and she has this lover, his name is Dodai, and she's fantasising about him and he's fantasising about her. And she sees him bounding over the mountain like a gazelle. Very poetic language, and she sings in her words, her love for him – 'as an apple tree among the wood, so is my beloved'. It's very beautiful. And it's also fresh and so new. It's unique; it's not based on anything. It's the first time poetry like that was written in the history of mankind.[50]

Arlen's *Song of Songs* is the only work he composed that was intended for performance. Its original orchestration was enormous and carried out as a student in 1950–51, with no thought of practicalities. Later, the orchestration was reduced to a more manageable size of some thirty-five to forty players. Arlen reduced the expansiveness of *The Song of Songs* to a central conflict: the love of the shepherdess for her shepherd lover Dodai, while at the same time being seduced into becoming part of King Solomon's harem. The music of Solomon is seductive and alluring, the music of Dodai is youthful and excitable, thereby reflecting the eternal conflict between raw carnal attraction and long-term security. It is orchestrated for double winds (including piccolo, alto flute, English horn and bass clarinet), two trumpets, two horns, percussion (side drum, triangle, glockenspiel, woodblock), harp, strings, women's chorus and vocal soloists (mezzo-soprano, baritone and tenor). Arlen's reduction of the work to the conflict between Solomon and Dodai allows the women's chorus ('Daughters of Jerusalem') to act as the narrative engine, underlining the shepherdess's conflict until Dodai comes bounding over the hills to her rescue: carnal attraction wins out in the end, leading to Arlen's main point that carnal love is the basis of monogamy, not the security of riches or dutiful maintenance of family standing. Very late in life, Arlen asked the conductor Kenneth Woods to add an ending to the work that makes this coupling more explicit. Woods did this by repeating the wordless women's chorus when the shepherdess is first brought to Solomon's bedchamber, only this time it trails away not with ululation but into a contented silence with all the wispy transparency of a post-coital cigarette. Inevitably, composing the work as a gay man in an environment unfriendly to gays, the question arises whether this episode also served as a metaphor. In an email to the author, Arlen added the following:

> Secular Jewishness and Jewish history had become a natural interest, part of my psyche, part of my being. *The Song of Songs*, when it first entered my consciousness, represented Judaism in its nascent beginnings, predating Christ by 900 years, representing Judaism in its original state. That meant it was in a sound world before the word Ashkenazy had come into being. My music had to be Sephardic, with a sound that had nothing to do with Europe, Chassidism, Klezmer, European instruments, or European *melos*. A tall order, if it had been conscious. But it was a subconscious mindset that allowed the emergence of this music, representing ancient times and at the same time the unfathomable 'modernity'

of *The Song of Songs*. What other culture, 900 years before Christ, produced a 'libretto' of such forward-looking sophistication? Who else fashioned a path, in a time of harems, that led to monogamy, a Jewish achievement, defying Solomon, the king of kings?[51]

Fürstenthal offers a contrast in both style, musical language and storyline while setting much of the same material. It would be fair to suggest that Fürstenthal's version is the view of a heterosexual man, with the conflict moved towards seduction by offering riches, status and security. As a result, Fürstenthal takes the love poetry of Solomon for Sulamith (the Shepherdess from Sulam) as his basis, relating the narrative from the point of view of Solomon; Arlen reads it from the point of view of Sulamith. Where Arlen sees monogamous love for Dodai, Fürstenthal shifts the interest to Solomon's pursuit of Sulamith. The original poem is ambiguous, made more so with both composers working from translation in different languages. In fact, 'Dodai' is a translation of any number of Semitic languages for '[my] beloved'. Who this 'beloved' is remains a mystery that has been debated over centuries.[52] In Fürstenthal's treatment, Sulamith is happy to be ravished by Solomon, though there are passages where it is implied that Sulamith actually misses and yearns for someone else, who is merely referred to as 'my beloved' or simply, 'beloved'. 'Des Nachts in meinem Bette, suchte ich ihn . . .' In Arlen's setting ('Upon my bed at night, I sought him . . .'), the 'ihn' (him) is not a clear reference to Solomon and the idea of another 'Geliebter' ('lover') is suggested. The Sulamith in Fürstenthal's setting is more complex: she clearly enjoys her passionate encounters with Solomon, while appearing to be yearning for someone else. Fürstenthal's version is set as twenty-seven individual songs, enough for an entire recital, spun out as a dialogue of love-poems. Françoise Fürstenthal offered the following account of its only performance:

Robert wrote 'Das Hohe Lied' in 1981/82. We had the great pleasure, in the summer of 1982, to have the visit of the superb Danish [mezzo-]soprano Birgitte Frieboe visiting La Jolla where she, together with the baritone Philip Larson, then Prof. at the UCSD Music Department, performed the 'Hohe Lied' fresh off the presses, at the Women's Clubhouse in La Jolla, to great applause.[53]

While Arlen sought expression via Sephardic *melos*, Fürstenthal remained squarely in *fin de siècle* Vienna, taking as his template Hugo Wolf's Italian and Spanish Songbooks with songs divided alternately between male and female singers. Yet it remains a point that goes beyond mere speculation that both Fürstenthal and Arlen were drawn to this quintessential passage in the Hebrew Bible. Arlen admitted in the interview above that in the late 1940s and early 1950s he strongly identified as a Jew and specifically looked for something that would affirm this self-identification without moving into the cantorial or liturgical. Fürstenthal's views have been expressed by his wife Françoise, who more than anyone was responsible for reviving his compositional gift. She would have preferred him to have had a closer connection with his culture and his religion, as the secular position taken by his parents arguably deprived him of who he felt himself to be once he was excluded from both country and culture. Françoise had originally wanted to go to Palestine as a young girl fleeing Hitler. She has continued to keep an element of Zionist identity, while her husband Robert was searching and, perhaps tacitly, found these Old Testament accounts a non-confrontational means of expressing a cultural continuum. Fürstenthal's musical language is so profoundly out of time with the age in which he lived that together with his observation that composition brought him spiritually back to Vienna, his setting of *Das Hohe Lied* returned him to a *Jewish* Vienna that existed before he was even born. Through his music,

Fürstenthal remained safe in a time and place over which his creative imagination had control. It was a place that Hitler could never enter.

In conclusion, secular Jewish refugee composers fell into several broad categories, often in parallel and occasionally intersecting. Composers such as Erich Zeisl, Paul Ben-Haim, Julius Chajes and others expressed their position in a post-1933 world by acquiescing to exclusion and embracing a Jewish musical identity that sought a synthesis of Western and Jewish *melos*. The new liturgical works commissioned by Rabbi Jacob Sonderling from secular composers offered a contemporary Universalist approach to the synagogue. Their experience of exclusion compelled them to write music that reached out to others. Composers such as Richard Fuchs and Robert Fürstenthal return us to a European-Jewish coexistence that was happily integrated. *Pace* Richard Wagner, the German and Jew were not mutually exclusive but complementary. Finally, it was the generation born in the 1920s that appeared to be the most traumatised. Most evaded references to the experiences they had as young adults or teenagers unless specifically commissioned to do so. It was the generation that looked forward, still too frightened by memories of disruption in childhood and adolescence to dwell on the past. The clearest expressions came from the two composers, Arlen and Fürstenthal, who were convinced nobody would ever hear anything they had written.

9

The Missionaries

*A vast crowd of Students [. . .] singing a final chorus 'Learning,
learning' (I could hear the music) gradually joined by choruses from
other countries all over the world representing other races and colors
[. . .] Chinese, Negroes, Indians, Whites, etc., all by and by taking up
the theme song 'Learning, learning', student choruses of the various
schools or 'colleges' in all those parts of the globe, and thus swelling it to
an enormous final song of great power, in an overwhelming expression of freedom and the beatuy of a 'higher race' (not a 'master race' in
the villainous sense of Hitler's misunderstood Nietzsche) . . .*
Austrian composer Ernst Kanitz (1894–1978),
in a letter dated 16 March 1945[1]

Before we start to look at musicians who through exile would end
up spreading the 'Gospel' of Austro-German music, it is worth
once again reviewing their options. In contrast to Chapter One, we
shall view these through contemporary eyes, rather than through the
prisms of hindsight. Which aspects of Austro-German traditions
were disseminated depended very much on fate and geography.

When compared with modern migration phenomena, the 500,000
individuals who fled Nazi-occupied Europe seem almost insignificant.[2]

This relatively small number was, however, something of an elite. It has already been mentioned that it was primarily musicians with international connections or funds held in foreign banks who managed to escape. Until 1938 and the annexation of Austria, the principal destinations of émigrés were countries in Europe. It was generally assumed that the Hitler regime would not be able to survive and it was best to remain relatively local and ready to return. About 160,000 found refuge in France, Switzerland, Czechoslovakia, the Netherlands and Scandinavia. The United States was not generally considered an option since it was geographically distant and considered a point from which there could be no return.[3] Only when Austria fell, the Sudetenland was subsumed by Nazi Germany and Czechoslovakia broken up in 1939, not to mention the continuing pogroms, including the so-called *Kristallnacht* of 9 November 1938, did the United States start to look more appealing as a destination. By the spring of 1939 it was looking as if war was unavoidable. The disastrous Évian Conference of July 1938 had not only signalled to Hitler that a policy of removing Jews was seen as reasonable, since so many countries had specifically ruled out taking Jewish refugees, it also signalled to Jews that the possibilities for flight were diminishing. European countries that had opened doors to refugees with the assumption they would soon return to their home country started to reconsider their policies as war looked inevitable.

Palestine and Turkey had started to take a limited number of refugees. In the case of Palestine, these were Zionists from the wealthy German bourgeoisie, and in the case of Turkey it was an attempt to modernise under the Atatürk dictatorship. Paul Frankenburger, later known as Paul Ben-Haim, along with Joseph Tal and for a brief time Stefan Wolpe and Julius Chajes, were the most prominent music émigrés to Palestine after 1933. Paul Hindemith left Germany for Istanbul in 1935, where he remained until he immigrated first to Switzerland in 1938 and then America in 1940. Other musicians arriving as teachers in Ankara were Eduard Zuckmayer, brother of the writer Carl Zuckmayer, and Ernst Praetorius.

Under the presidency of Franklin D. Roosevelt, the intake of immigrants was expanded in order to build up America's cultural and educational institutions. Previously, immigration was based on the potential contribution to American prosperity. The United States was still seen as a young country only gradually coming of age and recognising the need to shore up its own cultural institutions. With the expulsion of some 3,000 academics from German and Austrian universities, an effort was made by various public and private initiatives to bring them onto American campuses. For several musicians, such as Hanns Eisler, Ernst Toch, Rudolf Kolisch and the music critic Max Graf, Alvin Johnson's New School of Social Research and his 'University in Exile' set up in 1933 offered a lifeline. Great Britain started a similar attempt to profit from Germany's brain drain, but it could not compete with American funding and opportunities.

When it became clear that war was inevitable and countries started to close borders, few options were left to those intent on flight. As already mentioned, Mexico was the only country that regarded the annexation of Austria in 1938 as illegal. It took in several thousand Austrians, many of whom would later immigrate to other South American destinations or the United States. Japan also issued a number of visas, offering teaching opportunities to Thomas Mann's brother-in-law Klaus Pringsheim and the composer Manfred Gurlitt. Some 18,000 Austrian émigrés found refuge in Shanghai, one of the few destinations that did not require a visa. Others managed to flee to Australia and New Zealand, though a few of the musicians who arrived in Australia came as deportees from Great Britain. A few made it to India. A fair number made it to the Soviet Union and even managed to survive Stalin's purges. Nearly half of those fleeing Hitler after 1938 would head to South and Central America. Countries such as Cuba, the Dominican Republic and Bolivia took in over 100,000 refugees, though most viewed these countries as staging posts until American visas were issued. More important were Buenos Aires, Montevideo, Santiago and Rio de

Janeiro. Even Lima was able to assemble its National Orchestra of Peru under the Austrian Theo Buchwald. The ensemble was largely made up of refugees.

Attention, when given at all to music refugees in these distant parts of the world, invariably relates to contributions made post-immigration. Most became respected teachers or initiated European-style cultural institutions. The gains of host countries have filled many books, especially those regarding refugees arriving in the United States, Great Britain and Australia.[4]

Two processes are required in assessing the question of exile: emigration (leaving a country) and immigration (arriving in a new country). Each of these processes presented enormous difficulties, and created uncertainty and confusion. Mark Wischnitzer (1882–1955), Secretary General of the Hilfsverein der deutschen Juden (German Jewish Aid Society) in Berlin until his immigration to Paris in 1938, wrote an article published in the journal *Jewish Social Studies* in 1941, though written before the outbreak of war. Wischnitzer's article was on Jewish emigration from 1933 to 1938 and is particularly fascinating because it is written 'on the ground' without the benefit of hindsight.[5] It stands as a fascinating counterpoint to Chapter One, in which numbers are cited following decades of research. It also regards the Évian Conference as altogether more positive and does not view it as the propaganda coup later spun by the Nazi government. Wischnitzer uses the data acquired by the Hilfsverein as a basis for assessing the number of Jews leaving Germany after Hitler's appointment as chancellor and divides Jewish emigration into four periods: 1933–35; 1936–37; March–November 1938; and the period following the November pogroms in 1938. The article does not include Germany's absorption of Bohemia and Moravia, though it was written after the Nazi acquisition of Czechoslovakia's Sudetenland province. It also highlights the conditions required at the time for immigration into potential new homelands.

In summary, Wischnitzer mentions the initial panic with the appointment of Hitler as chancellor and four weeks later when parliament handed power to the executive. Physical violence against Jews as well as legislation restricted their ability to carry out certain professions, resulting in an initial wave of immigration into neighbouring countries. Wischnitzer refers to this initial period as creating a refugee crisis with as many as 80,000 Germans leaving the country. Concentration camps were already a reality as were physical threats aimed at individuals. This resulted equally in a crisis in Germany's neighbours until the autumn of 1933 when a large number of Jews could relocate to Palestine and the United States. Interestingly, during the autumn of 1933 emigration had started to fall considerably. Only ten to twenty applications were made to the Hilfsverein in early 1934, dropping from a high of 400–500 made in early 1933. The thinking was that Jews in Germany would merely learn to adjust to the new environment and, indeed, some local authorities such as Württemberg even issued orders prohibiting discrimination against 'non-Aryans' in November 1934. Indeed, police were instructed to protect Jews from attacks or hindrances to carrying out their trades. What was deemed acceptable was the removal of 'non-Aryans' from the civil service, while allowing the rest of the economy to carry on as before. By May 1934, the Hilfsverein was advising Jews to emigrate only in the interests of securing work abroad or securing a future for their children where they could be educated without exclusion. Otherwise, the view was 'to stay in their homeland, Germany, whose future was their own'.[6]

The passage of the Nuremberg Laws would result in a second wave of Jewish emigration. If most of the émigrés from 1933 to 1935 went to Palestine, from 1936 onwards, emigration started to expand further overseas, with North, Central and South America along with South Africa being the principal destinations. Nevertheless, it was at this time that nationalist policies, particularly those of the British Commonwealth, only allowed immigrants with specialist qualifications, leading to large retraining programmes being run by German and non-German Jewish organisations. The problem in Germany remained that highly qualified Jews in the professions found themselves excluded from employment altogether, while at the same time, their qualifications were not transferable to the extent that allowed possible entry and immigration into one of the Commonwealth nations. Also in 1937, Jews in Germany were having their passports taken away in order to stop them travelling short-term into neighbouring countries and force them into more permanent and distant immigration.[7]

At the start of 1938, the third period of emigration, 140,000 Jews had left Germany with an estimated 360,000 still remaining. With the annexation of Austria in March, this number rose to 540,000. Wischnitzer makes clear that what German Jews had progressively suffered over five years befell Austrian Jews overnight. A rush to the borders resulted in some 4,710 Austrian Jews managing to leave the country without any help at all from Jewish aid organisations. Without employment and with continued persecution, it was clear to Austrian Jews they needed to leave. By October 1938, 11,568 had emigrated.[8]

In the first half of 1938, emigration numbers were relatively low in the rest of Germany. With the *Gewerbeordnung* (Regulation of the Professions) of 6 July, restrictions were brought in that essentially rendered Jews unemployable. The 150 to 200 daily approaches for advice on emigration to the Jewish Aid Society in Berlin at the end of 1937 had exploded to thousands a day by April 1938. Countries that previously had absorbed Jewish immigrants had started to close their doors, leading President Roosevelt to convene the Évian Conference, 6–15 July 1938. Delegates from thirty-two governments attended, though those representing Jewish aid organisations were not invited. Nevertheless, the representative of Berlin's Jewish Aid Society submitted reports to the conference enumerating the current state of Jewish emigration. High hopes were placed in the resultant Intergovernmental Committee set up in London in August 1938, but what plans could be put in place, such as finding commonality in admission policies, priority offered to younger émigrés and financial help, were thwarted by further restrictive measures being imposed in Germany.

The fourth period of emigration followed the pogroms starting on 9 November 1938, resulting in the destruction of nearly all of the country's synagogues along with attacks on homes and those places of work still available to Jews. The costs for the damages were to be covered by the Jews as the German government openly blamed them for the 'nation's outrage'. This was ostensibly done in an effort to force remaining Jews to leave the country. The degree of Nazi chicanery is at this point breathtaking. George Rublee, who headed the Intergovernmental Committee in London, had attempted to negotiate with the German government in September 1938, only to be frustrated by the crisis of the Sudetenland. By December he had procured an agreement that would allow 30,000 wage-earning Jews to emigrate, with their families to follow. At this point, the German government estimated there were some 600,000 people defined as Jews by the Nuremberg Laws. The Nazi government gave a commitment to house and care for those Jews too elderly or infirm to emigrate and to find appropriate employment for those Jews still awaiting an opportunity to leave. A trust fund that enabled emigration would be managed by Nazi-appointed trustees consisting of two Germans and one foreign trustee.

As a frightening glimpse into the situation at the time of Wischnitzer's article, he stated that he was alarmed to learn that Jews who were designated for emigration were instead being forced into 'manual labour in special camps'. He also mentioned the difficulties of finding group-settlement schemes, with Palestine no longer accepting immigration by German Jews. In other words, it was considered feasible to try and set up colonies or groups of Jewish immigrants in different countries as an alternative to Palestine. Indeed, one such experiment was attempted in Argentina, while other countries considered for such 'group settlements' were Brazil, Costa Rica, Madagascar and Kenya. Referred to as *ordre du jour* was a scheme being considered in British Guiana. Wischnitzer went on to mention other places under consideration such as Bolivia and north-western Australia.

And finally, Wischnitzer mentioned the principal obstacle as being the inability of Jews to take money out of the country. Germany wanted to rid itself of Jews, but it intended to keep their money by imposing prohibitive emigration taxes called *Reichsfluchtsteuer* (Reich Flight Tax), making emigration of the middle classes nearly impossible.

Perhaps the most interesting points made in Wischnitzer's article were the conditions in potential places of refuge for fleeing German Jews. He broke them down into the specific rubrics of 'Asia', in which he included Palestine, China (Shanghai); the Philippines, India, Iraq, Iran, Hong Kong, Thailand and others; North America; Central America; the Caribbean; South America; Australasia and Africa, in which he included South Africa (including today's Namibia); Rhodesia (Zimbabwe) and Kenya.[9]

The scope of this chapter is limited given the huge diversity of new homelands and the equally diverse selection of musical refugees. For that reason, we shall look at some of the less familiar individuals in less familiar countries of refuge. Of interest is the unique impact of immigration within new environments. There was refuge in the Old World (Russia or the USSR); China (Shanghai), India and various European countries. There was also refuge in the New World: the Americas, South Africa and Australasia. Different individuals spotted different needs and different opportunities depending on who they were, what particular talents they brought, and where they ended up. As there is already a good deal of literature on immigration to the United States, the United Kingdom and Australia, this chapter will look at less familiar corners of the globe and the influence that music immigration could bring.

Austro-German New Musical Ideas in Distant Places

Schoenberg's arrival in America and his interactions as an émigré, including his dysfunctional relationship with local film studios, is well known. He was held in awe by fellow émigrés who knew him from Vienna, Berlin and Paris. Regardless of the validity of twelve-tone as a compositional language, he was highly regarded as a teacher, giving classes to some of America's brightest young students. To an almost comical degree he fit the stereotypical profile of the European master passing on knowledge and wisdom to a naïve generation of New World talent. The wider influence of Schoenberg's ideas to a diaspora beyond the United States, Austria and Germany is more surprising. Perhaps two of the most surprising places where Schoenbergian ideas would take hold were Shanghai and Moscow, cities in countries that by imposing Communism, rejected what it considered elitist, or 'formulaic', music. Under such systems, the composer was a servant of the people and was expected to write music whether simple or complex, that emboldened their respective societies. Perhaps it was a sense of being beyond local conventions that gave the Second Viennese School a certain *frisson*. In any case, serialism by its nature did not reflect Western European diatonic tonality, which alone may have facilitated pre-communist interest in China in Schoenberg's music, while offering an alternative tonal language to the decreed conventions of Soviet Russia. It appears to have allowed a certain ethnomusicological synthesis of musical languages.

The Second Viennese School in China

Returning to Wischnitzer's 1941 essay on German Jewish emigration, he writes regarding China:

In one spot in Asia, Jewish refugees from Germany entered without restriction. This was the International Zone in Shanghai.

Beginning with the last months of 1938, each boat arriving in Shanghai landed hundreds of Jews. Early in 1939, the number of the arrivals reached 4,000, of whom ten percent at the maximum could maintain themselves for the time being, the rest being dependent on the local welfare committee. The Shanghai emigration was mainly forced by the Gestapo.[10]

Surprisingly, three disciples of Vienna's Schoenberg School would arrive in Shanghai: the German composer Julius Schloß, the Viennese pianist Karl Steiner and the Berlin composer Wolfgang Fraenkel.[11] As mentioned by Wischnitzer, all three had been detained in concentration camps before arriving in Shanghai in 1939. Apart from Julius Schloß, who studied with Berg, neither Steiner nor Fraenkel had direct contact with Schoenberg or his primary circle prior to immigration, though Fraenkel met Schoenberg in his final years in Los Angeles. Steiner studied piano with the Schoenberg pupil Olga Novakovic (1884–1946), but Fraenkel appears to have moved toward twelve-tone composition based on ideas and theories he had come to second- or third-hand.

Similar to Richard Fuchs, Fraenkel was catapulted into composition by his participation in the Kulturbund. Although, like Fuchs, he was a thoroughly trained musician, he went into law and became a judge until all Jews on the public payroll were dismissed in April 1933. Where Fraenkel appears to differ from Fuchs (whose career as an architect was disrupted in the same manner as Fraenkel's as a judge) is in the character, number and scale of works he composed before participating in the Kulturbund. Despite composing twelve-tone works along with other works in a more general modernist style during the 1920s and early 1930s, there appears to be no evidence that Fraenkel had contact with either Schoenberg or any of his pupils during the years in which they were in Berlin simultaneously (1925–33). Of course, in a city like Berlin, it is possible that their paths crossed, but there is no evidence of this.

Fraenkel was interned in Sachsenhausen concentration camp following the pogroms of November 1938, but on the basis of being only 'half Jewish' he was released on the condition that he leave the country. Shanghai did not require a visa, meaning it was Fraenkel's only option at this late point. He arrived in either the last week of April or early May 1939, where he joined more than 12,000 German and Austrian Jews also seeking refuge in China. By 1945, it would have been home to between 18,000 and 20,000 refugees arriving from every corner of Nazi-occupied Europe. Cultural, social and hygienic conditions in China were vastly different from anything someone coming from Europe could comprehend, quite apart from language difficulties. In addition, refugees arriving in Shanghai came with little more than the clothes on their backs and only the equivalent of a few dollars in their pockets. Initially, new arrivals found themselves dependent on local Jewish aid organisations. Fraenkel lived in the so-called 'French Concession' of Shanghai in addition to other addresses in the cosmopolitan centre. The Japanese invasion and occupation of Shanghai had already taken place in 1937. The Japanese occupiers were subsequently pressured by their Nazi allies to move Jewish refugees into a concentration camp, the proposed location of which was to have been on one of the islands off the coast. This suggestion was never realised, though the Japanese did move stateless citizens (meaning Jewish refugees) into a ghetto in Hongkew in February 1943.

Fraenkel must have been able to start working as a musician soon after his arrival in Shanghai. He even played viola, occasionally violin, in the Shanghai Municipal Orchestra, an ensemble founded in the 1920s largely made up of Russians and initially intended for Shanghai's cosmopolitan population. The Italian conductor Mario Paci (1878–1946) was encouraging Shanghai's Chinese population to attend performances from as early as 1925, and by 1931 he was even hiring Chinese musicians as part of the ensemble. It gave weekly concerts, and despite being officially dissolved in 1942, the Japanese occupiers appear to have kept some of the ensemble intact. At least Fraenkel was spared the hardships of Karl Steiner, who was reduced to playing accordion in cafés and bars.

From 1945, Fraenkel also conducted a youth orchestra made up entirely of Chinese students from the local Conservatory, including a programme of Mendelssohn's Violin Concerto and Beethoven's 'Pastoral' Symphony.[12] Indeed, as early as 1941, Fraenkel was invited to join the faculty of Shanghai's Conservatory, teaching theory and composition. During the Japanese invasion and occupation, he seems to have managed an awkward diplomatic balance in order to keep the Conservatory operating, perhaps even considering immigrating to Japan, as his colleague Manfred Gurlitt had done thanks to the efforts of the Japanese conductor Hidemaro Konoe.[13] In addition to teaching in Shanghai, Fraenkel taught a few semesters in Nanjing as well as giving private lessons, enabling him to earn more than his salary at the Conservatory. Fraenkel taught traditional harmony, counterpoint and free counterpoint and often applied unconventional methods, once advising a student to toss dice as to where to go next in a harmonic progression rather than follow strict rules.[14] Nevertheless, it also appears, based on his lecture and teaching notes, that Fraenkel was inclined to follow modernist European trends of the period, including Schoenbergian ideas. These ideas imparted to various pupils began to result in a synthesis of the Viennese school and traditional Chinese music. Seen today, certain works can be viewed as the starting point of modernist Chinese composition. Fraenkel's own works would in turn start to incorporate characteristics of Chinese scales, intervals and harmonics within his broader dodecaphonic canvas.

Beyond some arrangements of Bach and Handel, however, Fraenkel's works were never performed in Shanghai. Nevertheless, he appears to have been reasonably productive, composing in nearly every genre, though almost everything he began during this period remained unfinished. His two completed works during his eight years in Shanghai were *Drei Orchesterlieder* (*Three Orchestral Songs*), based on Chinese poems from the Tang and Song dynasties translated into German by Vinzenz Hundhausen, and *Drei zweistimmige Praeludien* (*Three Two-Part Preludes*) for piano, twelve-tone works that Christian Utz speculates were used for teaching purposes.[15]

Nevertheless, following Fraenkel's departure from China in 1947, his fascination with Chinese and Japanese classical music continued. He made transcriptions of both from gramophone recordings and notated them with the intention of using Western orchestrations. Despite considerable recognition as a composer following his departure from China to the United States in the course of China's civil war, Fraenkel's true legacy remains his teaching and influence on a generation of Chinese composers. Yet as a composer he still won a number of prestigious international prizes, such as the Busoni Prize in 1957, the Queen Elisabeth of Belgium Prize in 1962 and the Teatro La Scala Prize in 1965.[16] His own writings on music all emphasised the idea of 'new music' being in opposition to 'classical music'. It is a concept he expressed in his main work, *A-Functional Music*, written in 1937–38 and revised in Shanghai, along with an article published in the German-language music journal *Der Kreis* in 1941 called 'Grundprobleme der neuen Musik' ('Fundamental Problems of New Music'), in addition to an English-language article published in the *Music Weekly*, a Shanghai publication as part of the *Guanghua Daily*. For Fraenkel, as Christian Utz explains, 'a-functional' was his own means of expressing 'a-tonal'.[17] 'New Music' was non-diatonic and as such potentially provided an interface with Western music with which Chinese composers could progress in their own traditions. Fraenkel even advised, in his article published in *Music Weekly*, that Western pre-classical music may also provide a suitable interface for modern Chinese music.

Julius Schloß would follow Fraenkel at Shanghai's Conservatory before his departure to Canada in 1948. Nevertheless, the impression Fraenkel and Schloß left on a number of Chinese composition students cannot be overestimated. Sang Tong (1923–2011) was their pupil and subsequent director of the Shanghai Conservatory. He is also seen as the composer of China's first 'atonal' work in 1947 called *Night Scenery*, most likely based on works by Fraenkel. A lengthy period followed the civil war and communist takeover of China in which further twelve-tone or atonal developments within Chinese music were suppressed. With the end of the Cultural Revolution in 1976, fresh opportunities opened for Chinese composers, who started exploring new directions including freeing up tonality. By 1979, Luo Zhongrong (1924–2021), now considered the father of contemporary Chinese music, published the first twelve-tone work in China with the title *Picking Lotus Flowers along the Riverside*.[18] The trajectory from Fraenkel to Luo Zhongrong is complex, but still traceable via the latter's composition teacher at Shanghai's National Vocational Music School (the name given to the Conservatory following the communist victory in the civil war), Tan Xiaolin (1911–48), who in turn taught at Yale University with his classmate Sang Tong. Dr Wong Hoi-Tan describes Luo Zhongrong's unique approach to twelve-tone composition as follows:

> Luo's twelve-note music can be categorised into two types: a pentatonic-related type and a non-pentatonic-related type. Pentatonic in this paper refers to the five-note collection with pitch classes related by tone–tone–tone–minor third–tone, where semitone and tritone are absent. Pentatonic tetrachords or trichords are subsets of this five-note collection.[19]

It was ultimately through the work of Wolfgang Fraenkel, who would compose 193 works altogether, and his successor at the Conservatory, Julius Schloß, along with piano recitals by Karl Steiner, that an important degree of cultural transfer occurred between Central Europe and China. This synthesis of musical languages still remains to be fully discovered. It remains, however, frustratingly difficult if not impossible to access or perform Fraenkel's own compositions. As part of the Moldenhauer Archives at Bavaria's State Library, Fraenkel's works are not available for performance without the permission of his remaining family members. The distant relatives of Fraenkel's wife, who remain his closest surviving relatives, are no longer culturally connected with Fraenkel and his legacy and have embargoed performances of his work, granting only limited access for educational purposes. This is a pity, as Fraenkel's music represents a pivotal point in the study of cultural transfer and relates a very specific episode within the story of Hitler's musical émigrés. It remains a sobering reality that the Nazis murdered most of Fraenkel's family in the 1930s and 1940s, leaving us with the paradox of the German government of today, through its public archive in Munich, striking an acquisition deal for Fraenkel's musical estate that fundamentally continues Hitler's attempt to silence him.[20]

The flight of Europe's musical elite to wherever refuge could be found would mean the Schoenberg School could take root across the world. Better known are the composers and teachers who arrived and taught in both the United Kingdom and the United States, such as Schoenberg himself, but also in Great Britain: Egon Wellesz, Peter Stadlen and Leopold Spinner. Less well-known was the influence of Guillermo (Wilhelm) Graetzer in Argentina and Philip Herschkowitz in the Soviet Union. The common factor with all of these disciples of Vienna's Schoenbergian School was the need to teach the very fundamentals of Western music in the same manner that Schoenberg insisted on teaching harmony and counterpoint – *Tonsatz* – to any pupil, no matter how talented and ambitious. Schoenberg pupils who did not follow his ideas, such as Paul Pisk, would nonetheless leave with a firm basis of music's material elements. It was a foundation that Schoenberg believed was essential before embarking on the building of new structures.

The Soviet Union and Philip Herschkowitz

Philip Herschkowitz (1906–89) was born into a Jewish family in Iaşi (Jassy) in Romania. He entered Vienna's Music Academy in 1927 to study with Joseph Marx while also taking private lessons with Alban Berg until 1931. In 1932 he completed a conducting course with Hermann Scherchen in Strasbourg. In the same year, Berg found a position for Herschkowitz at the music publishers Universal Edition (UE) where he could edit and produce the scores of Berg, Webern and Schoenberg. He remained an employee of UE until 1938. The greatest influence on Herschkowitz, however, was Anton Webern, with whom he studied in Vienna from 1934 to 1939. In correspondence, he even went so far as to write that he thanked Webern for his life's work and ultimately for his understanding of music.[21]

The annexation of Austria resulted in a situation that could only recall Kafka at his most cynical. UE was 'Aryanised', resulting in the loss of Herschkowitz's employment. Berg had died in 1935 and Webern's influence was limited, given his Nazi reputation as a 'Cultural Bolshevist', though at the same time Webern welcomed Austria's annexation by Germany. He no doubt sided with Social Democrats in the belief that Hitler was bad, but the clerical dictatorship of Schuschnigg was worse. Hitler, according to most of Austria's educated non-Jewish progressives, was easily dismissed as a cranky country yokel from Austria's border regions. He was more easily dealt with than the dictatorship of minor aristocracy and Catholic clergy that had consolidated power in 1933.

Worse was to come following Austria's annexation. Romania would not allow its Jewish citizens living abroad to return, and as a Romanian Jew, Herschkowitz had no means of immigrating elsewhere. A brief attempt to leave via Italy proved unsuccessful, resulting in a humiliating return to Austria. Only after the outbreak of war did Herschkowitz manage to escape via Yugoslavia. He returned to Romania after a short stay in Zagreb and lived in Bucharest for a year until the government of Ion Antonescu allied itself with Nazi Germany in 1940, forcing Herschkowitz to flee again, this time to Chernivtsi (former Austrian Czernowitz), which at that point was part of the Soviet Union and today is in Ukraine.

He acquired Soviet citizenship and began to compose again and teach at the local German-language Conservatory. Following Hitler's invasion of the Soviet Union, Herschkowitz fled first to Tashkent then Andižan. He became a member of the Soviet Composers' Collective and started work at Tashkent's Arts Institute in 1942 as an advisor on its collection of Uzbek folk music. His intention of returning to Vienna after the war was confounded by Soviet policies, leaving him with little option but to move to Moscow as the least undesirable option.

His background and compositional aesthetics identified him in the eyes of Soviet cultural arbiters as a composer with formulist influences from the West, not in accordance with the dictates of Socialist Realism and its requirement for the composer to work in the service of Soviet citizens. Put more simply, his music was viewed as elitist and incapable of instilling a sense of self-worth and patriotism. Indeed, it was not so very far from Hanns Eisler's criticism of his own teacher Arnold Schoenberg, leading to the breakdown in their relationship in the mid-1920s. Herschkowitz was unwilling to compromise and was ejected from the Soviet Composers' Collective in 1949. This led to a precarious existence during the dangerous years of Stalinist antisemitic paranoia. Herschkowitz survived under the radar by orchestrating film music until the late 1950s when he began to emerge as an important teacher offering an alternative view. It was during this time that he began writing his as yet unpublished book on composition. With the slow liberalisation of the Soviet Union, he began to be reintegrated into public life and was allowed to present a paper on Anton Webern in Leningrad in 1966. In 1968 and 1969 he took short-lived teaching positions in Kiev and Yerevan. He began to compose works for the piano and song cycles, notably based on the

Romanian poets Paul Celan and Ion Barbu. Towards the end of the 1960s, his pupil Edison Denisov even managed a performance of Herschkowitz works in Moscow.

This period of openness and liberalisation did not last and Herschkowitz was reduced to teaching privately in his tiny Moscow apartment, which the pianist Elisabeth Leonskaja described as taking hours to reach across the enormous expanse of the city. As with Wolfgang Fraenkel, it was the legacy Herschkowitz left with his pupils that remains more significant than his own compositions. Also in common with Fraenkel, his legacy as a composer has yet to be evaluated. The list of Herschkowitz pupils presents a 'who's who' of late Soviet composition, starting with Denisov and continuing with names such as Alfred Schnittke, Sofia Gubaidulina, Dmitri Smirnov, Leonid Hoffman and Valentin Silvestrov. In conversation with the author, Elisabeth Leonskaja also related how important Herschkowitz was to instrumentalists such as herself, Natalia Gutman and Alexei Lubimov. She went on to explain that Herschkowitz was not just important in discussions about the Viennese School, which was considered controversial and therefore attractive to young performers, but also important in teaching inter-pretation within the standard repertoire.

The Soviet system continued to thwart Herschkowitz's attempts to emigrate, or even to leave the country, if only for a short time. It took Perestroika in 1987 before he was permitted to accept an invita-tion from the Alban Berg Foundation to work on Berg's critical edition in Vienna. In 1989 Herschkowitz died of kidney failure in Vienna and left his musical estate to the City of Vienna, including his essays presently being edited and published by his wife Elena. His own compositions are slowly being recovered, with concerts in Vienna and Berlin and an important retrospective symposium that took place in Timişoara (Romania) in 2017. His music, in common with that of his teacher Webern, is concise and translucent in texture; fleeting and somehow impressionistic.

Latin America and Guillermo Graetzer

Returning to Wischnitzer's review of South and Central America in his report on immigration possibilities between 1933 and 1938, he mentions that by 1936, South and Central America, along with South Africa, had become the most important immigration destinations during the so-called 'Second Wave' of Jewish immigration. He highlights the improving and relatively strong Argentinian economy as a factor. Nevertheless, having absorbed thousands of Jewish refugees, by 1938, Argentina along with Brazil, Colombia and Uruguay had closed their doors. Indeed, out of the ten South American republics, which also included Bolivia, Ecuador, Paraguay, Peru, Chile and Venezuela, only Bolivia continued to pursue a liberal policy towards Jewish immigration. In order to immigrate to Brazil or Argentina, it was necessary to have family already living in the country as a prerequisite for entry. Chile followed a policy of selective immigration, making it one of the most difficult countries to enter. Colombia, similarly, was only granting visas in exceptional cases; Ecuador required immigrants to pay $100 landing money and show they were in possession of at least $400. Paraguay admitted farmers if they could show they had $250. Entry into Peru, as with Chile, was determined on a case-by-case basis, with few being admitted. Uruguay closed its doors entirely and Venezuela only granted 'reluctant' permission.

Even the Caribbean offered limited options. To immigrate to Barbados, Trinidad, San Domingo or Cuba, vast sums of money were required; Haiti was not a desirable option and prospects were in any case poor. Guatemala required $5,000 just to be considered and Honduras only allowed entry to farmers. Costa Rica and Nicaragua had closed their doors entirely.[22] At the time that Wischnitzer was compiling his report, South and Central America along with the Caribbean had taken in 47,600 refugees compared with Palestine's 45,100 and China's 4,000; North America had taken in 52,000. Of the South American countries, Argentina was far and away the most popular destination. Only Palestine and the United States had taken in more refugees. As the situation grew worse, immigration to South and Central America would, despite the above recounted difficulties, continue to increase. Occasionally, attempts to get to the other side of the Atlantic, and as far away from Europe as possible, ended in tragedy. An example of this was the case of the German ocean liner *St Louis* and its passengers of Jewish refugees desperate to get to Cuba in May 1939. Upon arrival, they were wrongly and illegally turned away, forcing the ship to return to Europe following countless failed attempts to find a North, South or Central American country prepared to allow the passengers to disembark and claim asylum. After the ship's return to Europe, over 250 of its passengers were subsequently arrested and murdered.

Such was the situation when Wilhelm Graetzer and his family arrived in Argentina on 2 January 1939, where they joined his sister Berta, who had moved to Buenos Aires much earlier. Wilhelm Graetzer soon acquired Argentinian citizenship and changed his name to Guillermo Graetzer.

Graetzer was born into a bourgeois Viennese Jewish family on 5 September 1914. As early as the age of thirteen, he had decided to study music in Berlin. At age seventeen, he began studying with Georg Schünemann, co-director of Berlin's Music Academy who recommended that he continue at the Public Music School in Berlin Neukölln (Volksmusikschule) where he studied composition with Paul Hindemith and Ernst-Lothar von Knorr until 1934.

With the arrival of Adolf Hitler as chancellor in 1933, Graetzer found it increasingly difficult to remain in Berlin and returned to Vienna where he continued his composition studies with Paul Amadeus Pisk, a former pupil of both Franz Schreker and Arnold Schoenberg. Despite isolation and increasing financial hardship, Vienna still offered some opportunities to modernist composers not available in Nazi Germany. Paul Pisk had started his series of concerts called *Musik der Gegenwart* (*Music of Today*). Ernst Krenek ran a parallel series called the 'Austrian Studio' which, in keeping with the *Zeitgeist*, was meant, as he explained to the head of Austrian liturgical music Joseph Lechthaler, 'to demonstrate that new music was not the exclusive preserve of lefties and Jews'.[23] It was a strange comment to make since Krenek was married at the time to the Jewish actress Berta Haas (though her stage name was Berta Hermann), having divorced Anna Mahler, daughter of Gustav and Alma. Neither wife would have been acceptably 'Aryan', but Krenek's blindness to such contradictions was emblematic of the age and city in which he lived. In any case, with such new music initiatives still taking place in Vienna, Graetzer managed a premiere of his Piano Sonata in B-flat in 1937.

With Pisk's departure to the United States in 1936, Graetzer continued his studies in the conducting class of Rudolf Nilius, while at the same time becoming ever more active in Vienna's Zionist Jewish National Front movement. It looked increasingly precarious for the family following Austria's annexation. Wilhelm moved to Budapest, unable to complete his course with Nilius, who nevertheless provided Graetzer with a recommendation. Having acquired Argentinian visas, the Graetzers left from Trieste on 15 December 1938, arriving two and half weeks later in Buenos Aires.

In May, Graetzer was soon giving courses in conducting at the Academia de Ópera despite initial struggles with the language. He was also working as an accompanist. Through the intervention of Paul Pisk, who was writing recommendations from his new home in California, Graetzer came into contact with the composer Juan Carlos Paz (1897–1972), through whom he encountered the conductor and composer Juan José Castro (1895–1968). Both men facilitated Graetzer's entry into Argentinian new-music circles. He went on to perform in Paz's ensemble *Agrupación nueva Música*, which led to work as composer and pianist with Joaquín Pérez Fernández and Otto Werberg's Dance Ensemble at the Teatro del

Pueblo. It was around this time that Graetzer was composing Zionist settings based on biblical texts.

In 1946 Graetzer hit upon the concept of Open Music Education, something he had profited from in Berlin with free access to composition lessons with Paul Hindemith and Ernst-Lothar von Knorr. It was an idea that was equally widespread in Vienna, where appending the prefix 'Volks' ('the people's') to schools, institutions and colleges meant they were open to all regardless of previous academic attainment or social position. It recognised the reality that high academic attainment in Austro-German societies was inevitably limited to those who could afford to pay for the best tuition. For that reason, early Social Democratic municipal councils strongly believed the potential for greater attainment in broader social segments lay in wider access to free education. With the founding of the Collegium musicum de Buenos Aires, Graetzer was able to offer children and adults courses in music, dance and pedagogy. He remained head of the institution until 1976. It was also a time when he began to adapt Carl Orff's music pedagogy for Latin Americans. In 1947, together with Alberto Ginastera, Julián Bautista and others, Graetzer became a founding member of the Liga de compositores de la Argentina, thus forming the Argentinian chapter of the ISCM. By 1955, he had become a full professor of composition and music theory at the Universidad Nacional de La Plata.

Until 1960, Graetzer's own compositions represented a wide range of contemporary European developments, with influences of Hindemith remaining dominant, but also representing polytonality and serialism. Nevertheless, there are a number of Lieder from his years in Berlin set to texts by Klabund,[24] Hans Bethge, Hermann Hesse, Rainer Maria Rilke and Friedrich Nietzsche. In addition, there are some piano works, including Graetzer's Sonata in B-flat, as well as a sonatina for recorder and piano. In common with a number of other émigré composers following arrival in new homelands, his works reflected a coming to terms with Judaism as a religion and

15. The renowned teacher and composer Guillermo Graetzer at the piano teaching a class in Buenos Aires, 1970.

culture along with its traditions. He composed a number of settings of biblical, Chassidic and Yiddish texts. Graetzer's love of music of the Renaissance and Baroque is reflected in his *Old Dances from the Spanish Court* from 1940, and his Bach arrangements of *The Art of Fugue* for large orchestra in 1950 and then chamber orchestra in 1985.

Carlos Graetzer, the son of Guillermo and also a noted Argentinian composer, describes his father's early works as being highly individual, yet showing clear influences of Hindemith and even Schoenberg. Guillermo Graetzer's neo-classicism remained dominant until his 1957 choral composition *De la sabiduría* (*On Wisdom*), based on the Book of Job. From the 1960s he became progressively more inspired by Latin American influences, setting many Argentinian and South American poets as well as developing a fascination with proto-Columbian culture.

This would result in two works based on the Creation myths of the Mayas: his 1962 choral work, *Preámbulo para al Popul Vuh de los Mayas* (*Preamble to the Popul Vuh of the Mayas*), and from 1989, his 'oratorio ballet' *La creación según el 'Pop Wuj Maya'* (*Creation according to 'Pop Wuj Maya'*). Carlos Graetzer considered this last work by his father as his masterpiece.

Graetzer's greatest contribution, despite his enormous output as composer, was to music education, founding and becoming vice-president of the *Sociedad Argentina de Educación Musical*, allowing him to take part in and influence music education throughout South America. He had become a major player throughout the region with seats on countless individual panels and juries, while chairing many international inter-American committees.

It would be difficult to overestimate Graetzer's significance in South American music. He published on a broad range of topics from Baroque ornamentation to pre-Columbian culture. The prizes and awards he received in his lifetime made him a household name. In 1986 he was awarded the *Gran Premio* of the *Sociedad Argentina de Autores y Compositores* (SADAIC) (*The Grand Prize of Argentinian Authors and Composers*). After his death in 1993, SADAIC launched a competition for composers with its prize named after Guillermo Graetzer.[25]

Unanswered Questions and Flight to Japan, the Philippines, India and Africa

There are many stories of strange and obscure places of refuge for émigrés from Nazi Germany. As already stated, American and British writers have published copiously on Hitler's musical diaspora and the effects it had on their cultural biotope. But there were many variables that determined which options were available for refugees. Just to consider a few, such as gender, age and location, would demand an entire book. There remain many open questions about which one can only speculate. Just take the example of two women composers: the Austrian Wally (later Vally) Weigl (1894–1982) and the German Julia Kerr (1898–1965), who composed under the name of Julia Kerwey. Both were married to men who in their previous homelands were exceptionally well regarded: Wally Weigl's husband, Karl Weigl (1881–1949), was a highly respected composer and teacher, while Alfred Kerr (1867–1948), Julia's husband, was arguably Germany's most distinguished cultural journalist and one of the Weimar Republic's most important writers. Yet consider the following: Wally Weigl composed far more in American exile after the death of her husband Karl than Julia Kerr in British exile, despite their respective husbands dying within a year of each other and leaving their wives to fend for themselves in new homelands. It could be argued that Julia Kerr already had a reputation as an opera composer in Germany. Her fairytale opera based on Eduard Mörike's story 'Die schöne Lau' ('The Lovely Lau') was the first opera to be broadcast on German radio in 1928, an event that was reported across Europe and even mentioned in the *New York Times*.[26] At the time of her flight from Berlin immediately after Hitler's appointment as chancellor, she and her husband were working on another opera called *Chronoplan*. Wally Weigl's later reputation rested on much smaller-scale works after the death of her husband. Julia Kerr had children to raise and Wally Weigl did not. But it would also be important to add questions of how the new homelands influenced their creativity. We again encounter the arguable influences of New versus Old World.

There was nothing binary about who went into exile and who didn't. Many good people could not leave and many questionable people did. Manfred Gurlitt (1890–1972) joined the Nazi Party in 1933 until he was ejected in 1937. His mother claimed he had not been fathered by her Jewish husband but by her second husband, Willi Waldecker. The ruse didn't work and Gurlitt immigrated to Tokyo with help from his friend the conductor Hidemaro Konoe, whose brother was an important government minister. Although Gurlitt was less established as a composer than Hindemith, their situations were equally ambivalent. Neither composer accepted the fate of exile and would have bent over backwards to have found an accommodation that allowed them actively to participate in Hitler's 'New Germany'. Perhaps the difference with Hindemith was his ability to recognise the scale of Nazi atrocities that had taken place.

Yet Gurlitt's immigration to Japan raises a question: did it start initially as a move to take up interesting professional opportunities before it was turned into exile? It was a situation that affected several German musicians invited to Japan, such as the Ukrainian Jewish pianist Leo Sirota (1885–1965) and the Jewish composer, teacher and conductor Klaus Pringsheim. Both Sirota and Pringsheim were invited to teach at the Imperial Conservatory in Tokyo before Hitler's appointment as chancellor. Following the Nazi takeover, Pringsheim decided not to return to Germany and extended his contract. In 1937 German pressure on Japanese authorities resulted in his dismissal. He left Japan for Thailand before returning to Japan where he earned a living by conducting the Tokyo Chamber Orchestra. In 1944 the German Embassy in Tokyo objected to the activities of a number of Jewish musicians living and working in Japan, such as Leo Sirota and the Russian-born but naturalised German pianist, Leonid Kreutzer (1884–1953), the conductor Joseph Rosenstock (1895–1985) and Pringsheim. The Nazi authorities expatriated them in 1944, rendering them 'stateless'. They were subsequently held in Karuizawa internment camp at various points and for varying lengths of time until the end of the war. Afterwards, and following a fruitless attempt to make a career in the United States, Pringsheim returned to Japan where he was offered a full professorship at the Musashino Academia Musicae in Tokyo. As with most other émigrés landing in distant, non-Eurocentric countries of refuge, his legacy was that of an influential and important teacher. His most lasting, and by no means insignificant, musical mark on German musical life was conducting the first complete Mahler cycle with the Berlin Philharmonic in 1923 and 1924. Rosenstock conducted the Nippon Philharmonic Orchestra immediately after the war before joining Sirota in 1946 in the United States. Kreutzer remained in Japan where he continued to teach, perform and conduct.

Likewise, the Joseph Marx pupil Herbert Zipper was invited in 1939 to take on the Manila Symphony Orchestra, facilitating his immigration to the Philippines. With the Japanese invasion of the Philippines in December 1941, Zipper was once again imprisoned, though this time only for a few months. Until the defeat of Japan, he and his wife Trudi barely managed to stay alive. Many of the orchestral members were killed in the fighting, but on 10 May 1945, Zipper made good on a vow he had undertaken in Dachau: with the fall of Hitler, he would conduct Beethoven's 'Eroica' Symphony. Its score was one of the few possessions he had managed to retain. Zipper left for the United States in 1946, but remained devoted to the Philippines, returning to conduct every summer. Like so many others, he would be remembered as an important and inspiring teacher.

The Czech composer Walter Kaufmann (1907–84) was a Berlin pupil of Franz Schreker and had developed an interest in the music of India as a student. His move to Bombay (Mumbai) in 1934 came after sensing it was only a question of when, not if, the Nazis would take over Czechoslovakia. According to the article by Mark Wischnitzer, by 1939 there were only 300 Jewish refugees in India, meaning musical opportunities would have been available to someone with Kaufmann's abilities. He easily procured a visa to India and within a year of arrival he was appointed head of European Music at All India Radio (AIR) where he composed the very Indian-sounding AIR theme[27] that is still used today. His interest in Indian music took him across the subcontinent and he published an ethnomusicological study on the music of Hindustan in 1944. The influence can be heard in some of his own works, and indeed he was once a composer for some of the films being made in what later became known as 'Bollywood'. Kaufmann was the founder and director of, occasional soloist in, and composer for, the Bombay Chamber Music Society.

After the war, his attempt to return to Prague was thwarted by a combination of Nazi brutality and the Beneš Decrees that expatriated and confiscated the possessions of German-speaking Czechs, including Kaufmann's mother who had converted to Judaism upon her marriage. AIR was a BBC affiliate and with post-war independence and the threat of partition promising instability, Kaufmann took up the offer of British citizenship that was his due as an AIR employee. He moved to the United Kingdom in 1946. The following year he moved to Canada and built up the Winnipeg Symphony Orchestra, which he conducted until 1957. From 1957 until 1978 he was a professor of musicology at Indiana State University in Bloomington and published extensively on ethnomusicology and the music of India.

Similar to Guillermo Graetzer, Kaufmann would not merely become a European missionary to distant corners of the globe but also a scholar and composer who explored the native music of his new homeland. If the definition of 'missionary' were to be applied, it would be in reverse – both men would become missionaries on behalf of the native societies in which they found themselves in their flight from Hitler. The influence of India is most acutely heard in the works of Kaufmann, while still inhabiting a largely Western European sound world.

South Africa accepted Jewish immigrants until the latter part of 1937, according to Wischnitzer's account.[28] By then, entry was restricted to people with close relatives already living there. Nevertheless, Friedrich H. Hartmann (1900–73), who was not Jewish but who had a partially Jewish wife, did manage to immigrate to South Africa after fleeing the Nazi takeover of Austria. Hartmann was a former pupil of Joseph Marx, Franz Schmidt and Felix Weingartner at Vienna's Music Academy. He published extensively on music theory, harmony and theory pedagogy in Vienna in the late 1930s, his most important publications being a book on harmony in 1934, one on counterpoint in 1936, and another called *Allgemeine Musiklehre für den Gebrauch an Lehranstalten* (*A General Music Primer for Use in Schools*) in 1937. As a supporter of the Schuschnigg regime, married to the 'non-Aryan' singing teacher Anny Hartmann née Schwed (1892–1972), Hartmann felt it essential to emigrate as quickly as possible. His initial plan was to head to Brazil, but when these plans fell through he applied to immigrate to South Africa. The application was successful and he was soon appointed head of Music at Rhodes University, followed by an appointment to the University of Johannesburg. He taught a generation of both white and black post-war South Africans, including the Black South African composer Michael Mosoeu Moerane (1904–80), before returning to Vienna in 1963 where he was appointed deputy head at Vienna's Music Academy.

It's extremely difficult to find information on Hartmann, possibly because his political background as a supporter of the Austro-Fascist government was not unblemished and possibly because his musical language remained deliberately in line with his teachers Joseph Marx and Franz Schmidt. He provided the incidental music for productions of Goethe's *Faust* and Hofmannsthal's *Der weiße Fächer* (*The White Fan*). His most astonishing, and unjustly neglected, work, however, is his *The Song of the Four Winds*, a symphony with vocal soloists that feels like a cross between Zemlinsky's *Lyric Symphony* and Marx's *Eine Herbstsymphonie* (*An Autumn Symphony*). The love of nature and landscape is apparent and even reminiscent of Mahler's *Das Lied von der Erde* (*The Song of the Earth*). The origin of the texts that Hartmann set is unclear but they appear to have been by the Nazi poet Hanns Johst (1890–1978). It is a similar case to that of Robert Fürstenthal, who was drawn to the poetry of Josef Weinheber, another Nazi poet. Today, and with hindsight, it is difficult to understand the thinking of a composer persecuted by the Nazis who nevertheless chose to set texts written by Nazi poets. Like Fürstenthal, it is most likely that Hartmann was drawn to the words and gave no thought to their provenance.

Openness to new environments was often, though not always, a question of the age of the individual émigré. Graetzer, Herschkowitz, Hartmann and Kaufmann were children of the first decade of the twentieth century. Younger composers such as Walter Arlen, Lukas Foss, Joseph Horovitz, André Previn, Franz Reizenstein and others, arriving in the United States or Great Britain, were receptive to their new cultures and thought of themselves as American or British composers. Of course, there were the exceptions such as Robert Fürstenthal who retreated into a *fin de siècle* Vienna he could never have known. But Fürstenthal considered himself an amateur and therefore free of aesthetic directives absorbed actively or passively by professional composers. Hartmann does not appear to have been drawn to African music, despite teaching the African nationalist Michael Moerane, uncle of the future South African president, Thabo Mbeki, but his *Song of the Four Winds* most definitely paints a musical picture of nature that is universal, and like Fraenkel, Graetzer and Herschkowitz, his legacy remains his pupils.

Hartmann's time in South Africa shows that the 'missionary' idea most often worked counter to his contemporaries Graetzer, Fraenkel and Kaufmann. It was most often a case of exiled composers seeing themselves as torchbearers of specific European traditions. But again, such concepts were dependent on how the host nations saw them-selves. New World nations were more ambivalent, welcoming Old World traditions but only insofar as they were useful in creating foundations for New World developments. It was more complex for those arriving in countries with established traditions, such as composers immigrating to the United Kingdom. Egon Wellesz, Hans Gál and others despaired at the lack of serious foundations in such countries, the shallowness of musicology and even a dearth of understanding of historiography or aesthetics. Nor did British musicians, scholars and composers always take kindly to being told how inconsequential their grasp of the very foundations of music was. As far as British, French or Russian musicians were concerned, they had established traditions of their own with little need of Central European interference. Hugh Allen, Professor of Music at Oxford, resisted Wellesz's inclusion onto the music faculty and insisted that musicology, history and aesthetics were of no use to the future cathedral organists studying at Oxford.[29] Vaughan Williams wrote to the Austrian pianist Ferdinand Rauter that wonderfully trained Central European musicians were in danger of 'trampling the tender flower of English music'.[30] Such nationalistic views frustrated and infuriated exiled composers, leaving many desperately trying to adapt and having to come to terms with the reality that they were unable to develop in the organic manner they would have, had they been allowed to remain in their home countries. The result was musical silence from the likes of Berthold Goldschmidt, or an attempt to move from a dominant genre (opera) to something more amenable to the new environment, as in the case of Hans Gál and Egon Wellesz.

In general, those who had been successful in their home countries found it more difficult to adjust to new environments. Kurt Weill and Erich Wolfgang Korngold were perhaps the obvious exceptions. But another question emerges: Would Joseph Kosma have been as successful had he remained in Berlin, Vienna or Budapest rather than immigrating to France and becoming the father of post-war French chanson? Would Antônio Carlos Jobim's bossa novas have emerged without the influence of his teacher Hans-Joachim Koellreutter (1915–2005)? On the other hand, Koellreutter was much the same age as Graetzer, and upon arriving in Brazil he had adapted more easily to the local musical environment. Nevertheless, he was a leading proponent in debates about nationalism versus serialism. Did a country's indigenous traditions take precedence over European developments?

Finally, there remains the matter of whether individuals who became noted interpreters had in fact intended to become composers. In a way, Georg Tintner's seminal work and masterpiece for string quartet and soprano, *The Ellipse*, must stand in for all of the works that couldn't be written, because composers such as himself, Walter Susskind and countless others found themselves having to work as jobbing musicians to pay the rent and put bread on the table. Had they remained in their homelands, there can be no knowing the treasures that might have followed. Tintner's *The Ellipse* is a representation of his life as seen through the retrospective prism of the 1950s. It is the geometrical shape that is not quite a circle. As an ellipse, it gives equal importance to that which is missing. It is a representation of Tintner's own life, but it could stand in for the lives of almost all the composers and performers mentioned in this book.

Is There a Conclusion to Be Drawn?

The vast vacuum that resulted from the musical brain drain from Europe along with much of the supportive public, means there are only awkward, often uncomfortable conclusions to draw. The conductor John Mauceri in his book *The War on Music*[31] argues persuasively that the organic transition that should have taken place, thus making the Schoenberg School just one development among many, occurred in the realms of applied music in Hollywood following the arrival of countless refugees. Moguls were not disconnected from their customers and they knew what sold – not just in America but worldwide. They knew that developments needed to take place in parallel not in isolation. If atonality or serialism had a place, it needed to be set in a context where it remained coherent. It is sobering to realise that such 'contexts' were horror movies and science fiction. Otherwise, Mauceri argues, Hollywood offered a more accurate timeline of twentieth-century music's natural development. Its organic progression was emerging from Strauss and Mahler. Other composers in Hollywood were on the verge of developing different music-to-visual aesthetics, but again, politics came into play with the House Committee on Un-American Activities inhibiting some of the most adventurous. Hanns Eisler was deported while others in his circle of left-leaning musicians kept their heads down if they wanted to remain in the USA. Indeed, the question of remigration, or the return to homelands by formerly exiled composers, demands its own thorough and exhaustive examination, and cannot be included here, which deals exclusively with the creative effects of exile.

It is impossible to say with certainty how the vacuum left by the expulsion of Europe's talented musicians has influenced developments today. Since the end of the Second World War, popular music developed not so much as an alternative to serious music, but as its aggressive, intended replacement. Had the gulf between the two been closer, as was arguably the case before Hitler, then the emergence of such destructive musical turf wars might not have dominated the second half of the twentieth century. Subjectively, there is a sense that composers today are showing a versatility that brings the two opposing elements closer together.

Yet the purpose of this examination was to challenge perceptions that the cultural divide was binary and only the 'good guys' fled Hitler while leaving the 'bad guys' to fiddle to the Nazi tune. We are in danger of losing much music that is of unquestionable value and, more importantly, reflective of its own time and circumstances. Dismissing all composers who remained in Hitler's Germany, with the exceptions of Richard Strauss and Carl Orff, is to lose yet another important chapter of European cultural history. To have written propaganda music for a despicable regime in order to have the wherewithal to continue composing music on a higher plane, needs to be judged by a different matrix. In other words, the best and most worthwhile music needs to be seen as work written under the terrible conditions imposed by a criminal and totalitarian regime. The experience of Dmitri Shostakovich offers a template of how one should assess genuine creativity when compliance was the only viable alternative. Not every musician or composer could emigrate and the risks of transplantation were enormous. Walter Bricht was not the only important voice to be silenced by exile.

The other point that needed to be made was no matter how great the contributions made by émigré musicians, they always came with a cost to the individual. This cost was rarely apparent to citizens of new homelands, and indeed, most composers and musicians would not have wanted it made known. They were grateful to have found refuge for themselves and their families. Yet in letters and oral histories, we know more about the true costs of saving a life but losing an audience, and hence the ability to continue creative development in a more organic manner. New homelands did gain enormously from Europe's brain drain, but the price that individual composers and musicians had to pay artistically is much more difficult to assess. In retrospect, it could be argued that everyone ultimately pays a price for the abrupt truncation of creativity.

Ultimately, there is also the reality of music that could only have been composed in exile. Merely looking at the nineteenth century already raises important questions. Would Chopin's Polonaises and Mazurkas have been as explosive had he been able to remain in Poland, or would they have become utilitarian works for local entertainment? Would Wagner have evoked German mythology and preached a malevolent, exclusionary racism had Germany been a nation state, at peace with itself and its neighbours? The music of exile is a special genre and in the twentieth century it covers much more than the functional demands of American cinema or the contained modernism of totalitarian Europe, or the defiance and self-analysis of works intended only for the desk drawer. The music of exile, in its many guises, ultimately expresses to some degree a yearning to return, with a plurality of 'returns' to be understood.

NOTES

Foreword

1. Lion Feuchtwanger, *Exil* (Aufbauverlag, 2013), p. 149.
2. Robert Fürstenthal: Born in Vienna, 27 June 1920–16 November 2016, died in San Diego, CA; Lieder and chamber music recordings are available on Toccata Classics.
3. *Vienna*, 1968, written, directed and produced by Orson Welles.
4. Ernst Bloch, *Das Prinzip Hoffnung*, vol. 3 (part 5: *Identität*), 1967, p. 1,628, original German: '[Heimat] sei "etwas" das allen in die Kindheit scheint und worin noch niemand war', quoted in Hartmut Krones (ed.), *Hanns Eisler: Ein Komponist ohne Heimat?* (Böhlau, 2012), p. 82.

Introduction

1. Frank Thiess was a prominent German writer born in 1890 in today's Latvia, who died in 1977 in Darmstadt.
2. NSDAP: Nationalsozialistische Deutsche Arbeiterpartei, which was shortened to the slang term 'Nazi' and originally frowned upon as disrespectful and too casual. 'National Socialist' was the acceptable term, though 'Nazi' is now generally used in all contexts and no longer seen as slang.
3. Some examples are as follows: Anthony Heilbut, *Exiled in Paradise: German Refugee Artists and Intellectuals in America from the 1930s to the Present* (The Viking Press, 1983); *The Intellectual Migration: Europe and America 1930–1960*, ed. Donald Fleming and Bernard Bailyn (Harvard University Press, 1963); *The Muses Flee Hitler: Cultural Transfer and Adaptation, 1930–1945*, ed. Jarrell C. Jackman and Carla M. Borden (Smithsonian Institution Press, 1983); Dorothy Lamb Crawford, *A Windfall of Musicians: Hitler's Émigrés and Exiles in Southern California* (Yale University Press, 2011); Joseph Horowitz, *Artists in Exile: How Refugees from Twentieth-Century War and Revolution Transformed the American Performing Arts* (Harper, 2008); Daniel Snowman, *The Hitler Émigrés: The Cultural Impact on Britain of Refugees from Nazism* (Chatto & Windus, 2002).

4. Schoenberg is the exception in this respect, as exemplified by the German musicologist Sabine Feisst's *Schoenberg's New World: The American Years* (Oxford University Press, 2011) and Kenneth H. Marcus's *Schoenberg and Hollywood Modernism* (Cambridge University Press, 2016).

5. John Mauceri, *The War on Music: Reclaiming the Twentieth Century* (Yale University Press, 2022).

6. Correspondence is held at the Universal Edition (UE) Archive, Wienbibliothek, Vienna.

7. *Le Lion amoureux*, composed as a commission by the Colonel de Basil Russian Ballet Company and performed at the Royal Opera House, Covent Garden, during their 1937–38 season. The Suite was premiered on 13 March 1938 by the BBC Symphony Orchestra conducted by Clarence Reynolds. The date corresponds with Austria's annexation by Nazi Germany. Rathaus continued to hold Austrian citizenship until this point, when he was rendered stateless.

8. Mark Latimer has identified the following members of the orchestra in the photograph who died as a result of exclusion or imprisonment: oboist Armin Tyroler; concertmaster Julius Stwertka; cellist Lucien Howitz; and violinist Paul Fischer. The following orchestra members from the photo immigrated to the United States: pianist Paul Wittgenstein; violinists Hugo Gottesmann, Max Rostal and Josef Geringer; clarinettist Viktor Polatschek; viola player Marcel Dick; and cellist Berner Heifetz. Horn player Gottfried von Freiberg, who had a Jewish grandparent, was a victim of constant harassment; he premiered Richard Strauss's Second Horn Concerto. Cellist Josef Zimbler died in exile in Argentina.

9. Lys Symonette (1914–2005) was present during the recording of Weill's *Dreigroschenoper* in Berlin with John Mauceri in 1989 and in conversation with the author, who was producer of the album, which featured Ute Lemper, Milva, René Kollo, Mario Adolf, Rolf Boyson, Susanne Tremper and Helga Dernesch and the RIAS Berlin Sinfonietta.

Chapter 1 The *'Hanswurst'* of Havoc

1. Vicki Baum, *Es war alles ganz anders: Erinnerungen* (Kiepenheuer & Witsch, 2018), pp. 435–37.

2. Richard Wagner, 'Ausführungen zu "Religion und Kunst": 1. "Erkenne dich selbst"', in *Sämtliche Schriften und Dichtungen*, vol. 10 (Breitkopf & Härtel, 1912), p. 265. I've paraphrased the actual quote, which is: '[...] die Juden ertheilte Vollberechtigung, sich in jeder erdenklichen Beziehung als Deutsche anzusehen-ungefähr wie die Schwarzen in Mexiko durch ein Blanket autorisiert wurden, sich für Weiße zu halten.'

3. See John Mauceri's *The War on Music*, p. 32, for further thoughts on the relationship between 'art' and 'artificial'.

4. 'Gesamtkunst' or 'total art' was a Wagnerian concept that saw music, drama, literature and staging coming together to create a 'total art' impression. Critics often complained that such ideas simply distracted from the music – the most holy of the arts.

5. Adolf Weißmann's views on Mahler in his publication *Musik in der Weltkrise* from 1922 stands out as a typical example.

6. Ernst Krenek in *Im Atem der Zeit* (Heyne Verlag, 1999), p. 1,015, mentions the view of the Catholic Church's head of music in the 1930s, Joseph Lechthaler, that atonal music was written by Jews for other Jews.

7. Christopher Hailey, *Franz Schreker, 1878–1934: A Cultural Biography* (Cambridge University Press, 1993), p. 290.

8. Österreichische Historikerkommission: *Schlussbericht der Historikerkommission der Republik Österreich. Band 1* (Oldenbourg Verlag, 2003), pp. 85–87.

9. https://www.annefrank.org/de/anne-frank/vertiefung/die-fehlenden-moglichkeiten-zu-fluchten-judische-emigration-1933

10. Conversation with the author.

11. https://www.wina-magazin.at/lissabon-ist-ausverkauft-exil-in-portugal-im-zweiten-weltkrieg

12. Called in English *Paris Gazette*, published by Viking Press in 1940. Its German title was *Exil* and was the third novel in his *Wartesaal – Waiting Room* trilogy. *Exil* was originally published in 1940.

13. Letter held at the Arnold Schoenberg Center in Vienna.

14. Later known as Eric Zeisl. His daughter Barbara married Schoenberg's son Ronald after the death of both Schoenberg and Zeisl.

15. Hans (later 'John') Kafka, 1902 (Vienna)–1972 (Munich).

16. The 1867 Constitution established the rights of all citizens within Habsburg Austria – similar rights were guaranteed in the Hungarian half of the Monarchy. It was a new constitution for establishing the configuration of the Dual Monarchy of Austria and Hungary.

17. Zeisl to H. Spiel, November 1938: '. . . In Paris. In der Stadt aller Städte. Dies ist ein Leben hier, von dem man sich gar keine Vorstellung machen kann. Absolutes Schlaraffenland.' *Musik des Aufbruchs: Endstation Schein-Heiligenstadt: Erich Zeisls Flucht nach Hollywood* (Mandelbaum, 2006).

18. 'Joseph Roths Roman *Hiob* ist mehr als seine historische Rück- und Vorschau: er ist eine Schau zum Anfang und zum Ende aller Zeiten hin, eine metaphysische Schau, die mythologische Zusammendrängung in ein Einzelschicksal des Geschicks eines ganzen Volks, und, in das Geschick eines Einzelvolks, des metaphysischen und mythologischen Volks Kat'exochen immerhin, das Schicksal des Menschen auf dieser Erde.'

19. Wilhelm Rettich, 1892 (Leipzig)–1988 (Sinzheim): his compositions are in a largely late-Romantic language and also include a sumptuous violin concerto.

20. For information on the Jewish Cultural League, see Chapter 2.

21. Georg Knepler, 'Music Exile in England', *Musica Reanimata*, no. 40 (June 2001); Peter Stadlen is cited in the exhibition catalogue *Musik des Aufbruchs: Hans Gál und Egon Wellesz: Continental Britons* (Mandelbaum, 2004), p. 94.

22. See Albrecht Dümling's *The Vanished Musicians: Jewish Refugees in Australia* (Peter Lang, 2016) for a detailed account of the *Dunera*.

23. See Louise London's *Whitehall and the Jews, 1933–1948* (Cambridge University Press, 2000) for documentation regarding Home Office policies.

Chapter 2 Exile in Germany: Of Jewish Destiny, the Composer Richard Fuchs and the Jewish Kulturbund

1. Certainly the most authoritative account is that by Lily E. Hirsch, *A Jewish Orchestra in Nazi Germany: Musical Politics and the Berlin Jewish Culture League* (University of Michigan Press, 2010).

2. *Central-Verein-Zeitung*, 28 September 1933. German original quoted in Ejal Jakob Eisler, Horst H.J.P. Bergmeier and Rainer E. Lotz, *Vorbei – Beyond Recall* (Bear Family Publication, 2001), p. 56.

3. Eva Weissweiler, *Ausgemerzt! Das Lexikon der Juden in der Musik und seine mörderischen Folgen* (Dittrich, 1999), p. 414.
4. As quoted in Jens Malte Fischer's essay 'Die Vitalität des Antisemitismus: Konstanten der Mahler-Rezeption', *Abhandlungen der Akademie der Wissenschaften und der Literatur* (Franz Steiner Verlag, 2021).
5. Born 1878 in Budapet, died 1962 in New York, best known for his dramas, including *The Play's the Thing.*
6. A Jewish 'service organisation' (similar to the Rotary or Lions Club) founded in 1843 in New York.
7. As quoted in Steven Sedley's short biography of Fuchs on the Richard Fuchs website.
8. Karl Wolfskehl, 1869 (Darmstadt)–1948 (Auckland, New Zealand); Süßkind von Trimberg, no biographical information is available beyond his authorship of the *Codex Manesse* from the second half of the thirteenth century.
9. Ibid.
10. Article by Kurt Singer from 4 May 1937 as quoted in *Central-Verein-Zeitung.*
11. Letter quoted in *Central-Verein-Zeitung,* 27 May 1937.
12. As quoted in Steven Sedley's short biography of Fuchs on the Richard Fuchs website.
13. Premiered in Wellington, New Zealand, 22 August 2014.
14. Letter of 15 June 1937, scans held at the Exilarte Center, Vienna.
15. Letter of 7 July 1937, scans held at the Exilarte Center, Vienna.
16. Turnbull Library, Manuscripts Collection, Fuchs, Richard (Dr) 1887–1947: Papers regarding *Vom jüdischen Schicksal* 1936–37, MS-Papers-6663-10. Translation by Alan Mulgan. The original poems are from the collection, Karl Wolfskehl, *Die Stimme Spricht.*
17. This and previous quoted correspondence was generously provided by Dr Jaleh Nili Perego and is held in the Fuchs Collection, Wellington, New Zealand, with scans also held by the Exilarte Center, Vienna.
18. See Tanya Buchdahl Tintner's *Out of Time: The Vexed Life of Georg Tintner* (UWA Press, 2011, and Wilfrid Laurier University Press, 2013).

Chapter 3 Exile in Germany: Inner Emigration

1. Quoted in Hermann Pölking, *Wer war Hitler: Ansichten und Berichte von Zeitgenossen* (Bebra Verlag, 2017), p. 267.
2. Alma Moodie to Werner Reinhardt, taken from *The Fractured Self: Selected German Letters of the Australian Violinist Alma Moodie,* ed. Kay Dreyfus, trans. Diana K. Weekes (Peter Lang, 2021).
3. *Leipziger Neueste Nachrichten,* no. 129, 9 May 1941, as quoted in Fred Prieberg, *Handbuch deutscher Musiker 1933–1945* (Musikwissenschaftliches Institut der Christian-Albrechts-Universität, 2004), p. 7,991.
4. Letter of 14 February 1935 to F.W. Herzog, held on microfilm and quoted by Fred Prieberg, *Handbuch,* p. 3,716.
5. Ibid, p. 3,717.
6. Paul von Klenau on *Michael Kohlhaas* in *Zeitschrift für Musik,* May 1934, p. 531.
7. Gerhard Scherler (1890–1950?) was advisor for theatre productions within the Ministry for Propaganda.
8. Franz Rommel, *Sommernachtstraum: Nationalzeitung Essen,* 31 May 1939.
9. Prieberg, *Handbuch,* pp. 2,795–2,803.
10. Toby Thacker, *Music after Hitler* (Ashgate, 2007), pp. 10–11.
11. Gerhart Göhler, *Zeitschrift für Musik,* CII/1 January 1935, p. 75.

12. Gerhard Schumacher, *Aktualität und Geschichtsbewußtsein als Vorgaben. Zu Wolfgang Fortners Kompositorischen Prinzipien*. Neue Zeitschrift für Musik CXMLIII/11, November 1982, pp. 20–28.

13. W. Stumme (ed.), *Schriften zur Musikerziehung* (Springer Verlag, 1941), W. Fortner quoted on p. 106.

14. Karl Grunsky, *Der Kampf um deutsche Musik* (Stuttgart, 1933), pp. 46–7.

15. Wolfgang Fortner in conversation with Fred Prieberg, 11 March 1963, Prieberg, *Handbuch*, p. 1,640.

16. Quoted in Prieberg, *Handbuch*, p. 2,889, taken from Carl Nissen's *Die deutsche Oper der Gegenwart* (Regensburg, 2004), p. 141.

17. 'Wenn Akademiker musizieren . . .', *Die Musik* XXVI/9, June 1935, p. 674.

18. Max Butting, memo no. 6, NSKA Dept. of Arts' Cultivation, 'List of Cultural Bolsheviks', as quoted in Prieberg, *Handbuch*, p. 860.

19. Christian Darnton, 'Max Butting (1888–1976)', *Tempo*, no. 119 (Cambridge University Press, 1976), pp. 44–46.

20. As per Prieberg's assessment in his *Handbuch*, p. 7,194.

21. *Zeitschrift für Musik* CII/3, March 1935, p. 302.

22. Wilhelm Hendel, *Die Schule der musizierenden Soldaten* DMMZ LXV/13, 14 June 1943.

23. Pfitzner to Erdmann in a letter from 19 August 1934, printed in *Begegnungen mit Eduard Erdmann*, ed. Christoph Bitter and Manfred Schlösser (Darmstadt, 1968).

24. Orel Website Dümling: http://orelfoundation.org/journal/journalArticle/what_is_internal_exile_in_music

25. *Die neue Zeitschrift für Musik*, March 1931, review of Raphael's *Te Deum* in Bremen on 6 March 1931, by Johann Weissenborn, p. 341.

26. Ibid, pp. 458–73.

27. *Signale*, 'Musik im Reich', no. 49, 1938, p. 667, review of the Orchestral Suite based on Smetana Dance Themes, op. 40.

28. *Vom rechten Glauben* and *Christus der Sohn Gottes*, as reported in *Die neue Zeitschrift für Musik*, August 1938, p. 924. References to performances of religious works in 1937 are found in *Die neue Zeitschrift für Musik*, August 1937, p. 932.

29. Letter from Günter Raphael to Hans Gál, 5 November 1946 (Bayerische Staatsbibliothek Munich, ANA 414).

30. H. Ungar, *Westdeutscher Beobachter*, no. 273; 30 April 1941, *Das Judentum im Musikleben Kölns*.

31. Hans Hinkel, German Federal Archive NS 15/187.

32. Correspondence collection of the Bavarian State Library, sig. 579.

33. Walter Braunfels, *Lebensabschnitt*, in *Bodensee-Zeitschrift*, Amriswil, February 1954, pp. 59–62.

34. Letter from Walter Braunfels to Werner Reinhardt, 5 December 1935, as quoted in Ulrike Thiele, 'Musikleben und Mäzenatentum im 20. Jahrhundert: Werner Reinhart', dissertation, University of Zurich, 2016, p. 163.

35. Ermatingen is a municipality in the district of Kreuzlingen in the canton of Thurgau in Switzerland.

36. Letter from 16 December 1935 quoted and translated in Dreyfus (ed.), *The Fractured Self*.

37. Letter from 2 February 1932 quoted and translated in Dreyfus (ed), *The Fractured Self*.

38. Quoted in Martin Wettges's *Walter Braunfels' musikalisches Testament*, L'annonce faite à Marie (Verkündigung); Archiv für Musikwissenschaft 1918–2020; Fritz Steiner Verlag, Heft 3, 2014.

39. Ibid, quoted from *Walter Braunfels, Der Künstler und das Leben* (Cologne, 1948), pp. 11–12.
40. Letter to de Simony undated from November 1933, as quoted in Wettges's *Walter Braunfels' musikalisches Testament*.
41. Michael Kater, *Composers of the Nazi Era: Eight Portraits* (Oxford University Press, 2000), pp. 86–111.
42. These are clearly explained in Alexander Rothe's excellent short article on Hartmann on the Orel Foundation website: http://orelfoundation.org/composers/article/karl_amadeus_hartmann
43. Prieberg, *Handbuch*, p. 2,681.
44. Letter from Hartmann to Wellesz, 2 January 1948 (Austrian National Library, Wellesz Fond, no. 2208).

Chapter 4 The Music of Resistance

1. Eisler in an interview with Hans Bunge: Hanns Eisler, *Fragen Sie mehr über Brecht: Gespräche mit Hans Bunge* (Luchterhand, 1986), p. 71.
2. Wolfgang Benz, *Information zur politischen Bildung*, 242, p. 8, quoted in Rebecca Meier's *Musik als Mittel des Widerstands in den Konzentrationslagern Theresienstadt und Auschwitz* (Grin Verlag, 2015), p. 3.
3. Meier, *Musik als Mittel des Widerstands*, p. 7.
4. Translation from the article by Guido Fackler, 'Concentration Camp Anthems', http://holocaustmusic.ort.org/places/camps/music-early-camps/moorsoldatenlied
5. Ibid.
6. Wilhelm Girnus as quoted in Jens Peitzmeier's *Musik in den Konzentrationslagern Auschwitz und Theresienstadt: Kunst als Widerstand gegen Grausamkeit und Unterdruckung* (Diplomica Verlag, 2014), p. 3.
7. Hans Gál, *Music Behind Barbed Wire: A Diary of Summer 1940* (Toccata Press, 2014).
8. The composer Hans Winterberg's recently discovered and recorded *Theresienstadt Suite* for piano is an example.
9. Joža Karas, *Music in Terezín 1941–1945* (Boydell & Brewer, 1985), p. 103.
10. http://david.juden.at/Kulturzeitschrift/66-70/67-Grigorcea.htm
11. My translation: transcript of original reproduced in Mark Ludwig, *Our Will to Live* (Steidl Verlag, 2021).
12. The Czech spelling of Petr Kien (1919–44) is not used as he was a German-speaking Czech who wrote in German.
13. This table is taken from Mindy Elicia Buckton, 'Re-Contextualizing Viktor Ullmann's *Kaiser von Atlantis* within Twentieth-Century Opera', dissertation, Laurentian University, 2010 – her table was itself based on that by Ingo Schulz.
14. Taken from the opening text in my free translation: https://collections.jewishmuseum.cz/index.php/Detail/Object/Show/object_id/1913
15. http://www.ghetto-theresienstadt.de/pages/k/kienp.htm
16. Ibid.
17. H.G. Adler, *Theresienstadt 1941–1945 das Antlitz einer Zwangsgemeinschaft* (Wallstein Verlag, 1960).
18. 'Kuhle Wampe' was a tent city in Berlin for the homeless. 'Wampe' is German dialect for 'stomach', suggesting the idea of 'empty stomach'.
19. Michael Haas and Marcus Patka, *Hanns Eisler, Mensch und Masse*, exhibition catalogue, Jewish Museum, Vienna, 2009, translation by the author, p. 161. In addition,

in his 1935 letter to Brecht, Eisler mentioned that the idea of the symphony came to him in Detroit. His later reference to Chicago was probably misremembered when speaking three decades later.

20. Ibid, p. 158, 'Trauer ohne Sentimentalität und Kampf ohne Militärmusik'.
21. In conversation with the author in 2009, the popular East German actress and singer Gisela May remembered being told by officials following the *Epilog*'s *Deutsche Symphonie*'s one and only performance in East Germany that the work was poor ('kein gutes Stück') and for that reason there would be no repeat performances.
22. Daniela Reinhold, *Im Schlagschatten des Krieges: Das Deutsche Miserere – eine Quellengeschichte*, Fokus Deutsches Miserere von Paul Dessau und Bertolt Brecht: Festschrift Peter Petersen zum 65. Geburtstag, ed. N. Ermlich Lehmann, S. Fetthauer, M. Lehmann, J. Rothkamm, S. Wenzel and K. Wille (Bockel, 2005), pp. 17–42.

Chapter 5 Kurt Weill and the Music of Integration

1. Nils Grosch (ed.), *Kurt Weill: Briefwechsel mit der Universal Edition* (Metzler Musik, 2002).
2. Berlin-based studios UFA (Universum Film AG), founded in 1917, was one of many European rivals to Hollywood during the interwar years.
3. The actual Korngold quote is provided thanks to his biographer Brendan Carroll and is taken from his interview with producer Henry Blanke. In answer to the question as to why he left Warner Bros, 'When I first came to Hollywood in 1934, I couldn't understand the dialogue. Now I can.' The quote was passed to the author on 11 April 2022.
4. 'Kuhhandel' is actually the German equivalent of the English expression 'horse-trading' – in other words, tricky bartering.
5. As quoted by David Drew, 'Reflections on the Last Years: *Der Kuhhandel* as a Key Work', in *A New Orpheus: Essays on Kurt Weill*, ed. Kim H. Kowalke (Yale University Press, 1986), pp. 218–19.
6. Ibid, p. 222.
7. Ibid, p. 221.
8. *Kurt Weill: Briefe an die Familie*, ed. Lys Symonette and Elma Juchem (J.B. Metzler, 2001).
9. 'ein merkwürdiger Knabe . . . nicht ganz sicher, ob er es wirklich kann'. Weill Lotte Lenya collection, W-LL(g), 198; translation emended from W-LL(e), 193–94 (6 May 1936), quoted in the Introduction to the KWF's critical edition of *Johnny Johnson*, ed. Tim Carter (New York: Kurt Weill Foundation for Music / European American Music Corporation, 2012), p. 30.
10. Letter dated 28 July 1937; *Kurt Weill: Briefwechsel*, ed. Grosch, p. 491.
11. Ibid, p. 15.
12. Ibid, p. 17.
13. Ibid.
14. *Über Kurt Weill*, translated into German from Blitzstein's article in *Modern Music* (New York, 1936), pp. 25–26.
15. Kurt Weill, *Musik und musikalisches Theater: Gesammelte Schriften* (Schott, 2000), p. 482, taken from the article 'Protagonist of Music in the Theater', *The American Hebrew*, New York, 8 January 1937.
16. Kurt Weill, *Musik und Theater: Gesammelte Schriften* (Henschelverlag, 1990), pp. 123–4, original title 'Notes for *Knickerbocker* Picture'.

17. In 1924 Ernst Toch founded the Gesellschaft für neue Musik – and the accompanying newsletter.
18. Elmar Juchem (ed.), *Kurt Weill und Maxwell Anderson* (Metzler, 2000), letter of 3 March 1939, pp. 132–33.
19. Letter in English of 10 May 1941 from Kurt Weill to his parents in Palestine, *Kurt Weill: Briefe an die Familie (1914–1950)*, ed. Nils Grosch, Joachim Lucchesi and Jürgen Schebera (J.B. Metzler Verlag, 2000), pp. 371–74.
20. Ibid, pp. 379–81.
21. Nils Grosch, 'Vom Weib des Nazisoldaten: Musik, Propaganda und Aufführung eines Brecht-Songs', *Song and Popular Culture*, vol. 50/51 (2005/06), p. 144.
22. See https://www.kwf.org/appreciations/one-touch-of-venus-an-appreciation
23. Otto Weininger, *Geschlecht und Charakter* (*Sex and Character*), was published in 1903 shortly after Weininger's theatrical suicide at the age of twenty-three in the house where Beethoven died. The book dominated ideas in Central Europe throughout the early decades of the twentieth century. At the time of his death, and following publication of *Geschlecht und Charakter*, Weininger was more widely regarded than Sigmund Freud.
24. Sven Kellerhoff, *Die Flamme brauste nur so zur Kuppel empor*, *Die Welt*, 29 July 2019.
25. 'Ich bin überzeugt, daß die große Kunst aller Zeiten [...] aktuell war: sie war nicht für die Ewigkeit bestimmt, sondern für die Zeit, in der sie entstand, oder mindestens für die nahe Zukunft, an deren Aufbau sie mitzuarbeiten bestimmt war.' *Melos: Zeitschrift für Musik*, Main VIII (1929), 'aktuelles Theater', p. 525.
26. Adorno, *Vortrupp und Avantgarde*, David Drew's entry on Weill in *The New Grove Dictionary of Music*, and Maurer Zenck's *Challenges and Opportunities of Acculturation: Schoenberg, Krenek and Stravinsky in Exile*, from *Driven into Paradise: The Musical Migration from Nazi Germany to the United States*, ed. Reinhold Brinkmann and Christoph Wolff (University of California Press, 1999).
27. William King, 'Composer for the Theater: Kurt Weill Talks about "Practical Music"', *New York Sun*, 3 February 1940, available at https://www.kwk.org/pages/wt-composer-for-the-theate-html
28. See Sotheby's sale of signed affidavits by Arnold Schoenberg: https://www.sothebys.com/en/auctions/ecatalogue/2008/music-108408/lot.90.html
29. King, 'Composer for the Theater'.
30. H.W. Heinsheimer: 'Opera for All the Valleys', *Educational Music Magazine* (March/April 1950), p. 25, as quoted in Kowalke (ed.), *A New Orpheus*, p. 297.
31. John Graziano, 'Musical Dialects in *Down in the Valley*', in Kowalke (ed.), *A New Orpheus*, p. 297.
32. Quoted in Naomi Graber, *Kurt Weill's America* (Oxford University Press, 2021), p. 273.
33. Weill writing to Chicago critic Irving L. Sablosky, quoted in Kowalke (ed.), *A New Orpheus*, p. 300.
34. Quoted in Graber, *Kurt Weill's America*, p. 276.
35. The work's correct title is *Mahagonny-Songspiel*, but with the opera *Aufstieg und Fall der Stadt Mahagonny* emerging in 1929, it was informally dubbed *Das kleine Mahagonny* (*The Little Mahagonny*) to differentiate it from the two-hour opera.
36. David Drew, *Kurt Weill: A Handbook* (Faber & Faber, 1987), p. 276.
37. Kim Kowalke, 'Today's Invention, Tomorrow's Cliché: *Love Life* and the Concept Musical', in '... dass alles auch hätte anders kommen können': Beiträge zur Musikgeschichte des 20. Jahrhunderts, ed. Susanne Schaal-Gotthardt, Luitgard Schader and Heinz-Jürgen Winkler (Schott, 2009), pp. 175–93.

38. Ibid, p. 186.
39. Stephen Hinton, *Weill's Musical Theater: Stages of Reform* (University of California Press, 2012), p. 407.
40. Alan Jay Lerner, 'Lerner's Life and *Love Life*', *PM*, 14 November 1948, quoted in Hinton, *Weill's Musical Theater*, p. 410.
41. Quoted in Mark N. Grant, '*Love Life*: An Apprecation', https://www.kwf.org/appreciations/love-life-an-appreciation
42. *Kurt Weill: Briefe an die Familie*, ed. Symonette and Juchem, p. 421.
43. Alan Paton, *Journey Continued: An Autobiography* (1989), p. 20, as quoted in Juchem (ed.), *Kurt Weill und Maxwell Anderson*, pp. 201–02.
44. Quoted in Foster Hirsch, *Kurt Weill on Stage* (Knopf, 2002), p. 316.
45. Graber, *Kurt Weill's America*, p. 266.
46. Ibid, p. 269, quoting Boris Goldovsky's interview at the Metropolitan Opera in 1949; transcript available at https://www.kwk.org/pages/wt-opera-news-on-th-air-1949.html
47. Lydia Goehr, '*Amerikamüde/Europamüde*: The Very Idea of American Opera', *Opera Quarterly*, vol. 22, issue 3–4 (Summer–Autumn 2006), pp. 398–432, p. 403.

Chapter 6 The Music of Inner Return

1. Interview with the author, September 2015.
2. Austria had a two-tier educational system that was itself often sub-divided: roughly, children heading for university attended the Gymnasium, or the Real-Gymnasium (for pupils going into the sciences, medicine or the arts), whereas others went to more vocational schools called Hauptschulen.
3. Czesław Miłosz, 'For Jan Lebenstein', in *New and Collected Poems* (HarperCollins, 2001), p. 462.
4. Brecht's work diaries (Aufbau Verlag, 1976) from 3 October 1942 in which he refers to Eisler's 'Brucknergeste'.
5. A combination of comments made in Brecht's diaries from 1 August and 22 October 1941, quoted in Werner Mittenzwei's *Das Leben des Bertolt Brecht*, vol. 2 (Suhrkamp Verlag, 1987).
6. Hanns Eisler and Ernst Bloch, 'Die Kunst zu erben', *Die neue Weltbühne* 34, 1 (6 January 1938), pp. 13–18.
7. A point made by Annette Thein in her chapter 'Dort wo du nicht bist . . .' in Krones (ed.), *Hanns Eisler*, p. 81.
8. Quoted in Albrecht Dümling's sleeve notes for the Decca recording with Matthias Goerne and Eric Schneider, a recording produced by the author as part of the *Entartete Musik* series.
9. String Quartet no. 3 in D major, op. 34 (1944–45).
10. To paraphrase Orson Welles in *Vienna* as quoted earlier in the chapter.
11. A selection of press quotes plus analysis of the symphony are available in Martin Schüßler's *Karol Rathaus* (Peter Lang Verlag, 1998), pp. 353–58.
12. Ibid, p. 357.
13. Ernst Toch, 'Glaubensbekenntnis eines Komponisten', *Deutsche Blätter* (March–April 1945), pp. 13–15. Ernst Toch Collection: Performing Arts Archive, UCLA, Box 106, item 22.
14. A concert with Henry Wood, BBC Symphony Orchestra, offering a first half with Wagner and a second half consisting of Toch's work, along with works by Hamilton Harty and Joaquín Turina, 20 August 1934.

15. Programme note for the performance in Berlin on 14 March 1948, Berlin Philharmonic.
16. *Am Beispiel Egon Wellesz: sein Briefwechsel mit Doblinger*, ed. Herbert Vogg (Doblinger, 1996), p. 142.
17. Quoted in booklet notes by Hannes Heher to the CPO recording with the Austrian Radio Orchestra under Gottfried Radl.
18. Letter from Ernst Toch to Kurt Stone (MGG), 30 May 1964, quoted in Constanza Stratz, 'Ernst Toch in Kalifornien', dissertation, University of Freiburg, 2010, p. 245.
19. Programme note for the performance by the Vienna Symphony on 11 January 1952.
20. Quote take from CPO booklet accompanying the recording by Alun Francis and RSO Berlin – the original Steinberg performance is available on EMI.
21. Toch, 'Glaubensbekenntnis eines Komponisten', *Deutsche Blätter* pp. 13–15. Ernst Toch Collection: Performing Arts Archive, UCLA, Box 106, item 22.
22. David Symons, *Egon Wellesz: Composer* (Florian Noetzl, 1996), p. 113.
23. Michael Haas, *Forbidden Music: The Jewish Composers Banned by the Nazis* (Yale University Press, 2013), p. 291.
24. 26 March 2003, BBC Symphony Orchestra, conductor Cristian Mandeal.
25. Quoted in CPO booklet notes by Hannes Heher accompanying the recordings made by ORF and Gottfried Rabl.

Chapter 7 Case Study: Hans Winterberg and his Musical Return to Bohemia

1. See note 8.
2. Perhaps a better-known Czech composer who retained his Austrian citizenship while continuing to live in Czechoslovakia was Viktor Ullmann (1898–1944). Erich Wolfgang Korngold (1897–1957) retained his Austrian citizenship and identity, despite his birth in Moravian Brno, having lived in Vienna from the age of four. Ernst Krenek, who was from Vienna, refused to become Czech, despite his entitlement to Czech citizenship.
3. Maria Maschat (1906–91), composer and pianist.
4. Oskar Frankl, 'Der deutsche Rundfunk in der Tschechoslowakischen Republik', *Der deutsche Rundfunk in der Tschechoslowakischen* (Urania Prague, 1937), pp. 49–50.
5. Today, Teplice.
6. The Nazis saw Jews as a different 'race' and they justified their policies forbidding the intermarriage of Jews and non-Jews as being the same as inter-breeding different races of cattle. It was an extention of the eugenics movement that had captivated much of the Western world – not just Nazi Germany. The Nazis simply used eugenics to accord their anti-Jewish prejudices with what was perceived as a 'scientific' basis.
7. Other composers murdered following the October transport were Hans Krása, Viktor Ullmann and Pavel Haas. Erwin Schulhoff, another important Czech composer of the same generation, died in 1942 in Wülzburg internment camp.
8. Questionnaire sent to Winterberg by Heinrich Simbriger on 10 January 1956; copies held by Peter Kreitmeir and the Sudeten German Music Institute, Regensburg.
9. See G.E.R. Gedye's *Fallen Bastions* (Faber, 2009), for his reports back to English readers as Prague correspondent in 1938 and 1939.
10. Letter to Heinrich Simbriger, dated 6 June 1955, held at the Sudeten German Music Institute, Regensburg. Yet in a letter to Rafael Kubelik from 2 September 1968,

Winterberg explained that he came from Jewish-German family with Czech as is "first mother tongue". Letter held at the Exilarte Center at Vienna's mdw.

11. According to Krenek's memoirs, *Im Atem der Zeit*, Hába was a passionate Czech nationalist and put pressure on Krenek to become a Czech citizen. Like Winterberg, Krenek maintained his Czech was too poor. Unlike Winterberg, Krenek had spent most of his life in Austria and Germany and not Czechoslovakia.

12. Letter from Dr Heinrich Simbriger to Sir Cecil Parrott, dated 5 January 1975, as well as a memorandum from the Bavarian Ministry of the Interior with responsibility for refugees, dated 6 October 1952. Copies provided by Peter Kreitmeir; Sudeten German Music Institute, Regensburg.

13. Letter to Heinrich Simbriger, dated 6 June 1955, the Sudeten German Music Institute, Regensburg.

14. Ibid.

15. See Harald Jähner, *Aftermath: Life in the Fallout of the Third Reich, 1945–1955* (W.H. Allen, 2021), chapter 3.

16. See note 8 to chapter seven.

17. Ibid.

18. Ibid.

19. Ibid.

20. Ibid; 'ich bin, so zu sagen, der typische Übergangsmusiker'. The concept of 'Übergangsmusiker' is difficult to translate and means in this context more than its literal translation of 'musician in transition'. In this case, it implies a musician who falls between two chairs.

21. Ibid.

22. Ibid.

23. Ibid.

24. Ibid.

25. Letter from Winterberg to Simbriger, 27 December 1955, Sudeten German Music Institute, Regensburg.

26. Letter from Simbriger to Sir Cecil Parrott, 5 January 1975. Parrott was the British ambassador to Czechoslovakia from 1960 to 1966. During this time he developed a deep interest in the country's music and intended to write a book on the subject in retirement. The letter eliciting information that was answered by Simbriger was research for the book, which sadly never reached publication.

27. Memorandum from the Bavarian Ministry of the Interior with responsibility for refugees, dated 6 October 1952. Copies provided by Peter Kreitmeir; Sudeten German Music Institute, Regensburg.

28. Fritz Rieger, conductor: born 1910, Horní Staré Město, Trutnov (formerly Trautenau), Austria, then Czech Sudetenland, died 1978, Bonn.

29. Letter to Simbriger from Hans Winterberg on 12 March 1956 regarding his legacy and the Esslinger Archive, Sudeten German Music Institute, Regensburg.

30. The contract, along with much of the documentation cited in this article, can be read in full at: https://forbiddenmusic.org/2021/05/27/the-winterberg-puzzles-darker-and-lighter-shades/

31. A BR Recording has been located of Maschat performing her Second Piano Sonata, as well as Maschat performing the Piano Suite from 1955 by Hans Winterberg. Lost works by Maschat include two fairytale operas, a good deal of chamber music, piano works, a large number of songs and choral works, a setting of the 23rd Psalm for women's chorus, and church music for two violins and organ in addition to the published works for recorder.

Chapter 8 'Hitler made us Jews': Israel in Exile

1. Lothar Gall, *Walter Rathenau: Porträt einer Epoche* (C.H. Beck, 2009), p. 53.
2. Arnold Schoenberg to Wassily Kandinsky, 19 April 1923, as quoted in the correspondence of Schoenberg and Kandinsky (*Korrespondenzen*, 3), ed. Jelena Hahl-Koch (Stuttgart, 1993), p. 80.
3. Letter from Schoenberg to Max Reinhardt, 23 May 1933, held at Vienna's Arnold Schoenberg Center.
4. Letter from Feuchtwanger to Bertolt Brecht, 16 February 1935, quoted in Guy Stern's chapter 'The Road to *The Eternal Road*', in *A New Orpheus*, ed. Kowalke, p. 270.
5. Interview printed in the *Jüdischer Rundschau* (a publication of the 'Kulturbund'), Berlin, February 1935, from Weill, *Musik und musikalisches Theater*, pp. 462–64.
6. Ibid.
7. See Guy Stern's fascinating chapter 'The Road to *The Eternal Road*', in *A New Orpheus*, ed. Kowalke, p. 279.
8. Quoted in ibid, p. 272.
9. Ibid, pp. 269–84.
10. Arnold Schoenberg to René Leibowitz, 5 November 1948, held by the Arnold Schoenberg Center, Vienna.
11. *Variety*, vol. 151, no. 7 (28 July 1943), p. 22.
12. Katina Paxinou (1900–73), Greek actress.
13. 'ungenannt und ungeminnt' – a quote from Wagner's *Tristan und Isolde*.
14. Ravel was often mistakenly listed as 'Jewish' during the Nazi years.
15. Helene Thimig (1889–1974), actress wife of Max Reinhardt, daughter of actor Hugo Thimig and sister to actors Hans and Hermann Thimig.
16. Lotte Walter (1903–70), Bruno Walter's daughter.
17. Letter held at Austria's National Library, ÖNB, 1283/12-5.
18. Quoted in Graber, *Kurt Weill's America*, p. 221.
19. Despite extensive press and publicity material, advertisements and posters, there seems to be some doubt that the pageant actually took place.
20. William A. Drake (1899–1965) was the screenwriter for the 1932 film *Grand Hotel*, which won the Academy Award for Best Picture. He went on to write the scripts for *Maria Galante* (1934), *The Three Musketeers* (1939) and *The Adventures of Sherlock Holmes* (1939).
21. Schüßler, *Karol Rathaus*, p. 377.
22. Corinne Chochem (1907–90), American choreographer of Russian-Jewish decent who researched and initiated works reflecting Hebrew folk-dancing.
23. *New York Times*, 5 October 2003.
24. David Putterman (1903–79) and Jacob (Jakob) Sonderling (1878–1964).
25. *Los Angeles Times*, 2 October 1938.
26. Ernst Toch Collection, UCLA Performing Arts Library, box 91.
27. Nathaniel Shilkret (born Natan Schüldkraut; 1889–1982), American musician, composer of Austro-Polish descent.
28. Marcus, *Schoenberg and Hollywood Modernism* (Cambridge University Press, 2018), pp. 165–70.
29. 'The Jews are Changing Their Music', *Los Angeles Times*, 2 October 1938.
30. Rudolf Stephan Hoffmann, *Erich Wolfgang Korngold* (Carl Stephenson Verlag, 1922), pp. 121–25.
31. *Musik des Aufbruchs: Endstation Schein-Heiligenstadt*, p. 49.

32. Marcus, *Schoenberg and Hollywood Modernism*, p. 173.
33. *Musik des Aufbruchs: Endstation Schein-Heiligenstadt*, p. 49.
34. Marcus, *Schoenberg and Hollywood Modernism*, p. 171.
35. Lecture by David Bloch at the Terezín Memorial Center on the occasion of the fiftieth anniversary of Ullmann's murder, 18 October 1994.
36. Franz Waxman was born Wachsmann in 1906 in Upper Silesia (today Poland) and died in 1967 in Hollywood. Already mentioned in the chapter on the Americanisation of Kurt Weill are the following important film scores by Franz Waxman: *The Bride of Frankenstein* (1935), *Captains Courageous* (1937), *Philadelphia Story* (1937), *Sunset Boulevard* (1950), *A Place in the Sun* (1951), *Prince Valiant* (1954) and *Peyton Place* (1957).
37. Mario Castelnuovo-Tedesco (1895, Florence–1968, Beverly Hills) went on to teach Nelson Riddle, Henry Mancini, André Previn, Jerry Goldsmith, John Williams and countless West Coast jazz musicians.
38. Alexandre Tansman (1897, Łódź–1986, Paris).
39. Darius Milhaud (1897, Marseilles–1974, Geneva).
40. Gina Genova, 'Reviewing a Cantor's Legacy: Newly Discovered Private Correspondence between Cantor David J. Putterman and Distinguished Composers, 1943–1970', *Musica Judaica*, vol. 19 (2009/2010), pp. 31–32.
41. Ursula Mamlok (née Meyer), born in Berlin in 1923, she returned there in 2006 where she died in 2016.
42. Ruth Schonthal, née Schönthal (1924, Hamburg–2006, Scarsdale, NY).
43. Lukas Foss, born Lukas Fuchs (1922, Berlin–2009, New York City), and Joseph Horovitz (1926, Vienna–2022, London).
44. https://www.wisemusicclassical.com/work/907/String-Quartet-No5--Joseph-Horovitz
45. Quote from the Milken recording of Foss's *Elegy for Anne Frank*, *Song of Anguish* and *Lammdeni*.
46. André Previn (1929, Berlin–2019, New York City); Ernest Gold (1921, Vienna–1999, Santa Monica).
47. Although Robert Furstenthal officially changed the spelling of his name after immigration, it is significant that he maintained the German spelling of 'Fürstenthal' for his compositions.
48. Email from Françoise Farron to the author, 20 August 2020.
49. 'Walter Arlen: A Film Score at 100 – The Lyric Feature', RTÉ broadcast, 16 August 2020.
50. Ibid.
51. Email to the author, 14 January 2016.
52. The reference in the original is 'my beloved', which in a variety of Semitic languages is transliterated as 'Dâdû', 'Dido', 'Dudu' and even 'David'. See Leroy Waterman, 'Critical Notes: The Song of Songs', *American Journal of Semitic Languages*, vol. 35, no. 2 (1919), pp. 102–03.
53. Email from Françoise Farron to the author, 28 August 2020.

Chapter 9 The Missionaries

1. Kanitz Papers, Special collections, USC, as quoted by Christopher Hailey in *Musik des Aufbruchs: Endstation Schein-Heiligenstadt*, p. 75. The letter was addressed to a friend named Margaret E. Bennett.

2. http://ieg-ego.eu/en/threads/europe-on-the-road/political-migration-exile/claus-dieter-krohn-emigration-1933–1945–1950
3. Ibid.
4. Just as examples, Crawford, *A Windfall of Musicians*; Heilbut, *Exiled in Paradise*; Dümling, *The Vanished Musicians*; Snowman, *The Hitler Émigrés*. See fn 3 from the Introduction for further examples.
5. Mark Wischnitzer, 'Jewish Emigration from Germany 1933–1938', *Jewish Social Studies*, vol. 2, no. 1 (1941), pp. 23–44.
6. Ibid.
7. The reason for taking Jewish passports away from German Jews seems puzzling in retrospect – but this is the account offered by Wischnitzer and one must assume his account is based on information at first hand and accurate at the time he was writing.
8. Wischnitzer is remarkably precise with the numbers he gives and bases these on monthly reports from Vienna's Jewish community.
9. Wischnitzer, 'Jewish Emigration from Germany 1933–1938', pp. 23–44.
10. Ibid, pp. 35–36.
11. Julius Schloß (1902–73); Karl Steiner (1912–2001); Wolfgang Fraenkel (1897–1983).
12. See Christian Utz's 'Cultural Accommodation and Exchange in the Refugee Experience', *Ethnomusicology Forum*, vol. 13, no. 1 (January 2004), pp. 119–51.
13. Hidemaro Konoe (1898–1973) was a former Franz Schreker composition pupil in Berlin and is remembered today as the founder of the NHK Orchestra, and for making the first electronic recording of a Mahler Symphony (no. 4).
14. Ibid, p. 133.
15. Ibid, p. 136.
16. The Busoni Prize was for *Variationen über ein Thema von Arnold Schönberg*, the Queen Elisabeth of Belgium Prize for *Musik für Streichquartett*, and the Teatro La Scala Prize for *Symphonische Aphorismen*.
17. See Utz, 'Cultural Accommodation', p. 142.
18. See Wong Hoi-Tan, 'Diversified Twelve-Note Technique in the Music of Luo Zhongrong', *Seventh Biennial International Conference on Music Since 1900* (2011).
19. Ibid, p. 165.
20. My thanks to my colleague Dr Ulrike Anton who helped initiate performances of Fraenkel's *Three Orchestral Songs* – heard for the first time in China and much enjoyed by Fraenkel's surviving students. Exilarte together with Chinese partners helped organise, and participated in, conferences and performances of works by Julius Schloß, Wolfgang Fraenkel and others in 2018 and 2019: https://exilarte.org/en/cd-serieslangen/the-exilarte-center-invited-to-china
21. Letter to Hanspeter Krellmann, quoted in Lena Herschkowitz and Klaus Linder, 'Philipp Herschkowitz über Musik Band 4', in *Die Musik in Geschichte und Gegenwart* (Bärenreiter/Metzler, 1997), p. 139.
22. Wischnitzer, 'Jewish Emigration from Germany 1933–1938', pp. 34–35.
23. Krenek, *Im Atem der Zeit*, p. 1,015.
24. Klabund was the pseudonym of the poet Alfred Henschke, 1890–1928.
25. For more information on music exile in Argentina, refer to Silvia Glocer, *Melodías del destierro: Músicos judíos exiliados en la Argentina durante el nazismo* (Gourmet Musical, 2016), for Graetzer, pp. 175–77.
26. Adolf Weißmann wrote about the broadcast for the *New York Times* on 19 February 1928.

27. https://www.youtube.com/watch?v=WuS-UiaKiVk
28. Wischnitzer, 'Jewish Emigration from Germany 1933–1938', p. 35.
29. Bojan Bujić, *Arnold Schoenberg and Egon Wellesz: A Fraught Relationship* (Plumbago Books, 2020), pp. 210–11.
30. Ralph Vaughan Williams letter to Rauter, 29 September 1942; Rauter Archive, Salzburg University.
31. Mauceri, *The War on Music.*

SELECT BIBLIOGRAPHY

Adler, H.G., *Theresienstadt 1941–1945 das Antlitz einer Zwangsgemeinschaft*, Göttingen: Wallstein Verlag, 1960, reprinted 2005

Beckerman, Michael, 'Ježek, Zeisl, Améry and the Exile in the Middle', *Music & Politics*, vol. 5, no. 2 (2011)

Beckerman, Michael, and Tadmor, Naomi, '"Lullaby", The Story of a Niggun', *Music & Politics*, vol. 10, no. 1 (2016)

Bockmaier, Claus, and Frühauf, Tina, *Jüdische Musik im süddeutschen Raum* (*Mapping Jewish Music of Southern Germany*), Munich: Buch & Media, 2022

Bohlman, Andrea F., and Schding, Florian, 'Hanns Eisler on the Move: Tracing Mobility in the "Reisesonate"', *Music & Letters*, vol. 96, 2015

Buchdahl Tintner, Tanya, *Out of Time: The Vexed Life of Georg Tintner*, Perth: UWA Press 2011, and Waterloo, ON: Wilfrid Laurier University Press, 2013

Bujić, Bojan, *Arnold Schoenberg and Egon Wellesz: A Fraught Relationship*, London: Plumbago Books, 2020

Cahn, Steven, 'A German-Jewish Tradition of Bildung and its Imprint on Composition and Music Theory', *Musical Quarterly*, vol. 101, nos 3–4 (2018)

Calico, Joy, *Arnold Schoenberg's 'A Survivor from Warsaw in Postwar Europe'*, Berkeley, CA: University of California Press, 2014

Castelnuovo-Tedesco, Mario, *Una vita di musica: un libro di ricordi*, vol. 2, ed. and trans. James Westby, Florence: Cadmo, 2005

Covach, John, 'The Americanization of Arnold Schoenberg? Theory, Analysis, and Reception', *Zeitschrift der Gesellschaft für Musiktheorie*, vol. 15, no. 2 (2018)

Covach, John, 'The Sources of Schoenberg's "Aesthetic Theology"', *19th-Century Music*, vol. 19, no. 3 (1996)

Crawford, Dorothy Lamb, *A Windfall of Musicians: Hitler's Émigrés and Exiles in Southern California*, New Haven, CT, and London: Yale University Press, 2011

Drew, David, *Kurt Weill: A Handbook*, London: Faber & Faber, 1987

Dreyfus, Kay (ed.), and Weekes, Diana K. (trans.), *The Fractured Self: Selected German Letters of the Australian Violinist Alma Moodie*, Bern: Peter Lang, 2021

Dümling, Albrecht, *The Vanished Musicians: Jewish Refugees in Australia*, Bern: Peter Lang, 2016

Eisler, Hanns, *Fragen Sie mehr über Brecht: Gespräche mit Hans Bunge*, Munich: Luchterhand, 1986

Fanning, David, and Levi, Erik, *The Routledge Handbook to Music under German Occupation 1938–1945*, London: Routledge, 2019

Feisst, Sabine, *Schoenberg's New World: The American Years*, Oxford University Press, 2011

Fetthauer, Sophie, *Musik und Theater im DP-Camp Bergen-Belsen. Zum Kulturleben der jüdischen Displaced Persons 1945–1950*, Neumünster: Von Bockel, 2012

Fetthauer, Sophie, *Musiker und Musikerinnen im Shanghaier Exil 1938–1949*, Neumünster: Von Bockel, 2021

Fischer, Jens Malte, 'Die Vitalität des Antisemitismus: Konstanten der Mahler-Rezeption', *Abhandlungen der Akademie der Wissenschaften und der Literatur*, Stuttgart: Franz Steiner Verlag, 2021

Fleming, Donald, and Bailyn, Bernard (ed.), *The Intellectual Migration: Europe and America 1930–1960*, Cambridge, MA: Harvard University Press, 1963

Fligg, David, *Don't Forget about Me: The Short life of Gideon Klein, Pianist and Composer*, London: Toccata Press, 2022

Frühauf, Tina, *Dislocated Memories: Jews, Music, and Postwar German Culture*, Oxford University Press, 2011

Gál, Hans, *Music Behind Barbed Wire: A Diary of Summer 1940*, London: Toccata Press, 2014

Ganani, Uri, and HaCohen, Ruth, 'Arnold Schoenberg, Richard Strauss and Other Alter Egos – or the Aesthetic of Inwardness and its Limitations', *Yearbook for European Jewish Literature Studies*, 2015

Gedye, G.E.R., *Fallen Bastions*, London: Victor Gollancz, 1939

Gilbert, Shirli, *Music in the Holocaust: Confronting Life in the Nazi Ghettos and Camps*, Oxford: Clarendon Press, 2005

Glocer, Silvia, *Melodías del destierro: Músicos judíos exiliados en la Argentina durante el nazismo*, Buenos Aires: Gourmet Musical, 2016

Goehr, Lydia, '*Amerikamüde/Europamüde*: The Very Idea of American Opera', *Opera Quarterly*, vol. 22, issue 3–4 (Summer–Autumn 2006), pp. 398–432

Graber, Naomi, *Kurt Weill's America*, Oxford University Press, 2021

Grosch, Nils (ed.), *Kurt Weill: Briefwechsel mit der Universal Edition*, Kraichtal, Metzler Musik, 2002

Guter, Eran, '"A Surrogate for the Soul": Wittgenstein and Schoenberg', *Synthese Library*, vol. 349, Springer, 2011

Haas, Michael, *Forbidden Music: The Jewish Composers Banned by the Nazis*, New Haven, CT, and London: Yale University Press, 2013

Haas, Michael, and Patka, Marcus, *Continental Britons, Hans Gál and Egon Wellesz*, exhibition catalogue, *JMW*, 2003

Haas, Michael, and Patka, Marcus, *Hanns Eisler, Mensch und Masse*, exhibition catalogue, Jewish Museum, Vienna, 2009

HaCohen, Ruth, 'Intercontextual Musical Currents and Performative Traditions in Twentieth-Century Palestine/Israel and Germany', in *Comparative Studies in the Humanities*, ed. Guy G. Stroumsa, Jerusalem: Israel Academy of Sciences and Humanities, 2018

HaCohen, Ruth, *A Theological Midrash in Search of Operatic Action: 'Moses and Aron' by Arnold Schoenberg*, Leiden: Brill, 2014

Hailey, Christopher, *Franz Schreker, 1878–1934: A Cultural Biography*, Cambridge University Press, 1993

Hall, Sharri K., 'The Personal Tragedy of Paul Hindemith's *Mathis der Maler*, *Musical Offerings*, vol. 9, no. 1 (2018)

Heilbut, Anthony, *Exiled in Paradise: German Refugee Artists and Intellectuals in America from the 1930s to the Present*, New York: The Viking Press, 1983

Hermanns, Doris, *'Und alles ist hier fremd': Deutschsprachige Schriftstellerinnen im Britischen Exil*, Berlin: AvivA Verlag, 2022

Hirsch, Lily E., *A Jewish Orchestra in Nazi Germany: Musical Politics and the Berlin Jewish Culture League*, Ann Arbor, MI: University of Michigan Press, 2010

Horowitz, Joseph, *Artists in Exile: How Refugees from Twentieth-Century War and Revolution Transformed the American Performing Arts*, New York: Harper, 2008

Jackman, Jarrell C., and Borden, Carla M. (ed.), *The Muses Flee Hitler: Cultural Transfer and Adaptation, 1930–1945*, Washington, DC: Smithsonian Institution Press, 1983

Jaczyński, Michał, 'The Presence of Jewish Music in the Musical Life of Interwar Prague', *Koło Naukowe Studentów Muzykologii, UJ*, 2017

Jähner, Harald, *Aftermath: Life in the Fallout of the Third Reich, 1945–1955*, London: W.H. Allen, 2022

Jakubczyk-Ślęczka, Sylwia, 'Musical Life of the Jewish Community in Interwar Galicia: The Problem of Identity of Jewish Musicians', *Koło Naukowe Studentów Muzykologii, UJ*, 2017

Juchem, Elmar (ed.), *Kurt Weill und Maxwell Anderson*, Berlin: Metzler, 2000

Karas, Joža, *Music in Terezín 1941–1945*, Martlesham, Suffolk: Boydell & Brewer, 1985

Kater, Michael, *Composers of the Nazi Era: Eight Portraits*, Oxford University Press, 2000

Kater, Michael, *Culture in Nazi Germany*, New Haven, CT, and London: Yale University Press, 2019

Kater, Michael, *The Twisted Muse*, Oxford University Press, 1997

Knapp, Alexander, 'Conceptualizing "Jewish Art Music" While Standing on One Leg: A Scholar's Dilemma', *Journal of the American Musicological Society*, vol. 65, no. 2 (2005)

Köhler, Kai, *Klassik in den Kämpfen ihrer Zeit*, Kassel: Mangroven Verlag, 2022

Kowalke, Kim H. (ed.), *A New Orpheus: Essays on Kurt Weill*, New Haven, CT, and London: Yale University Press, 1986

Krenek, Ernst, *Im Atem der Zeit*, Munich: Heyne Verlag, 1999

Krones, Hartmut (ed.), *Hanns Eisler: Ein Komponist ohne Heimat?* Leiden: Böhlau, 2012

Levi, Erik, *Music in the Third Reich*, London: Palgrave Macmillan, 1994

Levi, Erik, and Scheding, Florian (ed.), *Music and Displacement: Diasporas, Mobilities, and Dislocations in Europe and Beyond*, Lanham, MD: Scarecrow Press, 2010

Loeffler, James, 'In Memory of Our Murdered (Jewish) Children: Hearing the Holocaust in Soviet Jewish Culture', *Slavic Review*, vol. 73, no. 3 (2014)

London, Louise, *Whitehall and the Jews, 1933–1948*, Cambridge: Cambridge University Press, 2000

Ludwig, Mark, *Our Will to Live*, Göttingen: Steidl Verlag, 2021

Marcus, Kenneth H., *Schoenberg and Hollywood Modernism*, Cambridge University Press, 2016

Mauceri, John, *The War on Music: Reclaiming the Twentieth Century*, New Haven, CT, and London: Yale University Press, 2022

Meier, Rebecca, *Musik als Mittel des Widerstands in den Konzentrationslagern Theresienstadt und Auschwitz*, Munich: Grin Verlag, 2015

Overy, Richard, *Blood and Ruins: The Great Imperial War, 1931–1945*, London: Penguin, 2021

Parkin, Simon, *The Island of Extraordinary Captives: A True Story of an Artist, a Spy and a Wartime Scandal*, London: Sceptre Books, 2022

Peitzmeier, Jens, *Musik in den Konzentrationslagern Auschwitz und Theresienstadt: Kunst als Widerstand gegen Grausamkeit und Unterdruckung*, Hamburg: Diplomica Verlag, 2014

Perný, Lukáš, 'DAV (The Crowd) – Slovak Left-Wing Avant-Garde Group of the Interwar Period', *Academia Letters*, article 396 (March 2021)

Peschel, Lisa, *Performing Captivity, Performing Escape: Cabarets and Plays from the Theresienstadt Ghetto*, Kolkata: Seagull Books, 2014

Pölking, Hermann, *Wer war Hitler: Ansichten und Berichte von Zeitgenossen*, Berlin: Bebra Verlag, 2017

Potter, Pamela, *Art of Suppression*, Berkeley, CA: University of California Press, 2016

Potter, Pamela, *Music and German National Identity*, Chicago, IL: University of Chicago Press, 2002

Prieberg, Fred, *Handbuch deutscher Musiker 1933–1945*, Kiel: Musikwissenschaftliches Institut der Christian-Albrechts-Universität, 2004

Prieto, Eric, 'Adaptation and Adaptability in Arnold Schoenberg's "Moses and Aron"', *Forum for Modern Languages*, vol. 48, no. 2 (2012)

Rosenthal, Michael A., 'Art and the Politics of the Desert: German Exiles in California and the Biblical "Bilderverbot"', *New German Critique*, no. 118 (2013)

Ross, Alex, 'The Haunted California Idyll of German Writers in Exile', *New Yorker*, 2020

Rupprecht, Philip, '"Something Slightly Indecent": British Composers, the European Avant-Garde, and National Sterotypes in the 1950s', *Musical Quarterly*, vol. 91, nos 3–4 (2008)

Sands, Philippe, *East West Street: The Origins of Genocide and Crimes against Humanity*, London: Weidenfeld & Nicolson, 2017

Scheding, Florian, '"Problematic Tendencies": Émigré Composers in London, 1933–1945', in *The Impact of Nazism on Twentieth-Century Music*, ed. Erik Levi, Leiden: Böhlau, 2014

Schindler, Agatha, *Aktenzeichen 'Unerwünscht': Dresdner Musikerschicksale und national-sozialistische Judenverfolgung 1933–1945*, Dresden: S.S.G. Dresden, 1999

Schreffler, Anne, and Trippett, David, 'Kolisch and Schoenberg', *Musik Theorie*, vol. 24 (2009)

Schüßler, Martin, *Karol Rathaus*, Bern: Peter Lang Verlag, 1998

Seroussi, Edwin, *Hatikvah: Conceptions, Receptions and Reflections*, Yuval Online, 2015

Seter, Ronit, 'Israelism: Nationalism, Orientalism, and the Israeli Five', *Musical Quarterly*, vol. 97, no. 2 (Summer 2014)

Shelleg, Assaf, 'Imploding Signifiers: Exilic Jewish Cultures in Art Music in Israel, 1966–1970', *Hebrew Studies*, vol. 60 (2019)

Shelleg, Assaf, *Jewish Contiguities and the Soundtrack of Israeli History*, Oxford University Press, 2014

Snowman, Daniel, *The Hitler Émigrés: The Cultural Impact on Britain of Refugees from Nazism*, London: Chatto & Windus, 2002

Stefan, Paul, *Neue Musik und Wien*, Australia: Leopold Classic Library, 2016

Steinacher, Gerald, 'The University in Exile and the Garden of Eden: Alvin Johnson and His Rescue Efforts for European Jews and Intellectuals', in *Reassessing History from Two Continents: Festschrift Günter Bischof*, ed. Martin Eichtinger, Stefan Karner,

Mark Kramer and Peter Ruggenthaler, Innsbruck: Innsbruck University Press, 2013

Steiner, Zara, *The Lights That Failed: European International History 1919–1933*, Oxford University Press, 2007

Symonette, Lys, and Juchem, Elma, *Kurt Weill: Briefe an die Familie*, Berlin: J.B. Metzler, 2001

Symons, David, *Egon Wellesz: Composer*, New York: Florian Noetzl, 1996

Tarsi, Boaz, '*Moses and Aaron* as a Reflection of Arnold Schoenberg's Spiritual Quest', *Musica Judaica*, vol. 12, no. 5754 (1991–92)

Thacker, Toby, *Music after Hitler*, Farnham: Ashgate, 2007

Thiele, Ulrike, 'Musikleben und Mäzenatentum im 20. Jahrhundert: Werner Reinhart', dissertation, University of Zurich, 2016

Ticker, Carolyn S., *The Effects of Richard Wagner's Music and Beliefs on Hitler's Ideology*, Cedarville, OH: Cedarville University Press, 2016

Utz, Christian, 'Cultural Accommodation and Exchange in the Refugee Experience', *Ethnomusicology Forum*, vol. 13, no. 1 (January 2004)

Vogg, Herbert (ed.), *Am Beispiel Egon Wellesz: sein Briefwechsel mit Doblinger*, Vienna: Doblinger, 1996

Weill, Kurt, *Musik und musikalisches Theater: Gesammelte Schriften*, Mainz: Schott, 2000

Weissweiler, Eva, *Ausgemerzt! Das Lexikon der Juden in der Musik und seine mörderischen Folgen*, Munich: Dittrich, 1999

Wischnitzer, Mark, 'Jewish Emigration from Germany 1933–1938', *Jewish Social Studies*, vol. 2, no. 1 (1941)

Wynberg, Simon, 'From India to Indiana: On Reviving the Music of Walter Kaufmann', *Nivmag* (2020)

Youngerman, Irit, *Immigration, Identity, and Change: Emigré Composers of the Nazi Period and Their Perceptions of Stylistic Transformation in their Creative Work*, Berlin: Walter de Gruyter, 2009

Select Memoirs and Novels Reflecting the Experience of Exile

Baum, Vicki, *Es war alles ganz anders: Erinnerungen*, Cologne: Kiepenheuer & Witsch, 2018

Boschwitz, Ulrich Alexander, *Der Reisende*, Stuttgart: Klett-Cotta Verlag, 2019

Feuchtwanger, Lion, *Die Geschwister Oppermann*, Berlin: Aufbau, 2008

Feuchtwanger, Lion, *Exil*, Berlin: Aufbau, 2008

Mann, Klaus, *Der Vulkan*, Hamburg: Rororo, 1990

Mann, Klaus, *Mephisto: Roman einer Karriere*, Munich: Anaconda Verlag, 2020

Morgenstern, Soma, *Flucht in Frankreich*, Springe: Dietrich zu Klampen Verlag, 1998

Strouhal, Ernst, *Vier Schwestern: Fernes Wien, fremde Welt*, Vienna: Zsolnay Verlag, 2022

Zuckmayer, Carl, *Als wär's ein Stück von mir*, Frankfurt am Main: Fischer Verlag, 2016

Select Websites

http://americansymphony.org/hungary-torn
http://americansymphony.org/the-hungarian-jewish-composers-of-wwii
https://collections.jewishmuseum.cz
https://exilarte.org
https://forbiddenmusic.org

https://www.ghetto-theresienstadt.de
http://holocaustmusic.ort.org
http://ieg-ego.eu/en/threads/europe-on-the-road/political-migration-exile/claus-dieter-krohn-emigration-1933-1945-1950
https://www.kwf.org
https://leosmitfoundation.org/en/home
https://www.musica-reanimata.de/index.en.html
http://orelfoundation.org
https://www.ushmm.org/online/giving-tuesday-2022

INDEX

Locations for photos are entered in *italics*.

375